AF324632

KNOWLEDGE ENGINEERING

KNOWLEDGE ENGINEERING

S.C. Mehrotra

Ratnadeep R. Deshmukh

Sachin N. Deshmukh

Ramesh R. Manza

Department of Computer Science and Information Technology,
Dr. Babasaheb Ambedkar Marathwada University, Aurangabad

Narosa Publishing House
New Delhi   Chennai   Mumbai   Kolkata

S.C. Mehrotra

Ratnadeep R. Deshmukh

Sachin N. Deshmukh

Ramesh R. Manza

Department of Computer Science & Information Technology

Dr. Babasaheb Ambedkar Marathwada University

Aurangabad, Maharastra

Copyright © 2011, Narosa Publishing House Pvt. Ltd.

NAROSA PUBLISHING HOUSE PVT. LTD.

22, Delhi Medical Association Road, Daryaganj, New Delhi 110 002
35-36 Greams Road, Thousand Lights, Chennai 600 006
306 Shiv Centre, Sector 17, Vashi, Navi Mumbai 400 703
2F-2G Shivam Chambers, 53 Syed Amir Ali Avenue, Kolkata 700 019

www.narosa.com

All rights reserved. No part of this publication may be reproduced, stored in a retrieval system, or transmitted in any form or by any means, electronic, mechanical, photocopying, recording or otherwise, without prior written permission of the publisher.

All export rights for this book vest exclusively with Narosa Publishing House. Unauthorised export is a violation of terms of sale and is subject to legal action.

ISBN 978-81-8487-123-4

Published by N.K. Mehra for Narosa Publishing House,
22, Delhi Medical Association Road, Daryaganj, New Delhi 110 002

Printed in India

Preface

Knowledge Engineering (KE) is concerned with the application of computer systems to problems of human endeavor such as thinking, learning, problem solving, decision making, and knowledge transfer. At present, it refers to the building, maintaining and development of knowledge-based systems. With the dramatic advances in data acquisition and storage technologies, the problem of how to turn raw data into useful information has become one of the most daunting problems of KE.

This volume brings together academicians, researchers and scientists to discuss current status and future trends of Knowledge engineering who have highlighted pioneering advances in Knowledge Engineering and application of Data Mining.

The chapters in this book were contributed at the IEEE International Conference on Knowledge Engineering (ICKE-2011) organized by Department of Computer Science and Information Technology, Dr. Babasaheb Ambedkar Marathwada University, Aurangabad, (MS) India. The dates of the conference were chosen to coincide with the superannuation of our senior Professor and well known Scientist Dr. Suresh Chandra Mehrotra. The conference received an overwhelming response and after peer review, forty seven papers were selected for presentation. The key areas on which the papers were received are Web Mining, Data Mining Algorithm, Data Mining Security, Data Mining and Image Processing, HCI, Data Warehousing and Data Mining Applications. The contents of the book are segregated in **seven sections**. The split of topics between various sections is follows:

Section 1: Medical Imaging, Opinion Mining, PCA & LDA, Cross co-relation and phase based matching

Section 2: Data Mining like Data Cleaning, Weather forecasting and Web Mining

Section 3: HCI, ECG, Direct Manipulation Interface, Face Recognition in crowd, Gesture recognition for Mobile, Chaotic dynamics, epilepsy and Alzheimer's diagnosis, CAL, Devanagri character recognition and Speech Databases

Section 4: Web Mining related areas like Clustering, Web usage Mining, Web log analysis, BI, Web indexing, Crawlers and Link Mining

Section 5: The algorithms of Data Mining related to Decision Trees, Association Rules and Tries base Apriori algorithm, Decision support and GIS

Section 6: Security like density based approach, intrusion detection in Oracle, unbalanced datasets and dark block extraction

Section 7: Other allied areas of Data Mining for the applications like customer review, SOA-Governance & planning, Mobile Ad-Hoc networks, KE Framework for technical education institutes, time series analysis, extraction of genetic features, KD in Agriculture crop production, Earthquake prediction and Credit Card fraud detection.

We are confident that this volume will be useful for researchers, industry and academics to augment their knowledge on this topic

We would like to acknowledge and thank the contribution of IEEE, UGC, DST, CSIR, IETE, AICTE, MIT, DRDO, ISRO and CSI in making this conference a success. We would also like to thank all local organizations and Institutions for their sponsorship and support. The effort and contribution made by various officials and members of our parent organization Dr. Babasaheb Ambedkar Marathwada University, Aurangabad (MS) India deserves special mention and appreciation. We express our gratitude to all committee members, reviewers for spending their valuable time.

S.C. Mehrotra
Ratnadeep R. Deshmukh
Sachin N. Deshmukh
Ramesh R. Manza

Contents

Data Mining Algorithm

Security

Other Allied Topics

CHAPTER 1

Torn Document Reconstruction: A Review

Shubhangi D. Patil[1], R.R. Deshmukh[2], K.S. Bhagat[1] and D.K. Kirange[1]
[1]T.M.E. Society's J.T. Mahajan College of Engineering, Faizpur (MS) India, [2]Dr. BAM Unniversity, Aurangabad (MS) India
E-mail: shubhangi_4@hotmail.com; ratnadeep_deshmukh@yahoo.co.in; kanchanbhagat@rediffmail.com;
dkirange@rediffmail.com

ABSTRACT

Efficient and successful joining of torn pieces of papers to reconstruct the original documents is an important and challenging issue in many disciplines, especially in forensics and investigation sciences. This paper attempts to be the first paper for providing the review of various techniques for shredded document reconstruction. Automation of the process by means of appropriate techniques can speed up the problem solving substantially. An automated solution for this task can be divided into shape based matching techniques or techniques that analyze additionally the visual content of the fragments (pictorial). In the case of visual content techniques like texture based analysis are used. Depending on the application, shape matching techniques are suitable for entities of the puzzle problem with small numbers of pieces (e.g. up to 20). Also artifacts like broken and lost pieces or overlapping parts of fragments increase the error rate of shape based techniques since the matching of adjacent boundaries can fail. As a result additional features, e.g. color, document structure, have to be used.

Keywords: Shredded document reconstruction, shape based matching.

1. INTRODUCTION

The reassembling of torn documents is related to the traditional puzzle games like 2D pictorial cardboard puzzles [1]. A Jigsaw puzzle is defined in the online dictionary of Britannica as "any set of varied, irregularly shaped pieces that when properly assembled form a picture or map". The main difference to canonical jigsaw puzzle games is the irregular shape of the fragments and the content (mainly text in documents compared to images in jigsaw puzzles). Documents may be ripped up by hand or shredded by a machine. In both cases, the automatic or semiautomatic reconstruction of the original document would alleviate the manual effort, which is difficult and time-consuming. The amount of time necessary to reconstruct a document depends on the size and the number of fragments, and it can be measured in days or even weeks. Sometimes some fragments of the document can be missing, and for this reason the document can be only partially reconstructed. Even then, the manual effort of the forensic examiner, which is tedious and laborious, can be alleviated. One problem faced when reconstructing documents by hand lies in its manipulation. The physical reconstruction of a document modifies some aspects of the original document because products like glue and adhesive tape are added into it. This type of manipulation if known as destructive analysis. This paper focuses on the review of various techniques for reconstruction of documents ripped up by hand, as illustrated in Fig. 1.

Fig. 1 Ripped Up Documents Fragments

Figure 2 shows a general framework of techniques and tools, that enables semi-automatic reconstruction of a set of ripped-up documents. The individual components are controlled by global reconstruction approach (dotted lines); i.e., an interactive and iterative process of accepting, selecting or fine-tuning the obtained partial reconstruction results can be used. [2] This process consists of first trying to reconstruct the outer frames, followed by filling in the frames with non-border fragments if necessary.

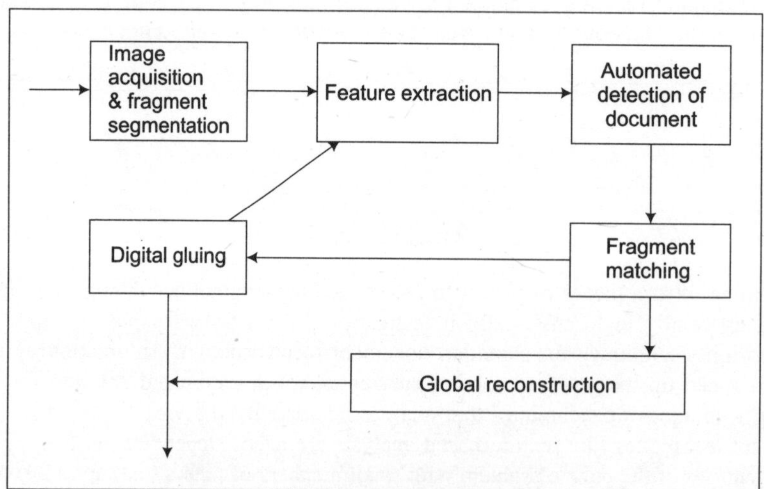

Fig. 2 General Framework for Document Reconstruction

We categorize various techniques of document reconstruction as shape based document reconstruction (A pictorial Reconstruction) and document reconstruction using pictorial information such as texture, color etc.

The paper is organized as follows: Section 2 deals with various techniques of torn document reconstruction Section 3 deals with the use of dynamic programming for document reconstruction. In Section 4, a global approach for reconstructing ripped-up documents is discussed. The global approach first finds candidate matches from document fragments using curve matching and then disambiguates these candidates through a relaxation process to reconstruct the original document.

2. A BRIEF REVIEW OF WORK

2.1 Florian Kleber [1] has proposed an automated assembly of torn documents. A precalculation of document snippets is described for clustering of the provided data. The main orientation is determined according to the printed or handwritten text information. Thus a combined shape and pictorial approach is used. To minimize the search space for matching the following calculations are performed on each snippet:

1. A rotational analysis to determine the alignment
2. The color of the ink/paper is distinguished

Advantages

1. The characteristics of snippets are calculated using combined shape and pictorial approach such that the tearing paper problem is solved.
2. The alignment is determined using rotational analysis for minimizing the search space for matching.
3. Using only shape information cannot solve large instances of problem.
   Hence color of the ink/paper is distinguished.

Disadvantages

1. It cannot solve very large instances of problem.
2. The algorithm does not work if the torn pieces are from multiple documents.
3. The system does not work for missing pieces.

2.2 Patrick De Smet [2] has proposed semi automatic reconstruction of a set of ripped up documents. The global reconstruction approach is used for controlling the individual components. An interactive and iterative process of accepting, selecting or fine tuning the obtained partial reconstruction results is used here. This process consists of first trying to reconstruct the outer frames followed by filling in the frames with non border fragments if necessary.

Advantages

1. A novel set of interactive tools have been implemented for global reconstruction
2. The page border results for merged fragments are computed more efficiently and intelligently.

Disadvantages

1. Large scale experiments are not considered.
2. New methods are yet to be incorporated for matching using color and text line detection.

2,3 Arindam Biswas [4] has proposed a fast, efficient and useful technique for the reconstruction of hand torn pages of documents from their images using countour descriptors for shape based matching. Chain code of the closed digital arc representing a countour and its Minkowski sum has been exploited.

Advantages

1. For each torn piece the corresponding scanned image can be of any one of its two surfaces.
2. Minkowski Sum, properly defined over the chain code [4] of the contour map, has been used judiciously for providing the necessary tolerance, which is a basic prerequisite for reconstruction of hand-torn documents.
3. Priori knowledge about the content of the document is not required.
4. The small gaps between the images of correctly matching pieces can be tolerated.

Disadvantages

1. The system does not work for missing pieces.
2. Multiple documents may be torn at a time. It is very difficult to handle this situation.
3. The corners for the torn piece may be topologically different from those of its counterparts, depending on the nature of hand movements and the behavior of the corner detection process.

2.4 Robin [5] has proposed a novel technique for the reconstruction of hand torn pages of documents using contour maps extracted from images of the torn pieces. The paper is aimed at automating the process for joining of the pieces which includes searching for the pieces in the memory, loading them into the program, matching the appropriate parameters and then joining them. After joining the image, presenting it to the user is the last part of the process. The whole paper is aimed at reducing the amount of effort required to join back pieces and at the same time increasing the efficiency of the whole process. As the jigsaw problem is similar the paper overcomes the problem of global consistency in which pieces are joined together because they match. It's quite a possibility that they are not the correct pair. The paper aim at making sure that no portion of the system violates the rule of global consistency.

Advantages

1. The method is fast, efficient, and robust, and has produced encouraging results on experimenting with a varied set of pieces
2. Appropriate tolerance has been included to suitably accommodate the jaggedness of the torn edges, thereby ensuring the robustness and efficacy of the system.

Disadvantages

1. Since no a priori information is there, for each torn piece, the corresponding scanned image can be of any one of its two surfaces
2. There will be unpredictable rigid transformation (translation and rotation) of scanned images of the torn pieces during image acquisition.
3. There can be small gaps between the images of correctly matching pieces.
4. There may be some shear while tearing off a piece of paper. The shear will occur due to twisting and skewing of the grip, and resultant tearing will proceed along the surface as well as the thickness of the paper. The torn apart counterparts, therefore, will have a partial overlap along their matching edges.

2.5 Carlos Solana [6] has described a procedure for reconstruction documents that have been shredded by hand. The method first applies a polygonal approximation in order to reduce the complexity of the boundaries and then extracts relevant features of the polygon to carry out the local reconstruction. In this way the overall complexity is reduced drastically because few features are used to perform matching. The ambiguities resulting from the local reconstruction are resolved and the pieces are merged together for a global solution. Advantages

1 The overall complexity is reduced because few features are used to perform the matching.
2 The results demonstrates that the methodology, in spite of the fact of using few features, is able to reconstructed documents shredded by hand

Disadvantages

The performance drops as the number of fragments gets bigger due to the scale used during the polygonal approximation.

3. DYNAMIC PROGRAMMING FOR DOCUMENT RECONSTRUCTION

Andre Pimenta [7] has proposed the use of dynamic programming for document reconstruction. Firstly, polygonal approximation is used to reduce the complexity of the boundaries and extract features from them. Thereafter, these features are used to feed the LCS dynamic programming algorithm. The scores yielded by the LCS algorithm are then used into a modified Prim's algorithm to find the best match among all pieces. Comprehensive experiments on a database composed of 100 shredded documents support the efficiency of the proposed methodology. When compared to global search algorithms, this approach brings an improvement of 18% in the number of fragments reconstructed.

Advantages

1 Polygonal approximation to reduce the complexity of the boundaries and overcome specific problems faced in document reconstruction.
2 The polygonal approximation reduces complexity and produces the features that feed the dynamic programming algorithm.
3 A strategy based on graphs is used to perform the image reconstruction, giving to the forensic expert a clear idea about the document, even when it is not totally reconstructed.

Disadvantages

1. Still considering the proposed strategy, t the use of other sequence chains produced by the LCS matrix can be used to solve some false positive problems.
2. The other kind of features such as texture and color can be added.

4. GLOBALLY CONSISTENT RECONSTRUCTION OF DOCUMENTS

One of the most crucial steps for automatically reconstructing ripped-up documents is to find a globally consistent solution from the ambiguous candidate matches. However, little work has been done so far to solve this problem in a general computational framework without using application-specific features.

Liangjia Zhu [8] propose a global approach for reconstructing ripped-up documents by first finding candidate matches from document fragments using curve matching and then disambiguating these candidates through a relaxation process to reconstruct the original document. The candidate disambiguation problem is formulated in a relaxation scheme in which the definition of compatibility between neighboring matches is proposed, and global consistency is defined as the global criterion. Initially, global match confidences are assigned to each of the candidate matches. After that, the overall local relationships among neighboring matches are evaluated by computing their global consistency. Then, these confidences are iteratively updated using the gradient projection method to maximize the criterion. This leads to a globally consistent solution and, thus, provides a sound document reconstruction. The overall performance of the approach in several practical experiments is illustrated. The results indicate that the reconstruction of ripped-up documents up to 50 pieces is possibly accomplished automatically.

Advantages

1. The reconstruction process would benefit greatly from the user interactions, which make it possible to reconstruct documents from a large number of fragments semi automatically in an efficient human-aided way.
2. A novel set of interactive tools have been implemented for global reconstruction.

Disadvantages

1. It would be better to make a more theoretical analysis on the global reconstruction approach because the validity of which is only supported by our tests and experience.
2. It is still an open problem to handle the issues of fibers along the fragment contours, especially when some fragments may only match well in three dimensions.
3. Some improvement should be made to the approach to tackle some complicated issues automatically. For example, the relaxation process may fail to distinguish some identical matches resulting from the presence of identical fragments without considering their color or text. In another case, if many fragments have nearly identical edges, the relaxation results will be highly dependent on the initial conditions.
4. Only disambiguating the candidate matches is not enough to reconstruct a seamless document. There are some inevitable gaps in the reconstructed documents. One reason is that sequentially merging of the fragments will accumulate the curve matching errors.

5. CONCLUSION

This paper attempts to be the first paper for providing the review of various techniques for automated document reconstruction. Although shape matching techniques work for documents with a small number of fragments (e.g. up to 20) this technique is also suitable for large instances (up to 1000s of fragments), aspects like erosion of the border and missing parts make it essential to expand the matching by using additionally content based features. Therefore for large instances information of the texture as well as the shape has to be considered.

As a future work the authors will work out different matching techniques working best for torn documents with a large number of fragments. Additionally methods to handle also constraints like holes in fragments or missing fragments will be treated as well as overlapping parts. For the reconstruction of torn documents/manuscripts an approach combined with document analysis methods will be used. Therefore the paper type (e.g. checked, lined), the skew, writing and paper color will be used as additional features to reduce the search space.

References

1. Florian Kleber, Markus Diem And Robert Sablatnig," Torn Document Analysis as a Prerequisite for Reconstruction", DOI 10.1109/VSMM.2009.27, IEEE 2009

2. Patrick De Smet," Semi-Automatic Forensic Reconstruction of Ripped-Up Documents", DOI 10.1109/ICDAR.2009.7, IEEE 2009

3. Florian Kleber and Robert Sablatnig, "A Survey of Techniques for Document and Archaeology Artefact Reconstruction", 2009 10th International Conference on Document Analysis and Recognition, IEEE 2009

4. Arindam Biswas, Partha Bhowmick, "Reconstruction of Torn Documents Using Contour Maps", Bengal Engg. & Sc. University, Shibpur, India, IEEE 2005

5. Robin, Sandeep Agarwal, Sameer & Poonam Tanwar, "Automated Mosiacing of Torn Paper Documents, "International Journal of Computer Science & Communication Vol. 1, No. 2, July-December 2010, pp. 129-132

6. Carlos Solana, Edson Justino, Luiz S. Oliveira, and Flavio Bortolozzi, "Document Reconstruction Based on Feature Matching", Proceedings of the XVIII Brazilian Symposium on Computer Graphics and Image Processing (SIBGRAPI'05), IEEE 2005

7. *Andre Pimenta, Edson Justino, Luiz S. Oliveira, and Robert Sabourin,* "Document Reconstruction Using Dynamic Programming", The National Council for Scientific and Technological Development, IEEE 2009

8. Liangjia Zhu, Zongtan Zhou, and Dewen Hu, "Globally Consistent Reconstruction of Ripped-Up Documents", IEEE Transactions on Pattern Analysis and Machine Intelligence, Vol. 30, No. 1, January 2008

Text Document Summarization Comparison, Using Query Dependent Clustering Techniques

[1]Rokade Prakash P., [1]Bewoor Mrunal S. and [2]Khairnar Snehal S.
[1]Bharti Vidyapeeth COE, Pune (MS) India, [2]AVCOE, Sangamner (MS) India
E-mail: prakashrokade2005@gmail.com, mrunalbewoor@yahoo.com, snehal1.khairnar1@gmail.com

ABSTRACT

World Wide Web is the largest source of information. Huge amount of data is present on the Web. There has been a great amount of work on query-independent summarization of documents. However, due to the success of Web search engines query-specific document summarization (query result snippets) has become an important problem. In this paper a method to create query specific summaries by identifying the most query-relevant fragments and combining them using the semantic associations within the document is discussed. In particular, first a structure is added to the documents in the preprocessing stage and converts them to document graphs. The present research work focuses on analytical study of different document clustering and summarization techniques currently the most research is focused on Query-Independent summarization. The main aim of this research work is to combine the both approaches of document clustering and query dependent summarization on a text document. The performance of the summary using different clustering techniques will be analyzed, compared and the optimal approach will be suggested.

Keywords: summarization, clustering, weighted graph, semantic parsing, information retrieval

1. PROBLEM DEFINITION

Document clustering methods usually represent documents as a term document matrix. This document matrix is further used to perform clustering by using clustering algorithms on it. Although these clustering methods can group the documents satisfactorily, it is still hard for people to capture the meanings of the documents since there is no satisfactory interpretation for each document cluster. In [1, 2, 3, 4] System for summarizing web pages, people have focused on generating query-independent summaries

The OCELOT system provides the summary of a web page by selecting and arranging the most (query-independent) "important" words of the page. OCELOT uses probabilistic *models* to guide the selection and ordering of words into a summary Furthermore, most summarization techniques are query-independent and follow one of the following two extreme approaches: [9, 10, and 11]

- Simply extract relevant passages viewing the document as an unstructured set of passages,

- Employ Natural Language Processing techniques.

2. WHAT IS SUMMARIZATION?

"An abbreviated, accurate representation of the content of a document preferably prepared by its author(s) for publication with it." Such abstracts are also useful in access publications and machine-readable databases (American National Standards Institute Inc., 1979).

2.1 Text Summarization:

Although there are as many different descriptions of what summarization is (or should be) as people may wish to have, there is in fact not so much disagreement in them. For example, text summarization may be described as "to reduce (long) textual information to its most essential points", "to condense information down to critical bit", or "to distill the most important information from a source or sources to produce an abridged version for a particular user (or users) and task (or tasks)" (Endres- Niggemeyer, 1998; Mani and MaybUry, 1999; Sparck-Jones, 1999).While some techniques exist for producing summaries for domain independent texts (Luhn, 1958; Marcu, 1997) it seems that domain specific texts require domain specific techniques [1] (DeJong, 1982; Paice and Jones, 1993). In order to address the issue of topic identification, content selection and presentation, we have studied alignments (manually produced) of sentences from professional abstracts with sentences from source documents.

Here a method to add structure, in form of a graph, to text documents in order to allow effective query specific summarization is discussed. That is a document is viewed as a set of interconnected text fragments. Main focus is on keyword queries since key word search is the most popular information discovery method on documents, because of its power and ease of use. This technique has the following key steps: First, at the preprocessing stage, a structure is added to every document, which can then be viewed as a labeled, weighted graph, called the document graph. Then, at query time, given a set of keywords, a keyword proximity search is performed on the document graphs to discover how the keywords are associated in the document graphs. For each document its summary is the minimum spanning tree on the corresponding document graph that contains all the keywords (or equivalent based on a thesaurus). So data from the minimum spanning tree nodes is collected and presented as a summary of the document.

Document clustering methods usually represent documents as a term document matrix and perform clustering algorithm on it. Although these clustering methods can group the documents satisfactorily, it is still hard for people to capture the meanings of the documents since there is no satisfactory interpretation for each document cluster. A single cluster can be represented as a node in the graph. The clusters which are related to each other can be connected with a weighted graph. The weights will be assigned based on the relativity among the clusters using the keywords from the query. The optimal spanning tree of the resulting graph can give the summary of the document.

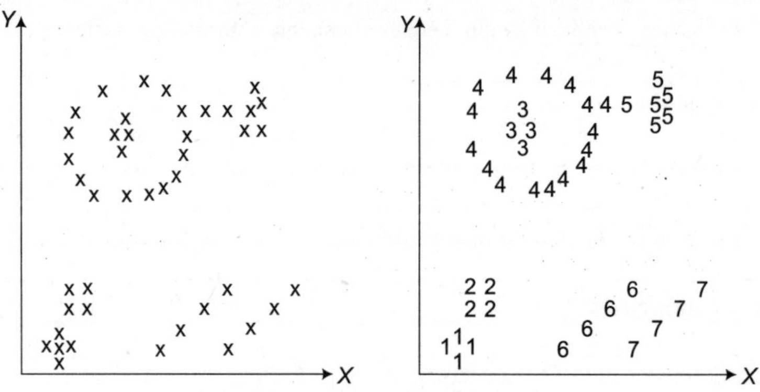

Fig. 1 Data Clustering

3. LITERATURE SURVEY

All prior work on text summarization was done primarily using statistical techniques which extract the most important words or sentences. Although work on summarization started as early as in 1960s (Luhn, [1]) much progress has not been made because of unavailability of computational power. With the advent of Internet as a major source of information, the work on text summarization has gained a new interest in the 1990s. Paice [2] gave an overview of the then significant approaches used for summarization.

Document Summarization is the task of deriving the gist of a source document by selecting the most salient 'content'.

The approaches followed for document summarization is classified in many ways:

- Abstractive Vs Extractive:
- Multi-Document Vs Single-Document .
- Query dependent Vs Query independent :

4. SYSTEM DESCRIPTION

4.1 Module 1: Clustering of Documents

Objective: Automatically group semantically related paragraphs in the documents into clusters.

4.1.1 Clustering Algorithms

A. Hierarchical Agglomerative Clustering

All the documents are splited into separate paragraphs of specific text size. The similarities (Distance) between two paragraphs are calculated by the occurrence of similar words + Semantic meaning of the paragraphs being compared. The semantic meaning of the sentence is calculated by "Semantic Parser Tool". The similarities (distances) are calculated between every pair of the paragraphs. Now we have a set of paragraphs, pronounce them as items.

Algorithm:

- Start by assigning each item to a cluster, so that if you have N items, you now have N clusters, each containing just one item. Let the distances (similarities) between the clusters the same as the distances (similarities) between the items they contain.
- Find the closest (most similar) pair of clusters and merge them into a single cluster, so that now you have one cluster less.
- Compute distances (similarities) between the new cluster and each of the old clusters.
- Repeat steps 2 and 3 until the maximum number of items in the cluster (User definable value) is reached.

B. Nearest Neighbor clustering

- Set $i = 1$ and $k = 1$. Assign pattern X_1 to cluster C_1
- Set $i = i + 1$. Find nearest neighbor of X_i among the patterns already assigned to clusters. Let d_m denote the distance from X_i to its nearest neighbor. Suppose the nearest neighbor is in cluster m.
- If d_m greater than or equal to t then assign X_i to C_m where t is the threshold specified by the user. Otherwise set $k = k + 1$ and assign X_i to a new cluster C_k.
- If every pattern has been considered then stop else go to step 2.

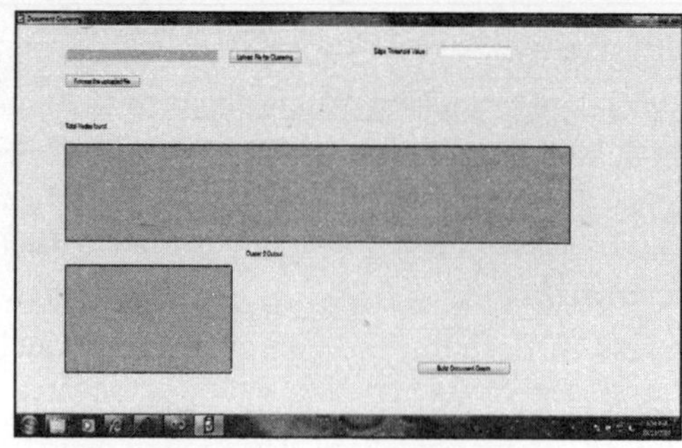

Fig. 2   Uploading a File

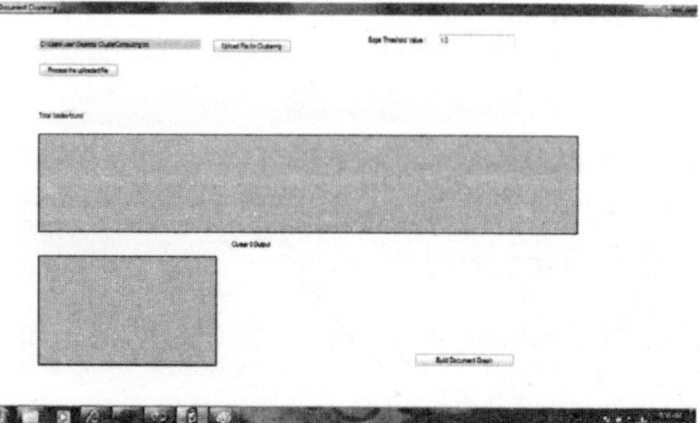

Fig. 3   Uploading a File and giving threshold Value

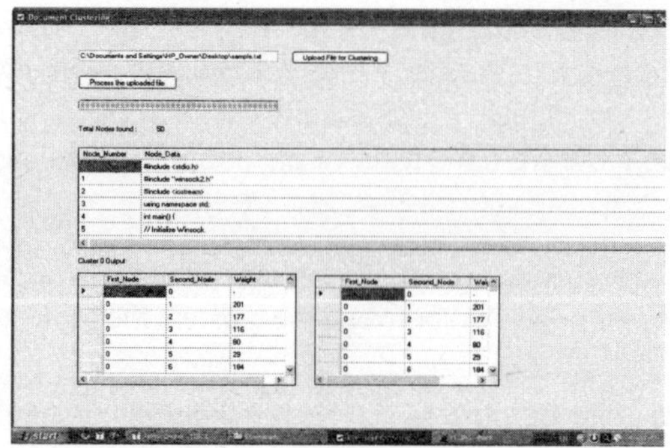

Fig. 4   After Running Parser

4.2   Module 2: Creating Document Graph

Each cluster becomes a node in the document graph. The *document graph G (V, E)* of a document *d* is defined as follows:

- *d* is split to a set of non-overlapping clusters *t(v)*, each corresponding to a node *v?V*.
- An edge *e(u,v)?E* is added between nodes *u, v?V* if there is an association between *t(u)* and *t(v)* in *d*.

Hence, we can view *G* as an equivalent representation of *d*, where the associations between text fragments of *d* are depicted.

A weighted edge is added to the document graph between two nodes if they either correspond to adjacent cluster node or if they are semantically related, and the weight of an edge denotes the degree of the relationship. Here two clusters are considered to be related if they share common words (not stop words) and the degree of relationship is calculated by "*Semantic parsing*". Also notice that the edge weights are **query-independent**, so they can be pre-computed.

Let $D = \{d1, d2,,\ldots, dn\}$ be a set of documents $d1, d2,,\ldots, dn$. Also let size (di) be the length of di in number of words. Term frequency $tf\,(d,w)$ of term (word) w in document d is the number of occurrences of w in d. Inverse document frequency idf (w) is the inverse of the number of documents containing term w in them.

A keyword query Q is a set of keywords $Q = \{w1,\ldots, wm\}$. A key component is the document graph $G\,(V, E)$ of a document d.

Notice that Q is only used in assigning weights to the nodes of G and not for assigning weights to the edges, which is a desirable property since the rest of G can be computed before queries arrive.

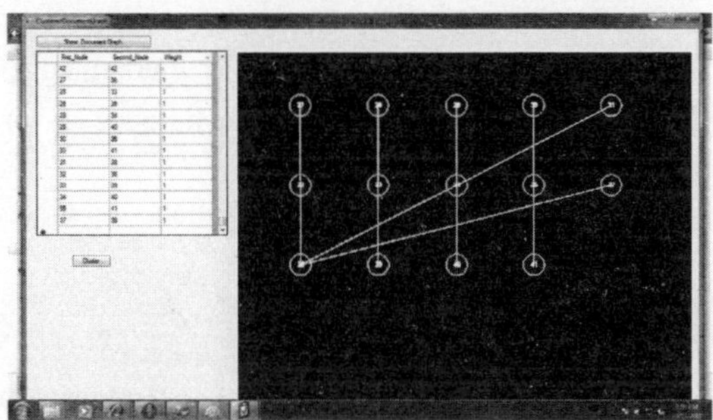

Fig. 5 Creating Document Graph

4.3 Module 3: Adding Weighted Edges to Document Graph

(Note: Adding weighted edge is query independent)

The following input parameters are required at the pre computation stage to create the document graph:

1. Threshold for edge weights. Only edges with weight not below *threshold* will be created in the document graph. (A threshold is user configurable value that controls the formation of edges)
2. Minimum text fragment size. This is used when a fragment is too long, which would lead to large nodes (text fragments) and hence large summaries. Users typically desire concise and short summaries.

Adding weighted edge is the next step after generating document graph. Here for each pair of nodes u, v we compute the association degree between them, that is, the score (weight) EScore (e) of the edge $e(u, v)$. If Score (e) = threshold, then e is added to E. The score of edge $e\,(u, v)$ where nodes u, v have text fragments $t(u)$, $t(v)$ respectively is:

$$\text{EScore} = \frac{\sum((\,tf\,(t(u), w) + tf\,(t\,(v), w)).idf\,(w)))\,w(t\,(u) \cap t\,(v))}{size\,(t\,(u)) + size\,(t\,(u))} \tag{1}$$

where $tf\,(d, w)$ is the number of occurrences of w in d,

$idf(w)$ is the inverse of the number of documents containing w, and size (d) is the size of the document (in words).That is, for every word w appearing in both text fragments we add a quantity equal to the tf *idf* score of w. Notice that stop words are ignored.

4.4 Module 4: Adding Weight to Nodes

When a query Q arrives, the nodes in V are assigned query-dependent weights according to their relevance to Q. In particular, we assign to each node v corresponding to a text fragment $t(v)$ node score NScore (v) defined by the Okapi formula.

4.5 Module 5: Creating MST and comparing the summary

Now this is the final stage to find out the minimal spanning tree. Here we are finding multiple results of spanning tree and top most result of spanning tree. The spanning tree whose score is the minimum is the top most result. Then we will compare the space complexity and time complexity of both algorithms. The algorithm giving the best result is our proposed final output.

5. CONCLUSION AND FUTUTER SCOPE

The clustering algorithm providing the less space and time complexity is proposed best suited clustering algorithm for query dependent text summarization.

We may apply all clustering algorithms to the text file and can suggest the best one for summarization by comparing space and tie complexity.

References

1. Luhn H.P. 1958, The automatic creation of literature abstracts, IBM Journal, pages 159-165
2. Paice, 1990, Constructing literature abstracts by computer Techniques & prospects, Information Processing and Management, 26:171- 186.
3. Daniel Marcu, December 1997, The Rhetorical Parsing, Summarization, and Generation of Natural Language Texts. PhD Thesis, Department of Computer Science, University of Toronto.
4. Grosz, Barbara, and Candy Sidner, 1986 "Attention, Intentions, and the Structure of Discourse", Computational Linguistics, Vol. 12, No. 3, pp. 175-204.
5. Mann and Thompson. Rhetorical Structure Theory: A theory of text organization. Technical Report ISI/RS-87-190, Information Sciences Institute, 4676 Admiralty Way, Marina del Rey, California 90290-6685, June 1987.
6. Chin-Yew Lin, Eduard Hovy. The automated acquistion of topic signatures for text summarization, Proceedings of the 18th conference on Computational linguistics-Volume 1, July 2000.
7. D.M. Zajic, B. Dorr, J. Lin, R. Schwartz, Sentence Compression as a Component of a Multi-Document Summarization System, Proceedings of the Document Understanding Conference, 2006.
8. Conroy, J., Schlesinger, J., O'Leary, D., & Goldstein, J. Back to basics: CLASSY 2006. In Proceedings of the 2006 document understanding conference (DUC 2006) at HLT/NAACL 2006, New York, NY, 2006.
9. H. Jing and K. McKeown. Cut and paste based text summarization. In Proc. of the 1st Meeting of the North American Chapter of the Association for Computational Linguistics, pages 178—185, 2000
10. Web URL: http://en.wikipedia.org/wiki/Part-of-speech_tagging
11. T. Hofmann. Probabilistic latent semantic analysis. In Proceedings of the 15th Conference on Uncertainty in AI, pages 289–296, 1999
12. T. Hofmann. Probabilistic latent semantic indexing. In Proceedings of SIGIR'99, 1999.
13. M. Brunn, Y. Chali, C.J. Pinchak. Text Summarization Using Lexical Chains. In Workshop on Text Summarization, ACM SIGIR Conference. September 13-14, 2001, New Orleans, Louisiana USA.
14. Barzilay, Regina and Michael Elhadad. 1997. Using lexical chains for text summarization. In Proceedings of the Workshop on Intelligent Scalable Text Summarization, pages 10-17, Madrid, Spain, August. Association for Computational Linguistics.
15. Chin-Yew Lin. 2004. Rouge: A package for automatic evaluation of summaries. In Proceedings of the ACL-04 Workshop: Text Summarization Branches Out, pages 74–81, Barcelona, Spain.

CHAPTER 3

Study and Evaluation of Multi-document Summarization Approaches: A Peer Review

[1]Sunita R. Patil and [2]Sunita M. Mahajan
[1]MPSTME, NMIMS, Vile Parle, Mumbai (MS) India, [2]ICS, MET, Bandra, Mumbai (MS) India
E-mail: sunita.patil.india@gmail.com; sunitamm@gmail.com

ABSTRACT

Automatic Multi-document Summarization is a crucial solution to reduce the information overload problem in the area of World Wide Web and online information services. Multi-document summarization is useful to give an outline of a topic from multiple related source documents and allow users to zoom in for more details as per interest. This paper is a survey of various approaches of multi-document summarization aiming at giving an overview of the researches of this area. So, the paper contains six parts which cover the introduction of multi-document summarization, summarization approaches, and related work of summary generation, research findings, evaluation and conclusion.

I. INTRODUCTION

Nowadays, people need much more information in work and life, especially the use of internet make information more easily gained. So, automatic summarization draws substantial interest since it provides a solution to the information overload problem people face in this digital era. Multi-document summary is the process of dealing with a large amount of information present in multiple related source documents by comprises only the essential material or main ideas in a document in less space. Researchers are investigating summarization tools and methods that automatically extract or abstract content from a range of information sources, including multimedia. Moreover, the source may not always have text for example; a sports event on videotape or tables displaying economic data and current tools cannot summarize nontextual media.

Multidocument Summarization is useful to give an outline of a topic from multiple related source documents and allow users to zoom in for more details as per interest which may be identifying the important concepts, entities, keywords, paragraphs, variables, relations or features in the text. The purpose of automatic summarization in technical literature is to facilitate quick and accurate identification of the topic of from multiple related documents. The objective is to save a prospective reader time and effort in finding useful information in a given article or report.

This paper is a survey of various approaches of multi-document summarization aiming at giving an overview of the researches of this area. The system outlined here consists of six sections as in first section we will give an overview of some approaches of multi-document summarization, its related research methods and then we will briefly introduce the types of summarization. In next section, we deal with the main approaches which have been used or proposed. The third section, will describe the basic idea of evaluation methods taken by some researchers. The last section is the conclusion.

II. SUMMARIZATION APPROACHES

This section will brief various approaches presented by researchers experimenting with the task tracks given by DUC's (Document Undertaking Conferences).

In the first approach, Latent Dirichlet Allocation and Singular Value Decomposition based Multi-Document Summarization by Rachit Arora and Balaraman Ravindran [1] presented Multi-Document Summarization using Latent Dirichlet Allocation which break down documents into different topics or events. Singular Value Decomposition is used to get the orthogonal representations of vectors and representing sentences as vectors can get the sentences that are orthogonal to each other in the LDA mixture model weighted term domain. Thus using LDA, the different topics in the documents and using SVD, the sentences that best represent topics are identified.

Algorithm

The algorithm works by decomposing the set of documents into individual sentences forming the candidate sentence set then applying Porter Stemmer to stem the words to their root form and remove the stop words using a standard stop-words list. Using LDA finds the probability distributions of the documents over the topics and of the topics over the vocabulary. For each topic constructed a term by sentence matrix by forming its sentence vector for the topic. Then Applying the Singular Value Decomposition on the term by sentence matrix weighted by LDA mixture model i.e. the matrix to get the new sentence matrix. Repeated this procedure for all the topics, formed the matrix and applied SVD on it to get the matrix. Then each sentence is represented by the column vector. Calculated the probability of topic and form a vector which stores the topics in the decreasing order of probability of topic. At the end left with a set of summary sentences, ordered them to represent a readable summary. Arranged the sentences in the relative order that they appear in their respective documents. If there is a tie, break it arbitrarily. In this way the summary based on LDA and Singular Value Decomposition is presented.

In the second approach, Query-focused Multi-document Summarization Using Keyword Extraction by Liang Ma,Tingting He, Fang Li, Zhuomin Gui1, Jinguang Chen[2] proposed a strategy of the summary sentence selection for query-focused multi-document summarization through extracting keywords from relevant document set. It calculates the query related feature and the topic related feature for every word in relevant document set, then obtains the importance of the word by combining the two features. The score of candidate sentence is computed through the importance of words which they contains, and the modified MMR technology is used to adjust the score of the candidate sentence, then the candidate sentence with the highest score is selected as the summary sentence, till the length of the summary is enough. The summary is generated through following steps:

    A. *Pre-processing-* Query and multi-documents are segmented into sentences.

    B. *Keyword Scoring-* [9] the summary is pieced together to answer a question using,

        B.1 *Query Related Feature-* constructed a matrix to record the relevant degree of words by their co-occurrence in multi-document set.

        B.2 *Topic Related Feature-*[10] extracted signature term by likelihood ratio of topics.

        B.3 *Keyword Scoring-* Keywords should correlate to the query sentence, and denote the main content of the multi-document set, feature fusing is used for keyword scoring.

    C. The Summary Generation

        C.1 *Candidate Sentence Scoring-* sorted the importance of the words, subsequently selected some keywords as important to the summary sentence extraction, then selected the candidate sentences which contains the most nuclear words as the summary sentence.

        C.2 *Summary Generation-* The modified MMR formula will be used to adjust the score of the candidate sentences.

In the third approach, IIIT Hyderabad at DUC 2007 By Prasad Pingali, Rahul K and Vasudeva Varma [3] focused on the query-focused multidocument summarization main task and in a pilot update summary generation tasks, used a term clustering approach to better estimate a sentence prior. Used only the sentence prior which is query independent, in the update summarization task and found that it's performance is comparable with the top performing systems.

A. *System*– The main task problem is defined as to synthesize from a small set of documents that are related to a given topic or query a brief, well organized, fluent answer to a need for information given, that cannot be met by just stating a name, date, quantity, etc. For the pilot task, an update summarization task that assumes that the user has already read previous documents related to a given topic, and the summary only provides new or update information is considered.

B. *Algorithm*– Uses a sentence extraction based approach, where extracted sentences verbatim from the given set of documents and concatenate them as a summary.

C. *Sentence Reduction*– Each sentence from the set is passed through set of rules which may result in reducing the length of the given sentences.

D. *Sentence Scoring*– The score of each sentence s is computed as a sentence prior score (or query independent score), and the score of a sentence answering the given query (query dependent score).

E. *Query-Dependent Score (QFocus)*– Compute the query dependent score of a given sentence using co-occurrence statistics of terms in the given document set.

F. *Entity Dereferencing*– Identify potential named entities (person names and organization names).

Then search the document set for acronymized version of organization names and partial person names (i.e. first name or last name). Finally replace repeated occurrences of a named entity with its shorter name.

In fourth approach, Using Cross-Document Random Walks for Topic-Focused Multi-Document Summarization by Xiaojun Wan, Jianwu Yang and Jianguo Xiao [4] proposed to integrate the relevance of the sentences to the specified topic into the graph-ranking based method for topic focused multi document summarization. The cross-document relationships and the within-document relationships between sentences are differentiated and applied the graph-ranking based method using each individual kind of sentence relationships and explore their relative importance for topic-focused multi-document summarization. This approach based only on the cross-document sentence relationships can perform better than or at least as well as the approaches based on both kinds of sentence relationships.

The proposed approach is a topic-sensitive extension of the graph-ranking based summarization methods [11,12,13] and consists of the three steps:

1. *Relevance Computing and Affinity Graph Building*

   The relevance of the sentences to the topic is computed, and affinity graphs are built to reflect different kinds of relationships between sentences in the document set respectively;

2. *Information Richness Computation*

   The information richness of the sentences is computed using the random walk model on each affinity graph;

3. *D iversity Penalty Imposition*

   A diversity penalty is imposed on the sentences and the affinity rank score of each sentence is obtained to reflect both information richness and information novelty of the sentence. The sentences with high affinity rank scores are chosen to produce the summary using the Porter's stemmer.

In fifth approach, Automatic multi-document summarization for digital libraries by Ou, S., Khoo, C. & Goh, D, D. Singh & A.S. Chaudhry (Eds.)[5] reports three types of multi-document summaries generated for a set of research abstracts, using different summarization approaches:

(a) A sentence-based summary generated by a MEAD summarization system[21] that extracts important sentences using various features,

(b) A sentence-based summary generated by extracting research objective sentences-

   (b.1) This approach uses of statistical and linguistic features to measure the significance of sentences thereby extracting the highest scoring sentences as the components of the summary.

(b.2) The well-known features used in most summarization work include frequent keywords, indicator phrases, title keywords, sentence position, extractive approach is statistics-based sentence extraction statistical and linguistic features used in sentence extraction include frequent keywords, title keywords, cue phrases, sentence position, sentence length, and so on.

(c) Variable-based summary-focusing on research concepts and relationships.

This framework contains four kinds of information:

    A. *Main concepts*

    B. *Research relationships between concepts*

    C. *Contextual relations*

    D. *Research methods*

In sixth approach, Language Model Passage Retrieval for Question-Oriented Multi Document Summarization by Jia-Ching Ying, Show-Jane Yen, Yue-Shi Lee, Yu-Chieh, Wu Jie-Chi Yang [6]. The goal of question-oriented text summarization aims at producing the informative short description according to the given queries. This is somewhat similar to the target of question answering which retrieves exact answers from large raw text collections. System presents a resource, and training data-free summarization model for DUC multi-document summarization task. Similar the method simplifies the two-pass retrieval as a passage retrieval task. At first the top-down clustering algorithm is used to merge similar passages into a set of groups. Then the passage retriever extracts relevant groups in response to the given query. Finally a maximizing scorer is used to re-form the sentences to the final summary.

There are four main components within the Model for summarization as,

1. *Passage Segmentation*- The sentences are first segmented; the words are not stemmed and tokenized. To represent the root of words, clustering and ranking steps are used. The sentences segmentation is carried out with a tool. This tool can successfully identify boundaries between sentences without tokenizing words.

2. *Passage/Sentence Clustering*- As multiple passages or sentences may describe the same concept meanings. To reduce the redundancy, a conventional clustering technique is applied to group similar passages into the same group. Used the top-down bisecting K-means algorithm (Zhao and Karypis, 2002) for clustering that splits the largest group into two sub-clusters.

3. *Passage Retrieval*- Passage retrieval components adopts the developed language model to extract important passages (clusters).Replaced the two pass framework with one-pass sentence ranking. However, in this way, it will cause the sentences too similar to make the reader over understanding.

4. *Summary Generation* Each retrieved cluster is treated as separable concept. Therefore for each cluster, extract an important sentence within it to represent the concept.

In seventh approach, Design and development of a concept-based multidocument summarization system for research abstracts by Shiyan Ou, Christopher S.G. Khoo and Dion H. Goh [7] reports abstractive approaches that involve text abstraction and generation to produce more coherent and concise summaries. Thus abstractive approaches seem more appropriate for multi-document summarization [14]. Abstractive approaches for multi-document summarization focus mainly on similarities and differences across documents, which can be identified and synthesized using various methods [15]. The MultiGen summarizer identified similar words or phrases across documents through syntactic comparisons and converted them into fluent sentences using natural language generation techniques [16].

The summarization process includes four major steps –

1. *Data pre-processing*

The input data are a set of dissertation records on a specific topic retrieved from the Dissertation Abstracts. Each sentence is parsed into a sequence of word tokens using the Conexor Parser [17].

Most dissertation abstracts have a clear structure containing five standard sections –

    • *background,*

    • *research objectives,*

- *research methods,*
- *research results* and
- *Concluding remarks.*

Each section contains one or more sentences.

2. *Macro-Level Discourse Parsing:* An automatic discourse parsing method was developed to segment a dissertation abstract into several macro-level sections and identify which sections contain important research information.

3. *Information Extraction:* An information extraction method was developed to extract research concepts and relationships as well as other kinds of information from the micro-level structure (within sentences).

   3.1 *Term Extraction:* Concepts, expressed as single-word or multi-word terms, usually take the grammatical form of nouns or noun phrases [18]. Sequences of contiguous words of different lengths are extracted from each sentence to construct *n*-grams. [20]

   3.2 *Relationship Extraction:* Two kinds of approach used for performing relation extraction. One uses linguistic patterns which indicate the presence of a particular relation in the text. The second makes use of statistics of co-occurrences of two entities [16].

4. *Information Integration* Information integration includes concept integration and relationship integration. To identify and cluster similar concepts based on two kinds of syntactic variations – *subclass modifier substitution* and *facet modifier substitution* [19] is used *internal insertion of modifiers, preposition switch* and *determiner insertion* to identify term variants.

5. *Information Integration:* To integrate similar concepts and relationships extracted from different abstracts information integrated.

   5.1 *Concept clustering and generalization*

   The multi-word terms (concepts) and the majority can be divided into the following two parts:

   (i) *Head noun* refers to the noun component that identifies the broader class of things or events to which the term as a whole refers.

   (ii) *Modifier* narrows the denotation of the head noun by specifying a subclass or a facet of the broader concept represented by the head noun.

   5.2 *Relationship normalization and conflation*

   To integrate relationships, identified different types of relationships found in the sample abstracts through manual analysis.

6. *Evaluation*

   The summarization system was evaluated as:

   A *Intermediate component evaluation:* evaluating the accuracy and usefulness of each summarization step.

   B *Final user evaluation:* evaluated the overall quality and usefulness of the generated summaries.

In eight approach, A Novel Chinese Multi-document Summarization Using Clustering Based Sentence Extraction by De-Xi Liu, Yan-Xiang He, Dong-Hong Ji, Hua Yang [8] proposes a strategy for Chinese multi-document summarization based on clustering and sentence extraction. To evaluate summarization strategy, following steps are performed,

1. *Term extraction-* A seeding-and-expansion mechanism is used to extract key terms from the texts. The procedure of term extraction consists of two phases, seed positioning (individual word) and term determination.

2. *Sentence clustering-* The terms extracted from the document collection are used to represent the features of vector in VSM.

3. *Representative sentence selection-* The terms extracted from the texts (sentence cluster or the whole document collection) are supposed to denote the main concepts in the texts, weighted the sentence based on the terms included in the sentence.

    3.1 *Local search strategy-* For local search strategies selected the representative sentences based on the clusters themselves. To select the representative sentence: centroid sentence, TF*IDF, TF are used.

    3.2 *Global search strategy-*For global search strategy, selected a sentence according to its contribution to the performance of the whole summary.

4. *Evaluation* -Adopted the extrinsic method to evaluate the quality of summarization by evaluating the results of classifying task.

III. RESEARCH FINDINGS

From the above discussion we have reached to the fact that multi-document summarization have two core tasks:

1. Determine what is salient (or relevant or important) in the source being summarized and
2. Decide how to reduce (or condense or abbreviate) it's content. But within and across these two categories, summaries differ according to function and target user.

A. Category of Summary

Many types of summary have been identified (Borko and Bernier 1975; Cremmins 1996; Sparck Jones 1999; Hovy and Lin 1999), as Extractive summaries, Abstractive summaries, Indicative summaries, Informative summaries, Topic-oriented or User Focused summaries and Generic summaries. At the most basic level, summaries differ according to whether they are extracts or abstracts.

- *Extractive summaries-* created by reusing portions (words, sentences, etc.) of the input text verbatim.
- *Abstractive summaries-* are created by regenerating the extracted content. *Extraction* is the process of identifying important material in the text, *abstraction* the process of reformulating it in novel terms, *fusion* the process of combining extracted portions, and *compression* the process of squeezing out unimportant material. The need to maintain some degree of grammaticality and coherence plays a role in all four processes.

Within and across these two categories, summaries differ according to function and target reader as indicative, informative, or critical:

- *Indicative* summaries follow the classical information retrieval approach: They provide enough content to alert users to relevant sources, which users can then read in more depth, provide an idea of what the text is about without conveying specific content
- *Informative* summaries act as substitutes for the source, mainly by assembling relevant or novel factual information in a concise structure.
- *Critical* summaries (or reviews), besides containing an informative gist, incorporate opinion statements on content. They add value by bringing expertise to bear that is not available from the source alone.

A summary can also be generic or user-focused:

- *Generic* summaries address a broad community; there is no focus on special needs because the summarizer is not targeting any particular group, it reflects the author's point of view.
- *Topic-oriented* or *User-focused* summaries, in contrast, are tailored to the specific needs or interest of an individual or a particular group.

Until recently, generic summaries were more popular, but with the prevalence of full-text searching and personalized information filtering, user-focused summaries are gaining importance. Many approaches discussed above support both user-focused and generic summarization.

B. Summarization Approaches & Methods

The various categories used by researchers mostly follow variable based approach, keyword extraction, text extraction, concept based approach, question answer based query systems, sentence extraction, paragraph extraction, relationship extraction, entity extraction, topic focused extraction, event indexing and feature extraction.

The techniques follow Discourse Parsing, N-gram, Latent Dirichlet Allocation, Singular Value Decomposition, Clustering, Segmentation, Affinity Graph Building, Lexical chains, Lead detection, collaborative filtering and Entity Dereferencing. All these techniques are basically used by all the multidocument summarization researchers.

IV. EVALUATION

All the above approaches used for multidocument summarization provides a way for summarizing information from multiple sources. The challenge in multidocument summarization is how to evaluate summarizers i.e. will the summaries generated by such systems actually help end-users to make better use? Multi document summaries should enable users to more efficiently find the information they need.

While evaluating above approaches,researchers were interested in whether this will be an effective tool for assisting the processing of large volumes of document contents to answer the following questions: [22]

- Do summaries help the user find information needed to perform a task of interest?
- Do users use information from the summary in gathering their facts?
- Do summaries increase user satisfaction with the online information services?
- Do users create better fact sets with an online information services which includes multi-document summarization than one that not?
- In the context of a every summary, what is the comparison of information quality in this task, and user satisfaction, when users have access to these summarization approaches versus minimal or human summaries?

V. CONCLUSION

This paper is a survey of various approaches of multi-document summarization in which we concentrated on summarization approaches which have been used and proposed. Generation and evaluation of multi-document summarization are also very important parts of this area. From the survey of multi-document summarization research tasks, we began by asking, Whether multi-document summaries help users to find the information they need? Our user study shows that when a system contains such summaries, there is a significant increase over the no-summary condition in the quality of information that they include in summarized document contents. Users feel that they are able to find substantially more of the information that is relevant. This result demonstrates that summaries do help subjects do a better job to assemble facts on given topics. Generating an effective summary requires the summarizer to select, evaluate, order and aggregate items of information according to their relevance to a particular subject or purpose. Most previous work in summarization attempted to use methods to select the important portion to use as summary. But it cannot be very coherent and comprehensible. We hypothesized that multi-document summary would enable end users to more effectively complete a fact-gathering task. Though true abstractive summarization remains a researcher's dream, the success of extractive summarizers and the rapid development of compressive and similar techniques testify to the effectiveness with which the research community can address new problems and find workable solutions to them.

References

1. Latent Dirichlet Allocation and Singular Value Decomposition based Multi-Document Summarization by Rachit Arora and Balaraman Ravindran, IEEE International Conference on Data Mining,2008(1550-4786/08 $25.00 © 2008 IEEE DOI 10.1109/ICDM.2008.55)

2. Query-focused Multi-document Summarization Using Keyword Extraction by Liang Ma, Tingting He, Fang Li, Zhuomin Gui1, Jinguang Chen, 2008 International Conference on Computer Science and Software Engineering, 978-0-7695-3336-0/ 08 $25.00 © 2008 IEEE

   DOI 10.1109/CSSE.2008.1323

3. IIIT Hyderabad at DUC 2007 By Prasad Pingali, Rahul K and Vasudeva Varma, in In Proceedings of the DUC 2007, Document Understanding Conference, http://duc.nist.gov.

4. Using Cross-Document Random Walks for Topic-Focused Multi-Document Summarization by Xiaojun Wan, Jianwu Yang and Jianguo Xiao, Proceedings of the 2006 IEEE/WIC/ACM International Conference on Web Intelligence (WI 2006 Main Conference Proceedings)(WI'06) 0-7695-2747-7/06 $20.00 © 2006

5. Automatic multi-document summarization for digital libraries by Ou, S., Khoo, C. & Goh, D, D. Singh & A.S. Chaudhry (Eds), in Asia-Pacific Conference on Library & Information Education & Practice 2006 *(A-LIEP 2006), Singapore, 3-6 April 2006* (pp.72-82).

6. Language Model Passage Retrieval for Question-Oriented Multi Document Summarization by Jia-Ching Ying, Show-Jane Yen, Yue-Shi Lee,Yu-Chieh, Wu Jie-Chi Yang in In Proceedings of the DUC 2007, Document Understanding Conference, http://duc.nist.gov.

7. Design and development of a concept-based multidocument summarization system for research abstracts by Shiyan Ou, Christopher S.G. Khoo and Dion H. Goh in Journal of Information Science OnlineFirst, published on December 3, 2007 as doi:10.1177/0165551507084630.

8. A Novel Chinese Multi-document Summarization Using Clustering Based Sentence Extraction by De-Xi Liu, Yan-Xiang He, Dong-Hong Ji, Hua Yang in Proceedings of the Fifth International Conference on Machine Learning and Cybernetics, Dalian, 13-16 August 2006(1-4244-0060-0/06/$20.00) ©2006 IEEE

9. Enrique Amigo, Julio Gonzalo, Victor Peinado, Anselmo Peñas and Felisa Verdejo. An Empirical Study of Information Synthesis Task. In Proceedings of ACL 2004.

10. Chin-Yew Lin and Eduard Hovy. The Automated Acquisition of Topic Signatures for Text Summarization. 2000. Proceedings of the 18th conference on Computational linguistics.

11. G. Erkan and D. Radev. LexPageRank: prestige in multidocument text summarization. In *Proceedings of EMNLP'2004*

12. I. Mani and E. Bloedorn. Summarizing Similarities and Differences among Related Documents. *Information Retrieval*, 1(1), 2000.

13. R. Mihalcea and P. Tarau. A language independent algorithm for single and multiple document summarization. In *Proceedings of IJCNLP'2005*.

14. S. Afantenos, V. Karkaletsis and P. Stamatopoulos, Summarization from medical documents: a survey, *Journal of Artificial Intelligence in Medicine* 33(2) (2005) 157–77.

15. J. Goldstein, M. Kantrowitz, V. Mittal and J. Carbonell, Summarizing text documents: sentence selection and evaluation metrics. In: F. Gey et al. (eds), *Proceedings of the 22nd ACM SIGIR International Conference on Research and Development in Information Retrieval* (ACM, New York, 1999) 121–8.

16. K. McKeown, R. Barzilay, D. Evans, V. Hatzivassiloglou, M.Y. Kan, B. Schiffman and S. Teufel, Columbia multi-document summarization: approach and evaluation. In: *Proceedings of the Document Understanding Conference 2001* (NIST, 2001). Available at: www nlpir.nist.gov/projects/duc/pubs. org.html (accessed 10 May 2006).

17. T. Pasi and J. Timo, A non-projective dependency parser. In: R. Grishman et al. (eds), *Proceedings of the 5th Conference on Applied Natural Language Processing* (Morgan Kaufmann, San Francisco, CA, 1997) 64–71.

18. T. Nomoto and Y. Matsumoto, Discourse parsing: a decision tree approach (1998). In: E. Charniak (ed.), *Proceedings of the 6th Workshop on Very Large Corpora*. Available at: http://acl.ldc.upenn.edu/W/W98/W98–1125.pdf (accessed 10 May 2006).

19. C.Y. Lin, Topic identification by concept generalization. In: H. Uszkoreit et al. (eds), *Proceedings of the 33rd Annual Meeting of the Association for Computation Linguistics* (ACL, Morristown, NJ, 1995) 308–10.

20. D. Borgigault and C. Jacquemin, Term extraction ??term clustering: an integrated platform for computeraided terminology. In: H. Thompson et al. (eds), *Proceedings of the 9th Conference of the European Chapter of the Association for Computational Linguistics* (ACL, Morristown, NJ, 1999) 15–22.

21. D. Radev, T. Allison, S. Blair-Goldensohn, J. Blitzer, A. Celebi, E. Drabek, W. Lam, D. Liu, H. Qi, H. Saggion, S. Teufel, M. Topper and A. Winkel, *The MEAD Multidocument Summarizer* (2003). Available at: www.summarization.com/mead/ (accessed 24 May 2006).

22. The Challenges of Automatic Summarization by *Udo Hahn, InderjeetMani, IEEE2000*

CHAPTER 4

A Novel Approach for Super Resolution Image Restoration in Medical Imagine

Ganesh Sable[1], Arun Gaikwed[2] and Ulhas Shinde[1]
[1]Savitraibai Phule Women's Engineering College, Aurangabad, [2]PICT, Pune (MS) India
E-mail: Sable.eesa@gmail.com; arungkwd47@gmail.com; shindeulhas1@yahoo.co.in

ABSTRACT

This paper gives the details of super resolution different methods.SR image reconstruction is one of the most spotlighted research areas, because it can overcome the inherent resolution limitation of the imaging system and improve the performance of most digital image processing applications. HR image can offer more details that may be critical in various applications to many sorts of digital image manipulations: reproduction of photographs, television display, image enhancement and many more.

All imaging systems have an upper limit on resolution. These limitations can arise in several ways:

- Diffraction of light limits resolution to the wavelength of the illuminating light.
- Lenses in optical imaging systems truncate the image spectrum in the frequency domain.
- Sampling of images limits the maximum spatial frequency to a fraction of the sampling rate.

Super-resolution (SR), also known as High-resolution (HR), means that pixel density within an image is high, and therefore an HR image can offer more details that may be critical in various applications.

The recent increase in the wide use of digital imaging technologies in consumer (e.g., digital video) and other markets (e.g., security and military) has brought with it a simultaneous demand for higher-resolution images. The demand for such high-resolution (HR) images can be met by algorithmic advances in super-resolution (SR) technology in tandem with hardware development. Such HR images not only give the viewer a more pleasing picture but also offer additional details that are important for subsequent analysis in many applications.

The current approach to obtaining HR images mainly relies on sensor manufacturing technology that attempts to increase the number of pixels per unit area by reducing the pixel size. However, the cost for high-precision optics and sensors may be prohibitive for general-purpose commercial applications, and there is a limitation to pixel size reduction due to shot noise encountered in the sensor itself. Therefore, a resolution enhancement (super-resolution) approach using computational, mathematical, and statistical techniques has received a great deal of attention recently.

One promising approach is to use signal-processing techniques to obtain an HR image (or sequence) from observed multiple low-resolution (LR) images. The major advantage of this approach is that it may cost less and the existing LR imaging systems can still be utilized.

Keywords: HR-High resolution, LR-Low Resolutions-Super Resolution, CCD-Charge coupled Device,MSE-Mean square error,PSNE-Peak signal to noise ratio,SSIM-Structural SIMilarity

1. INTRODUCTION

Any given set of source low resolution (LR) images only captures a finite amount of information from a scene, the goal of SR is to extract the independent information from each image in that set and combine the information into a single high resolution (HR) images. The only requirement is that each LR images must contain some information that is unique to that image.

Most methods in SR are strictly reconstructed based primarily on uniform and non-uniform sampling thermos and do not attempt to create any information not found in the LR images

SR techniques can prove useful in many different application, and these application can have different requirement in terms of both quality and complexity. The quality may also vary for different methods based on characteristics of the input image for these and other reasons choosing between SR methods is a complex task

2. LIMITATIONS OF EXISTING SYSTEM

There is much still and moving image content at a low resolution. Much current NTSC programming may be desired to play on future high definition television (HDTV) players. By the time HDTV sets are commonplace, consumers may have come to expect that level of resolution quality. (Just as consumers expect to see color images now, instead of the old black and white ones).

The current technology to obtain HR images mainly depends on sensor manufacturing technology that attempts to increase the number of pixels per unit area by reducing the pixel size. However, the cost for high-precision optics and sensors may be inappropriate for general-purpose commercial applications, and there is a limitation to pixel size reduction due to shot noise encountered in sensor itself.

It is usually not possible at the outset to achieve the desired resolution because of technology and cost constraints. For example, the technology of a CCD is limited by factors like physical dimension shot noise, and parasitic effects. In applications like astronomical imaging, the reduced size and weight of cameras in a spaceship or satellite affect its quality. The need for tradeoff between size, weight, and quality of the CCD array necessitates the design of SR algorithms to obtain the desired HR image of a common region of interest in the frames of a video sequence without modifying the physical characteristics of the CCD array.

3. LITERATURE SURVEY

Super-resolution is the problem of generating a high-resolution image from one or more low-resolution images.

Super resolution (SR) can be obtained by a technique whereby multi-frame motion is used to overcome the inherent resolution limitations of an LR camera system. Thus, most of the SR image reconstruction methods consist of three basic components: (i) motion compensation, (ii) interpolation, and (iii) blur and noise removal. The performance of motion-based SR algorithms will ultimately be limited by the effectiveness of motion estimation and modeling.

Another approach to obtain super resolution is by reconstructing frequency components, which lie above the cutoff frequency of the imaging system. Grid filters, which learn statistical properties of an image class, are able to exploit their prior knowledge to perform super-resolution.

One of the approaches is to use signal-processing techniques to obtain an HR image (or sequence) from observed multiple low-resolution (LR) images. The major advantage of this approach is that it may cost less and the existing LR imaging systems can still be utilized.

4. METHODS OF SUPER-RESOLUTION

There are many existing SR methods including non-uniform interpolation, frequency domain, deterministic and stochastic regularization, projection onto convex sets (POCS), hybrid techniques, optical flow, and other approaches [4][1][8].Additionally several methods provide parameters that can effect tradeoffs between such factors as fidelity and smoothness or quality and computation time.

4.1 Non-uniform Interpolation

The basis of non-uniform interpolation SR techniques is the non-uniform sampling theory which allows for the reconstruction of functions from samples taken at non-uniformly distributed locations. This was developed by Clark et al. [9] and later extended to two-dimensional signals by Kim and Bose [10]. SR image enhancement is a logical application of this new theory, but one that requires very accurate registration between images. Non-uniform interpolation is a basic and intuitive method of super-resolution and has relatively low computational complexity, but it assumes that the blur and noise Characteristics are identical across all LR images [4].

4.2 Frequency Domain

Tsai and Huang [11] proved that in the absence of noise or blurring it is possible to reconstruct a HR image from multiple LR images based on the aliasing present in the LR images. This was accomplished by relating the aliased discrete fourier transform coefficients of the LR images to a sampled continuous Fourier transform of an unknown HR image. Kim and Bose extended this to blurred and noisy LR images; provided the noise has zero mean and the blur and noise are identical across all LR images, using a recursive implementation based on the weighted least square theory [10].

4.3 Regularization

SR image reconstruction is generally an ill posed problem. However, it can be stabilized with a regularization procedure. Without loss of generality, we can define a model to relate LR images with the original HR image and additive noise as:

$$Yk = WkX + nk \text{ for } k = 1 \ldots p \tag{1}$$

By assuming that registration parameters are estimated, the inverse problem can be solved by deterministic regularization by taking proper prior information about the solution. For example, a constrained least square (CLS) method can be used to find x such that

$$\Sigma \|yk - Wkx\|^2 + \alpha \|Cx\|^2 \tag{2}$$

becomes minimum. In this method a smoothness constraint is used as priori knowledge for reconstruction. Parameter which is known as the regularization parameter controls the tradeoff between fidelity and smoothness in the solution. Current research focuse donsimultaneous blur identification and robust super-resolution.

4.4 Projection onto Convex Sets

Low resolution images usually suffer from blurring caused by a sensor's point spread function (PSF) and additionally from aliasing caused by under-sampling. Stark and Oskoui [12] have proposed a POCS technique that accounts for both the blurring introduced by the sensors as well as the effects of undersampling.In their model a low resolution image sequence is denoted by $g(m1, m2, k)$. It is assumed that an estimate of the high resolution image at time $k = tr$ is desired. A family of closed, convex constraint sets can be defined, one for each pixel within the low-resolution image sequence

$$Ctr \ (m1, m2, k) - y \ (n1, n2, tr) : |r(y)(m1, m2, k)| - do \tag{3}$$

Where

$$r^{(Y)}(m1, m2, k) = \ddot{y} \ g(m1, m2, k) - X\Sigma y \ (n1, n2, tr)\text{htr} \ (n1, n2; m1, m2, k) \tag{4}$$

is the residual associated with an arbitrary member, y, of the constraint set. htr combines the effect of the blur PSF and relative motion of object and sensor. The quantity _0 is an a priori bound reflecting the statistical confidence with which the actual image, y, is a member of the set Ctr $(m1, m2, k)$ this family of constraints is referred to as data consistency constraints. An estimate of the high-resolution version of the reference image is determined iteratively starting from some arbitrary initialization. Successive iterations are obtained by projecting the previous estimate onto the consistency set with an amplitude constraint set that restricts the gray levels of the estimate to the range [0, 255].

4.5 Optical Flow

Some applications can benefit from the generalization of SR techniques to support the imaging of objects that are non-planar, non-rigid, or which are subject to self-occlusion when rotated. One such applications SR reconstruction of facial images. Baker and Kande present optical flow as a solution to this problem [13]. Zhao and Sawhney present a comparison of three different flow methods: least-squares based flow, consistent flow (CONS), and bundled flow with CONS flow as initial input. They demonstrated that it worked well when small amount of noise were present, but that it was very sensitive to flow accuracy

5. PROPOSED RESEARCH WORK

I have keen interest in this area as well as inspiration to develop the relevant DSP techniques. In my work, I shall address the relevant signal processing technology for this SR approach to high-quality imaging. **I aim to develop a novel method for solving single-image super-resolution problems. Given a low-resolution image as input, recover its high-resolution counterpart.**

In my research work, the scope of techniques intended to achieve Super-resolution include: enhancement in spatial resolution for both gray-scale and color images, suppression of signal dependent noise, and various other associated artifacts.

6. METHODOLOGY

While most methods have been proposed for super-resolution based on multiple low-resolution images of the same scene (e.g., [2, 6, 8, 22]), the focus of my work will be on generating a high-resolution image from a single low-resolution image, with the help of a set of one or more training images from scenes of the same or different types. Commonly this is referred as the single-image super-resolution problem.

The single-image super-resolution problem arises in a number of real-world applications. A common application occurs when we want to increase the resolution of an image while enlarging it using a digital imaging software (such as Adobe Photoshop). Another application is found in web pages with images. To shorten the response time of browsing such web pages, images are often shown in low-resolution forms (as the so-called "thumbnail images"). An enlarged, high-resolution image is only shown if the user clicks on the corresponding thumbnail. However, this approach still requires the high-resolution image to be stored on the web server and downloaded to the user's client machine on demand. To save storage space and communication bandwidth (hence download time), it would be desirable if the low-resolution image is downloaded and then enlarged on the user's machine. Yet another application arises in the restoration of old, historic photographs, sometimes known as image in painting [5]. Besides reverting deteriorations in the photographs, it is sometimes beneficial to also enlarge them with increased resolution for display purposes.

7. RELATED PREVIOUS WORK

Simple resolution enhancement methods based on smoothing and interpolation techniques for noise reduction have been commonly used in image processing. Smoothing is usually achieved by applying various spatial filters such as Gaussian, Wiener, and median filters.

Commonly used interpolation methods include bicubic interpolation and cubic spline interpolation [13]. Interpolation methods usually give better performance than simple smoothing methods. However, both methods are based on generic smoothness priors and hence are indiscriminate since they smooth edges as well as regions with little variations, causing blurring problems and checkerboard effect. More recently, different researchers have proposed some learning-based methods. Some methods make use of a training set of images [1, 9, 10, 11, 12, 14, 19], while others do not require training set but require strong image priors that are either hypothesized [17] or learned from data [18]. The methods based on a training set are very similar in spirit. While the framework based on image analogies [12] was proposed for a wide variety of image texturing problems including super-resolution, the method is less effective than other super-resolution methods as no interaction between adjacent elements (pixels or image patches) in the high-resolution image is explicitly enforced to ensure compatibility.

Nevertheless, all these methods use the training data in a similar way. In particular, each element in the target high-resolution image comes from only one nearest neighbor in the training set. It should be noted that similar ideas have also been explored in the context of texture synthesis [7, 23, 24]. These methods typically require only one sample texture as input, possibly with some random noise [23] or a target model [24]. Similar to learning-based methods for super-resolution, only one nearest sample texture is selected to generate each synthesized pixel.

8. RESULTS AND DISCUSSION

A. *Experimental Setup*

8.1 Choice of Gain Factor K

The choice of k affects noise components which remain in the system. For $k = 1$, the number of nonzero coefficients remaining after thresholding decreases with each iteration, while the PSNR of the reconstructed image increases, until the signal converges. We consider that the signal has converged when $\hat{y}_i \cong \hat{y}_{i-1}$. The problem is that, because of the energy loss, the reconstruction quality attained when the system converges is limited. When $k > 1$, the energy of the final reconstructed image is closer to the energy of the original. This improves the reconstructed image's PSNR, but at the expense of more non-zero coefficients. We consider the number of non-zero coefficients to be a measure of efficiency because zero coefficients are very efficient to code, and so bit rate tends to be proportional to the number of non-zero coefficients. For implementation of the method we used $k = 1.6$ for better results.

8.2 Choice of Threshold

Initially we consider a large threshold $\theta = 64$ and decreasing at each iteration until target threshold, $\theta = 32$ is reached. A large starting threshold causes many coefficients to be eliminated initially. With the right balance between the energy gain k and the amount by which the threshold decreases each iteration, most insignificant coefficients remain significant, while the signal's energy is maintained and image reconstruction improves.

The control system, where the initial threshold 64 is reduced by 1 each iteration until $\theta_1 = 32$, performs best. Comparing the efficiency–distortion data for this system with the data corresponding to a threshold reduction of 4/iteration, the system with the slower threshold reduction rate produces a DDWT signal with noticeably fewer non-zero coefficients but the same reconstruction image quality.

8.3 Performance Measures

The performance of the reconstructed images for this method quantitatively compared using Peak Signal to Noise Ratio (PSNR) as

$$PSNR = 20 \log 10 \left(\frac{255}{RMSE} \right) \tag{5}$$

Where, RMSE is

$$RMSE = \sqrt{\frac{1}{MN} \Sigma_{i=1}^{N} (f(i,j) - \hat{f}(i,j))^2} \tag{6}$$

Eq.2 defines the PSNR of original image $f(i,j)$ with size $M \times N$ and reconstructed image $\hat{f}(i,j)$ with same size while Eq.3 gives the Root Mean Square Error (RMSE).

Table 1 and 2 shows the comparative results for CT brain image (256×256) and MRI image. Initially both PSNR and MSE is calculated for reconstructed image. The MSSIM measure in this case is the onlt the quality measurement favors

The results show that the reconstruction quality of the image with other is better than without noise shaping,. Visual quality for CT_brain and MRI image is shown in Fig. 2-5 respectively. Though the results obtained with this coding scheme are satisfactory, it is essential to extend the work to include different image coding method like EBCOT, TCE, and SPIHT to DDWT and DWT coefficients and calculating the S/N ratio.

Table 1 PSNR results for 256×256 CT brain image

Threshold	PSNR	MSE	S/NRatio	MSSIM
10	33.4112	8.481E3	320.575	0.66687
20	36.1046	1.005E4	270.72	0.66523
30	37.4852	1.118E4	152.46	0.67013
40	38.4606	2.561E4	124.332	0.54386
50	38.4606	2.561E4	105.768	0.52639

Table 2 PSNR results for 256×256 MRI_2 Image

Threshold	PSNR	MSE	S/NRatio	MSSIM
52	33.6039	2.882E4	110.550	0.51453
48	34.5108	2.665E4	115.230	0.54321
44	35.3029	2.558E4	118.220	0.53342
40	36.1532	2.432E4	124.332	0.54332
36	37.0902	2.182E4	134.321	0.6901

9. CONCLUSION

The threshold reduction rate affects the performance results. With decreasing threshold at each iteration, PSNR value increases that means with decreasing threshold the quality of image increases. And we get best results at **threshold** 30. The choice of gain factor k affects the noise components remains in the system. It is always better to choose k greater than one. When, $k > 1$ the energy of the final reconstructed image is closer to the energy of the original. This improves the reconstructed image's PSNR.

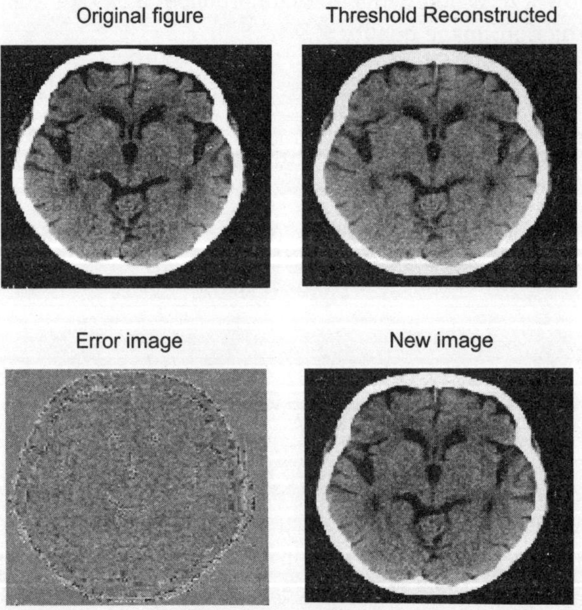

Fig.1 Visual Quality for CT brain Image at threshold=30

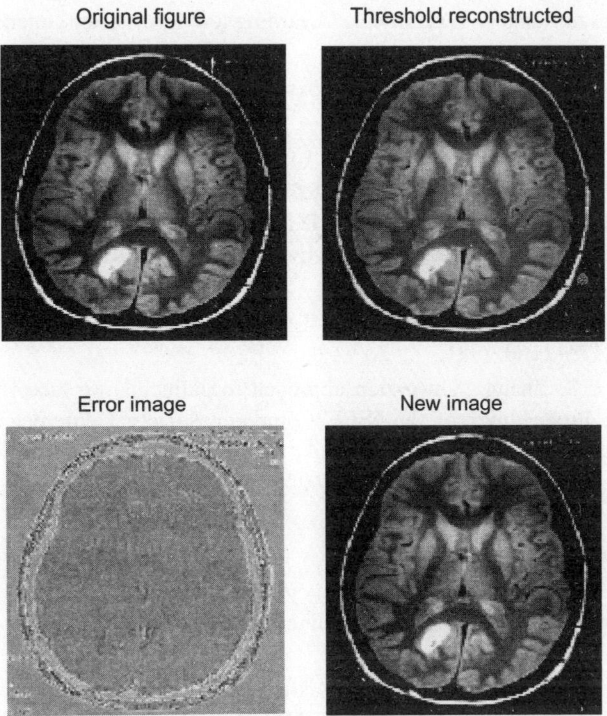

Fig.2   Visual Quality for MRI_2 Image at threshold=48

References

Magazine:

Digital Signal Processing, IEEE, May 2003; a special issue on Super Resolution Imaging

Papers:

1. C.B. Atkins, C.A. Bouman, and J.P. Allebach. Treebased resolution synthesis. In Proceedings of the Conference on Image Processing, Image Quality and Image Capture Systems, pages 405–410, Savannah, GA, USA, 25–28 April 1999.

2. S. Baker and T. Kanade. Limits on super-resolution and how to break them. In Proceedings of the IEEE Computer Society Conference on Computer Vision and Pattern Recognition, volume 2, pages 372–379, Hilton Head Island, SC, USA, 13–15 June 2000.

3. M. Belkin and P. Niyogi. Laplacian eigenmaps and spectral techniques for embedding and clustering. In T.G. Dietterich, S. Becker, and Z. Ghahramani, editors, Advances in Neural Information Processing Systems 14, pages 585–591. MIT Press, Cambridge, MA, USA, 2002.

4. M. Belkin and P. Niyogi. Laplacian eigenmaps for dimensionality reduction and data representation. Neural Computation, 15(6):1373–1396, 2003.

5. M. Bertalmio, G. Sapiro, V. Caselles, and C. Ballester. Image inpainting. In Proceedings of the Twenty-Seventh Annual Conference on Computer Graphics and Interactive Techniques (SIGGRAPH 2000), pages 417–424, New Orleans, LA, USA, 23–28 July 2000.

6. P. Cheeseman, B. Kanefsky, R. Kraft, J. Stutz, and R. Hanson. Super-resolved surface reconstruction from multiple images. Technical Report FIA-94-12, Artificial Intelligence Research Branch, NASA Ames Research Center, Moffett Field, CA, USA, December 1994.

7. A.A. Efros and T.K. Leung. Texture synthesis by non-parametric sampling. In Proceedings of the Seventh IEEE International Conference on Computer Vision, volume 2, pages 1033–1038, Kerkyra, Greece, 20– 27 September 1999.

8. M. Elad and A. Feuer. Super-resolution reconstruction of image sequences. IEEE Transactions on Pattern Analysis and Machine Intelligence, 21(9):817–834, 1999.

9. W.T. Freeman and E.C. Pasztor amd O.T. Carmichael.Learning low-level vision. International Journal of Computer Vision, 40(1):25–47, 2000.

10. W.T. Freeman, T.R. Jones, and E.C. Pasztor. Examplebased super-resolution. IEEE Computer Graphics and Applications, 22(2):56–65, 2002.

11. W.T. Freeman and E.C. Pasztor. Learning low-level vision In Proceedings of the Seventh IEEE International Conference on Computer Vision, volume 2, pages 1182–1189, Kerkyra, Greece, 20–27 September 1999.

12. A. Hertzmann, C.E. Jacobs, N. Oliver, B. Curless, and D.H. Salesin. Image analogies. In Proceedings of the Twenty-Eighth Annual Conference on Computer Graphics and Interactive Techniques (SIGGRAPH 2001), pages 327–340, Los Angeles, CA, USA, 12–17 August 2001.

13. R.G. Keys. Cubic convolution interpolation for digital image processing. IEEE Transactions on Acoustics,Speech, and Signal Processing, 29(6):1153–1160, 1981.

14. C. Liu, H.Y. Shum, and C.S. Zhang. A two-step approach to hallucinating faces: global parametric model and local nonparametric model. In Proceedings of the IEEE Computer Society Conference on Computer Vision and Pattern Recognition, volume 1, pages 192–198, Kauai, HI, USA, 8–14 December 2001.

15. S.T. Roweis and L.K. Saul. Nonlinear dimensionality reduction by locally linear embedding. Science, 290(5500):2323–2326, 2000.

16. L.K. Saul and S.T. Roweis. Think globally, fit locally: unsupervised learning of low dimensional manifolds.Journal of Machine Learning Research, 4:119–155, 2003.

17. R.R. Schultz and R.L. Stevenson. A Bayesian approach to image expansion for improved definition. IEEE Transactions on Image Processing, 3(3):233–242, 1994.

18. A.J. Storkey. Dynamic structure super-resolution. In S. Becker, S. Thrun, and K. Obermayer, editors, Advances in Neural Information Processing Systems 15, pages 1295–1302. MIT Press, Cambridge, MA, USA, 2003.

19. J. Sun, N.N. Zheng, H. Tao, and H.Y. Shum. Image hallucination with primal sketch priors. In Proceedings of the IEEE Computer Society Conference on Computer Vision and Pattern Recognition, volume 2, pages 729–736, Madison, WI, USA, 18–20 June 2003.

20. J.B. Tenenbaum. Mapping a manifold of perceptual observations. In M.I. Jordan, M.J. Kearns, and S.A. Solla, editors, Advances in Neural Information Processing Systems 10, pages 682–688. MIT Press, 1998.

CHAPTER 5

Opinion Mining: A Study on Automated Text Based Emotion Prediction

D.K. Kirange[1], [2]R.R. Deshmukh, T.I. Jain[1] and Shubhangi D. Patil[1]
[1]T.M.E. Society's JT Mahajan College of Engineering, Faizpur, [2]Dr. B A M University, Aurangabad (MS) India
E-mail: dkirange@rediffmail.com; ratnadeep_deshmukh@yahoo.co.in; tijain@rediffmail.com; shubhangi_4@hotmail.com

ABSTRACT

Opinion mining is a process for extracting the knowledge from text using Data Mining and Natural Language Processing techniques. In real world emotion plays a significant role. The goal of opinion mining is to make computer able to recognize and express emotions. Companies are interested to know about the people demand. They need to collect customer opinion about the products to know about the reputation of the company in the market. These surveys are then need to be summarized or categorized to produce the report about the good or bad aspects of particular products. Automatic detection of emotions in texts is becoming very important from applicative point of view. This research effort deals with a study of automatic emotion prediction using text modality along with the techniques, application challenges related to automated Opinion Mining.

Keywords: Opinion Mining, Natural Language Processing, Data Mining.

1. INTRODUCTION

Opinion Mining is a new and emerging area of research. Opinion Mining is a process, used for automatic extraction of knowledge from the opinion of others about some particular topic or problem. With the growing availability of online resources on web and popularity of fast and rich resources of opinion sharing such as online review sites and personal blogs, Opinion Mining has become an interesting area of research. World Wide Web is a fastest medium for opinion collection from users. Human perception and user opinion has greater potential for knowledge discovery and decision support.

Automated opinion-mining systems analyze and classify the opinions expressed in online documents on a topic-by-topic basis—for example, an article reviewing the stocks of technology companies such as Google, Microsoft, and Yahoo. In general, such systems have three advantages over traditional polling and focus groups [1].

1. They are consistent over time—companies using manual scoring will find that results change when their personnel turn over.

2. These systems can operate in near real time, assimilating vast amounts of information from the Web; this also makes them relatively inexpensive.

3. Some opinion mining systems are multilingual and can process documents that might prove difficult for a given group of human scorers.

Automatic detection of emotions in texts is becoming increasingly important from an applicative point of view. Survey, blogs and review site are used to collect customer opinion about products to get knowledge about the reputation of the company in the market. Companies are interested to know about the people demand. These surveys are to be then summarized to produce a report about the good and bad aspects of particular products. The summary reports are then to be used for decision making equally by manufacturer, customer and merchant. For business intelligence, it is useful to classify each opinion according to the aspect of the business or transaction e.g. product quality, ordering or credibility. This summarization task is different from traditional text summarization. On the other hand, OM is based on the features of the product on which the customers have expressed their opinions which helps to decide whether the opinions are positive or negative. OM can be used for recommendation system, government intelligence, citation analysis, human-computer interaction and its computer assisted creativity. Similarly information extraction from formally written scientific literature is as measurable by precision and recall process that is used to find levels of correctness and exhaustiveness [2].

The rest of the paper is organized as follows. In Section 2 we have discussed related work; Section 3 gives an introduction to various emotion categories along with the general frame work of OM. In section 4 challenges and issues are discussed along with some applications. Finally section 5 concludes the paper.

2. RELATED WORK

Much advanced research in this area has recently focused on several critical areas. The topics covered include related work in extracting opinion, sentiment in text modality.

2.1 Early Systems for Opinion Mining

Early binary opinion-mining systems were relatively simple. They performed a linguistic analysis of the sentences mentioning a topic, such as Google, and classified them as either positive or negative [1]. Research on opinion mining basically started with identifying opinion or sentiment bearing words, e.g. great, amazing, wonderful, bad, poor etc. For opinion extraction it is required to know the linguistic terms and get the idea from the text. Classification of contents of document into positive and negative, and subjective and objective terms is the basic problem of opinion mining. The terms are identified by syntactic features.

1. According to Livia Polanyi and Annie Zaenen, "The most salient clues about attitude are provided by the lexical choice of the writer, but the organization of the text also contributes information relevant to assessing attitude" [3].
2. Another main focus is on subjectivity detection. Subjectivity is used to express private states in the context of a text or conversation. Private state is a general term for opinions, evaluation, beliefs, perception, emotions, peculation and etc [4].
3. Objective statement conveys information in accordance with the intention of the author. If a user feedback has no judgment or opinion on the source content then it is called objective. Jaehui Park et al. in their work [5] categorized objective statements into summary and additional information.

2.2 Early Systems for Emotion Prediction for Text

The various approaches for emotion prediction for text are keyword spotting and feature-based statistical classification using machine learning methods [6].

1. In keyword spotting people tend to use specific words to express their emotions in human-human communication because they have learned how some words are related to the corresponding emotions. Intuitively, the presence of obvious emotional keywords like "happy," "sad," and "enraged" may be easily classified into the corresponding emotional category [7].
2. The statistical classification approach can reflect not only the emotional keywords as in the keyword spotting approach, but also useful features like n-gram and part-of-speech tag [8]. However, the problem of feature selection is still left to improve the performance of emotion recognition.

3. OVERVIEW OF OPINION MINING

Opinion is some attitude someone show about one topic. The research on OM is from word, phrase, and sentence to chapter and to address the issues which emotional words (also known as opinion). The target of OM is to mine out the opinions held by someone from documents.

3.1 Emotion Categories

Before starting on a research on emotion classification, the first question is "Which emotions should be addressed?" There are many different emotion sets exists in the literature including "happy", "sad", "surprise", "fear" and so on. These categories of emotions helps the conversational agent like chatbot or intelligent robot to give more human like responses based on the emotional state of user. Table 1 shows a deeper list of emotions as described in Parrot (2001), where emotions were categorised into a short tree structure [9].

3.2 A General Framework of Opinion Mining

Figure 1 shows a framework of opinion mining. It is logically derived from critical analysis of existing research in automated opinion mining [10]. As shown in the figure there are mainly two methods of OM. **Item Extraction:** Naturally, the first step is to know the item for which an opinion is required through item extraction. This only gives an overall positive/negative opinion about the item, without any specific details of what is actually being considered.

Nothing is known about the pros and cons of the features. In this step although it can be known that item A is good/bad, there is no apparent justification for this. **Feature Extraction:** Feature extraction is the identification of features of product which customers have expressed their reviews and feedbacks. This enables one to differentiate between good and bad features. In this step it can be known why item A is good/bad.

Consider monitor A as an example, whereas step 1 can inform us that the monitor is good/bad, step 2 can inform us about the zoom functionality, weight and size of the monitor. Based on this further detail, a more subjective opinion can be deduced.

Furthermore, as shown in Fig. 1, the output for item sentiment can be used as the input for item comparison and feature comparison. Figure 1, shows us that a reviewer can have the option of comparing item A with item B or the features of item A with those of item B.

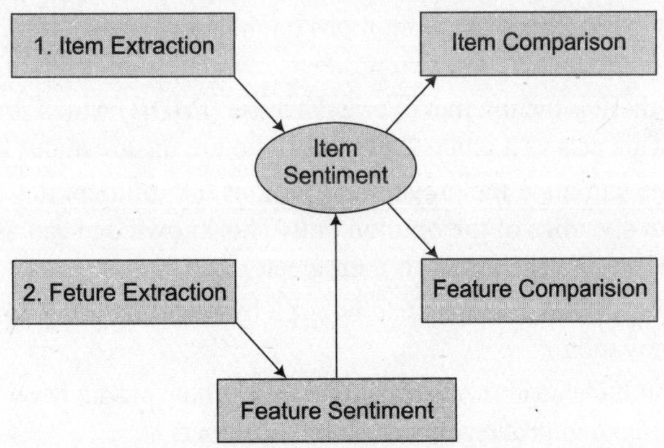

Fig. 1   Opinion mining framework

3.3 Opinion Mining as Applied to Emotion Prediction

Our main task is to classify the emotions listed in table 1 in various categories such as happiness, sadness, anger, disgust, surprise and fear. For this classification we can use various classifiers such as Naive Bayes, Support Vector Machines, and Vector Space Model.

Figure 2 shows how the opinion mining can be used for predicting emotions using set theory. The set theory deals with collection of abstract objects to find the intersections and set differences of objects in a given set [11]. For the graphical simplicity, we only show 3 emotional classes (anger, disgust and fear).

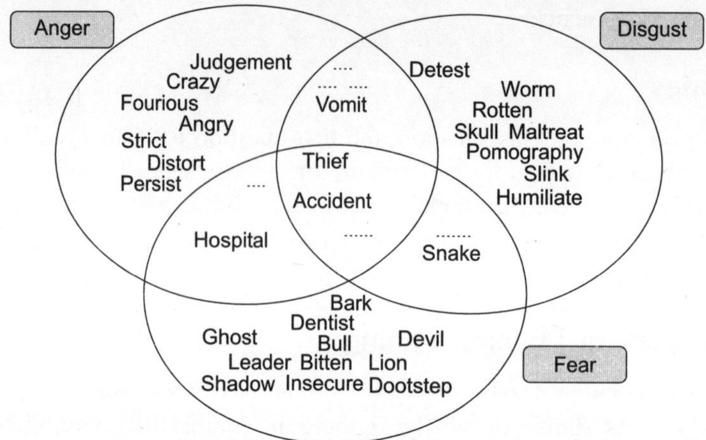

Fig. 2 Emotion prediction using opinion mining

4. APPLICATIONS AND FUTURE CHALLENGES

Opinion mining can be used in various fields to meet different goals. In this section we take the opportunity to present some of the common ones. In spite of recent advances and many applications, there are still several promising new directions for developing and advancing new opinion research.

4.1 Applications

Opinion mining is useful for government enterprise and even personal to come to know the public sentiments and it helps to make decisions. Following are the various application areas for OM [12].

1. Shopping: Consumers are actively involved in comparison shopping over the internet. Popular web sites like amazon.com allow customers to express their opinions on their websites. Customers can easily view the opinions for products and identify how features between products compare with each other.

2. Entertainment: Currently, there is the internet movie database (IMDB) which provides online reviews for movies as well as TV programs. This acts as a guide for people who are unsure about which movies to watch.

3. Government: Governments can mine the prevailing opinions on public policy. Election candidates can become more knowledgeable about specifics of the opinion poll. This knowledge can assist politicians to identify where their strengths and weaknesses lie according to their electorate.

4. Research and Development: Product reviews can be used by manufacturing companies to improve features and provide a platform for innovation.

5. Marketing: Companies can have customer's feedback about their products on their web sites. Analyzing these reviews can help them to make improvements in quality products.

6. Education: The online reviews of the students in e-learning systems can help the tutor to improve the performance of academic as well as institution.

4.2 Future Challenges

OM suffers from several different challenges, such as determining which segment of text is opinionated, identifying the opinion holder, determining the positive or negative strength of opinion. Following are the general challenges pointed out by different authors:

1. Authority[13]
2. Non Expert opinion
3. Domain Dependent [14]
4. Language differences
5. Effects of syntax on semantics [15]

Sentence document Complexity, Contextual Sentiments, Heterogeneous documents, Reference Resolution, Modal operators: might, could, and should are still remain challenging problems in this area.

5. CONCLUSIONS

Emerging opinion mining technologies makes it possible to aggregate and financially leverage the opinions of vast number of peoples. Automated OM analyzes and classifies the opinion expressed in online documents on topic by topic basis. This paper mainly focuses on the automated system for the text based emotion prediction using OM. The various systems have been implemented but building on what have been done so far, need to build integrated systems that try to deal with all the problems together.

References

1. V.S. Subrahmanian, "Mining online opinions", Published by the IEEE Computer Society, IEEE 2009
2. Khairullah Khan, Baharum B.Baharudin, Aurangzeb Khan, Fazal-e-Malik, "Mining Opinion from Text Documents: A Survey", 3rd IEEE International Conference on Digital Ecosystems and Technologies, 2009
3. Livia Polanyi and Annie Zaenen, "Contextual valence shifter", Computing Attitude and Affect in Text: Theory and Applications Chapter 1, pages 1–10. Springer, 2006.
4. Nitin Jindal and Bing Liu, "Mining Comparative Sentences and Relations", American Association for Artificial Intelligence, www.aaai.org., 2006.
5. Jaehui Park et al., "web content summarization using social bookmarks", WIDM08, 2008.
6. Cheongjae Lee and Gary Geunbae Lee, "Emotion Recognition for Affective User Interfaces using Natural Language Dialogs", Regional Technology Innovation Program of the Ministry of Commerce, Industry and Energy (MOCIE), 2006.
7. X. Zhe and A.C. Boucouvalas, "Text-to-emotion engine for real time internet communication," International Symposium on Communication Systems, Networks and DSPs, 2000, 354-357.
8. C.H. Lee and S. Narayanan, "Toward detecting emotions in spoken dialogs," IEEE transactions on Speech and Audio Processing, Vol. 13, no. 2, 2005, 293-303.
9. Parrott, W. (2001), Emotions in Social Psychology, Psychology Press, Philadelphia
10. Yee W. LO, Vidyasagar POTDAR, "A Review of Opinion Mining and Sentiment Classification Framework in Social Networks", 3rd IEEE International Conference on Digital Ecosystems and Technologies, 2009
11. Taner Danisman1 and Adil Alpkocak1, "Feeler: Emotion Classification of Text Using Vector Space Model", Scientific and Technological Research Council of Turkey (TUBITAK) Project No: 107E002.
12. Haji Binali, Vidyasagar Potdar, Chen Wu, "A State of the Art Opinion Mining and its Application Domains", Digital Ecosystems and Business Intelligence Institute, 2008.
13. Jack G. Cornrad et al. 'Professional Credibility: Authority on the web', WICOW08, 2008.
14. G. Salton, "Automatic Text Processing: The Transformation, Analysis and Retrieval of Information by Computer", Addison-Wesley, 1989.
15. Bo Pang and Lillian Lee, "Opinion Mining and Sentiment Analysis", Foundations and Trends in Information Retrieval Vol. 2, Nos. 1–2 (2008) 1–135 2008.

CHAPTER 6

Comparative Study of Face Recognition Methods: PCA and LDA

Sushma R. Sonawane[1], Madhuri A. Jawale[2] and Niket P. Borade[3]
[1]Marathwada Institute of Technology, Aurangabad (MS), India-431028, [2]SRES College of Engineering, Kopargaon,
[3]Yanbu Industrial College, Yanbu, KSA.
E-mail: sushma.borade@yahoo.com, jawale.madu@gmail.com, nborade@yic.edu.sa

ABSTRACT

Face recognition is one of the most successful applications of image analysis and understanding and has gained much attention in recent years. This paper presents comparative study of two most popular appearance-based face recognition methods PCA (Principal Components Analysis) and LDA (Linear Discriminant Analysis). It is generally believed that algorithms based on LDA are superior to those based on PCA. In this paper we show that this is not always the case. Our conclusion is that when the training data set is small, PCA can outperform LDA and, also, that PCA is less sensitive to different training data sets.

Keywords: Face Recognition, PCA, LDA.

1. INTRODUCTION

A biometric system provides automatic identification for an individual based on a unique feature or characteristics possessed by the individual. Biometric systems have been developed based on fingerprints, voice, hand geometry, handwriting, the retina, the eye gaze and the one presented in this paper, the human face. Over the last ten years or so, face recognition has become a popular area of research in computer vision and one of the most successful applications of image analysis and understanding. Face recognition is such a challenging yet interesting problem that it has attracted researchers who have different backgrounds: psychology, pattern recognition, neural networks, computer vision, and computer graphics. Although very reliable methods of biometric personal identification exist, for example, fingerprint analysis and retinal or iris scans, these methods rely on the cooperation of the participants, whereas a personal identification system based on analysis of frontal or profile images of the face is often effective without the participant's cooperation or knowledge. In general, face recognition techniques can be divided into two groups based on the face representation they use [1]:

1. Appearance-based, which uses holistic texture features and is applied to either whole-face or specific regions in a face image;

2. Feature-based, which uses geometric facial features such as mouth, eyes, brows, cheeks etc. and is based on geometric relationships between them.

Among the various approaches to face recognition, appearance-based subspace analysis, although one of the oldest, gives the most promising results. Subspace analysis is done by projecting an image into a lower dimensional space (subspace) and after that recognition is performed by measuring the distances between known images and the image to be recognized. In this paper, two most popular appearance-based subspace projection methods for face recognition will be presented, they are: Principal Component Analysis (PCA) and Linear Discriminant Analysis (LDA). PCA finds a set of the most representative projection vectors such that the projected samples retain most information about original samples [2]. LDA uses the class information and finds a set of vectors that maximize the between-class scatter while minimizing the within-class scatter [3], [4]. Comparison is done using AR face database. Euclidean distance is used as a distance metrics.

The aim of this paper is to provide a comparative study of these two projection methods. For comparison, same preprocessed images are the input into these algorithms. It is interesting to note that the literature on this subject is contradictory. And this is another reason to perform a study of this kind. Beveridge *et al.* claim that in their tests LDA performed worse than PCA [5], Martinez and Kak state that LDA is better [6], and Belhumeur *et al.* claim that LDA outperforms PCA [3].

The rest of this paper is organized as follows: Section 2 gives a brief description of the algorithms to be compared, Section 3 gives the details of methodology, Section 4 presents the results and Section 5 concludes the paper.

2. ALGORITHMS

A face image in 2-dimension with size m $\times$ n can also be considered as one dimensional vector of dimension N. ($N = m \times n$). Since space derived this way is highly dimensional, recognition in it is unfeasible. Therefore, recognition algorithms derive lower dimensional spaces to do the actual recognition while retaining as much information from the original images as possible. An illustration of building a general subspace appearance based face recognition system is shown in Figure 1. Training of the system is shown in the left part of the figure and the procedure for projecting gallery images onto a subspace (projection matrix W^T) is shown in the right part of the figure; X is a matrix containing the images expressed as vectors in its columns, x_{mean} – mean image (as a vector), Φ – matrix containing mean-subtracted images in its columns, W^T – projection matrix, x_g – gallery image (as a vector). During the training phase, the projection matrix (containing the basis vectors of the subspace) is calculated and then the gallery images (the images of known persons) are projected onto that subspace and their projections are stored in a database. Later, in the recognition phase (Fig. 2), new image is normalized, mean-subtracted, projected onto the same subspace as the gallery image was and its projection is then compared to stored gallery projections. The nearest neighbor is determined by calculating the distances (d) from a probe image projection to all gallery images projections. Then the minimum distance is chosen as a similarity measure. The identity of the most similar gallery image is then chosen to be the result of recognition and the unknown probe image is identified.

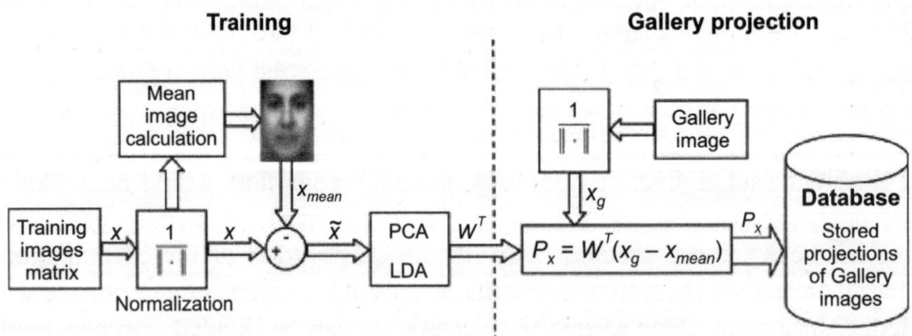

Fig. 1 An illustration of general subspace appearance-based face recognition system.

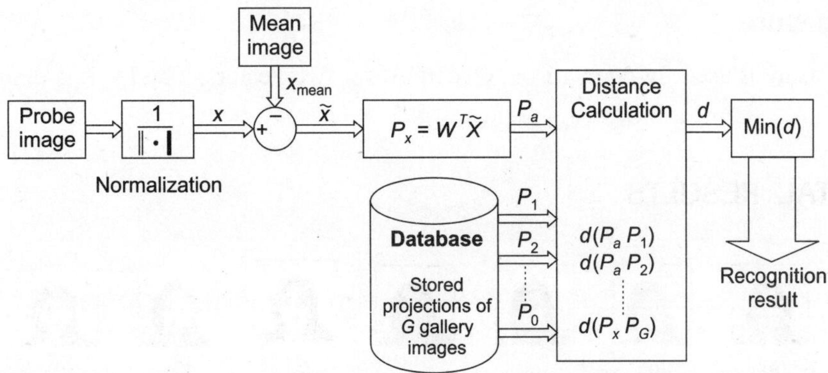

Fig. 2   The recognition phase of a general subspace face recognition system.

2.1   Principal Component Analysis (PCA).

We implemented Principal Component Analysis (PCA) procedure as described by Turk and Pentland [2]. Given s-dimensional vector representation of each face, PCA finds a t-dimensional subspace whose basis vectors correspond to the maximum variance direction in the original space. This new subspace is lower dimensional (t<< s). New basis vectors define a subspace of face images called face space. All images of training set are projected onto the face space to find sets of weights that describe the contribution of each vector. To identify an unknown image, that image is projected onto the face space to find its set of weights. The face is recognized by comparing a set of weights of unknown face with sets of weights of known faces.

The projection matrix is composed of t eigenvectors corresponding to t largest eigenvalues. This creates a t-dimensional face space. As these eigenvectors look like ghostly faces they are called as eigenfaces.

2.2   Linear Discriminant Analysis

Unlike PCA method that extracts features to best represent face images; the LDA method tries to find the subspace that best discriminates different face classes. The within-class scatter matrix represents variations in appearance of the same individual while the between-class scatter matrix represents variations in appearance due to difference in identity. Images are projected from N^2-dimensional space (where N^2 is the number of pixels in the image) to C dimensional space (where C is the number of classes of images). The between-class scatter matrix S_b and the within-class scatter matrix S_W are defined by

$$S_w = \Sigma_{j=1}^{c} \Sigma_{i=1}^{Nj} (\Gamma_i^j - \mu_j)(\Gamma_i^j - \mu_j)^T \tag{1}$$

$$S_b = \Sigma_{j=1}^{c} (\mu_j - \mu)(\mu_j - \mu)^T \tag{2}$$

where Γ_i^j is the ith sample of class j, μ_j is the mean of class j, C is the number of classes, N_j is the number of samples in class j and μ represents the mean of all classes [3].

The goal is to maximize S_b while minimizing S_W, in other words, maximize the ratio $det|S_b|/det|S_w|$. It is maximized when the column vectors of the projection matrix (W_{LDA}) are the eigenvectors of $S_W^{-1} S_b$. i.e

$$W_{opt} = [w_1 \ w_2 \ .... \ w_m] \tag{3}$$

where $\{w_i \mid i = 1, 2, ...m\}$ is the set of generalized eigenvectors of S_b and S_w corresponding to set of decreasing generalized eigenvalues $\{?_i \mid i = 1, 2, ...m\}$

Upper bond on m is C-1 where C is the number of classes.

In order to prevent S_W to become singular, PCA is used to reduce dimension of feature space to $M - C$ and then, apply standard FLD (i.e LDA) defined by Eq.(3) to reduce dimension to $C - 1$. More formally, W_{opt} is given by

$$W_{opt} = W_{LDA} \ W_{pca} \tag{4}$$

2.3 Distance Measure

Euclidean distance measure is used for comparison. Generally, for two vectors, x and y, it is defined as:

$$d_{L2}(x, y) = \|x - y\|^2 \tag{5}$$

3. EXPERIMENTAL RESULTS

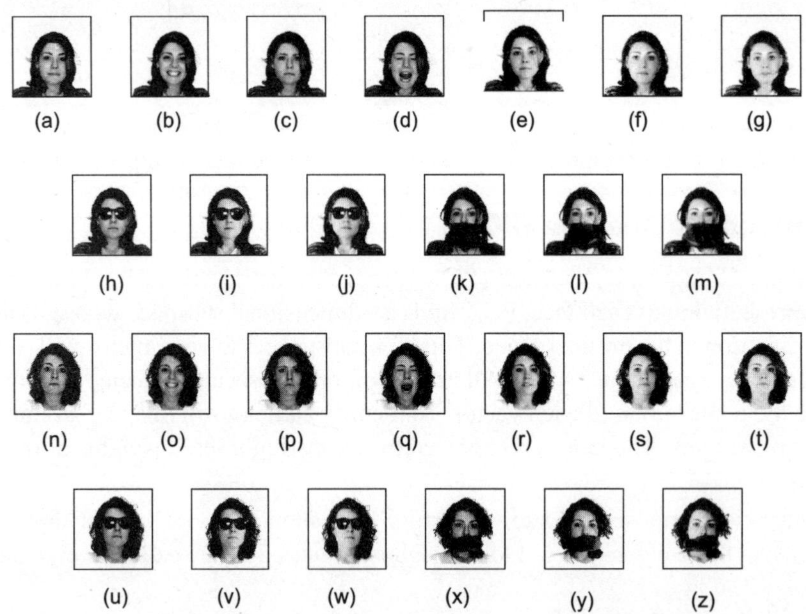

Fig. 3 Images of one person in the AR face database.

3.1 Data

We used standard AR-face database (a publicly available dataset) for recognition tests. This database consists of over 3200 color images of the frontal images of faces of 126 individuals. There are 26 different images for each individual. For each individual, these images were recorded in two different sessions separated by two weeks, each session consisting of 13 images. For illustration, images for one person are shown in Figure 3. The images (a)-(m) were taken during one session and the images (n)-(z) at a different session. All images were taken by the same camera under controlled conditions of illumination and viewpoint. All images in the database are of size 768×576 pixels.

3.2 Preprocessing

For implementation, we randomly selected 50 different individuals (25 males and 25 females) from this database. We morphed images to the size of 85×60 and converted them to gray-level images.

3.3 Small Training Data Set

We used two images per person for training and five for testing. Here we used only the nonoccluded images recorded during the first session. For example, for the person shown in Figure 3, only Figures 3a through 3g are used. There are 21 different ways to select two images for training and five for testing. We used all these ways to create 21 different training and testing data sets. We applied 1) PCA, 2) PCA without first three eigenvectors and 3) LDA. Testing is done using nearest-neighbor algorithm (Euclidean distance measure). Let f be the dimensionality of the final subspace in which face identification takes place.

Table 1 summarizes the results for all 21 cases of training and testing data sets for the case of low-dimensionality. And, Table 2 shows results for the case of high-dimensionality. For each value of the dimensionality parameter f, the top row shows the number of cases for which the basic PCA outperformed the other two algorithms, the middle row shows the number of cases for which PCA without the first three eigenvectors was the best, and the last row shows the number of cases for which LDA outperformed PCA.

Table 1 shows that if we limit the dimensionality of the final subspace to between roughly 1 and 6, PCA (including PCA without the first three eigenvectors) can outperform LDA. For high-dimensional spaces, we can conclude that, LDA has a greater chance of outperforming PCA. Finally we observe that the performance of both PCA and LDA gets better as value of f increases.

Table 1   Results of 21 Training and Testing Sets

Method	f = 1	f = 2	f = 3	f = 4	f = 5	f = 6	f = 7	f = 8	f = 9	f = 10
PCA	6	9	13	9	9	9	7	4	4	3
PCA w/o 3	4	1	0	0	0	0	0	0	0	0
LDA	11	11	8	12	12	12	14	17	17	18

Table 2   Results for the 21 Cases of Training and Testing Sets (High –Dimensional Spaces)

Method	f = 20	f = 30	f = 40
PCA	3	2	2
PCA w/o 3	0	0	0
LDA	18	19	19

3.4   Using Larger and Representative Samples per Class

In this section we used all the 26 images for each person in the AR database. The first 13 of these (Figures 3a through 3m), were taken in one session; these are used for training now. The last 13 (Figures 3n through 3z), were taken in a second session; these are used for testing. Figure 4 shows that LDA outperforms PCA when a large and representative training data set is used.

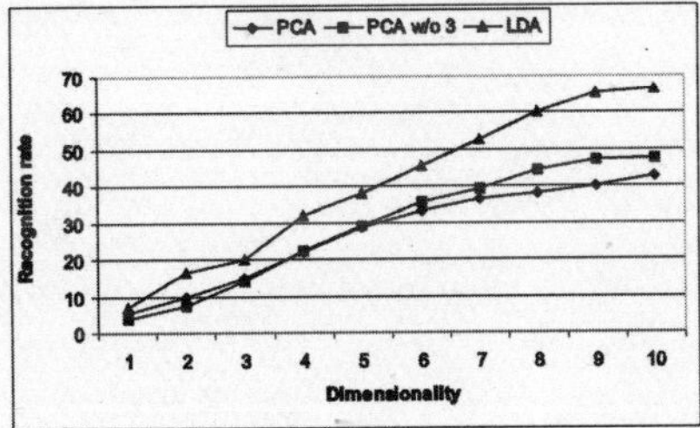

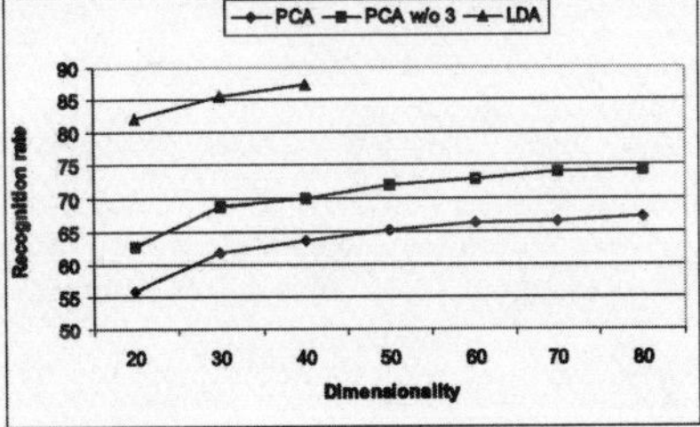

Fig. 4   Results for PCA and LDA algorithms using larger and representative training set.

4.   CONCLUSIONS

This paper presented a comparative study of two most popular appearance-based face recognition methods (PCA and LDA) using Euclidean distance metrics. Although one might think that LDA should always outperform PCA (since it deals directly with class discrimination), our experimental results suggests otherwise. PCA might outperform LDA when the number of samples per class is small or when the training data nonuniformly sample the underlying distribution. Practically one never knows in advance the underlying distributions for the different classes. Therefore in practice it is difficult to ascertain whether or not the available training data is adequate for the job.

References

1. Zhao, W., Chellappa, R., Phillips, A.: Face Recognition in Still and Video Images: A Literature Survey. ACM Comput. Surv. 35, 399—458 (2003)
2. Turk M., Pentland A.: Eigenfaces for Recognition. J. Cogn. Neurosci. 3, 71—86 (1991)
3. Belhumeur, P., Hespanha, J., Kriegman, D.: Eigenfaces vs. Fisherfaces: Recognition using Class Specific Linear Projection. In: Proc Fourth Eur. Conf. Computer Vision, vol. 1, pp. 45—58. Cambridge, UK (1996)
4. Zhao, W., Chellappa, R., Krishnaswamy, A.,: Discriminant Analysis of Principal Components for Face Recognition. In: 3rd IEEE International Conference on Automatic Face and Gesture Recognition, pp. 336—341. Nara, Japan (1998)
5. Beveridge, J., She, K., Draper, B., Givens, G.,: A Nonparametric Statistical Comparison of Principal Component and linear Discriminant Subspaces for Face Recognition. In: IEEE Conference on Computer Vision and Pattern Recognition, pp. 535—542. Kauai, HI (2001)

CHAPTER 7

Face Recognition with Principal Component Analysis and Cross-Correlation Techniques

[1]Srinivasulu Asadi, [2]K Lalitha and [2]K.Hazarathaiah

[1]Dept of IT, SVEC, Tirupati, J.N.T. University, Anantapur, (AP) India, [2]Dept of CSSE, SVEC,
Tirupati J.N.T. University, Anantapur (AP), India
E-mail: srinu_asadi@yahoo.com, lalitha_psr@yahoo.com, azaroop@gmail.com

ABSTRACT

Automated face recognition has become a major field of interest. Face recognition algorithms are used in a wide range of applications viz., security control, crime investigation, and entrance control in buildings, access control at automatic teller machines, passport verification, identifying the faces in a given databases. This paper discusses different face recognition techniques by considering different test samples. The experimentation involved the use of Eigen faces and PCA (Principal Component Analysis). Another method based on Cross-Correlation in spectral domain has also been implemented and tested. Recognition rate of 90% was achieved for the above mentioned face recognition techniques.

General Terms: Image Processing, Artificial Intelligence, Biometric, Signal Processing.

Keywords: Face Recognition, Principal Component Analysis, Cross-Correlation Technique.

1. INTRODUCTION

Face recognition is biometric identification by scanning a person's face and matching it against a library of known faces. Face recognition is defined as the identification of a person from an image of their face. Face Recognition systems can be of two types. Firstly, Face Identification: Given a face image that belongs to a person in a database and to tell whose image it is. Secondly, Face Verification: Given a face image that might not belong to the database, verify whether it is from the person it is claimed to be in the database.

The main aim of most commercial face recognition is to increase the capability of security and surveillance systems. In theory, security systems involving face recognition would be impossible to hack, as the identification process involves unique identification methods, and thus only authorized users will be accepted. Face recognition has N classes, where each class represents one person from N individuals that mean multi class classification (one person vs. all the others). Face recognition must discriminate between the subtle differences of human faces. Face recognition is performed in order to determine the identity of each face. Applications of face recognition are access control, face databases, face identification, human computer interaction, law enforcement, smart cards and multimedia management.

2. RELATED WORK

Currently there are many methods of biometric identification viz., fingerprint, eye iris, retina, voice, face etc. Each of these methods has certain advantages and disadvantages, which must be considered in biometrical system developing: system reliability, price, flexibility, necessity of physical contact with scanning device and many others. Selecting the certain biometrical identification method or using the multi-biometrical system can help to support these, often discrepant, requirements. Face identification can be an important alternative for selecting and developing optimal biometrical system. Its advantage is that it does not require physical contact with image capture device (camera). Face identification system does not require any advanced hardware; it can be used with existing image capture devices like web cams, security cameras etc.

Face is not so unique as fingerprints and eye iris, so its recognition reliability is slightly lower. However, it is still suitable for many applications, taking into account its convenience for user. Also it can be used together with fingerprint identification or another biometrical method for developing more security critical applications. Multi-biometrical approach is especially important for identification (1: N) systems. Identification systems are very convenient for using, because they do not require any additional security information (smart cards, passwords etc.). On the other hand, 1: N-matching routine usually accumulates False Acceptance probability, which may become unacceptable for applications with large databases.

3. PRINCIPAL COMPONENT ANALYSIS

PCA also known as Karhunen Loeve projection. PCA calculates the Eigen vectors of the covariance matrix, and projects the original data onto a lower dimensional feature space, which is defined by Eigen vectors with large Eigen values. PCA has been used in face representation and recognition where the Eigen vectors calculated are referred to as Eigen faces. In gel images, even more than in human faces, the dimensionality of the original data is vast compared to the size of the dataset, suggesting PCA as a useful first step in analysis. There are many approaches to face recognition ranging from the Principal Component Analysis (PCA) approach (also known as Eigen faces). Prediction through feature matching. The idea of feature selection and point matching has been used to track human motion. Eigen faces have been used to track human faces. They use a principal component analysis approach to store a set of known patterns in a compact subspace representation of the image space, where the subspace is spanned by the Eigen vectors of the training image set.

PCA is a useful statistical technique that has found application in fields such as face recognition and image compression, and is a common technique for finding patterns in data of high dimension. The basic goal is to implement a simple face recognition system, based on well-studied and well-understood methods. One can choose to go into depth of one and only one of those methods. The method to be implemented is the PCA (Principle Component Analysis). It is one of the more successful techniques of face recognition and easy to understand and describe using mathematics. This method involves using Eigen faces.

The first step is to produce a feature detector (dimension reduction). Principal Components Analysis (PCA) was chosen because it is the most efficient technique, of dimension reduction, in terms of data compression. This allows the high dimension data, the images, to be represented by lower dimension data and so hopefully reducing the complexity of grouping the images.

3.1 Methodology

3.1.1 Data acquisition

A database of different image sets of faces was constructed. It's only got 2 dimensions, and the reason why one can have chosen this is so that one can provide plots of the data to show what the PCA analysis is doing at each step.

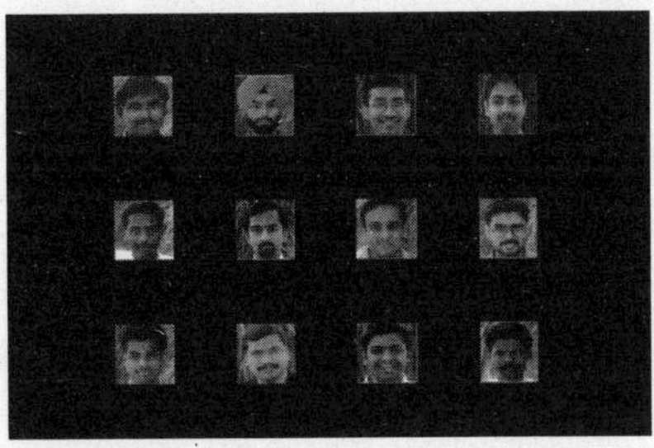

3.2   Subtract the Mean Image Data

For PCA to work properly, you have to subtract the mean from each of the data dimensions. The mean subtracted is the average across each dimension. So, all the x values have x' (the mean of the x values of all the data points) subtracted, and all the y values have y' subtracted from them. This produces a data set whose mean is zero.

3.3   Find the Covariance Matrix

This is done in exactly the same way as was discussed in Section 2.2.2. Since the data is 2 dimensional, the covariance matrix will be 2 * 2 as shown below:

Since the non-diagonal elements in this covariance matrix are positive, both the x and y variable increase together.

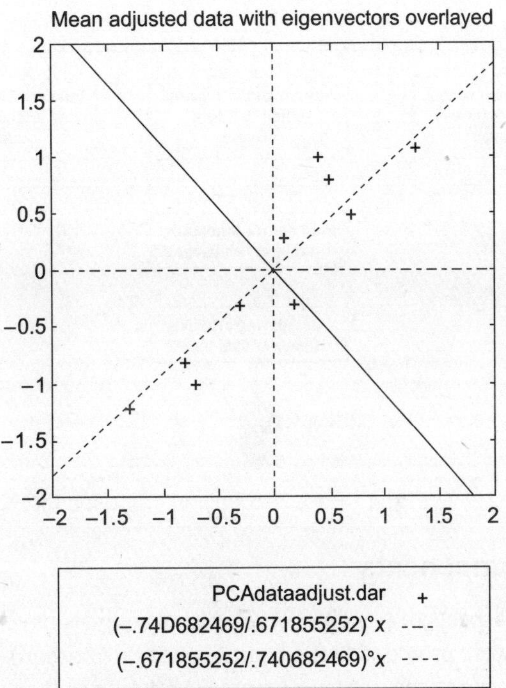

Fig.1   A plot of the normalized data (mean subtracted) with the Eigen vectors of the covariance matrix overlayed on top

3.1.2   Recognition process in eigen faces Approach

Step 1   Form a face database that consists of the face images of known individuals.

Step 2   Choose a training set that includes a number of images (M) for each person with some variation in pose and different faces.

Step 3   Calculate the $M \times M$ matrix L, find its Eigen vectors and Eigen values, and choose the M' Eigen vectors with the highest associated Eigen values.

Step 4 Combine the normalized training set of images to produce M' Eigen faces.

Step 5 Store these Eigen faces for later use.

Step 6 For each member in the face database, compute and store a feature vector.

Step 7 Choose a threshold value e that defines the maximum allowable distance from any face class. Optionally choose a threshold f that defines the maximum allowable distance from face space.

Step 8 For each new face image to be identified, calculate its feature vector and compare it with the stored feature vectors of the face library members.

Step 9 If the comparison satisfies the threshold for at least one member, then classify this face image as "known", otherwise a miss has occurred and classify it as "unknown" and add this member to the face library with its feature vector.

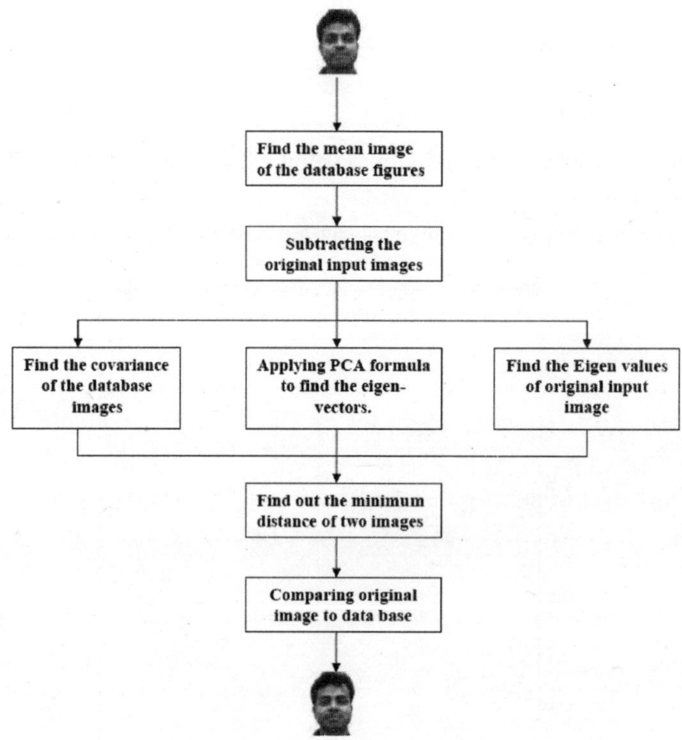

Fig. 4 Face recognition proposed for PCA

3.4 Extracting Principal Components

The details about the computational aspects of principal components analysis have been skipped in this section, as it has been mentioned before. (references were provided at the beginning of this section). However, basically, the extraction of principal components amounts to a variance maximizing (varimax) rotation of the original variable space. For example, in a scatter plot one can think of the regression line as the original X axis, rotated so that it approximates the regression line. This type of rotation is called variance maximizing because the criterion for (goal of) the rotation is to maximize the variance (variability) of the new variable (factor), while minimizing the variance around the new variable.

3.5 Benefits of PCA

- The basic Benefit in PCA is to reduce the dimension of the data.
- No data redundancy as components is Orthogonal.
- With help of PCA, complexity of grouping the images can be reduced.

- Application of PCA in the prominent field of criminal investigation is beneficial.
- PCA also benefits entrance control in buildings, access control for computers in general, for automatic teller machines in particular, day-to-day affairs like withdrawing money from bank account, dealing with the post office, passport verification, and identifying the faces in a given databases

PCA Features
- PCA computes means, variances, covariance's, and correlations of large data sets
- PCA computes and ranks principal components and their variances.
- Automatically transforms data sets.
- PCA can analyze datasets up to 50,000 rows and 200 columns

4. CROSS-CORRELATION TECHNIQUE

4.1 Cross-Correlation Technique

Correlation is often called Template matching. Correlation can be used to locate features within an image which is closely related to convolution. It is a standard of estimating the degree to which two series are correlated. The use of cross-correlation for template matching is motivated by the distance measure (squared Euclidean Distance) Correlation of two functions $f(x, y)$ and $h(x, y)$ is defined as

$$f(x, y) * h(x, y) = 1/(M * N) * \sum_{n=0}^{N-1} \sum_{m=0}^{M-1} f * f^*(m, n) \, h(x + m, y + n)$$

Where f^* is complex conjugate of f

        $f(x, y), h(x, y)$ are convolution of two functions

        M, N are the size of matrices limit is $m = 0$ to

        $m - 1$ and $n = 0$ to $n - 1$

Cross-Correlation and Euclidean Distance are two of the most common statistical techniques used for target matching. Calculation of the Cross-Correlation can be carried out in both the spatial and Fourier domain. Significant performance benefits are achieved by computing the Fourier domain Cross-Correlation using the Mixed Radix Fast Fourier Transform (FFT). This paper provides further results of a comparison of these techniques undertaken in the Meteorological Product Extraction Facility environment, by comparing the displacement vectors derived from pseudo-real imagery data, including analysis of behavior in different contrast regions. The results show that the two techniques are well matched. In assessing the relative benefits of alternative matching techniques, this paper additionally provides results for the Euclidean Distance method. It includes comparison with Cross-Correlation of the displacement vectors in different contrast regions and analyses where maximum discrepancy is observed between the two methods. The results indicate that differences between the two techniques are more apparent in lower contrast regions.

Matching Images
It can deal with two similar tasks:
1. Given a point in one image, to find its matching point in the other image, feature matching or optical flow.
2. Find the transformation mapping one image to the other Image alignment or Image registration.

Cross Correlation Function: The cross correlation of random processes $X(t)$ and $Y(t)$ is

$$RXY(t; c) = E\,[X(t)\,Y(t + c)]$$

A neighborhood operation in which each output pixel is a weighted sum of neighboring input pixels. The weights are defined by the computational molecule. Image processing operations are implemented with convolution which includes smoothing, sharpening, and edge enhancement. Correlation is closely related mathematically to convolution.

Issues of Correlation: In many image identification processes the mask may need to be rotated and scaled at each position. The process is very similar to 2D filtering except in that case the image is replaced by an appropriately scaled version of the correlation. The process can be extremely time consuming. The 2D cross correlation needs to be computed for every point in the image.

4.2   Implementation Method

The Fourier transform can also be used to perform correlation, which is closely related to convolution. Correlation can be used to locate features within an image in this context [15] correlation is often called Template matching.

For instance, suppose you want to locate occurrences of the letter "*a*" in an image containing text. This example reads in text.tif and creates a template image by extracting a letter "*a*" from it,

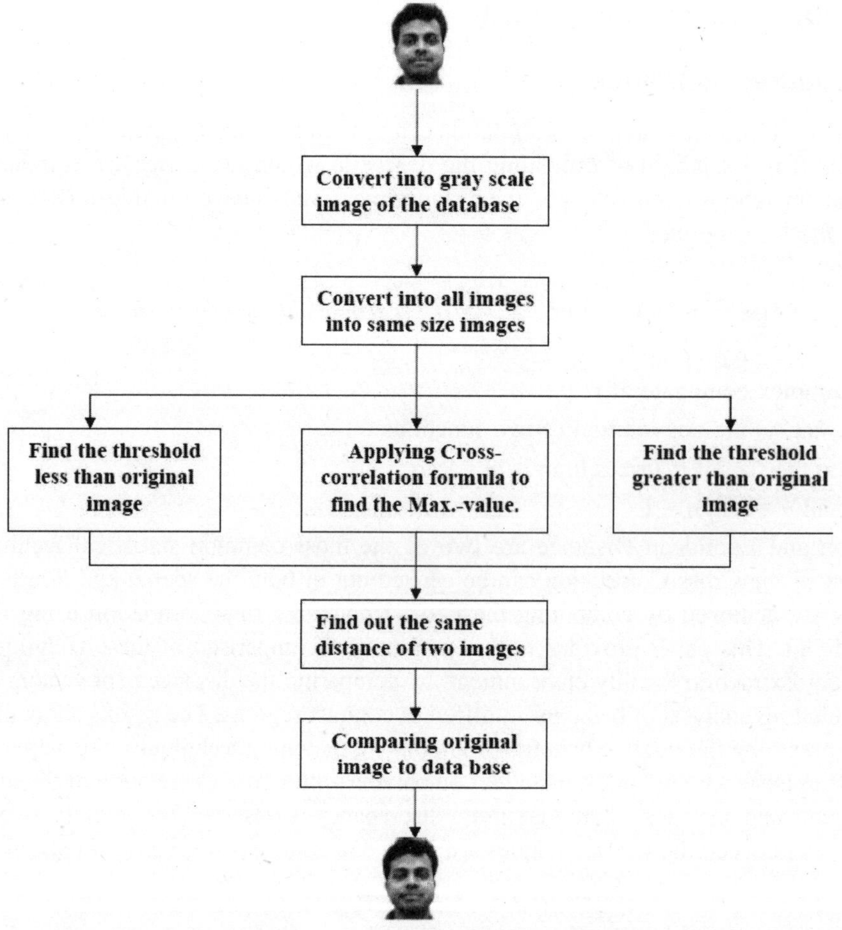

Fig. 5   Face Recongnition proposed for cross-correlation technique process

The correlation of the image of the letter "*a*" with the larger image can be computed by first rotating the image of "*a*" by 180° and then using the FFT-based convolution technique [13].

To match the template to the image, you can use the fft2 and ifft2 functions.

Use this formula C = real(ifft2(fft2(bw)* fft2(rot90(a,2),256,256))); calculate C value.

Display, scaling data to appropriate range. Figure, imshow(C, a)

Find max pixel value in C. max(C(:)).

Use a threshold that's a little less than max. thresh = 45;

Display showing pixels over threshold. Figure, imshow($C >$ thresh)

Comparing with input image to the database image set.

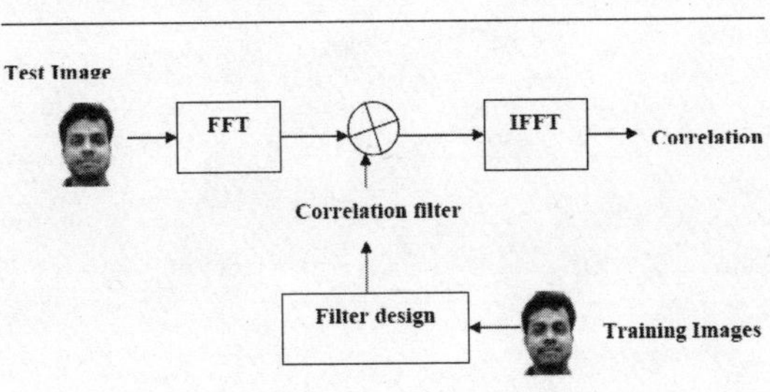

Figure 6: Block diagram showing the Correlation process

Fig. 6   Block diagram showing the correlation process

5.   RESULTS AND DISCUSSION

The performance of the two methods was accessed by testing. The face images of 12 people with different poses (48 Images) were taken for testing. By using PCA (Principal Component Analysis) the recognition accuracy was 90% on a very small set of faces. However the accuracy might decrease with increase in the number of samples. The recognition accuracy of Eigen face method can be improved by using a Neural Network for classification rather than taking the Euclidean Distance of the features. By using Cross-Correlation Technique the recognition accuracy was 85% on a very small set of faces. However the accuracy might decrease with increase in the number of samples. The recognition accuracy of Eigen face method can be improved by using a Wavelet Networks for classification rather than taking the Euclidean Distance of the features

The results of the testing process are documented below.

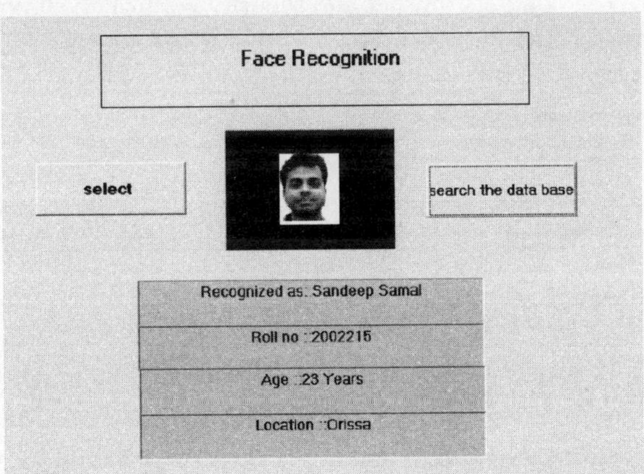

Fig. 7   Recognized face using prinicipal component analysis

Principle Component Analysis (PCA), a frequently used statistical technique for optimal lossy compression of data under least square sense; provide orthogonal basis vector space to represent original data This dissertation includes research and experimentation with face recognition techniques tested with different faces principally; experimentation involved the use of Eigen faces and PCA (Principal Component Analysis). Another method based on Cross-Correlation in spectral domain has also been implemented and tested.

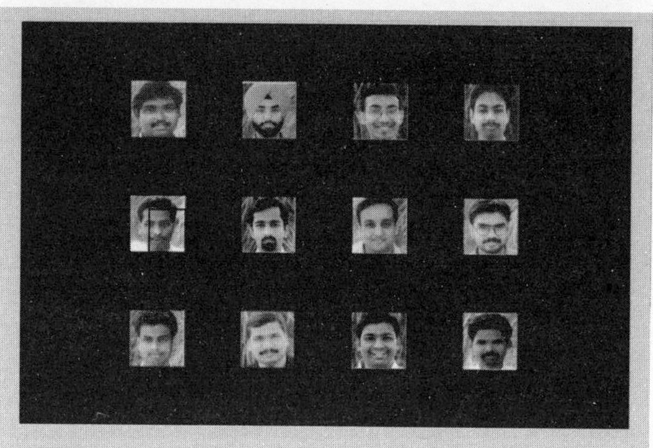

Fig. 9 Recognized face using cross-correlation technique

Efficiency of the Algorithm & Suitability for Industry Use: Recognizing faces could theoretically be very fast, because it consists only of a matrix subtraction, one matrix multiplication and a bit of comparison. On the other hand, training new faces is a comparably complicated calculation, especially if the "face-space" has to be recalculated as soon as new persons are added.

6. CONCLUSION

Two face recognition strategies i.e. PCA (Principal Component Analysis) and Cross-correlation technique were implemented. Principal Component Analysis gave better results for varying poses. Cross-correlation technique can recognize faces even when they are rotated. But this method fails when faces with quite different poses are taken into account. The results are pretty good for the test samples that we have considered.

Face recognition is quickly emerging as a viable authentication method today. With the adoption of standards and community awareness, this technology will become more and more acceptable. Current implementations of this technology are visible in airports, ATM counters, border and security control checkpoints, crime investigation, entrance control in buildings, access control for computers in general, day-to-day affairs like withdrawing money from bank account, passport verification etc. Hence, in this contemporary world, face recognition is playing an important role and can be concluded as an upcoming technology.

Further, we can improve the system by integrating with other biometric methods like speaker recognition, finger print, eye iris, and retina and voice recognition. Further it is suggested to use neural networks and wavelet networks for improving the accuracy of Eigen face method rather than taking Euclidean distance into account

References

1. Jackson, J.E., "A Users Guide to Principal Components", John Wiley and Sons, pp. 1-25, 1991.
2. Kyungnam Kim, "Face Recognition using Principal Component Analysis", USA, June 2000.
3. Geof Givens, J Ross Beveridge, Bruce A. Draper and David Bolme," A Statistical Assessment of Subject Factors in the PCA Recognition of Human Faces", April 2003.
4. Bruce A. Draper, Kyungim Baek, Marian Stewart Bartlett and J. Ross Beveridge," Recognizing Faces with PCA and ICA", 2002.
5. J. Ross Beveridge, Kai She and Bruce A. Draper and Geof H. Givens"A Nonparametric Statistical Comparison of Principal Component and Linear Discriminant Subspaces for Face Recognition".
6. Matthew Turk, Alex Pentland, "Eigen faces for Recognition" Vision and Modeling Group, the Media Laboratory, Massachusetts Institute of Technology; September 1990.
7. Imola K. Fodor," A survey of dimension reduction techniques", June 2002.

8. W. Yambor, B. Draper and R. Beveridge, Analyzing PCA-based Face Recognition Algorithms: "Eigen vector Selection and Distance Measures", July 2000.

9. Christopher James Cobb, "Face Recognition Project", December, 2001.

10. Geof H. Givens, J. Ross Beveridge, Bruce A. Draper and David Bolme, "Using A Generalized Linear Mixed Model to Study the Configuration Space of a PCA+LDA Human Face Recognition Algorithm", April 2003.

11. B.V.K. Vijaya Kumar, "Tutorial survey of composite filter designs for optical correlators," Appl. Opt. 31, pp. 4773-4801 (1992).

12. B.V.K. Vijaya Kumar, and D. Casasent, A. Mahalanobis, "Minimum average correlation energy filters," Appl. Opt. 26, pp. 3633-3630 (1987).

13. Gonzales, R and Woods R,"Digital Image Processing, 2nd Edition Prentice-Hall Englewood cliffs, NJ, 2002.

14. Mario's Savvides and B.V.K. Vijaya Kumar and Pradeep Khosla, "Face verification using correlation filters", U.S.A.

15. Greg Dew and Ken Holmlund, "Investigations of Cross-Correlation of and Euclidean Distance Target Matching Techniques in the MPEF environment".

16. Beata J Wysocki, Tadeusz A Wysocki "Orthogonal Binary Sequences with Wide Range of Correlation Properties", Australia.

17. John W. Fisher III, "Nonlinear Extensions to the Minimum Average Correlation Energy-Filter" University of Florida, 1997.

18. Ahmet Bahtiyar Gul "Holistic Face Recognition by Dimension Reduction", May 2002.

19. Ilker Atalay, "Face Recognition using Eigen Faces", January 1996.

20. Mat lab 6.0 "Image Processing Tool Box".

CHAPTER 8

Iris Biometric for Person Identification Using Phase-Based Image Matching

Sarika B. Solanke

MIT, Engineering College, Aurangabad (MS) India

E-mail: sarikaso@yahoo.com

ABSTRACT

Iris recognition is one of the most accurate and reliable biometric method. Compared with other biometric features, iris can obtain high accuracy due to the rich texture of iris patterns. Iris recognition system includes the preprocessing system, segmentation, feature extraction and recognition. Iris localization aims to isolate the iris region from the original eye image, it includes finding both iris boundaries and detecting eyelids. Daugman (1993) built a recognition system; the system used an integro differential operator to locate the iris boundaries. Wildes (1997) used Hough transform method and a voting procedure in order to locate the iris boundaries. This paper presents an efficient algorithm for iris recognition using phase-based image matching technique using phase components in 2D Discrete Fourier Transforms(DFT's)of given images. Experiments are performed using iris images obtained from CASIA database. (Institute of Automation, Chinese Academy of Sciences) and Matlab application for its easy and efficient tools in image manipulation. I have studied various well known algorithms for iris recognition. Four algorithms due to Avila, Li Ma, Tissue and Daugmann are implemented and compared on the CASIA iris image database. The results show that the daugman's algorithm gave the highest accuracy of 99.9%.

Keywords: Biometrics, iris recognition, Phase-based image matching, phase-only correlation, phase-only matched filtering.

I. INTRODUCTION

Iris recognition is a proven, accurate means to identify people. It examines automated iris recognition as a biometrically based technology for personal identification and verification. In particular, the biomedical literature suggests that irises are as distinct as fingerprints or patterns of retinal blood vessels [1] [2]. Iris recognition system includes the pre-processing system, segmentation, feature extraction and recognition. Especially it focuses on image segmentation and statistical feature extraction for iris recognition process. The performance of iris recognition system highly depends on segmentation. For instance, even an effective feature extraction method would not be able to obtain useful information from an iris image that is not segmented properly. It presents a straightforward approach for segmenting the iris patterns. The human iris is the annular part between the dark pupil and the white sclera, it is unique and stable throughout life[1]. Iris localization aims to isolate the iris region from the original eye image, it includes finding both iris boundaries and detecting eyelids. The localization accuracy is very important for later iris normalization, feature extraction and patterns matching. It costs nearly more than half of the recognition time, therefore, iris localization is crucial for the performance of an iris recognition system. Daugman (1993) built a recognition system; the system used an integro differential operator to locate the iris boundaries [2]. Wildes (1997) used Hough transform method and a voting procedure in order to locate the iris boundaries. Most of previous localization methods, however, require to search the iris boundaries over large parameter space exhaustively.

A. Necessity

Whenever people log onto computers, access an ATM, pass through airport security, use credit cards, or enter high-security areas, they need to verify their identities. People typically use user names, passwords, and identification cards to prove that they are who they claim to be. However, passwords can be forgotten, and identification cards can be lost or stolen. Thus, there is tremendous interest in improved methods of reliable and secure identification of people. Biometric methods, which identify people based on physical or behavioural characteristics, are of interest because people cannot forget or lose their physical characteristics in the way that they can lose passwords or identity cards. Biometric techniques constitute efficient solutions to security problems as the features used in the control decision are based on the intrinsic characteristics of the persons [1] [2].These techniques are already widely used for the recognition of persons using distinct physical characteristics, such as fingerprints, voice and hand shape. Recently, the recognition of individuals based on characteristics of the iris has attracted significant attention from the research community, mainly for being non-invasive. Some other important characteristics of the iris that are extremely usefully in recognition are the stability, as the iris suffers very few changes along aging and is reasonably protected against external aggressions, and the high robustness, as has extraordinarily details and individual specificities.

B. Objectives

The system is to be composed of a number of sub-systems, which correspond to each stage of iris recognition. These stages are segmentation-locating the iris region in an eye image, normalisation-creating a dimensionally consistent representation of the iris region, and feature encoding-creating a template containing only the most discriminating features of the iris.

The input to the system will be an eye image, and the output will be an iris template, which will provide a mathematical representation of the iris region.The objective of this work has been the development of an algorithm for identification of persons through iris recognition from features in its inner region, since this region present most of its specific characteristics. The objective will be to implement an open-source iris recognition system in order to verify the claimed performance of the technology. The development tool used will be MATLAB, and emphasis will be only on the software for performing recognition, and not hardware for capturing an eye image. A rapid application development (RAD) approach will be employed in order to produce results quickly. MATLAB provides an excellent RAD environment, with its image processing toolbox, and high level programming methodology [3] [4].

C. Performance of Iris Biometric Systems

Four modules of an iris biometrics system:
1. Image Acquisition,
2. Segmentation of the iris region,
3. Analysis and representation of the iris texture, or
4. Matching of iris representations.

To appreciate the richness of the iris as a pattern for recognition, it is useful to consider its structure in a bit more detail. The iris is composed of several layers. Its posterior surface consists of heavily pigmented epithelial cells that make it light tight (i.e. impenetrable by light). Anterior to this layer are two cooperative muscles for controlling the pupil. Next is the stromal layer, consisting of collagenous connective tissue in arch-like processes. Coursing through this layer are radially arranged corkscrew like blood vessels. The most anterior layer is the anterior border layer, differing from the stroma in being more densely packed, especially with individual pigment cells called chromataphores. The visual appearance of the iris is a direct result of its multilayered structure. The anterior surface of the iris is sent to be divided into a central pupillary zone and a surrounding cilliary zone.The border of these two areas is termed the collarette; it appears as a zigzag circumferential ridge resulting as the anterior border layer ends abruptly near the pupil. The cilliary zone contains many interlacing ridges resulting from stromal support [1].

The aim of biometrics is to identify individuals using physiological or behavioural characteristics such as fingerprints, face, iris, retina, and palmprints. Among many biometric techniques, iris recognition is one of the most promising approaches due to its high reliability for personal identification [1], [2], [3], [4]. The human iris, which is the annular part between the pupil and the white sclera, has a complex pattern determined by the chaotic morphogenetic processes during embryonic development. The iris pattern is unique to each person and to each eye and is essentially stable over a lifetime. Furthermore, an iris image is typically captured using a noncontact imaging device, which is of great importance in practical applications. A major approach for iris recognition today is to generate feature vectors corresponding to individual iris images and to perform iris matching based on some distance metrics [2].

D. Daugman's Approach

Most of the commercial iris recognition systems implement a famous algorithm using iriscode, which was proposed by daugman [2]. In this algorithm, 2D Gabor filters are used to extract a feature vector corresponding to a given iris image. Then, the filter outputs are quantized to generate a 2 Kbit iriscode. The dissimilarity between a pair of iriscodes is measured by their Hamming distance based on an exclusive-OR operation.The iriscode is very compact and can be accommodated, even on the magnetic stripe implemented on the back of typical credit cards. In addition, exclusive-OR comparison allows us to perform extremely rapid recognition. On the other hand, one of the difficult problems in feature-based iris recognition is that the matching performance is significantly influenced by many parameters in the feature extraction process (for example, spatial position,orientation, center frequencies, and size parameters for 2D Gabor filter kernels), which may vary, depending on the environmental factors of iris image acquisition. Given a set of test iris images, extensive parameter optimization is required to achieve a higher recognition rate.

Daugman's patent states that "the system acquires through a video camera a digitized image of an eye of the human to be identified" near-infrared illumination. The system assesses the focus of the image in real time by looking at the power in the middle and upper frequency bands of the 2D Fourier spectrum. The algorithm seeks to maximize this spectral power by adjusting the focus of the system, or giving the subject audio feedback to adjust their position in front of the camera. Given an image of the eye, the next step is to find the part of the image that corresponds to the iris. Recently, Daugman has studied alternative segmentation techniques to better model the iris boundaries.Even when the inner and outer boundaries of the iris are found, some of the iris still may be occluded by eyelids or eyelashes.Upon isolating the iris region, the next step is to describe the features of the iris in a way that facilitates comparison of irises. The first difficulty lies in the fact that not all images of an iris are the same size. The distance from the camera affects the size of the iris in the image.

The goal of image acquisition is to acquire an image that has sufficient quality to support reliable biometrics processing. The goal of segmentation is to isolate the region that represents the iris. The goal of texture analysis is to derive are presentation of the iris texture that can be used to match two irises. The goal of matching is to evaluate the similarity of two iris representations.

E. Wildes' Approach

Wildes describes an iris biometrics system developed at Sarnoff Labs that uses a very different technical approach from that of Daugman. Whereas Daugman's system acquires the image using "an LED-based point light source in conjunction with a standard video camera," the Wildes system uses "a diffuse source and polarization in conjunction with a low light level camera." When localizing the iris boundary, Daugman's approach looks for a maximum in an integro-differential operator that responds to circular boundary. By contrast, Wildes' approach involves computing a binary edge map followed by a Hough transform to detect circles. In matching two irises,Daugman's approach involves computation of the normalized Hamming distance between iris codes, whereas Wildes applies a Laplacian of Gaussian filter at multiple scales to produce a template and computes the normalized correlation as a similarity measure. Wildes briefly describes the results of two experimental evaluations of the approach, involving images from several hundreds of irises.

There are advantages and disadvantages to both Daugman's and Wildes' designs. Daugman's acquisition system is simpler than Wildes' system, but Wildes' system has a less-intrusive light source designed to eliminate specular reflections. For segmentation, Wildes' approach is expected to be more stable to noise perturbations; however, it makes less use of available data, due to binary edge abstraction,and therefore might be less sensitive to some details. Also,Wildes' approach encompassed eyelid detection and localization.For matching, the Wildes approach made use of more of the available data, by not binarizing the bandpass filtered result, and hence might be capable of finer distinctions; however,it yields a less compact representation.Furthermore, the Wildes method used a data-driven approach to image registration to align two instances to be compared, which might better respond to the real geometric deformations between the instances, but comes at increased computation.

F. Image acquisition

These generally fall into one of two categories, corresponding to the first two subsections. The first category is engineering image acquisition to make it less intrusive for the user. The "Iris on the Move" project is a major example of this . The other category is developing metrics for iris image quality, in order to allow more accurate determination of "good" and "bad" images. All current commercial iris biometrics systems still have constrained image acquisition conditions. Near-infrared illumination, in the 700–900 nm range, is used to light the face, and the user is prompted with visual and/or auditory feedback to position the eye so that it can be in focus and of sufficient size in the image. In 2004, Daugman suggested that the iris should have a diameter of at least 140 pixels. The International Standards Organization (ISO) Iris Image Standard released in 2005 is more demanding, specifying a diameter of 200 pixels.

II. THE USEFUL METHOD FOR IRIS RECOGNITION USING PHASE-BASED IMAGE MATCHING

This method proposes an efficient iris recognition algorithm using phase-based image matching, that is, an image matching technique using only the phase components in 2D Discrete Fourier Transforms (DFTs) of given images. The technique of phase-based image matching has so far been successfully applied to high-accuracy image registration tasks for computer vision applications [3], [4], [5], where the estimation of sub pixel image translation is a major concern. The proposed matching algorithm assumes the use of iris images registered in the system to achieve high performance. In order to reduce the size of iris data and to prevent the visibility of individual iris images, we introduce the idea of 2D Fourier Phase Code (FPC) for representing iris information. The 2D FPC is particularly useful for implementing compact iris recognition devices using the state-of-the-art Digital Signal Processing (DSP) technology. By changing the degree of phase quantization, we can optimize the trade-off between iris data size and recognition performance flexibly while avoiding the visibility of individual iris images.

Flow diagram of the proposed algorithm.

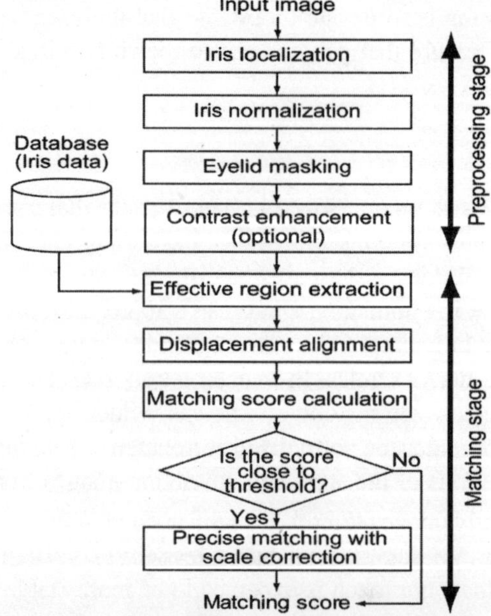

Fig. 1 Flow diagram of the Proposed Algorithm.

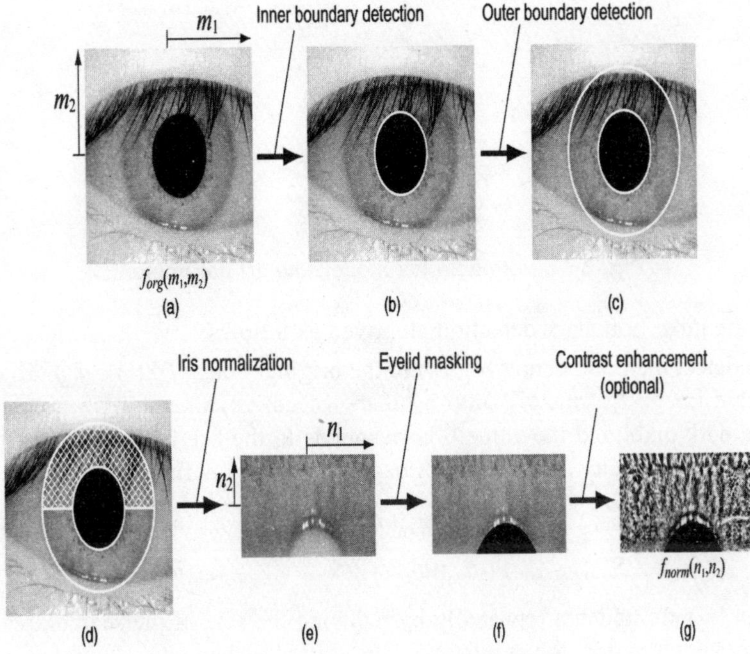

Fig. 2 Iris image pre-processing.

(a) Original image $f_{\mathrm{org}}(m_1, m_2)$.

(b) Detected inner boundary.

(c) Detected outer boundary.

(d) Lower half of the iris region for matching.

(e) Normalized image.

(f) Normalized image with eyelid masking.

(g) Enhanced image $f_{\mathrm{norm}}(n_1, n_2)$.

The algorithm consists of two stages:

1. The Pre-processing stage and

2. The Matching stage.

The purpose of pre-processing is to localize the iris region in the captured image and to produce a normalized iris texture image with a fixed size (256×128 pixels). A typical eye image contains some irrelevant parts, which cause significant degradation of the matching performance. The preprocessing step is designed to remove these irrelevant parts correctly from the given image and to extract only the iris region. In addition, the size of the extracted iris varies, depending on the camera-to-eye distance and light brightness level. Therefore, the size should be normalized before the matching operation.

1. Iris Localization

This step detects the inner boundary (the boundary between the iris and the pupil) and the outer boundary (the boundary between the iris and the sclera) in the original gray-scale image $f_{\mathrm{org}}(m_1, m_2)$ shown in Fig. 2a.

Figure 3 shows the deformable iris model with 10 parameters used in our system, where the inner boundary and the outer boundary of an iris are represented by a pair of independent ellipses. We found that the accuracy of the iris localization step has significant impact on the overall system performance. Hence, the highly flexible iris model with 10 parameters is employed in our system.

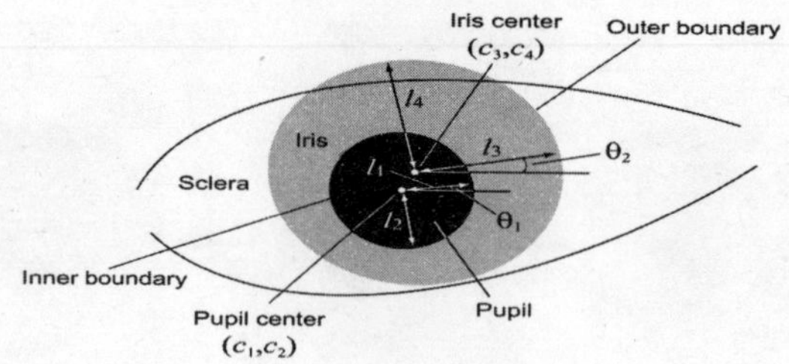

Fig. 3 Deformable iris model with 10 parameters.

The detailed steps of the inner boundary detection are given as follows:

1. The first step is to detect the pupil center (c_1, c_2) in the original image $f_{org}(m_1, m_2)$. To do this, we first transform the given gray-scale image $f_{org}(m_1, m_2)$ into a binary (negative) image $f_{bin}(m_1, m_2)$ where the pixel value 1 corresponds to the dark pixel and the value 0 corresponds to the bright pixel. Then, the pupil center (c_1, c_2) is estimated as the center of gravity of the binary image $f_{bin}(m_1, m_2)$ defined as follows:

$$c_1 = S_{(m1,\ m2)\epsilon W}\ m_1 f_{bin}(m_1, m_2)/S_{(m1,\ m2)\epsilon W} f_{bin}(m_1, m_2) \tag{1}$$

$$c_2 = S_{(m1,\ m2)\epsilon W}\ m_2 f_{bin}(m_1, m_2)/S_{(m1,\ m2)\epsilon W} f_{bin}(m_1, m_2) \tag{2}$$

The coordinates (c_1, c_2) are updated repeatedly by reducing the size of the search area W until they converge to a certain point. For every iteration, the search area W is shifted to the updated pupil center (c_1, c_2). In addition, the size of W is reduced until it covers the whole pupil region with a moderate margin. The obtained coordinates (c_1, c_2) for the pupil centre are used as the initial values for the optimization in Step 2.

The accuracy of pupil center detection depends on the threshold value used for image binarization. That is, if many nonpupil regions (for example, the eyelashes) have pixel value 1 (that is, a dark pixel) in the binary image $f_{bin}(m_1, m_2)$, (1) and (2) may choose a pixel (c_1, c_2) that is in the nonpupil region, resulting in false detection of the inner boundary in Step 2. Thus, it is important to determine the appropriate threshold value for binarization.

2. The next step is to find the optimal estimate $(l_1, l_2, c_1, c_2, \theta_1)$ for the inner boundary by maximizing the following absolute difference:

$$|S\ (l_1 + \Delta l_1, l_2 + \Delta l_2, c_1, c_2, \theta_1) - S\ (l_1, l_2, c_1, c_2, \theta_1)| \tag{3}$$

Here, Δl_1 and Δl_2 are small constant and S denotes the N-point contour summation of pixel values

$$S\ (l_1, l_2, c_1, c_2, \theta_1) = \Sigma\ n = 0 \text{ to } N-1 \text{ for } (p_1(n), p_2(n)), \tag{4}$$

where $\quad p_1(n) = l_1 \cos \theta_1.\ \cos(2\Pi/Nn) - l_2 \sin \theta 1.\ \sin(2\Pi/Nn) + c_1$

and $\quad p_2(n) = l_1 \sin \theta_1.\ \cos(2\Pi/Nn) + l_2 \cos \theta 1.\ \sin(2\Pi/Nn) + c_2$

Thus we will detect the inner boundary as the ellipse on the image for which there will be a sudden change in luminance summed around its perimeter.

2. Iris Normalization

The next step is to normalize the extracted iris region and to compensate for the elastic deformations in iris texture. We unwrap the iris region to a normalized rectangular block with a fixed size (256 × 128 pixels). To avoid having the iris region be occluded by the upper eyelid and eyelashes, we use only the lower half of the iris region, as shown in Fig. 2d. This iris region is transformed into the normalized image by the parameters $(l_1, l_2, l_3, l_4, c_1, c_2, c_3, c_4, \theta_1, \theta_2)$ as shown in Fig. 2e, where the n_1 axis corresponds to the angle of the polar coordinate system and the n_2 axis corresponds to the radius.

3. Eyelid Masking

This process masks the irrelevant eyelid region in the normalized iris image. In general, the iris/eyelid boundary can be modeled as an ellipse contour in the normalized image. Hence, the same method for detecting the inner boundary can be applied to iris/eyelid boundary detection. The detected eyelid region is masked as shown in Fig. 2f.

4. Contrast Enhancement

In some situations, the normalized iris image has low contrast. Histogram equalization transforms the pixel value so that the resulting image has an approximately flat histogram. To do this, we use a cumulative histogram of the image as the pixel value mapping function. Let $H(u)$ be the cumulative histogram of the image, where u denotes the pixel value (e [0, 255]). We convert the pixel value u in the iris image to the pixel value 255 $H(u)$/Ntotal to have a contrast-enhanced iris image, where Ntotal denotes the total counts of pixels. In our algorithm, we transform the pixel value by using the local cumulative histogram evaluated within a small image block (of size 15 × 15 pixels) centered at the pixel to be converted.

We proposed the idea of the Band-Limited POC (BLPOC) function for an efficient matching of fingerprints, considering the inherent frequency components of fingerprint images. Through a set of experiments, we have found that the same idea is also very effective for iris recognition. Our observation shows that the 2D DFT of a normalized iris image sometimes includes meaningless phase components in high-frequency domains and that the effective frequency band of the normalized iris image is wider in the k_1 direction than in the k_2 direction, as illustrated in Fig.4

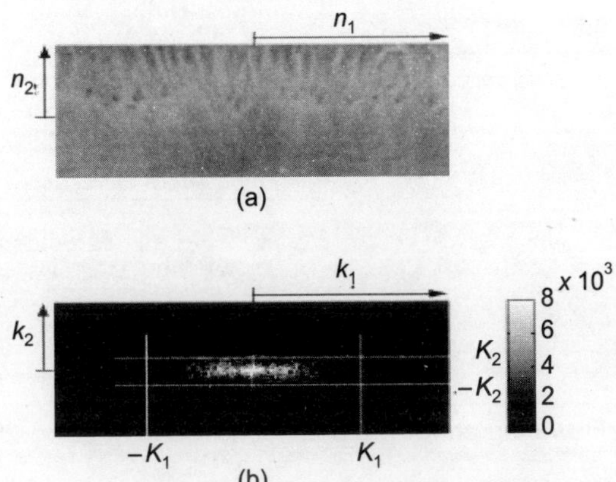

Fig. 4 Normalized Iris Image in(a) The spatial domain and (b) The frequency domain

The original POC function $r_{fg}(n_1, n_2)$ emphasizes the high-frequency components, which may have less reliability.This reduces the height of the correlation peak significantly, even if the given two iris images are captured from the same eye. On the other hand, the BLPOC function allows us to evaluate the similarity by using the inherent frequency band of the iris texture.

Assume that the ranges of the inherent frequency band of iris texture are given by

$$k_1 = -K_1, \cdots, K_1 \text{ and } k_2 = -K_2 \cdots, K_2, \text{ where } 0 <= K_1 <= M_1, \text{ and } 0 <= K_2 <= M_2.$$

Thus the effective size of frequency spectrum is given by $L_1 = 2K_1 + 1$ and $L_2 = 2K_2 + 1$.The BLPOC function is defined as

$$r_{fg}^{K_1 K_2}(n_1, n_2) = \frac{1}{L_1 L_2} \sum_{k_1=-K_1}^{K_1} \sum_{k_2=-K_2}^{K_2} R_{FG}(k_1, k_2) \times W_{L_1}^{-k_1 n_1} W_{L_2}^{-k_2 n_2} \tag{5}$$

where $n_1 = -K_1, \cdots, K_1$ and $n_2 = -K_2, \cdots, K_2$. When two images are similar, their BLPOC function gives a distinct sharp peak.

The maximum value of the correlation peak of the BLPOC function is always normalized to 1 and does not depend on L_1 and L_2.In addition ,the translational displacement between the two images can be estimated by the correlation peak position.

III. IMPLEMENTED-ORIENTED IRIS RECOGNITION ALGORITHM

The proposed matching algorithm assumes the use of iris images directly in the system to achieve high recognition performance. In order to reduce the size of iris data and to prevent the visibility of individual iris images, we introduce here the idea of 2D FPC for representing iris information. The 2D FPC is particularly useful for implementing compact iris recognition devices using state-of-the art DSP technology. By changing the degree of quantization in the 2D FPC, we can optimize the trade-off between the iris data size and recognition performance flexibly while avoiding the visibility of individual iris images. The 2D FPC corresponds to the quantized version of the phase spectrum of a normalized iris image, which is essential for phase-based iris recognition. Instead of using iris images directly, the system registers 2D FPCs as biometric data.

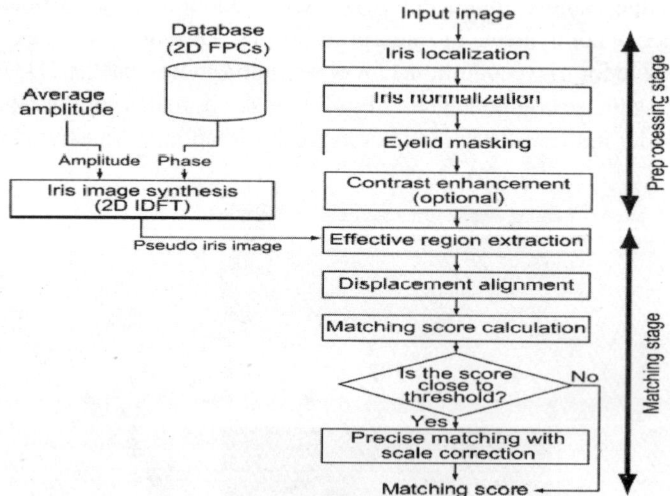

Fig. 5 Flow diagram of the proposed algorithm using 2DFPCs

A major problem of this approach is that the 2D FPC does not contain amplitude spectrum and the actual iris image cannot be reconstructed from the 2D FPC.

This property is particularly useful for reducing the iris data size while keeping a sufficient level of performance. In our algorithm, the iris region is normalized into a rectangular image block of 256×128 pixels. Assuming 8-bit (256-level) quantization of pixel value, the total data size of an iris image becomes $256 \times 128 = 32$ Kbytes. On the other hand, the size of the 2DFPC with 4-bit quantization can be reduced to 8 Kbytes by utilizing the symmetry of the phase spectrum. Similarly, the sizes of 2D FPCs with 3-bit, 2-bit, and 1-bit quantization are 6, 4, and 2 Kbytes, respectively (Figs. 6b, 6c, and 6d).

The performances of iris recognition algorithms using 2D FPCs are evaluated for the CASIA iris image databases (versions 1.0 and 2.0) and ICE 2005 database with various levels of phase quantization.

We use the baseline algorithm for CASIA version 1.0 and the modified

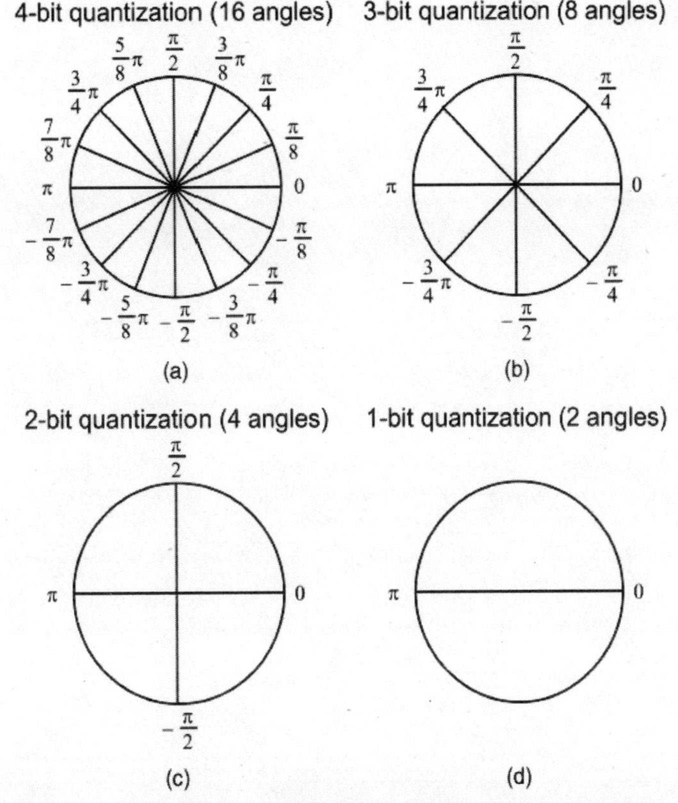

Fig. 6   Phasequantization. (a) Four-bit quantization. (b) Three-bit quantization. (c) Two-bit quantization. (d) One-bit quantization

Algorithm for CASIA version 2.0 and ICE 2005. The original phase-based iris recognition algorithm is particularly suitable for implementing high-accuracy iris verification/identification systems, for which the recognition performance is a major concern.

ACKNOWLEDGMENTS

Portions of the research use the CASIA iris image databases (versions 1.0 and 2.0) collected by the Institute of Automation, Chinese Academy of Sciences, and the ICE 2005 database collected by the National Institute of Standards and Technology.

References

1. R. Wildes, "Iris Recognition: An Emerging Biometric Technology," Proc. IEEE, Vol. 85, no. 9, pp. 1348-1363, Sept. 1997.

2. J. Daugman, "High-Confidence Visual Recognition of Persons by a Test of Statistical Independence," IEEE Trans. Pattern Analysis and Machine Intelligence, vol. 15, no. 11, pp. 1148-1161, Nov. 1993.

3. L. Ma, T. Tan, Y. Wang, and D. Zhang, "Efficient Iris Recognition by Characterizing Key Local Variations," IEEE Trans. Image Processing, Vol. 13, no. 6, pp. 739-750, June 2004.

4. C. Tisse, L. Martin, L. Torres, and M. Robert, "Person Identification Technique Using Human Iris Recognition," Proc. 15th Int'l Conf. Vision Interface, pp. 294-299, 2002.

5. K. Miyazawa, K. Ito, T. Aoki, K. Kobayashi, and H. Nakajima, "An Efficient Iris Recognition Algorithm Using Phase-Based Image Matching," Proc. 12th IEEE Int'l Conf. Image Processing, Vol. 2, pp. 49-52, Sept. 2005.

6. R.C. Gonzalez and R.E. Woods, Digital Image Processing, second ed. Prentice Hall, 2002.

CHAPTER 9

Data Cleaning: Current Approaches and Issues

[1]Vaishali Chandrakant Wangikar and [2]Ratnadeep R. Deshmukh

[1]MCA Department, Maharashtra Academy of Engineering, Alandi, Pune (MS), India,
[2]Deptartment of Computer Science & IT, Dr. Babasaheb Ambedkar Marathwada University, Aurangabad (MS), India
E-mail: vaishali.wangikar@gmail.com, ratnadeep_deshmukh@yahoo.co.in

ABSTRACT

The data cleaning is the process of identifying and removing the errors in the data warehouse. While collecting and combining data from various sources into a data warehouse, ensuring high data quality and consistency becomes a significant, often expensive and always challenging task. Without clean and correct data the usefulness of Data Mining and data warehousing is mitigated. This paper analyzes the problem of data cleansing and the identification of potential errors in data sets. The differing views of data cleansing are surveyed and reviewed and a brief overview of existing data cleansing techniques is given. We also give an outlook to research directions that complement the existing systems.

Keywords: Sorted Neighborhood Methods, Fuzzy Match, Clustering and Association, Token-Based Data, Record Linkage.

1. INTRODUCTION

Common data quality problems(anomalies) include inconsistent data conventions amongst sources such as different abbreviations or synonyms; data entry errors such as spelling mistakes inconsistent data formats, missing, incomplete, outdated or otherwise incorrect attribute values, data duplication, irrelevant objects or data. Data that is incomplete or inaccurate is known as "dirty" data.

The various types of anomalies occurring in data that have to be eliminated. The type of anomalies can be classified under several types of it. Based on this classification we evaluate and compare existing approaches for data cleansing with respect to the types of anomalies handled and eliminated by them.

The paper categorizes the data cleansing into two categories: cleansing string data and record or attribute de-duplication.

Data cleaning offers the fundamental services for data cleaning such as attribute selection, formation of tokens, selection of clustering algorithm, selection of similarity function, selection of elimination function and merge function etc.

The paper is organized as follows. Related Research Work describes various existing data cleaning techniques, Comparison of existing techniques, Conclusion and Future Work.

2. RELATED RESEARCH WORK

2.1 Cleansing String Data

This category of data cleaning removes 'dirt' in strings (words). Algorithm that identifies a group of strings that consists of (multiple) occurrences of a correctly spelled string plus nearby misspelled strings. All strings in a group are replaced by the most frequent string of this group.

2.1.1 Data Cleaning for Misspelled Proper Nouns (Border Detection Algorithm)

The method is proposed by Arturas Mazeika and Michael H.B¨ohlen in 2006. The method targets proper noun databases, including names and addresses, which are not handled by dictionaries. *Center Calculation* and *Border Detection algorithms* [1] are suggested. Data cleansing is done in two steps. First, the string data is clustered by identifying center and border of hyper-spherical clusters, and second, the cluster strings are cleansed with the most frequent string of the cluster. All strings within the overlap threshold from the center of the cluster are assigned to one cluster.

Border Detection algorithm is a simple and effective strategy to compute clusters in string data. One starts with a string in the database and selects the border that separates the cluster from the other clusters. If the initial string was chosen close to the center of the cluster, the border detection will yield good and robust results. If one chooses the initial string close to the border, two separate clusters might be assigned. As the cluster size increases, the relative clustering error decreases. The algorithm successfully identifies borders of clusters provided a sufficient sample size. The robustness of the algorithm is not affected by the cluster size.

Experiments show that the border detection is robust provided a sufficient sample size. The investigation indicates that very few q-grams of the center strings are sufficient to identify strings of the cluster. An algorithm that robustly finds the identifying q-grams of the cluster is an interesting challenge.

2.1.2 Robust and Efficient Fuzzy Match for Online Data Cleaning(Fuzzy Match similarity Algorithm)

To ensure high data quality, data warehouses must validate and cleanse incoming data tuples from external sources. In many situations, clean tuples must match acceptable tuples in reference tables. A significant challenge in such a scenario is to implement an efficient and accurate fuzzy match operation that can effectively clean an incoming tuple if it fails to match exactly with any tuple in the reference relation. A few similarity function which overcomes limitations of commonly used similarity functions is proposed, and an efficient fuzzy match algorithm is developed in 2003 by Surajit Chaudhuri, Kris Ganjam, Venkatesh Ganti Rajeev Motwani. Edit distance similarity [2] is generalized by incorporating the notion of tokens and their importance to develop an accurate fuzzy match similarity function for matching erroneous input tuples with clean tuples from a reference relation. The error tolerant index [2] and an efficient algorithm is developed for identifying with high probability the closest fuzzy matching reference tuples. Using real datasets, demonstration of the high quality of proposed similarity function and the efficiency of algorithms given.

2.1.3 Data Cleaning by Clustering and Association Methods (Data Mining Algorithms)

The two applications of data mining techniques in the area of attribute correction: context-independent attribute correction implemented using clustering techniques and context-dependent attribute correction using associations are proposed by Lukasz Ciszak, 2008 IEEE[3].

Attribute correction solutions require reference data in order to provide satisfying results.

Context-independent attribute correction means that all the record attributes are examined and cleaned in isolation without regard to values of other attributes of a given record.

Context-dependent means that attribute values are corrected with regard not only to the reference data value it is most similar to, but also takes into consideration values of other attributes within a given record

Experimental results of both algorithms created by the author show that attribute correction is possible without an external reference data and can give good results. As it was discovered in the experiments, the effectiveness of a method depends strongly on its parameters. The optimal parameters discovered here may give optimal results only for the data examined and it is very likely that different data sets would need different values of the parameters to achieve a high ratio of correctly cleaned data.

2.2 Record or Attribute De-duplication

A process for determining whether two or more records defined differently in a database, actually represent the same real world object. During data cleaning, multiple records representing the same real life object are identified, assigned only one unique database identification, and only one copy of exact duplicate records is retained.

2.2.1 A Token-Based Data Cleaning Technique

Most existing work on data cleaning, identify record duplicates by computing match scores compared against a given match score threshold. Some use the entire records for long string comparisons that involve a number of passes. Determining optimal match score threshold in a domain is hard and straight long string comparisons with many passes is inefficient.

The proposed token based technique proposed by Timothy E., Ohanekwu and C.I. Ezeife eliminates the need to rely on match threshold by defining smart tokens that are used for identifying duplicates. This approach also eliminates the need to use the entire long string records with multiple passes, for duplicate identification.

Existing algorithms use token keys extracted from records for only sorting and/or clustering. The results from the experiments show that the proposed token-based algorithm [5] outperforms the other two algorithms.

2.2.2 Record Linkage: Similarity Measures and Algorithms

In the presence of data quality errors, a central problem is the ability to identify whether two entities (e.g., relational tuples) are approximately the same The techniques used here are record linkage and approximate join in the sequel.

A variety of approximate match predicates that have been proposed to quantify the degree of similarity or closeness of two data entities. The authors Nick Koudas, Sunita Sarawagi, Divesh Srivastava have compared and contrasted them based on their applicability to various data types, algorithmic properties, computational overhead and their adaptability. Most approximate match predicates return a score between 0 and 1 (with 1 being assigned to identical entities) that effectively quantifies the degree of similarity between data entities. Such approximate match predicates will consist of three parts.

Atomic Similarity Measures: This part measures to assess atomic (attribute value) similarity between a pair of data entities. Several approximate match predicates including edit distance, phonetic distance (soundex), the Jaro and Winkler measures, tf.idf and many variants thereof. Several approaches to fine tune parameters of such measures are considered.

Functions to combine similarity measures : Given a set of pairs of attributes belonging to two entities (tuples), in which each pair is tagged with it's own approximate match score (possibly applying distinct approximate match predicates for each attribute pair), how does one combine such scores to decide whether the entire entities (tuples) are approximately the same. For this basic decision problem several proposed methodologies like statistical and probabilistic, predictive, cost based, rule based, user assisted as well as learning based are given. Moreover, several specific functions including Naive Bayes, the *Fellegi-Sunter model, linear support vector machines* (SVM) and approaches based on voting theory are covered.

Similarity between linked entities: Often the entities over which we need to resolve duplicates are linked together via foreign keys in a multi-relational database. Author has presented various graph-based similarity measures that capture transitive contextual similarity in combination with the intrinsic similarity between two entities.

Record Linkage Algorithms: Once the basic techniques for quantifying the degree of approximate match for a pair (or subsets) of attributes have been identified, the next challenging operation is to embed them into an approximate join framework between two data sets. A common feature of all such algorithms is the ability to keep the total number of pairs (and subsequent decisions) low utilizing various pruning mechanisms. These algorithms can be classified into two main categories.

1. *Algorithms inspired by relational duplicate elimination and join techniques including sort-merge, band join and indexed nested loops*: In this context, techniques like Merge/Purge [9] (based on the concept of sorted neighborhoods), Big Match (based on indexed nested loops joins) and Dimension Hierarchies (based on the concept of hierarchically clustered neighborhoods) are reviewed .

2. *Algorithms inspired by information retrieval that treat each tuple as a set of tokens, and return those set pairs whose (weighted) overlap exceeds a specified threshold:* In this context, a variety of set join algorithms are reviewed [6].

2.2.3 Adaptive Sorted Neighborhood Methods for Efficient Record Linkage

A variety of record linkage algorithms have been developed and deployed successfully. Often, however, existing solutions have a set of parameters whose values are set by human experts off-line and are fixed during the execution. Since finding the ideal values of such parameters is not straightforward, or no such single ideal value even exists, the applicability of existing solutions to new scenarios or domains is greatly hampered. To remedy this problem, an argument is made by Su Yan, Dongwon Lee, Min-Yen Kany, C. Lee Giles that one can achieve significant improvement by adaptively and dynamically changing such parameters of record linkage algorithms. To validate the hypothesis, a classical record linkage algorithm, the Sorted Neighborhood Method (SNM)[7] are used and demonstrated how one can achieve improved accuracy and performance by adaptively changing its fixed sliding window size.

Two adaptive versions of the SNM algorithm, named as the incrementally-adaptive SNM (IA-SNM) and the accumulatively-adaptive SNM (AA-SNM) are proposed, both of which dynamically adjust the sliding window size, a key parameter used in SNM, during the blocking phase to adaptively fit the duplicate distribution. Comprehensive experiments with both real and synthetic data sets of three domains validate the effectiveness and the efficiency of the proposed adaptive schemes.

3. COMPARISON

3.1 The following table shows comparison of three different algorithms especially used for cleaning *string type of data*.

	Border Detection Algorithm	Data Mining Algorithm- Attribute Correction Algorithm	Fuzzy Match Similarity Function Algorithm
Features	(1) Simple, effective to compute clusters in the string data. (2) It helps in selection of border that separates one cluster from the other. If the initial string was chosen close to the center of the cluster, the border detection will yield good and robust results . If one chooses the initial string close to the border, two separate clusters might be assigned	(1) The given attributes are validated against reference data to provide cleansing solution (2) fuzzy match similarity (*fms*) function that explicitly considers IDF token weights and input errors while comparing tuples.	(1) If the tuple or attribute fails to match the reference data then fuzzy match operation is applied on it. (2) The two applications of data mining techniques in the area of attribute correction are: *context-independent* attribute correction implemented using clustering techniques and *context-dependent* attribute correction using associations.
Significance/ Performance	It produces good cleansing results for string data with large distances between centers of clusters and small distances within the clusters.	Quality of *fms* is better than *ed* (edit distance) using two Datasets. The algorithms are 2 to 3 orders of magnitude faster than the naïve algorithm	The algorithms displays better performance for long strings as short strings would require higher value of the parameter to discover a correct reference value. This method produces as 92% of correctly altered elements which is an acceptable value.

| Limitations | Our data cleansing algorithm is less is applicable for natural language databases. | There is always cost associated with transformations of IDF tokens. | The major drawback of this method that may classify as 'incorrect a value that is correct in context of other attributes of this record, but does not have enough occurrences within the cleaned data set |

3.2 The following table shows comparison of three different algorithms used *for cleaning duplicate entries of attributes as well as records.*

	Token-Based Algorithm and Algorithms	Record Linkage Similarity Measures Linkage	Adaptive Sorted Neighborhood Methods For Efficient Record
Features	For finding duplicates of attributes as well as records smart tokens are used instead match score comparison against match threshold. This approach also eliminates the need to use the entire long string records with multiple passes, for duplicate identification.	Approximate match and approximate join techniques are proposed to quantify the degree of similarity Atomic Similarity Measures, Functions to combine similarity measures, Similarity between linked entities are considered for matching Two approximate join techniques proposed, the first is concerned with procedural algorithms operating on data, applying approximate match predicates, without a particular storage or query model in mind. The second is concerned with declarative specifications of data cleaning operations.	Among many parameters of record linkage algorithms, the main focus is on the size of the sliding window in *SNM* and the adaptive version of *SNM* is proposed. The size of the window in SNM amounts to the size of the block, which in turn is related to the aggressiveness of a blocking method. Two adaptive versions of the *SNM* algorithm, named as the incrementally-adaptive *SNM (IA-SNM)* and the accumulatively-adaptive *SNM* (AA-SNM) are proposed.
Significance /Performance	By using short lengthened tokens for record comparisons, a high recall/precision is achieved. It has drastically lowers the dependency of the data cleaning on match "threshold" choice. It has a recall close to 100%, as well as negligible false positive errors. It succeeded in reducing the number of token tables to a constant of 2, irrespective of the number of fields selected by the user. The smart tokens are more likely applicable to domain-independent data cleaning, and could be used as warehouse identifiers to enhance the process of incremental cleaning and refreshing of integrated data.	A non-declarative specification offers greater algorithmic flexibility and possibly improved perform-ance (e.g., implemented on top of a file system without incurring RDBMS overheads). A declarative specification offers unbeatable ease of deployment (as a set of SQL queries), direct processing of data in their native store (RDBMS) and flexible integration with existing applications utilizing an RDBMS	Adaptive sorted neighborhood methods significantly outperform the the original SNM method. AA-SSNM has better performance than *IA-SNM*. The F-score of *AA-SNM* is 49% larger than that of *SNM*. The F-score difference between *IA-SNM* and *AA-SNM* is about 4%, but the PC difference is around 13%. This shows that AA-SNM is a better blocking method than IA-SNM since it finds more potential duplicate pairs with similar F-score

Limitation	Existing algorithms use token keys extracted from records for only sorting and/or clustering Token-based cleaning technique on unstructured, and semi-structured data yet to be considered.	The output of the approximate join needs to be post processed to cluster together all tuples that referto the same entity. The approximate join operation above might produce seemingly inconsistent results like tuple A joins with tuple B, tuple A joins with tuple C, but tuple B does not join with tuple C. A straightforward way to resolve such inconsistencies is to cluster together all tuples via a transitive closure of the join pairs. In practice, this can lead to extremely poor results since unrelated tuples might get connected through noisy links.	The adaptive schemes are robust to the variance in the size of each individual block, which can range from moderate to severe. Besides, the adaptive schemes show better resistance to the errors in the blocking fields. The performance of the algorithm depends upon the appropriate size of window. Several methods for adjusting window sizes, which are used in the adaptive methods, are proposed and compared. Among them, the full adjustment method is shown to be near optimal.

4. CONCLUSION

Various data cleaning algorithms and techniques are presented in the paper but each method can be used to identify a particular type of error in the data. The technique suitable for one type of data cleaning may not be suitable for the other. As data cleaning has a wide variety of situations that need to cater efficiently by some comprehensive data cleaning framework. Future research directions include the review and investigation of various methods to address wide area of data cleaning. A better integration of data cleaning approach in the frameworks and data decision processes should be achieved.

Acknowledgements

For reviewing different algorithms of data cleaning, experiments and contributions done by several authors are referred. The papers are enlisted in the references.

References

1. Arturas Mazeika Michael H.B¨ohlen: Cleansing Databases of Misspelled Proper Nouns, Clean DB, Seoul, Korea, 2006

2. Surajit Chaudhuri, Kris Ganjam, Venkatesh Ganti Rajeev Motwani: Robust and Efficient Fuzzy Match for Online Data Cleaning. ACM, SIGMOD 2003, June 9-12, 2003, San Diego__CA.

3. Rohit Ananthakrishna1 Surajit Chaudhuri Venkatesh Ganti,: Research Eliminating Fuzzy Duplicates in Data Warehouses. Proceedings of the 28th VLDB Conference, Hong Kong, China, 2002.

4. Lukasz Ciszak: Application of Clustering and Association Methods in Data Cleaning .Proceedings of the International Multiconference on ISBN 978-83-60810-14-9 Computer Science and Information Technology, pp. 97 – 103.

5. Timothy E. Ohanekwu, C.I. Ezeife: A Token-Based Data Cleaning Technique for Data Warehouse Systems.

6. Nick Koudas, Sunita Sarawagi, Divesh Srivastava: Record Linkage: Similarity Measures and Algorithms. SIGMOD 2006, June 27–29, 2006, Chicago, Illinois, USA.

7. Su Yan, Dongwon Lee, Min-Yen Kany, C. Lee Giles: Adaptive Sorted Neighborhood Methods for Efficient Record Linkage. JCDL'07, June 17.22, 2007, Vancouver, British Columbia, Canada.

8. M. Hernandez and S. Stolfo :The Merge/Purge Problem for Large Databases. Proc. ACM SIGMOD Int'l Conf. Management of Data. pp. 127-138, May 1995.

9. M.A. Hernandez and S.J. Stolfo,:Real-World Data Is Dirty: Data Cleansing and the Merge/Purge Problem. Data Mining and Knowledge Discovery, Vol. 2, pp. 9-37, 1998.

CHAPTER 10

Characterization of Models for Application of Data Mining to University Databases

P.U. Bhalchandra, S.D. Khamitkar, S.N. Lokhande, N.K. Deshmukh, R.P. Rathod and S.S. Phulari

School of Computational Sciences, Swami Ramanand Teerth Marathwada University, Nanded (MS) India, 431606.

E-mail: srtmun.parag@gmail.com, s.khamitkar@gmail.com, nileshkd@yahoo.com, lokhande_sana@rediff.com

ABSTRACT

This work is an executive summary of the minor research project being initiated at Swami Ramanand Teerth Marathwada University, Nanded, MS, India to introduce models for data mining and outlining their characterization. It has been observed that the Data mining models suggested here enables University like higher educational organization to use their current reporting capabilities to uncover and understand hidden patterns in vast databases. This will definitely help universities to have a predictive foresight for resource allocations.

Keywords: Data Mining, Educational Analytics, KDD

1. INTRODUCTION

The emerging fields of academic analytics and educational data mining are rapidly producing new possibilities for gathering, analyzing, and presenting educational data. This is mainly due to the reason that the basic data available with any organization has become a key source of intelligence and also has competitive advantage for that organization. With the explosion of electronic data available to educational organizations and the demand for better and faster decisions, the role of data driven intelligence is becoming central in educational organizations. This is the demand side.

Now days, there is a boom in the field of statistical or predictive sciences, called Data Mining alias KDD. This is the process of converting the raw data into useful knowledge required for supporting decision-making [1]. It automates the process of knowledge discovery, making us orders of magnitude more productive in our search for useful information than we would be otherwise. It also increases the confidence with which we can make business decisions. Virtually every educational organization, these days, is in the process of exploring and implementing data mining solutions to core problems including student support, course registration processes, alumina associations, designing new courses, etc. This is the application side.

A combined reading of demand and application side make one observation firm that though all educational organizations, institutions or Universities have been computerized or they have database systems capturing all essential data, possibility of automatic knowledge discovery is missing. Higher educational Institutions would like to have predictive foresight to know, for example, which students will enroll in particular course programs, and which students will need assistance in order to graduate or postgraduate?, etc.

One way to effectively address these challenges is through the analysis and presentation of data, or data mining. Data mining enables higher educational organizations to use their current reporting capabilities to uncover and understand hidden patterns in vast databases. These patterns are then built into data mining models and used to predict individual behavior with high accuracy. This will help these institutions to better allocate resources, for example, give an institution the information necessary to take action before a student drops out, or to efficiently allocate resources with an accurate estimate of how many students will take a particular course.

The objective of the study undertaken at SRTMUN is to introduce models for data mining processes and sketch their characterization. Using these models, one can realize what data has to be captured, what surrounding information has also to be captured, how mining can be carried out, etc. It is a feasible process because over the years, University like SRTMUN has accumulated a vast amount of data in their databases- information management systems. These data typically represent daily operations and transactions within education, administration contexts. It is easy to see that all the business intelligence and rules are, in some way, embedded in these data.

We feel that such investigation can be easy with data mining due to the ability to uncover hidden patterns in large databases. By using this colleges and universities can build models that predict with a high degree of accuracy the behavior of population clusters. Thus the research project undertaken is essential for all interested in understanding how to get the maximum value from data, especially when abundant data are available

2.   LITERATURE REVIEW

Analytics or Mining in educational environment is called Educational Data Mining, concern with developing new methods to discover knowledge from educational databases [2, 3]. We have not found any one roof effort to understand data mining requirements of university like organizations. This may be due to the lack of deep and enough knowledge in higher educational system which prevents system management to achieve quality objectives. However we found some efforts taken in mining individual spheres of university databases, like to analyze student's trends and behaviors toward education [4]. Data mining is also an emerging methodology used in educational field to enhance our understanding of learning process to focus on identifying, extracting and evaluating variables related to the learning process of students [3]. *K*-means clustering [5] is a widely used method that is easy and quite simple to understand. A recognized work [2] gave a case study that use students data to analyze their learning behavior to predict the results and to warn students at risk before their final exams. Another work [6] explained that *k*-means is a well known clustering algorithm tends to uncover relations among variables already presented in dataset. One more study [3] used educational data mining to identify and enhance educational process which can improve their decision making process. Some studies like [7] concluded that clustering was effective in finding hidden relationships and associations between different categories of students.

3.   INTRODUCTION TO DATA MINING TOOLS

Data mining is the semi-automatic discovery of patterns, associations, changes, anomalies, rules, and statistically significant structures and events in data. Data mining differs from traditional statistics in several ways: formal statistical inference is assumption driven in the sense that a hypothesis is formed and validated against the data. Data mining in contrast is discovery driven in the sense that patterns and hypothesis are automatically extracted from data. Results of the data mining process may be insights, rules, or predictive models [1, 8]. The field of data mining draws upon several roots, including statistics, machine learning, databases, and high performance computing. Statistical and machine learning principles suggest the need for substantial user input (specifying meta-knowledge necessary to acquire highly predictive models from small data sets). Data mining serves two goals:

1. **Insight**: identify patterns and trends that are comprehensible, so that action can be taken based on the insight.
2. **Prediction**: a model is built that predicts (or scores) based on input data.

It is observed that the majority of research in data mining has concentrated on building the best models for prediction [6]. It is so because a prediction task is well defined and can be objectively measured on an independent test-set.

Following common terms are used in data mining process. A very lucid note is appeared in [8]. Considering the scope of this paper, we have discussed them in a simple and general overview. Readers are encouraged to explore them further depending on their interest.

- **Data exploration and visualization** Raw data and algorithm results can be visualized through tables and graphics such as graphs and histograms as well as through more specific techniques such as symbolic data analysis (which consists in creating groups by gathering individuals along one attribute). The aim is to display data along certain attributes and make extreme points, trends and clusters obvious to human eye.

- **Clustering algorithms** aim at finding homogeneous groups in data. We can use k-means clustering and its combination with hierarchic clustering [6]. Both methods rest on a distance concept between individuals. We can also use Euclidian distance.

- **Classification** is used to predict values for some variable. For example, given all the Information about a student, we may want to predict whether the student will perform well in the final exam. Commonly used method is $C\,4.5$ decision tree. The tree can be represented by a set of rules such as: *if $x = v1$ and $y > v2$ then $t = v3$*. Thus, depending on the values an individual takes for, say the variables x and y, one can predict its value for t. The tree is built taking a representative population and is used to predict values for new individuals.

- **Association rules** find relations between items. Rules have the following form: $X->Y$, *support* 50%, *confidence* 70%, which could mean '*if students get X incorrectly, then they get also Y incorrectly*', with a support of 50% and a confidence of 70%. Support is the frequency in the population of individuals that contains both X and Y. Confidence is the percentage of the instances that contains Y amongst those which contain X.

- **Decision tree** is a tree-shaped structure that visually describes a set of rules that caused a decision to be made.

- **Genetic algorithms** are optimization techniques that can be used to improve other data mining algorithms so that they derive the best model for a given set of data.

- **Neural networks** are non-linear predictive models that learn how to detect a pattern to match a particular profile through a training process that involves interactive learning, using a set of data that describes what you want to find. Neural networks are good for clustering, sequencing, and predicting patterns, but their drawback is that they do not explain why they have reached a particular conclusion.

- **Data warehouse** enables us to tap into knowledge hidden in the massive amounts of data to understand business trends and make timely strategic decisions.

- **Predictive modeling** can be used to identify patterns, which can then be used to predict the odds of a particular outcome based upon the observed data.

- **Rule induction** is the process of extracting useful if/then rules from data based on statistical significance.

- **Fuzzy logic** handles imprecise concepts and is more flexible than other techniques. For example, it can help determine students that are likely to respond to a course or a subject

- **K-NN or K-Nearest Neighbor** is a classic technique for discovering associations and sequences when the data attributes are numeric.

4. OUR WORK

In this study, we mainly address the capabilities of data mining and its applications to the higher education data of SRTMUN, with a view that data mining is a powerful tool for academic intervention. We will be suggesting a model and an algorithm for every sphere we found while analyzing university database [9]. Characterization of modeling processes will be our main outcome. In routine sense, our work relies on four basic methods of data mining: Classification, Categorization, Estimation, and Visualization. While dealing with modeling processes we will use Classification to identify associations and clusters to separates subjects under study. Categorization uses rule induction algorithms to handle categorical outcomes, such as "persist" or "dropout," and "transfer" or "stay." Estimation includes predictive functions or likelihood and deals with continuous outcome variables. Visualization uses interactive graphs to demonstrate mathematically induced rules and scores, and is far more sophisticated than pie or bar charts. We are hopeful that for the institutions like SRTMUN, we can come with some modeling processes that use classification for a comprehensive analysis of student or course characteristics or use estimation to predict the likelihood of a variety of outcomes, such as transferability, persistence, retention, and course success, etc. Since nobody knows how to derive these results and what data one must pick from university database to derive these results, we will suggest a model for every process found. Then we will be elaborating the characterization of the models.

This work needs a survey to analyze university database and sources of university database rigorously. Initially, we will view every database (department wise) i.e., data mart and come with a model. This model can be made up of main processes in SRTMUN, which usually occur in most of the higher educational systems, including evaluation, planning, registration, consulting, marketing, performance and examination. Each process can be categorized into some sub-processes also. The main idea in this model is identifying how each of these traditional processes can be improved through data mining techniques. If so, enhanced processes achieved through data mining will be presented as research outcome. The techniques appropriate in achieving these enhanced processes can also be presented as modeling processes. Then we throw some light on the analytics associated with the modeling process. This is because of the fact that some Analytics is always associated with a scientific, hypothesis-driven approach.

While doing this, we will simply stick up to the general life cycle of data mining model. In the early days, "build a warehouse first, mine later" paradigm was followed by organizations [8, 9]. This helps in understanding the data before mining it. This approach ensures that data mining complements a data warehouse.

5. MODEL FORMULATIONS

In this study, data gathered from university administration will be analyzed. It is followed by supporting data preparation activities, such as data cleansing, data description, data transformation, data sampling and data pruning [9, 10].

- **Data Set:** The data set used in this study will obtained from all departments
- **Database:** The database management system used in this study will be Microsoft SQL server 2005. This software is used because it is compatible and efficient to use with the database management system i.e. relational database [11, 12].
- **Application Software:** The programming environment used for application will be Visual studio 2005 for building data mining model. It is suitable for development of mining model and is compatible with SQL Server 2005, in which data will be maintained/stored.

The Data mining process can consist of following steps:

1. Preparations: In this step data stored in different tables will be joined in a single table after joining process errors will be removed.
2. Data Selection and Transformation: In this step we determine the fields of study used for analysis. Data is inform of yes/no is transformed in form of 1/0.

6. IMPLEMENTATION OF MINING MODEL

Some models like below will be suggested for every sphere we find in the university database [9].

1. Prediction Model
   - Predicting students learning outcome
   - Student- Subject- Score prediction
   - Labeling students Slow – Medium- Good
   - Lecturers' teaching style, qualification and
   - Expertise and prediction of score level of students

2. Classification Model
   - Classification of students – Rank wise
   - Classification of courses to various students
   - Student's home background and courses opted
3. Clustering Model
   - Prediction of continuation of student's performance
4. Association Model
   - Association of student's personal information or Educational information of his/her parents with the score
   - Association of students attendance with the score

7. CHALLENGES

Data mining in university databases is not an easy task [11]. Some challenges we found includes,

1. Make Data Mining Models Comprehensible to University Administration. Administrative users need to understand the results of data mining.
2. Make Data Transformations and Model Building Accessible to Users. We need to translate user's questions into a data mining problem in relational format. This often requires writing SQL, Perl scripts, or small programs. Even defining what the desired transformations and features should be is a knowledge-intensive task requiring significant understanding of the tasks, the algorithms, and their capabilities. Can we design a transformation language more accessible to business users? Can we automatically transform the data?
3. Scale algorithms to large volumes of data. University database could be in terabytes. Most data mining algorithms can handle a few gigabytes of data at best, so there are three to four orders of magnitude to grow before we can attack the largest databases that exist today
4. Cope with privacy issues. Data collection can also lead to abuses of the data, rising with many social and economic issues.

Conclusion

This paper demonstrates the ability of data mining in improving the quality of higher educational processes by offering a model for every process found. To retain qualified in educational domain, a deep understanding of the knowledge hidden among the data is required. It is witnessed that the data mining can be utilized in a number of ways in higher education as indicated by above discussions in this paper. It is also clear that models must be rebuilt or at least validated each year, since processes at universities are continually changing. For all models discussed in this paper, the majority of time spend on each modeling will be mainly for building the dataset to be used. Creation of these datasets required at least one year of historical data and in some cases as many as ten years of data.

References

1. Book on Data *Mining*. Adriaans, P., & Zantinge, D. (1996). Addison-Wesley Longman.
2. Galit.et.al (2007) Examining online learning processes based on log files analysis: a case study. Research, Refelection and Innovations in Integrating ICT in Education.
3. Erdogan and Timor (2005) A data mining application in a student database. Journal of Aeronautic and Space Technologies July 2005 Volume 2 Number 2 (53-57)
4. Alaa el-Halees (2009) Mining Students Data to analyze e-Learning Behavior: A Case Study.
5. Kifaya(2009) Mining student evaluation using associative classification and clustering. Communications of the IBIMA Vol. 11 IISN 1943-7765.
6. Han, J. and Kamber, M., (2006) "Data Mining: Concepts and Techniques", 2nd edition. The Morgan Kaufmann Series in Data Management Systems, Jim Gray, Series Editor.

7. Henrik (2001) Clustering as a Data Mining Method in a Web-based System for Thoracic Surgery: © 2001

8. Ron Kohavi, Data Mining and Visualisation, Appeared in the National Academy of Engineering (NAE) US Frontiers of Engineering, 2000

9. Naeimeh Delavari, Application of Enhanced Analysis Model for Data Mining Processes in Higher Educational System, IEEE sponsored ITHET 6th Annual International conference, July 7-9, 2005, Juan Dolio, Dominican Republic

10. Behrouz et.al., (2003) Predicting Student Performance: An Application of Data Mining Methods with the Educational Web-Based System Lon-CAPA © 2003 IEEE, Boulder, CO.

11. Connolly T., C. Begg and A. Strachan (1999) Database Systems: A Practical Approach to Design, Implementation, and Management (3rd Ed.). Harlow: Addison-Wesley.687

12. ZhaoHui. Maclennan J, (2005). Data Mining with SQL Server 2005 Wihely Publishing, Inc.

CHAPTER 11

Distributed Database for Weather through Tini Microcontroller

[1]M.A. Joshi, [2]M.R. Jathar and [1]S.C.Mehrotra

[1]Department of Computer Science and Information Technology, Dr. Babasaheb Ambedkar Marathwada University, Aurangabad (MS) India,

[2]LESD, Raja Ramanna Centre for Advanced Technology, Indore (MP) India.

E-mail: dixitmb@gmail.com

ABSTRACT

Weather monitoring and forecasting require a considerable amount of climate data. In the present work, the data is acquired through a dedicated Tini microcontroller connected to the Network using Ethernet technology. One wire devices like temperature sensor is connected to the Tini microcontroller. The system collects the data over a distributed network. The data is analyzed and results are stored in a central database. The interactive features are also included through users for complete control.

Keywords: Distributed Database, TINI, 1-Wire, distributed database

1. INTRODUCTION

Cheap, reliable, portable and automatic data acquisitions systems are required for remote rural based applications. For example, devices which can automatically probe quality of soil in agricultural fields and send these data to a central database have to very cost affective to be used in mass scale and without skill manpower to create useful interactive database. Similarly to describe accurately current weather conditions and predict coming events, meteorologists need to install multiple suitable devices for collecting reliable data at a central database. Much of this information is collected from weather stations. The problem is that conventional meteorological instrument systems are inefficient and expensive and these systems mostly need manual supervision. Each sensor in a weather station requires its own wiring and power supply. The sensor output must be signal conditioned before transmission. And adding sensors to an existing station is a complex problem. The thermometers were used to record the maximum and minimum temperature and they need to reset each time. In this case possibility of error is not neglected. Automation of these monitoring methods can not only increase the reliability but also improve the timely availability of data.

The paper describes a distributed embedded system which can be used for such applications where data has to be collected and transmitted at multiple locations and at regular time interval. The system can be operated independently and automatically with minimum human interaction.

2. METHODOLOGY

For development of embedded system, we need many components; the most important is the processor. Hundreds of processors are available, having processing power as 8 bit, 16 bit, 32 bit, and 64 bit microcontrollers. For developing such an embedded system, we have used TINI (Tiny Internet Interface) microcontroller [1] [2], DS18B20 1-wire sensors, and display device. The microcontroller is having Ethernet support so we can access the system via internet. The board has onboard memory & also embedded java. We are using 1-wire sensors for sensing the parameters. 1-wire devices provide network connectivity to entities that lack the ability to communicate with the outside world. An object connected to a 1-wire chip is capable of joining a 1–wire network. In a 1-wire network one or more devices are connected which are uniquely addressable that share a single conductor for communication and power. The sensors are placed at different locations. The use of display device is optional [3] [4].

3. EXPERIMENTS AND RESULTS

The experiments are carried out for three parameters-Temperature, Humidity, and Wind Direction.

3.1 Temperature Monitoring

To establish communication between the sensors and microcontroller we have used the 1-wire communication protocol. To use this protocol we need such a sensor that supports the 1-wire communication. The DS18B20 digital thermometer provides the solution for this. For monitoring the temperature of the environment, we have used DS18B20 [5] 1-wire temperature sensor. Four temperature sensors are connected as a 1-wire network. This 1-wire network [6] is interfaced with the microcontroller. The temperature sensed by the sensor is read by microcontroller and sent via serial port to TINI for making it available on internet. The same is done for other parameters.

3.2 Humidity Monitoring

Humidity measurement is the more difficult problems in basic meteorology. For humidity monitoring we have used hall HF3223 sensor [7]. The humidity sensor gives output in the form of frequency for relative humidity. This sensor proposes dual functionality to monitor humidity and temperature. The sensor is mostly used where reliable and accurate measurement is needed. It is cost effective and easy to connect. We can connect this sensor directly to microcontroller; hence we have interfaced this sensor to 89C51RD2 microcontroller. This microcontroller along with the other sensors and display device is interfaced with the TINI microcontroller.

3.3 Weather Cock for Wind Direction

For the development of our weather cock we have used eight reed switches [8] [9] for detecting eight main directions and a magnet. The magnet is placed on a cock, which is fixed on a small ball bearing for free movement, in such a way that at any given time it is over one of the reed switches. The closure placement of magnet gives information about wind direction. The fly wheel placed at the tail of the cock is fitted with hall sensor for wind speed information. These signals, from reed switches are fed to ports of embedded system whenever the system gets a request from TINI it transfers all the parameter in a string format.

4. ACTUAL WORKOUT OF THE SYSTEM

The working out of the weather station is explained in the form of system flow chart. The flowchart shows that weather server is started and it waits for client connection. When the client sends requests to the web server then HTTP page containing applet is then sent to the client. This process is handled by TINI HTTP server thread. By the end of this process the socket server is started. This socket server waits for socket connection. Once the connection has established the server client communication starts. The data is sent to the clients on request. The weather server starts and HTML pages containing applet are sent to the client. This is a continuous process. This applet is handled by TINI socket server thread.

The data is sent to client and central database after certain time interval. Whenever there is any change in weather parameters, it will be transferred. If the system is running without errors this process is repeated continuously. If there is any problem with the system in case of Hardware failure the same is intimated to server and will be solved accordingly. If the problem occurs in case of software the same can be solved by the experts at the server only. And the weather monitoring thread will run.

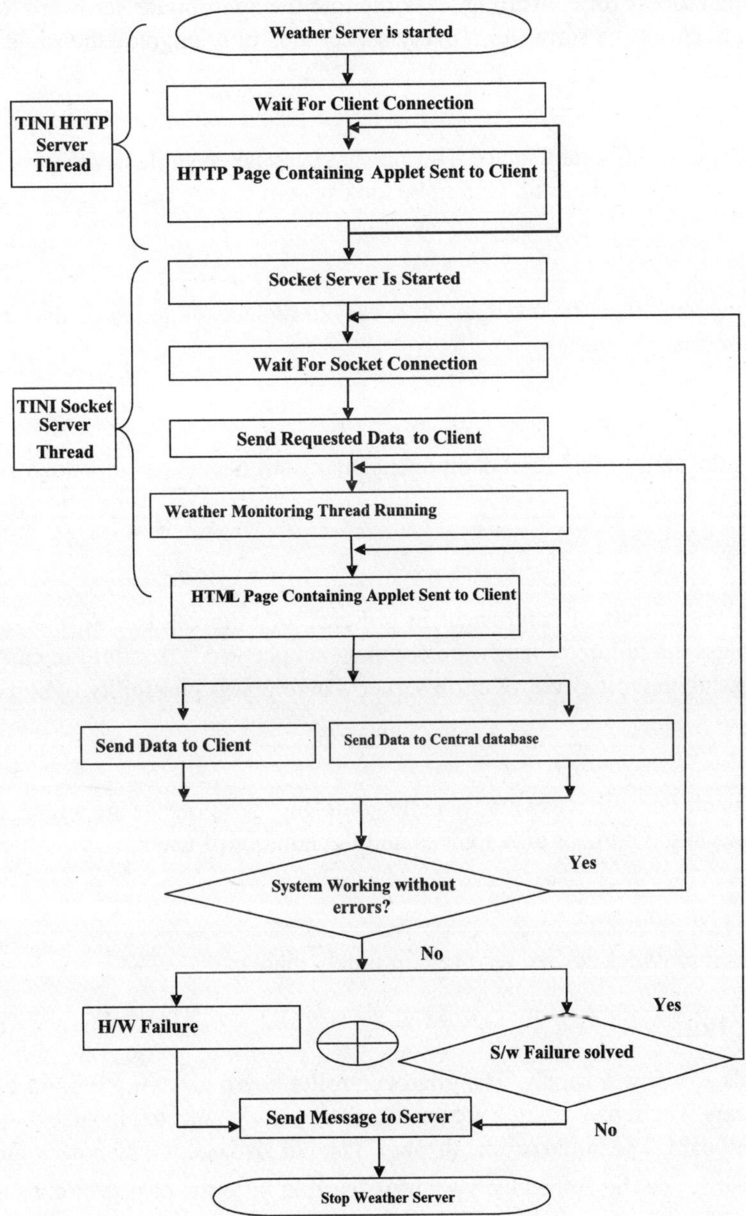

Fig. 1   System Flowchart

5. FEASIBILITY OF THE SYSTEM

The feasibility of the embedded system is studied [10] with respect to the following points:

5.1 Software Up Gradation Capabilities

For developing our embedded system we have used advanced microcontroller and development environment tools, so the embedded system software development became easy. Further we can modify and upgrade the software as well as hardware. As the conversion process for converting class file into the appropriate hardware format is difficult and time consuming hence we need to check the software in every aspect then only upgrade the same.

5.2 Size

The size of embedded system is the important factor. The care has been taken while developing the embedded system that it should be portable, easy to handle and install. Our embedded system is very small in size, portable and easy to install.

5.3 Fault Tolerant

The system can recover from component failure if any. It is easy to replace the failed component and resume the system with newly installed components.

5.4 Recoverable

The failed processes during the fault or failure of component can restart hence the embedded system we have developed is recoverable.

5.5 Consistency

The system can coordinate the actions of component in presence of failures also. So the users need not to visit the weather station location unless the failure of hardware components occurred. If failure in case of software occurred, it can be done easily by accessing the microcontroller on server. There is less possibility of software failure.

5.6 Scalable

The system is said to be scalable because it can also operate while new components are added. It remains effective when there is a significant increase in the number of resources and the number of users.

5.7 Predictable

The system is predictable as it provides desired response in timely manner.

5.8 Power Consumption

The embedded system needs +5v power supply. The microcontroller board is having lithium battery cell, which if once charged will work for 10 years. The sensors which are used here they are connected in such a way that they uses parasite power from microcontroller board. The liquid crystal display [11] will also needs +5v power supply. In all the embedded System consumes less power hence the embedded system is feasible in terms of power consumption.

5.9 Cost

While designing an embedded system cost is the most important factor. Initial cost of developing, debugging and testing the hardware and software cost is a one –time non recurring cost. Our embedded system costs around 10000/- which is very less as compared to the other embedded systems developed for weather monitoring.

Considering all the points, our embedded system is feasible technically, operationally and economically.

6. CONCLUSION

An automated weather monitoring system is more reliable and accurate way of monitoring the Weather parameters such as Temperature, Humidity, Wind Direction and Wind Speed of any area compared to existing manual systems. This is particularly useful in remote areas those are not connected to cities by means of roads and where the manual supervision of weather parameters is inconvenient.

References

1. TINI Design and Implementation Developers guide –By Don Loomis.
2. http://www.maximic.com
3. "Designing of Distributed System using TINI for Temperature Monitoring", M.A. Joshi, M.R. Jathar, S.C. Mehrotra, International Journal of Instrumentation Society of India, pg.39-40, Vol-I, March 2010.
4. "Multichannel Temperature Monitoring Using 1-Wire Sensors", International Journal of Computer Science and Applications, pg. 195-196, Jun 2010.
5. http://www.ibutton/sensor
6. http://www.midondesign.com/Documents/1wire_weather_stn.PDF
7. http://www.hw-group.com/products/Sensors/Humid-1Wire_en.html
8. http://www.reed-sensor.com/Notes/General_Reed_Switch_Theory.htm
9. http://en.wikipedia.org/wiki/Reed_switch
10. http://en.wikipedia.org/wiki/Feasibility_study
11. http://www.datasheetcatalog.com/datasheets_pdf/8/9/C/5/89C51RD2.shtml

Use of Search Engine Result Count for Similarity, Duplicate and Substitution Detection in Web Mining: A Survey

Sonal Deshmukh[1], R.R. Deshmukh[2] and Sachin Deshmukh[2]
[1]MCA Department, Jawaharlal Nehru Engineering College, Aurangabad (MS)-431002 India,
[2]Department of CS and IT, Dr BAM University, Aurangabad (MS)-431003 India
E-mail: sonal_deshmukh@ymail.com, ratnadeep_deshmukh@yahoo.co.in, sndeshmukh@hotmail.com

ABSTRACT

With a huge amount of information available on the Web, it has become a fertile area of mining research. Search engines are developing and adopting different mining algorithms for different communities of research like web content mining, web structure mining and web usage mining. In this paper we are focusing on Duplicate web page detection and word substitution for hiding the real information in the web page or in E-mail. These problems can be solved using different categories of algorithms. For the survey, we focused on the algorithms that are using search engine result count for solving these problems.

Index Terms: Web mining, data mining, duplicate detection, text substitution, page similarity.

1. INTRODUCTION

The World Wide Web is the widely known largest heterogeneous dynamic database available publicly. Due to the huge information available, we are drowning in information and facing information overload [1]. This overload presents the problems like finding relevant information, creating new knowledge out of the information available, personalization of the information and learning about consumers or individual users [2]. Web mining is the use of data mining techniques to automatically discover and extract information from web document and services. The task of web mining can be subdivided into Resource finding, Information selection and preprocessing, Generalization and Analysis [3].

The major categories of Web Mining can be stated as web content mining, web structure mining and web usage mining [4]. Web content mining is described as the discovery of the useful information from web data or web documents or web contents. Web structure mining [5] is to discover the model underlying the link structures of the web. The model is based on the topology of the hyperlinks with or without description of the links. The model can be used to categorize the web pages and is useful to generate information such as the similarity and relationship between the web sites. Web usage mining tries to make sense of the data generated by web surfer's sessions or behaviors. Web usage data includes data from server access logs, proxy server logs, browsers logs, user profiles, registration data, user sessions or transactions, cookies, user queries, bookmark data, mouse clicks and scrolls and any other data as an interaction. Today many of the search engines are using the search queries for fine tuning their search algorithms. If the most wanted query results are arranged for easy access, the searching time decreases drastically. Hence the popular searches of the day (like special news) are retrieved fast in the search engines.

2. GOOGLE AND ITS PAGE RANK

Although many factors determine Google's overall ranking of search engine results, Google maintains that the heart of its search engine software is Page Rank [6]. A few quick searches on the Internet reveal that both the business and academic communities hold PageRank in high regard. The business community is mindful that Google remains the search engine of choice and that PageRank plays a substantial role in the order in which webpages are displayed. Maximizing the PageRank score of a webpage, therefore, has become an important component of company marketing strategies. The academic community recognizes that PageRank has connections to numerous areas of mathematics and computer science such as matrix theory, numerical analysis, information retrieval, and graph theory. As a result, much research continues to be devoted to explaining and improving PageRank [7].

The PageRank algorithm assigns a PageRank score to each of more than 25 billion webpages [8]. The algorithm models the behavior of an idealized random Web surfer [9, 10]. This Internet user randomly chooses a webpage to view from the listing of available webpages. Then, the surfer randomly selects a link from that webpage to another webpage. The surfer continues the process of selecting links at random from successive webpages until deciding to move to another webpage by some means other than selecting a link. The choice of which webpage to visit next does not depend on the previously visited webpages, and the idealized Web surfer never grows tired of visiting webpages. Thus, the PageRank score of a webpage represents the probability that a random Web surfer chooses to view that webpage. To model the activity of the random Web surfer, the PageRank algorithm represents the link structure of the Web as a directed graph. Webpages are nodes of the graph, and links from webpages to other webpages are edges that show direction of movement. The process for determining PageRank begins by expressing the directed Web graph as the n x n "hyperlink matrix" 1t, where n is the number of webpages. To model the overall behavior of a random Web surfer, Google forms the matrix $G = aS + (1- a)$ 1?, where $0 \cdot = a <1$ is a scalar, 1 is the column vector of ones, and ? is a row probability distribution vector called the personalization vector. The damping factor, a, in the Google matrix indicates that random Web surfers move to a different webpage by some means other than selecting a link with probability $1 - a$. The majority of experiments performed by Brin and Page during the development of the PageRank algorithm used $a = 0.85$ and ? = ** ( ) [9, 10]. Values of a ranging from 0.85 to 0.99 appear in most research papers on the PageRank algorithm. Assigning the uniform vector for ? suggests Web surfers randomly choose new webpages to view when not selecting links. The uniform vector makes PageRank highly susceptible to link spamming, so Google does not use it to determine actual PageRank scores. Link spamming is the practice by some search engine optimization experts of adding more links to their clients' webpages for the sole purpose of increasing the PageRank score of those webpages. This attempt to manipulate PageRank scores is one reason Google does not reveal the current damping factor or personalization vector [8]. The Google matrix for the entire Web has more than 25 billion rows and columns, so computing the exact solution requires extensive time and computing resources. The power method converges for most starting vectors when the dominant eigenvalue is not a repeated eigenvalue . Since ? = 1 is the dorninant eigenvalue of G and p is the dominant left eigenvector in the eigensystem $pG = p$, the power method applied to G converges to the PageRank vector. This method was the original choice for computing the PageRank vector. Given a starting vector $p(0)$ e.g. $J p(0) = ?$, the power method calculates successive iterates

$$(k) = (k-1)G, \text{ where } k = 1, 2, ...,$$

until some convergence criterion is satisfied. Notice that $p(k) = p(k-1)G$ can also be stated $(k) = (0)Gk$.

3. THE STRING SIMILARITY

A. Kolomogory Complexity

The Kolomogorv complexity of a string x is the length, in bits, of the shortest computer program of the fixed reference computing system that produces x as output. The choice of computing system changes the value of $K(x)$ by an additive fixed constant at most. Since $K(x)$ goes to infinity with x, this additive fixed constant is an ignorable quantity if we consider large x. One way to think about the Kolmogorov complexity $K(x)$ is to view it as the length, in bits, of the ultimate compressed version from which x can be recovered by a general decompression program. Compressing x using the compressor gzip results in a file xg with (for files that contain redundancies) the length $|xg| < |x|$. Using a better compressor bzip2 results in a file xb with (for redundant files) usually $|xb| < |xg|$; using a still better compressor, like PPMZ, results in a file xp with (for again appropriately redundant files) $|xp| < |xb|$. The Kolmogorov complexity $K(x)$ gives a lower bound on the ultimate value: For every existing compressor, or compressors that are possible but not known, we have that $K(x)$ is less than or equal to the length of the compressed version of x. That is, $K(x)$ gives us the ultimate value of the length of a compressed version of x (more precisely, from which version x can be reconstructed by a general purpose decompresser), and our task in designing better and better compressors is to approach this lower bound as closely as possible.

B. Information Distance and Normalized Information Distance

Information can be in different forms. Single word can be information, a set of words can be information (e.g. John F Kennedy) and a meaningful sentence can be information. Depending on the type of data that is to deal with, there are different similarity measures available. Examples of character based similarity metrics are

> Edit Distance or Levenshtein Distance
> Affine Gap Distance
> Smith Waterman Distance
> Jaro Distance Metrics and
> Q-gram Distance

Different implementations of edit distance gives different time complexities ranging from $O(|s1|, |s2|)$ for two strings of length $|s1|$ and $|s2|$ to $O(\max\{|s1|, |s2|\}.\ k)$ time for checking whether two strings have edit distance less than k. In case of truncation of the strings, Affine gap distance works fine requiring $O(a.|s1|\ .\ |s2|)$ time when the maximum length of a gap $a << \min\{|s1|, |s2|\}$ and in general it is $O(a2.\ |s1|\ .\ |s2|)$. Smith Waterman distance is an extension to Edit distance and Affine Gap distance providing lower cost for mismatches at the ends. Its time complexity can be given as $O(|s1|\ .\ |s2|)$. Jaro comparison value is given as

$$\text{Jaro}\,(\sigma1,\ \sigma2) = \frac{1}{3}\left(\frac{c}{|\sigma_1|} + \frac{c}{|\sigma_2|} + \frac{c - t/2}{c}\right)$$

requiring $O(|s1|\ .\ |s2|)$ time. With the appropriate use of hash-based indexes, the average time required for computing the q-gram overlap between two strings $s1$ and $s2$ is $O(\max\{|s1|, |s2|\})$ [11]. Character based similarity metrics have limitations. When words are reassembled (e.g. John Smith and Smith, John), character based similarity metrics does not work. For this type of data, generally token based metrics are used. Common metrics are WHIRL and Q-grams with tf/idf. A similarity measure in WHIRL is given by

$$\text{sim}\,(\sigma1,\ \sigma2) = \frac{\sum_{j-1}^{|D|} v_{\sigma_1}(j) \cdot v_{\sigma_2}(j)}{\left\|v_{\sigma_1}\right\|2 \cdot \left\|v_{\sigma_2}\right\|2}$$

Information distance, denoted as $E(x, y)$, is defined as the length of the shortest binary program in the reference universal computing system that computes output y from input x and output x from input y where x and y are two different strings. Estimation of information distance is given as

$E(x, y) = K(x, y) - \min\{K(x), K(y)\}$ where $K(x, y)$ is a length of the shortest binary program that produces a pair x, y and tell that how much they are apart. This distance $E(x, y)$ is actually a metric: Up to close precision, we have $E(x, x) = 0$, $E(x, y) > 0$ for $x ? y$, $E(x, y) = E(y, x)$, and $E(x, y) = E(x, z) + E(z, y)$, for all x, y, z. We now consider a large class of admissible distances: All distances (not necessarily metric) that are nonnegative, symmetric, and computable in the sense that, for every such distance D there is a prefix program that, given two strings x and y, has binary length equal to the distance $D(x, y)$ between x and y. Then,

$E(x, y) = D(x, y) + cD$ where cD is a constant that depends only on D but not on x, y, and we say that $E(x, y)$ minorizes $D(x, y)$ up to an additive constant [12].

The information distance mentioned above can be seen as dependant of the length of the strings that are being compared. More the length more will be the distance and so on. Hence information distance itself is not sufficient to judge the similarity. This distance is to be normalized. Such approach was first proposed by [13]. The normalized information distance (NID) has values between 0 and 1, and it inherits the universality of the information distance in the sense that it minorizes, up to a vanishing additive term, every other possible normalized computable distance. NID is defined by

$$\text{NID}(x, y) - \frac{K(x, y) - \min(K(x), K(y))}{\max(K(x), K(y))}$$

4. GOOGLE SIMILARITY DISTANCE

Every text corpus or particular user combined with a frequency extractor defines its own relative frequencies of words and phrases usage. In the WWW and Google setting, there are millions of users and text corpora, each with its own distribution. In the sequel, we show (and prove) that the Google distribution is universal for the entire individual Web users distributions. The number of Web pages currently indexed by Google is approaching 1010. Every common search term occurs in millions of Web pages. This number is so vast, and the number of Web authors generating Web pages is so enormous, that the probabilities of Google search terms, conceived as the frequencies of page counts returned by Google divided by the number of pages indexed by Google, approximate the actual relative frequencies of those search terms as actually used in society. Based on this premise, the theory developed states that the relations represented by the normalized Google Distance approximately capture the assumed true semantic relations governing the search terms.

In contrast to strings x where the complexity $C(x)$ represents the length of the compressed version of x using compressor C, for a search term x (just the name for an object rather than the object itself), the Google code of length $G(x)$ represents the shortest expected prefix-code word length of the associated Google event x. The expectation is taken over the Google distribution g. In this sense, we can use the Google distribution as a compressor for the Google semantics associated with the search terms. The normalized Google distance (NGD), is then defined by

$$\text{NGD}(x, y) = \frac{G(x, y) - \min(G(x), G(y))}{\max(G(x), G(y))}$$

$$= \frac{\max\{\log f(x), \log f(y)\} - \log f(x, y)}{\log N - \min\{\log f(x), \log f(y)\}},$$

where $f(x)$ denotes the number of pages containing x, and $f(x, y)$ denotes the number of pages containing both x and y, as reported by Google [12].

At the time of doing the experiment, a Google search for "horse" returned 46,700,000 hits. The number of hits for the search term "rider" was 12,200,000. Searching for the pages where both "horse" and "rider" occur gave 2,630,000 hits, and Google indexed 8,058,044,651 Web pages. Using these numbers in, we derive below, with $N = 8,058,044,651$, a Normalized Google Distance between the terms "horse" and "rider" as follows:

NGD (horse, rider) ~ 0.443 NGD is a normalized semantic distance between the terms in question, usually in between 0 (identical) and 1(unrelated) [12].

5. PROBLEM OF WORD SUBSTITUTION

Terrorist groups or criminals involved in illicit acts generally use word substitution to hide their existence of communication and content of their communication. For example al-Qaeda was using the word 'wedding' for the word attacks. The substitutions of the words can be detected by human using semantic and deep contextual information. But to write software for such detection is very difficult. For such type of detection [14] has proposed an algorithm on the basis of frequency difference of the words.

Now a days, Web repository is being used for checking spellings and Grammar [15]. Google can be thought as a tool to search the web repository. To view the relationship between the word and its context, [14] has designed a set of measures. The measures are as follows.

A. Sentence Oddity

This measure considers a sentence as a whole and the relationship between the entire sentence and sentence with particular word of interest deleted. *SO* is based on the observation that if we remove contextually appropriate word from the sentence then it should not change the frequencies of resulting bag of words in comparison with frequency of entire sentence because it co-occurs frequently. But if remove contextually inappropriate word from the sentence it may produce large frequency of remaining bag of words because it co-occurs rarely. *SO* is given by

$$SO = \frac{\text{Frequency of bag of words, target word removed}}{\text{Frequency of entire bag of words}}$$

Here *SO* should be large for a sentence with substituted word.

B. Enhance Sentence Oddity

While calculating *SO* it may happen that target word may include in the sentence in numerated, then it will be helpful to calculate ESO where the numerator explicitly exclude the target word. So ESO can be calculated as

$$ESO = \frac{\text{Frequency of bag of words with target word excluded}}{\text{Frequency of entire bag of words}}$$

C. K-gram Frequencies

In this measure a sentence is divided into two parts i.e. a frequency of left k gram word and right k gram word. Left k gram of a word is the string starting with the word & extends left in the sentence. Right k gram of a word is the starting with the word & extends right in the sentence. Here our example is "we expect that the attack will happen tonight".

The left k gram of attack is "expect that the attack". Its frequency is $f = 50$ & right k gram is "attack will happen" and its frequency is 9260. The sentence with the substitution is "we expect that campaign will happen tonight". Here left k gram of campaign is "expect that the campaign" and its frequency is $f = 77$ and right k gram is "campaign will happen" and its frequency is $f = 132$. Here we are expecting that k gram will be smaller for a sentence containing a substitution. But here only right k gram is smaller not the left k gram. So left and right k gram is giving different information about the structure of sentences.

D. Hypernym Oddity

The hypernym of any word means the word with more general meaning. For e.g. hypernym of dog is "Tommy", house dog, carnivore, eutherian mammal. So we can take hypernym instead of the original word and also hypernym instead of the substituted word. If the word is contextually appropriate then the sentence with hypernym seems to be more unusual and if the is contextually inappropriate then the sentence with hypernym seems to be more usual so we define hypernym oddity as $HO = fh - f$ Here fh is frequency of the sentence with the hypernym and f is the frequency of a sentence as bag of words. If the word is inappropriate then result must be zero, close to zero or negative and if the word is appropriate then the result must be positive.

In the example hypernym of attack is operation and hypernym for campaign is race. The frequency of sentence with attack is $f = 2.42$ M and with its hypernym is $fh = 1.31$M. The frequency of sentence with campaign is $f = 1.63$ M and with its hypernym is $fh = 1.97$ M. The HO is -1.11Mfor ordinary sentence and 340000 for the sentence containing a substitution.

E. Point Wise Mutual Information

PMI is used to measure the strength of an association between a word that may be a substitution and adjacent region of a sentence. We can calculate PMI by the following formula

$$PMI = \frac{P\,(word)\,P\,(adjacent\,region)}{P\,(word + adjacent\,region)}$$

Here $p(\ )$ is the probability and $+$ is the concatenation of word and adjacent region in either direction . Here PMI will be too small so we can also take the frequencies

$$PMI = \frac{f\,(word)\,f\,(adjacent\,region)}{f\,(word + adjacent\,region)}$$

Here PMI value for a word which is unusual will be larger.

The intuition behind applying PMI measure is that if the target word is appropriate (not substituted) then it should be part of some stable phrase. Such stable phrase should occur on web more often.

We calculate a family of PMI measure using nested adjacent region that increase in length until their observed frequencies drop to zero.

6. CONCLUSION

In this survey, we have tried to present the use of search engines for carrying out unconventional tasks. As on today, similarity page search is highly needed. The research is going on finding semantically similar pages. Using Google similarity metrics adds another dimension to the research. As well the techniques discussed above can be used for other problems like word substitution and others.

Though the research is going on in this dimension, there is a requirement of obtaining more precise results. For example, different search engines have different indexed database and that to varying in count. As per our thinking, normalization depending on multiple search engine results is highly required. Search engines today rely basically on the textual data. But information can be stored in different forms. Mining of other type of data also is a need of today. Hence this field can attract attention of researchers.

References

1. P. Maes, "Agents that reduce work and information overload", Communication of the ACM, 37(7), 30-40,1994

2. Raymond Kosala, Hendrik Blockeel, "Web Mining Research: A Survey", ACM SIGKKD, Volume 2, Issue 1, 1-15, July 2000

3. O. Etzioni, " The World Wide Web: Quagmire or gold mine", Communication of ACM, 39(11):65-68,1996

4. S.K. Madria, S.S. Bhowmik, W.K. Ng, E.P. Lim, "Research issues in web data mining", A proceedings of Data Warehousing and Knowledge Discovery, First International Conference, DaWaK'99, pages 303-312, 1999

5. S. Chakrbarti, B. Dom, D. Gibson, J. Kleinberg, S. Kumar, P. Raghawan, S. Rajgopalan and A. Tomkin, " Mining the link structure of World Wide Web", IEEE Computers, 32(8), 60-67, 1999

6. http://www.google.com/technology/index.html, Our Search: Google Technology.

7. Rebecca S Wills, "Google's PageRank: The Math Behind the search Engine", The Mathematical Intelligence, Springer Publication, Volume 28, 4 November 2006, pp 6-11

8. http://www.webrankinfo.com/english/seo-news/topic-16388.htm,January 2006, Increased Google Index Size?

9. Sergey Brin and Lawrence Page, "The anatomy of a large-scale hypertextual Web search engine", Computer Networks and ISDN Systems 33 (1998), 107-117

10. Lawrence Page, Sergey Brin, Rajeev Motwani, and Terry Winograd, "The PageRank citation ranking: Bringing order to the Web", Technical report, Stanford University, 1998.

11. Ahmed K. Elmagarmid," Duplicate Record Detection: A Survey", Journal of Data Mining and Knowledge Discovery, Springer, Aug 2006

12. Rudi L Cilibrasi, Paul M.B. Vitanyi, "The Google Similarity Distance", IEEE transaction on Knowledge and Data Engineering, Vol. 19 No. 3, March 2007, pp 370-383

13. M. Li, J.H. Badger, X. Chen, S. Kwong, P. Kearney, and H. Zhang, "An Information-Based Sequence Distance and its Application to Whole Mitochondrial Genome Phylogeny," Bioinformatics, Vol. 17, no. 2, pp. 149-154, 2001.

14. SzeWang Fong,Dmitri Roussinov and David B Skillicon, "Detecting Word Substitution in Text", IEEE transaction on Knowledge and Data Engineering, Vol 20, No. 8, August 2008, pp. 1067-1076

15. K. Olsen and J. Williams, "Spelling and rammar checking using the Web as a Text Repository", J. Am. Soc. For Information Science and Technology, Vol. 5, no. 11, pp. 1020-1023, 2004

Non-invasive Brain Computer Interface Application Using Electroencephalograph Signal Analysis

S.B. Jadhav[1], S.B. Vanajale[1] and S.T. Patil[3]
[1]Computer Engineering Department, Bharati Vidyapeeth University, Pune (MS) India,
[2]Rajarshi Shahu Engineering College, Pune (MS) India
E-mail: shital_jadhav81@rediffmail.com, sbvanjale@bvucoep.edu.in, stpatil99@gmail.com

ABSTRACT

A Brain-Computer Interface (BCI) is a system that acquires and analyzes neural signal with goal of creating a communication channel directly between the brain and the computer .The electroencephalograph (EEG) signals are obtained from the brain through non-invasive methods .In bioengineering applications non-invasive BCI used for human subject monitoring for disorders, neurological diseases ,attention monitoring and overall mental state. This research work aims at sensing and recognizing typical change in the state of brain of person during pranayama . Anulom vilom is one part of the Pranayama, involves much more than merely breathing for relaxation.

A wavelet transformation is applied to EEG records from persons under anulom vilom. Correlation dimension, largest lyapunov exponent, approximate entropy and coherence values are analyzed. This model & software is used to keep track on the improvement of the persons mind, balance, flexibility, mental values, social values, love, sex, knowledge, weight reduction and body fitness.

Keywords: Non-invasive, anulom vilom, approximate entropy, EEG, coherence, largest lyapunov exponent, correlation dimension, wavelets.

1. INTRODUCTION

1.1 Non-Invasive BCI

A Brain-Computer Interface (BCI) , sometimes called a direct neural interface or brain machine interface , is a direct communication pathway between the brain and an external device. BCI applications are often aimed at assisting, augmenting or repairing human cognitive or sensory-motor functions.

There are three types of BCI research invasive , partially invasive and non-invasive. Invasive BCIs are implanted directly into the grey matter of brain during the neurosurgery. Partially invasive BCI devices are implanted inside the skull but rest outside the brain rather than within the grey matter. In non-invasive BCI Signals recorded using non invasive neuroimaging technology. EEG is the most studied potential non-invasive interface.

1.2 Electroencephalography

The brain generates rhythmical potentials, which originate in the individual neurons of the brain. Electroencephalograph (EEG) is a representation of the electrical activity of the brain.

1.3 Anulom Vilom

Anulom vilom is a term with a wide range of meanings. "The regulation of the incoming and outgoing flow of breath with retention.". Anulom vilom also denotes cosmic power. Because of this connection between breath and consciousness. The word anulom vilom means stretch, extension, expansion, length, breadth, regulation, prolongation, restraint and control to create energy, when the self-energizing force embraces the body, fast inhalation and fast exhalation, followed by inhaling through right nostril and performing kumbhaka with bandhas and exhaling through left nostril.

1.4 Experimental Setup

Medic-aid systems, Chandigarh (India), machine was used to aquire 32-channel eeg signal with the international 10-20 electrode coupling. The sampling frequency of the device is 256 Hz with 12-bit resolution and stored on hard disc. 32 channel EEG data was recorded simultaneously for both referential and bipolar montages. Recordings are made before, meanwhile and after the person is doing anulom vilom, and also we have kept track on recording the EEG data after one, two and three months of the same persons doing anulom vilom. Such 10 persons data is collected for analysis.

2. PARAMETERS

The present work pertains to the analysis of the EEG signal using various characteristic measures like Correlation Dimension (CD), Largest Lyapunov Exponent (LLE), Hurst exponent (HE) & Approximate Entropy (AE).

Correlation Dimension:

The dimension of a graph can give much more information about the nature of the signal Grassberger & Procaccia Algorithm is used

$$C(r) = \frac{2}{N(N-1)} \Bigg) \sum_{i=1+w}^{N} \theta\left(r - /\, x_i - x_j\, /\right) \tag{1}$$

    N-no. of data points

    θ-Heaviside function

    r- radial distance

    w-Tac $x\,j$ step away from $x\,i$

Approximate Enropy

Amount of disorder in the system. Amount of information stored in a more general probability distribution. Steyn-Ross algorithm is used

$$AE(m, r, l) = \frac{1}{L-m} \sum_{i=1}^{L-m} Log^{m+1} C_i(r) - \frac{1}{L-(m+1)} Log^m C_i(r) \tag{2}$$

where m = pattern Length = 2

             r = noise threshold = 15%

             L = time interval between two datasets

         $Ci(r)$ = correlation integral

Largest Lyapunov Exponent

It is rate at which the trajectories of a signal separate one from other.

Wolf algorithm is used to calculate Largest Lyapunov Exponent

$$\delta Z\,(t) = e\lambda t\,/\,\delta z_0\,/ \tag{3}$$

$$\delta z0 = \text{Initial seperation}$$

$$\lambda = \lambda1,\ \lambda2,\ \lambda3,\ \dots\ \lambda n\ \text{Phase spaces}$$

Hurst Exponent

Evaluates presence or absence of long range dependence and it degree. Hurst algorithm is used

$$H = Log\left(\frac{R}{S}\right)\,/\,Log\,T \tag{4}$$

R/S - Rescaled Range,

T- Duration of sample of data

3. RESULTS

Artifactual currents may cause linear drift to occur at some electrodes. To detect such drifts, we designed a function that fits the data to a straight line and marks the trial for rejection if the slope exceeds a given threshold. The slope is expressed in microvolt over the whole epoch (50, for instance, would correspond to an epoch in which the straight-line fit value might be 0 μv at the beginning of the trial and 50 μ v at the end). The minimal fit between the EEG data and a line of minimal slope is determined using a standard *R*-square measure.

We usually apply the measures described above to the activations of the independent components of the data. As independent components tend to concentrate artifacts, we have found that bad epochs can be more easily detected using independent component activities. The functions described above work exactly the same when applied to data components as when they are applied to the raw channel data

It is more interesting to look at time-frequency decompositions of component activations than of separate channel activities, since independent components may directly index the activity of one brain EEG source, whereas channel activities sum potentials volume-conducted from different parts of the brain. to visualize only frequencies up to 30 Hz. decompositions using FFTs allow computation of lower frequencies than wavelets, since they compute as low as one cycle per window, whereas the wavelet method uses a fixed number of cycles (default 3) for each frequency.

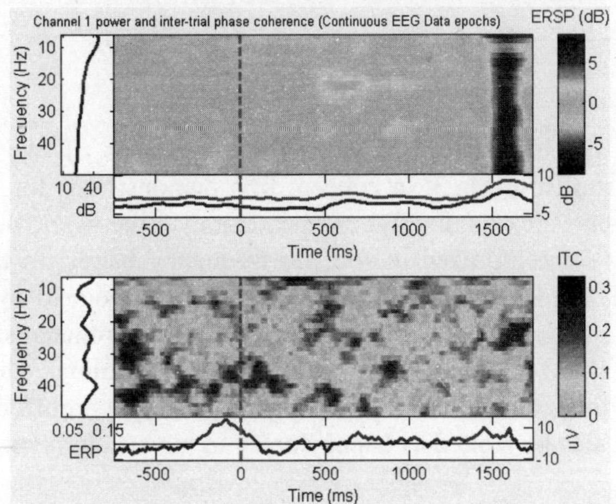

Fig. 1 time frequency components

The above time window appears in Fig.1. The ITC image (lower panel) shows strong synchronization between the component activity and stimulus appearance, first near 15 Hz then near 4 Hz. The ERSP image (upper panel) shows that the 15-Hz phase-locking is followed by a 15-Hz power increase, and that the 4-Hz phase-locking event is accompanied by, but outlasts, a 4-Hz power increase.

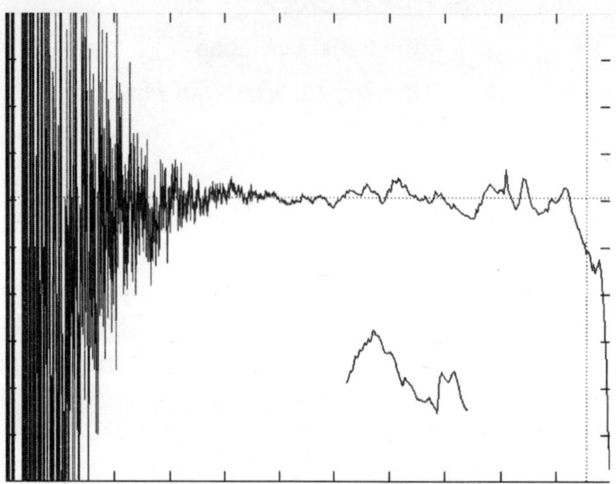

Fig. 2   correlation dimension

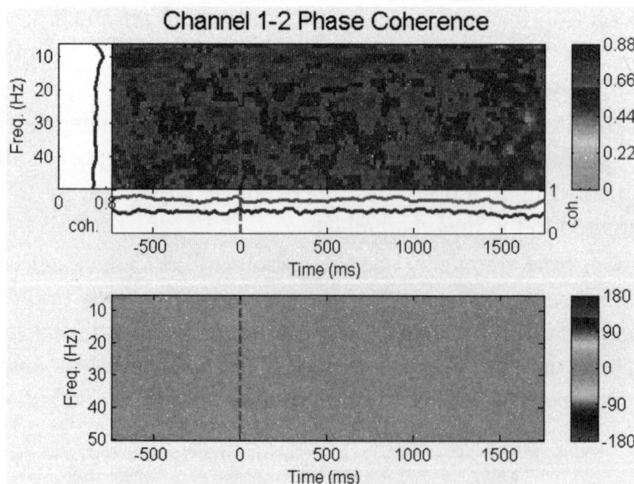

Fig. 3   cross-coherence

To determine the degree of synchronization between the activations of two components, we may plot their event-related cross-coherence as shown in Fig.3. (a concept first demonstrated for EEG analysis by Rappelsberger). Even though independent components are (maximally) independent over the whole time range of the training data, they may become transiently (partially) synchronized in specific frequency bands. In the cross window below, the two components become synchronized (top panel) around 11.5Hz (click on the image to zoom in). The upper panel shows the coherence magnitude (between 0 and 1, 1 representing two perfectly synchronized signals). The lower panel indicates the phase difference between the two signals at time/frequency points where cross-coherence magnitude (in the top panel) is significant. In this example, the two components are synchronized with a phase offset of about -120 degrees (this phase difference can also be plotted as latency delay in ms, using the minimum-phase assumption.

Channel statistics may help determine whether to remove a channel or not. To compute and plot one channel statistical characteristics.

4. CONCLUSION

From this model & software we conclude that, the EEG signal after anulom vilom becomes less complex. Correlation dimension, Largest lyapunov exponent, Approximate entropy & Hurst exponent decreases.Less parallel functional activity of the brain predictability of the EEG signal increases.

References

1. Prof. S.T. Patil & Dr. D.S. Bormane, "Dynamic EEG Analysis Using Multi-resolution Time & Frequency" (BIOCON-September, 2005, Pune)

2. Prof. S.T. Patil & Dr. D.S. Bormane, "Fast Changing Dynamic & High Non-stationary EEG Signal Analysis Using Multi-resolution Time & Frequency. In January 2006 at Government College of Engineering, Aurangabad.

3. Prof. S.T. Patil & Dr. D.S. Bormane, "EEG Analysis during Bramari using wavelet, selected in **CIT, International conference,** Bhubaneshwar, December 2006.

4. Prof. S.T. Patil **"Enhanced adaptive mesh generation for image representation,** ETA-2006, **National conference,** Rajkot, October 2006.

5. Chatrian et al., "A glossary of terms most commonly used by clinical electroencephalographers", Electroenceph.and Clin. Neurophysiol., 1994, 37:538-548.

6. Susumo Date, "A Grid Application for an Evaluation of Brain Function Using ICA" Proceedings of the International conference, IEEE - 2002.

7. Daubechies, Ingred. Ten Lectures on Wavelets SIAM (Society for Industrial and Applied Mathematics), Philadelphia, Pennsylvania, 1992.

8. S. Mallat, "A Theory for Multiresolution Signal Decomposition: The Wavelet Representation", IEEE Trans. on Pattern Analysis and Machine Intelligence, vol. 14, pp710-732, July 1992.

9. John G. Proakis, "Digital Signal Processing", Maxwell Macmillan International Edition.

10. http/www/health and yoga.com/pranayama/breathing.

11. http/www/life positive.com/yoga philosophy.

12. http/www/spiritual age.com/yoga/ pranayama/onkar yogasan.

CHAPTER 14

A Cognitive Account of Direct Manipulation Interfaces

R.G. Pawar, Kiran S. Kale and Ajit S. Ghodke
Sinhgad Institute of Business Administration & Computer Application, Pune (MS), India
E-mail: rgpawar@rediffmail.com, kiranskale@rediffmail.com, ghodke.a@gmail.com

ABSTRACT

Direct manipulation interfaces involves continuous representation of objects of interest, and rapid, reversible, incremental actions and feedback. The term was introduced by Ben Shneiderman in 1983 within the context of office applications and the desktop metaphor. Direct manipulation is closely associated with interfaces that use windows, icons, menus, and a pointing device (WIMP GUI) as these almost always incorporate direct manipulation to at least some degree.
Keywords: Direct manipulation, cognitive modeling, directness, interfaces

1. INTRODUCTION

One of the most significant developments of the 1980's in human computer interaction (HCI) was the emergence of 'direct manipulation' as a theoretical concept and design practice. At the heart of this development is the promotion of graphic and manual forms of interaction overand above more abstract and linguistic ones, on the grounds that the former place less load on the human cognitive system and are preferred by users. This philosophy has had a massive and largely beneficial impact on the face of personal computing and continues to exert a strong influenceon the design of interactive software today

The three most ubiquitous transformation widgets are mostly standardized and are:

(i) The Translation widget, which usually consists of three arrows aligned with the orthogonal axes centered on the object to be translated. Dragging the center of the widget translates the object directly underneath the mouse pointer in the plane parallel to the camera plane, while dragging any of the three arrows translates the object along the appropriate axis. The axes may be aligned with the world-space axes, the object-space axes, or some other space.

(ii) The Rotation widget, which usually consists of three circles aligned with the three orthogonal axes, and one circle aligned with the camera plane. Dragging any of the circles rotates the object around the appropriate axis, while dragging elsewhere will freely rotate the object.

(iii) The scale widget, which usually consists of three short lines aligned with the orthogonal axes terminating in boxes, and one box in the center of the widget. Dragging any of the three axis-aligned boxes effects a non-uniform scale along solely that axis, while dragging the center box effects a uniform scale on all three axes at once.

There are systems with attractive features, and claims for the benefits of systems that give the user a certain sort of feeling, and even lists of properties that seem to be shared by systems that provide that feeling, but no account of how particular properties might produce the feeling of directness. The mail purpose of this paper is to study the underlying basis for direct manipulation systems. On the one hand, what provides the feeling of "directness?" Why do direct manipulation systems feel so natural? What is so compelling about the notion? On the other hand, why can using such systems sometimes seem so tedious?

The notion of "direct manipulation" is not a unitary concept, nor even something that can be quantified in itself. "Directness" is an impression or a feeling about an interface. The efforts to character-ize the space of interfaces can be seen. The goal is to give cognitive accounts of these phenomena. At the root of our approach is the assumption that the feeling of directness results from the commitment of fewer cognitive resources. To put the other way around, the need to commit additional cognitive re-sources in the use of an interface leads to the feeling of indirectness can also be observed. Some of the production of the feeling of directness is due to adaptation by the user, so that the designer can neither completely control the process, nor take full credit for the feeling of directness that may be experienced by the user. The feeling of directness is always relative; it is often due to the interaction of a number of factors. There are costs associated with every factor that increases the sensation of directness. There are no ways to measure the trade-off values, but attempt can be made to provide a framework within which one can say what is being traded off against what.

3. TWO ASPECTS OF DIRECTNESS: DISTANCE AND ENGAGEMENT

There are two distinct aspects of the feeling of directness. One involves a notion of the distance between one's thoughts and the physical requirements of the system under use. A short distance means that the translation is simple and straightforward, that thoughts are readily translated into the physical actions required by the system and that the system output is in a form readily interpreted in terms of the goals of interest to the user. We use the term directness to refer to the feeling that results from interaction with an interface. The term distance is used to describe factors which underlie the generation of the feeling of directness.

The second aspect of directness concerns the qualitative feeling of engagement, the feeling that one is directly manipulating the objects of interest. There are two major metaphors for the nature of human-computer interaction, a conversation metaphor and a model-world metaphor.

In a system built on the conversation metaphor, the interface is a language medium in which the user and system have a conversation about an assumed, but not explicitly represented world. In this case, the interface is an implied intermediary between the user and the world about which things are said. In a system built on the model-world metaphor, the interface is itself a world where the user can act, and which changes state in response to user actions. The world of interest is explicitly represented and there is no intermediary between user and world. Appropriate use of the model-world metaphor can create the sensa-tion in the user of acting upon the objects of the task domain themselves. We call this aspect of directness direct engagement.

3.1   Distance

The underlying aspect of directness distance to emphasize the fact that directness is not a property of the interface alone, but involves a relationship between the task the user has in mind and the way that task can be accomplished via the interface. The critical issues involve minimizing the effort required to bridge the gulf between the user's goals and the way they must be specified to the system. An interface introduces distance to the extent there are gulfs between a person's goals and knowledge and the level of description provided by the systems with which the person must deal. These are termed as the gulf of execution and the gulf of evaluation. The gulf of execution is bridged by making the commands and mechanisms of the system match the thoughts and goals of the user. The gulf of evaluation is bridged by making the output displays present a good conceptual model of the system that is readily perceived, interpreted, and evaluated as shown in Fig. 1. The goal in both cases is to minimize cognitive effort.

The feeling of directness is inversely proportional to the amount of cognitive effort it takes to manipulate and evaluate a system and moreover, cognitive effort is a direct result of the gulfs of execution and evaluation. The better the interface to a system helps bridge the gulfs, the less cognitive effort needed and the more direct the resulting feeling of interaction.

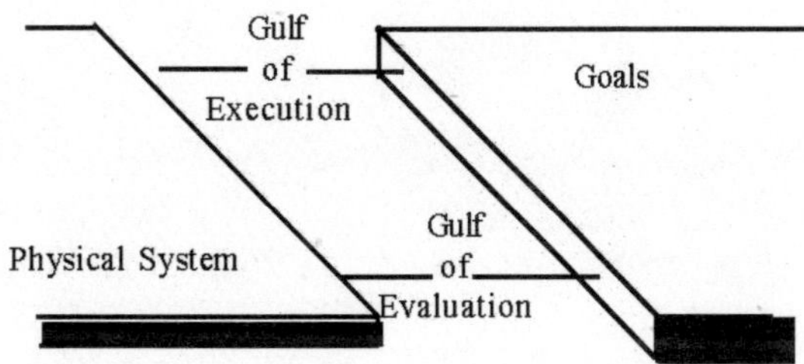

Fig. 1   The gulfs of execution and evaluation

3.2   Direct Engagement

The description of the nature of interaction at this point begins to suggest how to make a system less difficult to use, but it misses an important point, a point that is the essence of direct manipulation. The analysis of the execution and evaluation process explains why there is difficulty in using a system, and it says something about what must be done to minimize the mental effort required to use a system. But there is more to it than that. The systems that best exemplify direct manipulation ail give the qualitative feeling that one is directly engaged with control of the objects- not with the programs, not with the computer, but with the semantic objects of our goals and intentions. This is the feeling that Laurel discusses: a feeling of first personness, of direct engagement with the objects that concern us.

4.   CONCLUSION

Direct manipulation was clearly a large and important step beyond programming languages. However, it is not a panacea for human computer interaction as even the earliest of commentators point out since there are situations in which manipulation is clumsy to perform. The key to taking the next step beyond manipulation lies in recognizing that these situations are the very same ones in which language is more graceful as an interaction method, and that a one sided 'programming' of computers by people can be replaced by a two-sided conversation conducted in the context of some visual framework.

References

1. Ankrah, A, Frohlich, n.M., & Gilbert, G.N. 1990. Two ways to fill a bath, with and without knowing it. Proceedings of INTERACT '90, 73-78..

2. Black, J.B., & Sebrechts, M.M. (1981). Facilitating human-computer communication. AppliedPsycholinguistics, 2, 149-17 7.

3. Cawsey, A 1989. Explanatory dialogues. Interacting with Computers 1, 69-92.

4. Disessa, A.A. (1985). A principles design for an integrated computational environment. Human-Computer Interaction, 1, 1-47.

5. Hollan, J.D., Stevens, A., & Williams, M.D. (1980). Steamer: An advanced computer-assisted instruc-tion system for propulsion engineering. Proceedings of Summer Computer Simulation Conference, 400-404. Arlington, VA: AFIPS Press.

6. Kay, A. (1984, September). Computer software. Scientifzc American, 52-59.

7. Shneiderman, B. (1974). A computer graphics system for polynomials. The Mathematc Teacher, 67(2), 11 1-1 13.

8. Shneiderman, B. (1982). The future of interactive systems and the emergence of direct manipulation.Behauiorand Znfownation Technology, 1, 237-256.

9. Shneiderman, B. (1983). Direct manipulation: A step beyond programming languages. ZEEE Computer, 16(8), 57-69.

10. Andrea Leganshuk, Shumin Zhai, and William Buxton. Bimanual direct manipulation in areasweeping tasks. http://www.dgp.utoronto.ca/people/andrea/bimanual.html, 1996.

CHAPTER 15

Recent Advances for Recognition of Faces in the Crowd

D.K. Kirange[1], A.M. Patil[1], R.R. Deshmukh[2] and Shubhangi D. Patil[1]
[1]T.M.E. Society's J.T. Mahajan College of Engineering, Faizpur (MS) India, [2]Dr. B A M University, Aurangabad (MS) India
E-mail: dkirange@rediffmail.com; ratnadeep_deshmukh@yahoo.co.in; shubhangi_4@hotmail.com

ABSTRACT

Facial recognition technology has emerged as an attractive solution to address many contemporary needs for identification and the verification of identity claims. The amount of work going in the field of face recognition is very vast and huge. Hence it is very difficult to summarize all of this work. The problems of variable lighting, pose, facial expression, aging affects more on the desired performance of the face recognition. This paper attempts to provide a survey of the various problems faced by the face recognition technology and hence gives an idea of the recent advances for improving the performance of the face recognition systems.

Keywords: Face Recognition, facial expression, pose, lighting.

1. INTRODUCTION

Automatic recognition of individuals based on their biometric characteristics has attracted researcher's attention in recent years due to the advancement in image analysis methods and the emergence of significant commercial applications. There is an ever increasing demand for automated personal identification in a wide variety of applications ranging from low to high security such as: Human Computer Interaction (HCI), access control, surveillance, airport screening, smart card and security.

Fig. 1 Easy Scenarios in Face Recognition

Broadly speaking, the approaches proposed in the last years have been able to *solve* specific still face images recognition applications. Examples of scenarios where face recognition achieves very good results are given in Figure 1.

When the scenario departs from the *easy* scenario, then face recognition approaches experience severe problems. Face recognition in an uncontrolled environment is a complex problem because many issues occur. For Example more than 1 face can appear, lighting conditions vary, facial expressions, different scale, position, orientation, facial hair, make-up, glasses, Occlusion.

In other words, current algorithms are yet to be developed. Figure 2 shows different images which present some of the problems encountered in face recognition.

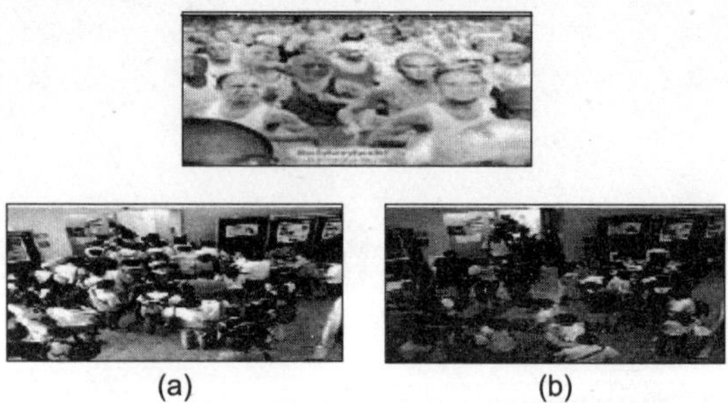

(a)   (b)

Fig 2   Difficult scenarios in Face Recognition

The rest of the paper is organized as follows: Comparing two faces with different illumination is one of the fundamental problems for face recognition systems. Section 2 deals with existing techniques for recognizing faces invariant to illumination. Section 3 addresses the problem of comparing faces under varying pose which is one of the fundamental challenges for the face recognition. Section 4 describes a problem of recognizing faces with different facial expressions. Age is one of the challenging task because human faces can vary a lot over time in many aspects, including facial texture (e.g. wrinkles), shape (e.g. weight gain), facial hair, presence of glasses, etc. Section 5 lists various approaches dealing with recognizing faces under age invariance.

2. RECOGNIZING FACES INVARIANT TO ILLUMINATION

Comparing two faces with different illumination is one of the fundamental problems for face recognition systems. It is well known that the differences in pixel values caused by different lighting conditions can be greater than the differences between two different people under the same lighting condition. Figure 3 shows how a face can vary under different illuminations. Adini, Moses, and Ullman [1] were the first who observed the problem. But, Zhao and Chellappa [2] gave a theoretical proof of it on the basis of eigenface system projection.

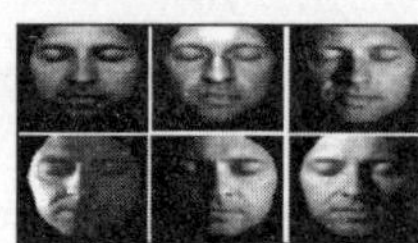

Fig. 3   Example of a face under various illuminations

2.1 Review of Related Work for Illumination Invariance

To handle such problems, the researchers have already proposed various approaches during these years.

1. Belhumeur et al. [3] and Bartlett et al. [4] adopted the PCA by discarding the first few principal components. In [5], a hybrid approach based on the use of PCA and correlation filters was proposed. Advantage: achieved better performance for images under different lighting conditions.
2. In [6], the Discrete Cosine Transform was employed by Chen et al. to compensate for illumination variations in the logarithm domain.
3. Jacobs et al. [7] presented a method based on the fact that, for point light sources and objects with Lambertian reflectance, the ratio of two images from the same object is simpler than the ratio of images from different objects.

3. Nanni et al. [8] proposed local based methods based on the Gabor filter. In Du et al. [9] a wavelet based normalization method was presented.

4. Liu et al. [10] used a ratio image to solve the illumination variation. Similar method had been proposed by Wang, et al. [11], which aimed to acquire an illumination-invariant face feature image for a group of images of the same subject.

5. Multi-resolution LBP [12] was presented where neighborhoods of different sizes are considered to deal with textures at different scales, and the uniform LBP, characterized by at most one 0–1 or 1–0 transition, to better represent primitive structural information such as edges and corners. Zhang et al. [13] proposed to couple the LBP representation with Gabor phases. Local ternary pattern (LTP)[14] was proposed by Tan and Triggs, which was also an extension of LBP.

6. Recently, in [15], an effective method of handling illumination variations was presented by using illumination cone. This method also dealt with shadowing and multiple lighting conditions which was on the basis of 3D linear subspace.

3. RECOGNIZING FACES INVARIANT TO POSE

Comparing faces under varying pose is another fundamental challenge for the face recognition system. Figure 4 shows how a face image can change under modest pose variations.

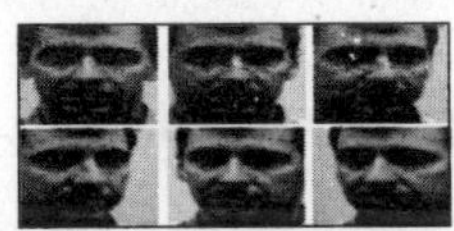

Fig. 4 Example of faces in various pose

3.1 Review of Related Work for Pose Invariance

New AAM methods [16] have been proposed to handle both varying pose and expression. In [17], Eigen light-fields and Fisher light-fields method was proposed to do pose invariant face recognition. A method by 3D model of the entire head for exploiting features like hairline, which handled large pose variations in head tracking and video-based face recognition was presented [18]. Computing the Kullback-Leibler divergence between testing image sets and a learned manifold density was the other thought [19]. In [20] learns manifolds of face variations for face recognition in video. In [21], the research said they achieved pose robustness by decomposing each appearance manifold into semantic Gaussian pose clusters, comparing the corresponding clusters and fusing the results by RBF network.

4. COMPARING FACES WITH DIFFERENT FACIAL EXPRESSIONS

Comparing faces with different facial expressions is another problem for some face recognition applications. Figure 5 gives an example of a face with many different expressions.

Fig. 5 Examples of a face with various expressions

4.1 Review of related work for comparing faces with different facial expressions

There are various approaches to dealing with expressions that are based on the idea of building a model of the changes that faces undergo through expression variations.

1. A morphable model (2D or 3D) [22] or active appearance model [23] can be used to capture expression variations. The morphable model or active appearance model is fit to the input face, and then either the face can be expression normalized to yield an image of a face under neutral expression.

2. Singular Value Decomposition (SVD) can be extended to multi dimensional tensors. [24, 25]. Given a set of images for each person that varies over expressions as well as possibly over lighting and pose, different subspaces can be learned for each mode of variation. A new face is projected to this model and the closest gallery face in that space is found.

5. AGE INVARIANT FACE RECOGNITION

Face recognition across ages is an important problem and has many applications, such as passport photo verification, image retrieval, surveillance, etc. This is a challenging task because human faces can vary a lot over time in many aspects, including facial texture (e.g. wrinkles), shape (e.g. weight gain), facial hair, presence of glasses, etc. Figure 6 shows several images of the same person with different age gaps.

Fig. 6   Face images of the same person with different age

5.1   Related Work for Face Recognition Invariant to Age

In computer vision, most aging approaches are example based and can be divided into three types.

The prototype method [26], [27] computes average face image of each age group as prototype and defines the differences between prototypes as aging transformation. Wang et al. [28] applied this prototype approach in PCA space instead of on image directly and Park et al. [29] applied it to 3D face data. Prototype method is able to extract average patterns, but many details (e.g., wrinkles, pigments, etc.) crucial for age perception are ignored.

The function-based method describes relationships between a face image and its age label with an explicit function, such as quadratic function [30], support vector regression [31], kernel smoothing method [32], or an implicit function [33]. Jiang and Wang [34] directly built a mapping function between young faces and their appearances at later ages. All of those functions need considerable real aging sequences to learn the function parameters.

Distance based methods [35] formulate aging simulation as an optimization problem. They synthesize a face close to the images of intended age in age space and close to the input individual in the identity space simultaneously. The algorithm in [35] adopted global AAM model and simple similarity metrics, simulation results are not realistic enough.

6. CONCLUSIONS

A lot of work has been done in the area of face recognition. But despite the existence of numerous commercial face recognition systems there are still important challenges for further research. The problems such as variable lighting conditions, age invariance, pose invariance, illumination invariance are of significant importance. This paper provides a survey of recent advances in face recognition systems to improve the robustness of face recognition systems to change in illumination, pose, expression, and age.

Acknowledgments

The authors would like to thanks Huafeng Wang, Yunhong Wang, And Yuan Cao for providing a useful survey paper on video based face recognition. Also we would be very thankful to Michael Jones for his paper study paper regarding face recognition at Microsoft research laboratories. Also the authors would like to welcome any comments and suggestions from the anonymous reviewers.

References

1. Y Adini, Y Moses, S Ullman, "Face recognition: the problem of compensating for changes in illumination direction", IEEE Transactions on Pattern Analysis and Machine, Vol. 19: 721-732,1997.

2. WY Zhao, R Chellappa "Illumination-insensitive face recognition using symmetricshape-from-shading" IEEE Conference on Computer Vision and Pattern Recognition, 2000.

3. PN Belhumeur, JP Hespanha, DJ Kriegman, "Eigenfaces vs. Fisherfaces: recognition using class specific linear projection" IEEE Transactions on pattern analysis and machine, Vol 19: 711-720, 1997.

4. Bartlett, M. Stewart, & Sejnowski, T., 1997. Viewpoint invariant face recognition using independent Component analysis and attractor networks. In M. Mozer, M. Jordan, & T. Petsche, Eds.,Advances in Neural Information Processing Systems 9. Cambridge, MA: MIT Press: 817-823.

5. Chen, W., Er, M. J., & Wu, S. Illumination compensation and normalization for robust face recognition using discrete cosine transform in logarithm domain. IEEE Transactions on Systems, Man and Cybernetics-Part B: Cybernetics, 36(2), 458-466, 2006.

6. Jacobs, D.W., Belhumeur, P.N., & Barsi, R.. Comparing images under variable illumination. In Proceedings, IEEE conference on computer vision and pattern recognition pp. 610-617. 1998.

7. Nanni, L., & Maio, D. Weighted Sub-Gabor for Face Recognition. Pattern Recognition Letters, 28(4), 487-492 2007.

8. Liu, D.H., Shen, L.S., Lam, K.M., & Kong, X. Illumination invariant face recognition. Pattern Recognition, 38, 1705-1716. 2005.

9. Wang, H., Li, S.Z., & Wang, Y. Face recognition under varying lighting conditions using self quotient image. In Proceedings of the IEEE international conference on automatic face and gesture recognition pp. 819-824, 2004.

10. Savvides, M., Kumar, B.V., & Khosla, P.K. Corefaces-robust shift invariant PCA based correlation filter for illumination tolerant face recognition. In Proceedings of the international conference on computer vision and pattern recognition Vol. 2, pp. 834-841, 2004.

11. Du, S., & Ward, R. Wavelet based illumination normalization for face recognition. In Proceedings of international conference on image processing Vol. 2, pp. 954-957,2005.

12. Ojala, T., Pietikainen, M., & Maenpaa, T. Multiresolution gray-scale and rotation invariant texture classification with local binary patterns. IEEE Transactions on Pattern Analysis and Machine Intelligence, 24(7), 971-987. 2002.

13. Zhang, W., Shan, S., Chen, X., & Gao, W. Are Gabor phases really useless for face recognition? In Proceedings of international conference on pattern recognition Vol. 4, pp. 606-609,2006.

14. Tan, X., & Triggs, B. Enhanced local texture feature sets for face recognition under difficult lighting conditions. In Proceedings of the IEEE international workshop on analysis and modeling of faces and gestures pp. 168-182.2007.

15. Georghiades, A., Kriegman, D., & Belhumeur, P. From few to many: Generative models for recognition under variable pose and illumination. IEEE Transactions Pattern Analysis and Machine Intelligence, 40, 643-660. 2001.

16. T. Cootes, K. Walker, and C. Taylor. View-based active appearance models. In Proceedings of the IEEE International Conference on Automatic Face and Gesture Recognition, pages 227-232, 2000.

17. I. Matthews, R. Gross, and S. Baker, Appearance-based face recognition and light-fields, IEEE Transactions on Pattern Analysis and Machine Intelligence, vol. 26, no. 4, pp. 449-465,2004.

18. M. Everingham and A. Zisserman, Identifying individuals in video by combinig 'generative' and discriminative head models, in Proceedings of the 10th IEEE International Conference on Computer Vision (ICCV '05), vol. 2, pp. 11031110, Beijing,China, October 2005.

19. O. Arandjelovic, G. Shakhnarovich, J. Fisher, R. Cipolla, and T. Darrell, Face recognition with image sets using manifold density divergence, Proceedings of the IEEE Computer Society Conference on Computer Vision and Pattern Recognition (CVPR '05), vol. 1, pp. 581-588, San Diego, Calif, USA.

20. O. Arandjelovic and R. Cipolla, An illumination invariant face recognition system for access control using video, in Proceedings of the British Machine Vision Conference (BMVC '04), pp.537-546, Kingston, Canada, September 2004.

21. Arandjelovic O, Cipolla R A pose-wise linear illumination manifold model for face recognition using video; Computer Vision And Image Understanding,Vol:113(1), pp: 113-125,2009.

22. V. blanz and T. Vetter: "Face Recognition Based on fitting a 3D morphable model", IEEE Trans. Patt. Anal. Mach. Intell. Vol 25, No 9, 2003

23. T.F. Cootes, G.J. Edwards and C.J. Taylor, " Active Appearance Models", IEEE Trans. Patt. Anal. Mach. Intell. Vol 23, No 6, 2001

24. J. Lee, B. Moghaddam, H. Pfister and R. Machiraju, " A bilinear Illumination model for robust face recognition", IEEE Intl. Conf. on Comp. Vis., Vol 2, No 2, pp-1177-1184, 2005.

25. M.A.O. Vasilescu and D. Teraopoulos, "multilinear analysis of image Ensembles: Tensorfaces", Proc. of the European Conference on Computer vision, pp 446-460, 2002

26. D.M. Burt and D.I. Perrett, "Perception of Age in Adult Caucasian Male Faces: Computer Graphic Manipulation of Shape and Color Information," Proc. Royal Soc. of London, Vol. 259, pp. 137-143, Feb. 1995.

27. B.P. Tiddeman, M.R. Stirrat, and D.I. Perrett, "Towards Realism in Facial Prototyping: Results of a Wavelet mrf Method," Proc. 24th Conf. Theory and Practice of Computer Graphics, pp. 105-111, 2006.

28. J. Wang, Y. Shang, G. Su, and X. Lin, "Age Simulation for Face Recognition," Proc. 18th Int'l Conf. Pattern Recognition, Vol. 3, pp. 913-916, 2006.

29. U. Park, Y. Tong, and A.K. Jain, "Face Recognition with Temporal Invariance: A 3D Aging Model," Proc. Eighth Int'l Conf. Automatic Face and Gesture Recognition, 2008.

30. E. Patterson, K. Ricanek, M. Albert, and E. Boone, "Automatic Representation of Adult Aging in Facial Images," Proc. Sixth IASTED Int'l Conf. Visualization, Imaging, and Image Processing, p. 612, 2006.

31. J. Wang and C. Ling, "Artificial Aging of Faces by Support Vector Machines," Proc. 17th Canadian Conf. Artificial Intelligence, pp. 499-503, 2004.

32. J.B. Pittenger and R.E. Shaw. "Aging faces as viscal-elastic events: Implications for a theory of nonrigid shape perception". *J. of Exp. Psychology: Human Perception and Performance*, 1(4): 374-382, 1975.

33. A.C. Berg, F.J.P. Lopez, and M. Gonzalez, "A Facial Aging Simulation Method Using Flaccidity Deformation Criteria," Proc. 10th Int'l Conf. Information Visualization, pp. 791-796, July 2006.

34. F. Jiang and Y. Wang, "Facial Aging Simulation Based on Super Resolution in Tensor Space," Proc. 15th Int'l Conf. Image Processing, pp. 1648-1651, 2008.

35. A. Lanitis, "Comparative Evaluation of Automatic Age- Progression Methodologies," EURASIP J. Advances in Signal Processing, vol. 8, no. 2, pp. 1-10, Jan. 2008.

36. Huafeng Wang, Yunhong Wang, And Yuan Cao, "Video Based Face Recognition", World Academy Of Science, Engineering And Technology 60 2009

37. Michael Jones, "Face Recognition: Where We Are And Where To Go From Here", Mitsubishi Electric Research Laboratories, Tr2009-023 June 2009.

CHAPTER 16

Surround Sense Hand Gestures for Mobile Device

Snehal S. Golait[1] and R.V. Dharaskar[2]
[1]Priyadarshini College of Engineering, Nagpur, (MS) India, [2]Department of Computer Science & Engineering
(PG & UG), G.H. Raisoni College of Engineering (MS) India
E-mail: dalal_snehal@rediffmail.com, rvdharaskar@rediffmail.com

ABSTRACT

Mobile Computing is a technology that allows transmission of data, via a computer, without having to be connected to a fixed physical link. Mobile voice communication is widely established throughout the world. This paper proposed system is used to note down small pieces of information, quickly and ubiquitously, can be useful. This system use Mobile phone as pen and able to write a short message in the air. The system uses mobile phone with the in-built accelerometer to recognize human writing by holding the or even draw simple diagrams in the air. The acceleration due to hand gestures can be converted into an image, and sent to the user's Internet email address for future reference. Feature extraction is one of the basic function of handwritten gestures. It involves measuring those features of the input pattern are relevant to classification. For recognition of character use a stork grammar.

Keywords: Accelerometer, Stork Grammar, Hand Gestures.

1. INTRODUCTION

Imagine this scenario. A person parks car in one of the many levels of an airport parking lot. While rushing to catch flight, glances towards the ceiling, and catches the parking lot number – "Level 5, Row A". Walking briskly with luggage in one hand, takes out mobile phone using the other. Holding the phone like a pen, writes the word "5A" in the air, and puts the phone back into pocket. When inside flight, checks email one last time before turning off the phone. An email in mailbox says "PhonePoint Pen – 5A". Now assured to remember her parking lot number when returns to the airport a week later. The above is a fictional scenario, however, representative of a niche in the space of mobile computing applications. To be specific, believe that there is a class of applications that will benefit from a technology that can ubiquitously and quickly "note down" short pieces of information. Although existing technologies have made creative advances towards this direction, deficiencies remain. Proposed system is used to note down small pieces of information, quickly and ubiquitously, can be useful. This system use Mobile phone as pen and able to write a short message in the air. The system uses mobile phone with the in-built accelerometer to recognize human writing by holding the or even draw simple diagrams in the air. The acceleration due to hand gestures can be converted into an image, and sent to the user's Internet email address for future reference. Existing system shows that system is feasible if the user is restricted to a few simple constraint. Discuss some of these deficiencies, and motivate the potential of PhonePoint Pen.

1. Typing an SMS, while popular among the youth, has been unpopular among a large section of society. Many studies report user dissatisfaction with mobile phone typing [1]. The major sources of discomfort arise from small key sizes, short inter-key spacing, and the need for multi-tapping in some phone keyboards. With increasingly smaller phones, Keyboard sizes will decrease, exacerbating the problem of physical typing. Even if keyboard innovations improve the typing experience (virtual keyboards [18]), problems may still arise while noting information on the fly. While driving or walking fast, or while having one hand occupied, typing information may not be feasible. Using the mobile phone accelerometer to capture hand gestures, and carefully laying them out in text or geometric images, can be useful. The utility may be greater due to nature of phones, and their seamless connectivity to the Internet.

2. Keyboards do not permit drawing. While styluses have been the proposed approach, they have not been successful because they are tedious to pull out and push back after every usage. Moreover, the palette for drawing is limited by the phones display, making the interface unattractive. The ability to draw on air, with natural movements of the hand, can circumvent these problems.

3. Current approaches are largely ad-hoc. People use whatever is quickly reachable, including pen-and-paper, sticky notes, one's own palm, etc. None of these scale because they are not always handy, and more importantly, not always connected to the Internet. Thus recorded information gets scattered, making information search and retrieval hard.

2. PROPOSED APPROACH

Proposed approach uses mobile phone within built accelerometer that detects acceleration in the X, Y, and Z directions. The accelerometers measure linear movement along each axis, but cannot detect rotation. To detect the rotation require gyroscope. To begin with a brief functional explanation of the gyroscope, Consider the position of a gyroscope-enabled phone (GEP) [17] at time $t = t_0$ in 2D space. Consider Figure 1, at this initial position, the GEP's axes are aligned with the earth's reference axes (i.e., gravity is exactly in the negative Y direction). The accelerometer reading at this position is $< Ix\,(t_0);\ Iy\,(t_0) - g >$, where $Ix\,(t_0)$ and $Iy\,(t_0)$ are the instantaneous accelerations along the x and y axes at time t_0 respectively, and g is gravity.

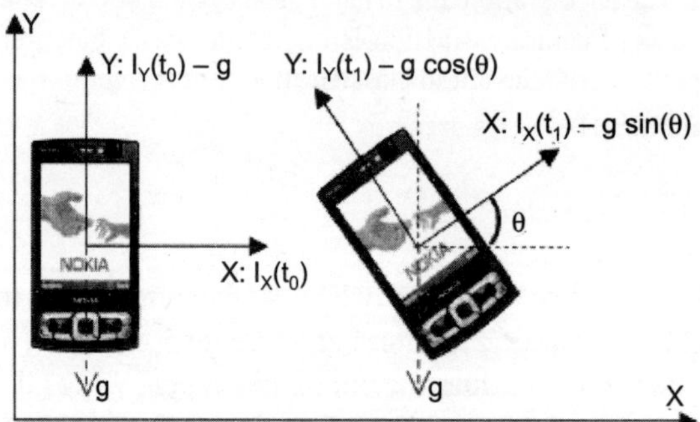

Fig. 1   Earth's gravity projected on the XY axes

Now, the phone may rotate at the same physical position at time t_1. The phone now makes an angle ? with the earth's reference frame, and the accelerometer readings are $< Ix\,(t_1) - g\sin(?\,);\ Iy\,(t_1) - g\cos(?\,) >$. However, it is possible that the phone moved along the XY plane in a manner that induced the same acceleration as caused by the rotation. This leads to an ambiguity that gyroscopes and accelerometers can together resolve (using angular velocity detection in gyroscopes). However, based on the accelerometer readings alone, linear movements and rotation cannot be easily discriminated.

This is a difficult problem and cope with this by imposing a soft constraint on the user. (i) The simpler approach is to pretend that one of the corners of the phone is the pen tip, and to hold it in a non-rotating grip. Some users also found it easier to hold it like a white-board eraser – this grip also reduced wrist-rotation. (ii) Alternatively, while writing an alphabet, users may briefly pause between two "strokes". The pause is often natural because the user changes the direction of movement (from one stroke to another). For example, while writing an "A", the pause after stroke "/" and before the starting of stroke "\" can be exploited. An accelerometer snapshot at this paused instant can identify the components of gravity on each axes, and hence, the angular orientation ? can be determined. Knowing ? the phone's subsequent movement can be derived.

The phone identifies the hand gestures as one of multiple strokes, compares the sequence of strokes against a grammar, and recognizes the air-written alphabets. The entire process requires negligible training, and can run entirely on the phone's processor. The written message is displayed on the phone-screen, and may also be emailed to the user if she desires.

3. COMPUTING DISPLACEMENT

The phone's displacement translates to the size of the air-written character, as well as their relative positions (such as in equations, figures, etc.). The displacement d is essentially computed as

$$= \bullet \, (\bullet \, a \; dt) \; dt$$

where a is the instantaneous acceleration. In other words, the algorithm first computes the velocity (the integration of acceleration), followed by the displacement (the integration of velocity). Noise in the acceleration readings will reflect on the velocity computation, and will get magnified in the computation of displacement. For instance, an erroneous short positive impulse in the accelerometer (i.e., acceleration becoming positive and then returning to zero),results in a positive velocity. Unless a negative impulse compensates for the positive impulse, the phone would continue to be in a state of constant velocity. When this velocity is integrated, the displacement error will be large.

4. DIFFERENTIATING "A" FROM A TRIANGLE

The imaginary slate in the air has no global reference frame for position. While writing character "A", assume the writer has already drawn the "/" and "\", and now lifts the pen to draw the "–". Observe that the phone has no idea about the global position of "/\". Hence, upon drawing the "–", the pen does not know whether it is meant to be added in the center (to indicate an "A"), or at the bottom (to indicate a triangle, ?). This ambiguity underlies several other characters and shapes.

This is a difficult problem, and we plan to jointly exploit the accelerations along the X, Y, and Z axes. Consider the intent to write an "A". Also assume that the user has just finished writing "/\". The pen is now at the bottom of the "\". The user will now lift the pen and move it towards the up-left direction, so that it can write the "–". The lifting of the pen happens in 3D space, and generates an identifiable impulse on the Z axis. When the acceleration in Z axis is above a certain threshold, we label that stroke as a "lifting of the pen". This pen-lifting can be used as a trigger for the user going off the record. User movements in the XY plane are still monitored for pen repositioning, but do not get included in the final output. When the phone is in position to write "–", a small pause can be used as an indication for going back on the record.

5. IDENTIFYING CHARACTER TRANSITION

If pen-lifts are recognized, certain ambiguities remain. For instance, "B" and "13" may have the exact same hand-movement, including the pen-lift. The user's intention is difficult to recognize, making character.

6. STROKE DETECTION

Characters can be viewed as a sequence of strokes. The alphabet "A", for instance, is composed of 3 strokes, namely "/", "\", and "—". If the discrete strokes can be pulled out from the seemingly continuous movement of the hand, it would be possible to infer the characters. To this end, we have analyzed the English alphabets and characterized the basic set of strokes. Some basic storks of English alphabets are shown in Fig. 2.

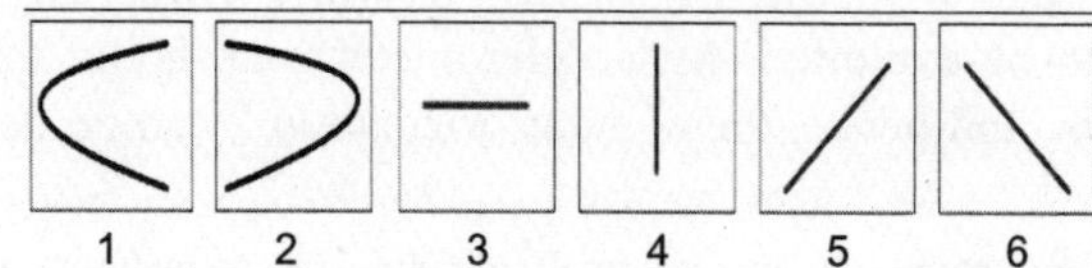

Fig. 2 Basic strokes for English characters.

To identify the strokes, computes a running variance of the accelerometer readings. When this variance falls below a threshold, marks those regions as a pause of the hand. The pauses demarcate the human-strokes, allowing to operate on each of them individually. For stroke-detection, our basic idea is to correlate the human-strokes against each of the basic strokes. This form of correlation is not new, and has been used as standard primitives in classification and matching techniques [9, 10, 11]. The correlation is performed over a varying window size of accelerometer readings. This is because the hand often rotates towards the end of the stroke, and the samples corresponding to the rotations should ideally be pruned out. In such cases, a shorter window size offers better correlation, in turn yielding the exact size of the human-stroke. Besides, even when the pauses are short between strokes, varying the window-size identifies the stroke boundaries. The intuition is that two consecutive strokes are typically different in the English alphabet, and thereby, correlating across the boundaries of the strokes reduces the correlation value. Performance results, reported later, show reasonable reliability in stroke detection. The natural question, then, pertains to combining the strokes into a character.

7. CHARACTER AND WORD RECOGNITION

For character recognition adopt a stroke grammar for English alphabets and digits. The grammar is essentially a tree, and expresses the valid sequence of strokes to Forman alphabet. Moreover, the grammar also helps in stroke-recognition because it provides with an ability to anticipate the next stroke. For instance, observing strokes "| \ / " in succession, can anticipate an "*M*" and expect the next stroke to be a "|". Thus, by correlating "|" to the stream of accelerometer readings (and ensuring a high correlation), the system can better identify the end-points of the next stroke. This helps in identifying the residual samples, which in turn helps in tracking the re-positioning of the hand in-between strokes.

8. CONCLUDING REMARK

This paper attempts to exploit the accelerometer in mobile phones to develop a new input technology. While today's users are mostly used to keyboards and touch-screens, we propose to mimic a pen. By holding the phone like a pen, the user should be able to write short messages in the air. The phone identifies the hand gestures as one of multiple strokes, compares the sequence of strokes against a grammar, and recognizes the air-written alphabets. The entire process requires negligible training, and can run entirely on the phone's processor. The written message is displayed on the phone-screen, and may also be emailed to the user if she desires.

References

1. "PhonePoint Pen: Using Mobile Phones to Write in Air" MobiHeld'09, August 17, 2009, Barcelona, Spain.
2. V. Balakrishnan and P.H.P. Yeow, "A study of the effect of thumb sizes on mobile phone texting satisfaction," in Journal of Usability Studies, 2008.
3. V. Balakrishnan and P.H.P. Yeow, "Sms usage satisfaction: Influences of hand anthropometry and gender," in Human IT 9.2, 2007.
4. J. Liu, Z. Wang, L. Zhong, J. Wickramasuriya, and V. Vasudevan, "uWave: Accelerometer-based personalized gesture recognition and its applications," in IEEE PerCom, 2009.
5. "SurroundSense: Mobile Phone Localization via Ambience Fingerprinting "MobiCom'09, September 20–25, 2009, Beijing, China.

6. " EyePhone: Activating Mobile Phones With Your Eyes" MobiHeld 2010, August 30, 2010, New Delhi, India.

7. Naveen Santhapuri_ Justin Manweiler_ Souvik Sen_Xuan Bao_ Romit Roy Choudhury_ Srihari Nelakuditiy_ Duke University University of South Carolina "Sensor Assisted Wireless Communications".

8. Paul Keir, John Payne, Jocelyn Elgoyhen, Martyn Horner, Martin Naef, and Paul Anderson, "Gesture-recognition with non-referenced tracking," in 3DUI '06: Proceedings of the 3D User Interfaces, 2006.

9. Juha Kela, Panu Korpipää, Jani Mäntyjärvi, Sanna Kallio, Giuseppe Savino, Luca Jozzo, and Di Marca, "Accelerometer-based gesture control for a design environment," Personal Ubiquitous Comput., 2006.

10. "Virtualkeyboard,"http://www.unwiredview.com/wpcontent/uploads/2008/01/nokia-virtualkeyboard-patent.pdf.

11. Xuan Bao, Department of ECE, Duke University, Romit Roy Choudhury, Department of ECE, Duke University "MoVi: Mobile Phone based Video Highlights via Collaborative Sensing" MobiSys'10, June 15–18, 2010, San Francisco, California, USA.

12. Andrew Ofstad Emmett Nicholas Rick Szcodronski Romit Roy Choudhury Dept. of Electrical and Computer Engineering Duke University "AAMPL: Accelerometer Augmented Mobile Phone Localization" MELT'08, September 19, 2008, San Francisco, California, USA.

13. Nishkam Ravi and Nikhil Dandekar and Preetham Mysore and Michael L. Littman Department of Computer Science Rutgers University Piscataway, NJ 08854 "Activity Recognition from Accelerometer" Data Copyright c 2005, American Association for Artificial Intelligence (www.aaai.org).

14. Youngbum Lee, Student Member, IEEE, Jinkwon Kim, Muntak Son, and Myoungho Lee "Implementation of Accelerometer Sensor Module and Fall Detection Monitoring System based on Wireless Sensor Network" Proceedings of the 29th Annual International Conference of the IEEE EMBS Cité Internationale, Lyon, France August 23-26, 2007.

15. Vimala Balakrishnan1, Paul, H.P. Yeow2 Multimedia University, Jln Ayer Keroh Lama, 75450 Melaka, Malaysia " HAND-SIZE VARIATIONS EFFECT ON MOBILE PHONE TEXTING SATISFACTION " Ubiquitous Computing and Communication Journal.

16. Emiliano Miluzzoy, Cory T. Corneliusy, Ashwin Ramaswamyy, Tanzeem Choudhuryy, Zhigang Liux, Andrew T. Campbelly "Darwin Phones: the Evolution of Sensing and Inference on Mobile Phones" MobiSys'10, June 15–18, 2010, San Francisco, California, USA. Copyright 2010 ACM 978-1-60558-985-5/10/06.

17. S. Agrawal, I. Constandache, S. Gaonkar, and R. Roy Choudhury. Phonepoint pen: using mobile phones to write in air. In MobiHeld '09: Proceedings of the 1st ACM workshop on Networking, systems, and applications for mobile handhelds, 2009.

18. Nokia, "virtual keyboard," loads/2008/01/nokia-virtual-keyboardpatent.Pdf ..http://www.unwiredview.com/wpcontent/

CHAPTER 17

Modeling of Chaotic Dynamics in Social Systems

R.P. Rastogi[1] and Pankaj Mathur[2]

[1]Insa Hon. Scientist, Chemistry Department, Gorakhpur University, Gorakhpur, India,
[2]Department of Mathematics and Astronomy, Lucknow University, Lucknow, India
E-mail: rprastogi@yahoo.com, pankaj_mathur14@yahoo.co.in

ABSTRACT

Recent developments in the experimental and theoretical studies of dynamics of non-equilibrium phenomena generated some interest in the analogous phenomenon in social systems although not up to expected level. However, much more interest was developed in Chaos theory which attracted greater attention since its inception (1963). Nevertheless, great emphasis was given to philosophical discussion of concepts related to determinism and metaphor analysis as compared to application of models for chaos to similar phenomena in social systems.

In view of the fact, that most of the non-equilibrium phenomena including bi-stability, temporal oscillations, chemical waves, Lorenz's model, Rössler's model, Chua's model involve cross-catalysis or autocatalysis. In this communication, following strategy has been suggested for the development of models and semi-quantitative theories, for Chaos in social systems which involves:

- identification of cause effect sequence of key processes (positive and negative feedback)
- identification of key-variables (target variables)
- development of three-variable models (semi-quantitative and quantitative treatment)
- application to specific non-equilibrium Chaotic phenomenon.

The approach is useful for decision-making (crisis management) and Management science.

Keywords: Chaos, mathematical modeling, autocatalysis, cross-catalysis.

1. INTRODUCTION

There have been significant advances in the development of dynamics of open systems in non-equilibrium both from theoretical and experimental angles [1]-[3] which has potential applications for Social sciences. In recent communications [4]-[6], variety of phenomena from regions close to equilibrium to very far from equilibrium have been analyzed from philosophical angle involving Causality Principle supported by theoretical considerations and formally designed experiments. It is felt that there should be no difficulty in utilizing these concepts in analyzing non-equilibrium phenomena including Chaos in Socio-political and Socio-economic systems. However, detailed mathematical analysis of analogous phenomena in social systems may not be easy in view of involvement of number of variables.

Although there had been some impact of researches in non-equilibrium Science [3], Chaos theory attracted good deal of interest in social sciences, when Lorenz model and Rössler's model were postulated. However, since the literal meaning of chaos is related to 'great confusion or disorder', the clarification of terminology in the context of different disciplines led to good deal of philosophical discussion on conceptual basis, such as metaphor analysis, sociology of knowledge generation through various disciplines [7]-[10], Historiography [11], Time series [12] and philosophical discussion related to following two versions of theory,

   (i) Order out of chaos (Ilya Prigogine)

   (ii) Hidden-order within chaos (Lorenz, Menderbolt) .

In order to avoid such difficulties, there is need to adopt proper strategy to obtain meaningful results. Under the circumstances, it is desirable to adopt semi-quantitative models with emphasis on key processes and key variables in the search of three-variable or four-variables models. In this communication, we illustrate this approach by examining the application of Lorenz model [13] and Rössler model [14] of deterministic chaos along with their modified forms to analogous phenomena in Social systems.

2.   CHAOS IN SOCIAL SYSTEMS

Unlike the variables like temperature and pressure in Physico-chemical systems, which are well defined, this is seldom so in social systems. Sometimes as in the present case, the variables have many attributes which needs to be specified although subjectivity in identifying the variables as well as their "importance" is an important deterrent in planning. In socio-political and socio-economic systems, the variables are likely to be too many but their identification is not easy. However, their relative importance can easily be assessed. Keeping this in view, we have attempted to classify attributes of each variables viz., corruption, bad governance and political will.

Corruption promotes bad governance and in turn bad governance promotes corruption. Further both corruption and bad governance are contagious, self generating and promote autocatalysis. The third important factor, the Political will or Administrative will, counters the effect of corruption and bad governance. We can define the above mentioned variables as:

2.1   Corruption

It may be defined [15] as a kind of illegitimate favour for immediate or future personal gains for doing an official work which one is supposed to do free of charge and objectivity. Thus, misappropriation of public assets or misuse of office for personal gain is corruption.

In a narrow sense, it is limited to the illegitimate transaction in cash or kind but in a broader sense, it also includes nepotism (parochialism)- favouring family, caste, creed, language, place of birth or region and cronyism (favouring friends). One factor responsible for corruption in developing societies is consumerism. Consumerism encourages corruption which again encourages consumerism. Lust of quick money and erosion of moral and ethical values are additional factors.

N. Vittal, Ex-Chief Vigilance Commissioner, Govt. of India, remarked "Corruption which began with the corrupting of the institutions has led to the institutionalization of corruption." Subhash Sharma adds that "before the corruption of institutions, individuals and groups were corrupted (espetially since colonial period) and after the institution, the society at large has been corrupted."

2.2   Bad Governance

It is epitomised by [15]

   (a) unnecessary delaying tactics (red tapism)

   (b) digression of the matter

   (c) twisting wrong interpretation of laws, rules and regulations

(d) unnecessary referring for opinion/concurrence to other agencies/officers/departments (like law, finance, personnel etc.)

(e) making/covering the real issue with bad intension

(f) demanding irrelevant papers/documents for verification

(g) directly demanding cash or kind or directly demanding percentage (p.c.) share in the deal.

2.3   Political and Administrative Will

In view of the nature of corrupt society and bad governance, one can legitimately expect these to catalyse the process of corruption and bad governance by themselves just as living species self multiplies. Evil influence of corruption and bad governance is usually countered by Political Will which has following attributes:

Political will is governed by Political and committed leadership and supported by social leadership which provides good governance. World Bank defined in 1994: "Good governance is epitomised by predictable, open and enlightened policy making (i.e., transparent process); a bureaucracy imbued with a professional ethos; an executive arm of government for its action; and a strong civil society participating in public affairs and all behaving under the rule of law".

For recovery from the evil influence of corruption and mismanagement the society needs devoted and dedicated leaders of high integrity and objectivity having vision and foresight.

2.4   Public Opinion

At the macro-level, public opinion is reflected through print and electronic media, while at the micro-level, forces at macro level, forces of social psychology influence the public opinion. At the intermediate level, carefully organised opinion surveys provide the required information. Public opinion in a sense is a measure of permissiveness of moral and ethical values.

3.   TARGET AND SECONDARY VARIABLES

For illustration, we will use the phenomena of corruption to differentiate between significant and less significant variables.

Corruption promotes bad governance and in turn bad governance promotes corruption. Further both bad governance and corruption are contagious, self-generating and promote autocatalysis. The third important factor, the political will or administrative will counters the effect of bad governance and corruption in the system. Thus these are the three target/ primary variables. However, level of moral and ethical values, public opinion, social psychology, quality of leadership are some of the additional (secondary) variables as illustrated below

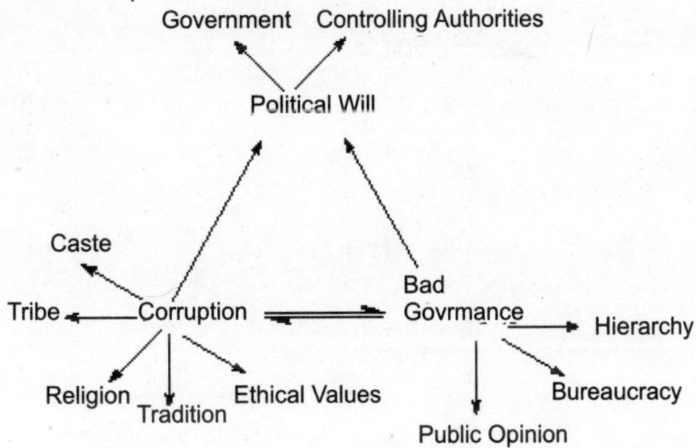

Fig. 1   Primary and secondary variables

4. DIFFERENT MODELS

In this section we give models where Chaos has been

4.1 Lorenz Model

The non-linear system of differential equations involved in Lorenz attractor [13], [16], [17] are given by

$$\frac{dx}{dt} = \sigma\,(y - x) \tag{1}$$

$$\frac{dy}{dt} = x\,(\rho - z) - y \tag{2}$$

$$\frac{dz}{dt} = xy - \beta z \tag{3}$$

where $x,\ y,\ z$ are variables and $\sigma,\ \rho,\ \beta$ are constants. Taking

x = amplitude of convective motion

y = temperature difference between ascending and descending current

z = distortion of vertical profile from linearity

and the value of the constants $\sigma = 10$, $\beta = 8/3$ and $\rho = 28$, with the initial conditions (0, 0.01, 0), the above set of differential equations leads to the Lorenz attractor on solution. Here s is called the Prandtl number and r is the Rayleigh number. The Lorenz model aims to describe the stability and the onset of the convective or turbulent motion in a fluid heated from the bottom and cooled from the top. The variables x (t), y (t), z (t) are not spatial variables, but refer to the remixing of the fluid and to the horizontal and vertical variations in temperature.

When the three variable models is applied to the social system then **x (t) denotes Corruption, y (t) denotes bad governance and z (t) denotes the political and administrative will.**

We first consider Lorenz equations (1), (2), (3) and assume that it can also be used for chemical systems. The above mathematical relations can be expressed in the form of chemical reaction as illustrated below, in order to identify cross-catalysis or autocatalysis if any.

$$y \xrightarrow{\ generates\ } x\,; \qquad \frac{dx}{dt} = \sigma y$$

$$x \xrightarrow{\ decays\ }\,; \qquad \frac{dx}{dt} = -\sigma x$$

$$x \xrightarrow{\ generates\ } y\,; \qquad \frac{dy}{dt} = \rho x$$

$$y \xrightarrow{\ decays\ }\,; \qquad \frac{dy}{dt} = -y$$

$$x + z \xrightarrow{\ decays\ }\,; \qquad \frac{dy}{dt} = -(x + z)$$

$$x + y \xrightarrow{\ generates\ } z\,; \qquad \frac{dz}{dt} = xy$$

$$z \xrightarrow{\ decays\ }\,; \qquad \frac{dz}{dt} = -\beta z$$

Similarly we can describe the other models as well.

4.2 Modified Lorenz Model

In equation number (1) and (2) of the Lorenz model cross catalalysis occurs between x and y i.e., x generates y and y generates x, but there is no autocatalysis. We have modified [18] the Lorenz model by taking into the consideration the autocatalysis of both x and y, which is obtained by adding terms "cx" and "ey" in equations (1) and (2) respectively. Then the set of differential equation turn up to be

$$\frac{dx}{dt} = \sigma(y - x) + cx \tag{4}$$

$$\frac{dy}{dt} = x(r - z) - y + ey \tag{5}$$

$$\frac{dz}{dt} = xy - \beta z \tag{6}$$

where c and e are additional constant to the original model. Here Fig. 2(a) correspond to the Lorenz type strange attractor when the constants have the values $\sigma = 10$, $\beta = 8/3$, $\rho = 28$, $c = 2.2$ and $e = 0.3$ while Fig. 2(b) yields the beginning of the strange attractor when $\sigma = 10$, $\beta = 8/3$, $\rho = 28$, $c = 0.2$; $e = 7.3$.

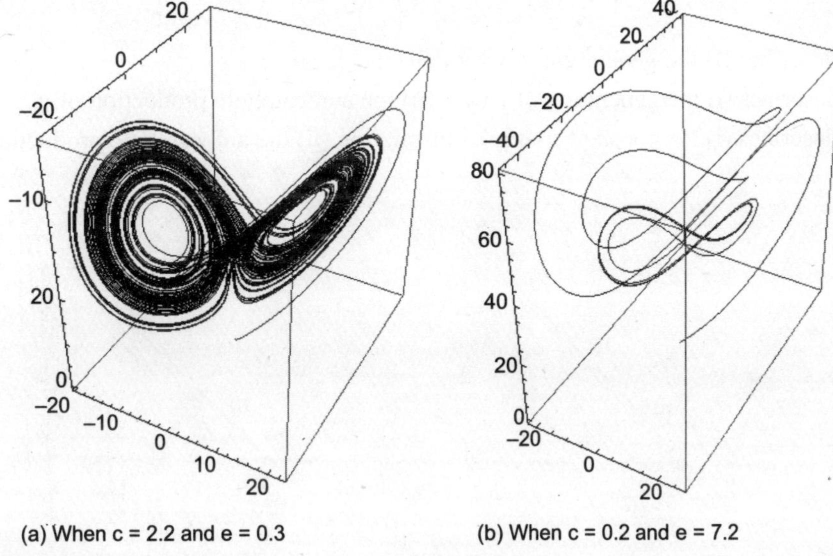

(a) When c = 2.2 and e = 0.3   (b) When c = 0.2 and e = 7.2

Fig. 2 Attractors with constants $\sigma = 10$, $\beta = 8/3$, $\rho = 28$, initial conditions (0, 1, 0) and (a) $c = 2.2$, $e = 0.3$, (b) $c = 0.2$, $e = 7.3$

4.3 Rössler Model

Rössler considered the following set of non-linear differential equations

$$\frac{dx}{dt} = -(y + z) \tag{7}$$

$$\frac{dy}{dt} = x + ay \tag{8}$$

$$\frac{dz}{dt} = b + xz - cz \tag{9}$$

where x, y, z are variables and a, b, c are constants. If $a = 0.2$, $b = 0.2$, $c = 5.7$, then the above system of non-linear differential equations lead to the Rössler's attractor on solution under the initial condition (–1, 0, 0).

When the above model is applied to social system *x*(t) denotes **Corruption,** *y*(t) denotes **bad governance and** z **(t) denotes the political and administrative will.** Further **b** denotes the public opinion, moral and ethical values which remain constant during a certain perid of time. Thus, Rössler model in effect acts as a four variable model.

4.4 Modified Rössler Model

The second term on the right hand side of equation (8) represents autocatalysis of *y* while the second term on the right hand side of the equation (9) represents the autocatalysis of *z*. There is no *cyclic term or cross-catalysis*. We have modified the Rössler's by considering the following system of non-linear differential equations

$$\frac{dx}{dt} = p\,y - qz \tag{10}$$

$$\frac{dy}{dt} = x + ay \tag{11}$$

$$\frac{dz}{dt} = b + r\,xz - cz \tag{12}$$

where *p, q, r* are additional constants to original Rössler model. In this system of the following processes have been expressed

   (a) Equation (10) describes (i) the generation of *x* by *y* (ii) the decay of *x* by *z*.
   (b) Equation (11) describes (i) the generation of *y* by *x* (ii) the autocatalytic production of *y*.
   (c) Equation (12) describes (i) the constant source of inspiration (ii) the autocatalytic production of *z* (iii) the decay of *z*.

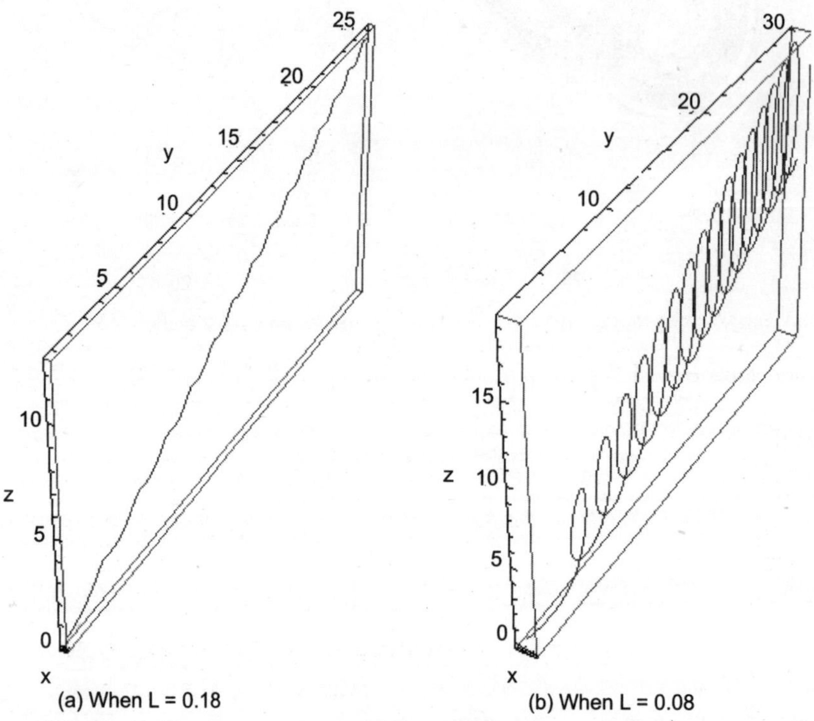

Fig. 3   Attractors with constants *B* = 0.1, *P* = 0.2, *F* = 0.001, *H* = 0.8, *J* = 0.2, initial conditions (0, 1, 0) and
(a) *L* = 0.18, (b) L = 0.08

If we fix the value of the constants have the values $B = 0.1$, $P = 0.2$, $F = 0.001$, $H = 0.8$, $J = 0.2$ and the value of L is varied then the strange attractor occurs if $0 < L < 0.15$. If $L < 0$ the chaotic character does not exist, whereas if $L > 0.15$ stability is achieved. Fig. 3(a) and 3(b) show the situation just mentioned. It is also seen that if the constants have the values $B = 0.1$, $F = 0.001$, $H = 0.8$, $J = 0.2$, $L = 0.03$ and the value of the constant P is varied then for very small values of P chaos does not exist whereas it exists for higher values of P.

5. CONCLUSION

Since number of Non-equilibrium phenomena far from equilibrium are governed by autocatalysis and inhibitory reactions [3] which is also true for analogous phenomena in social systems, it would be advisable to look for mathematical models for the analysis of chaotic phenomena for social systems. For such a strategy, it would be necessary to identify key processes and the relevant causal sequence involved in a particular situation. Such an approach would obviously be useful for Decision making and Management science. Further, planned work is still needed to examine in depth, the implications of chaos theory in social and global systems.

Rössler's model (original model and the modified model) is the best model to explain the social conditions if we put x = bad governance, y = corruption and z = control system (political will). Even when we ignore the generation of x by y and generation of y by x Chaos can prevail in social systems. However, it is obvious that mathematical models developed above are quite relevant in exploring the mechanism of development of social chaos.

Acknowledgement

Thanks are due to Indian National Science Academy for supporting the project.

References

1. Prigogine I, Introduction to Thermodynamics of Irreversible Processes, Wiley, New York, 1968.
2. de Groot SR and Mazur P, "Non-Equilibrium Thermodynamics", North-Holland, Amsterdem, 1962.
3. Rastogi R.P., Introduction to Non-equilibrium Physical Chemistry-Towards Complexity and Non-linear Science, Elsevier, Amsterdem, 2008.
4. Rastogi R.P and R.C. Srivastava, J. Sci. Ind. Res. 67 (2008) 747-758.
5. Rastogi R.P, J. Sci. Ind. Res., 40(1981) 565-570
6. Rastogi R.P, J. Sci. Ind. Res., 43(1984) 357-360.
7. Weingart Peter and Maasen Saberia, The Order of Meaning: The Career of Chaos as a Metaphor, Configurations 5.3 (1997) 463-520, John Hopkins University Press.
8. Kellert Stephan H., Science and Literature in Philosophy: The Case of Chaos theory and Deconstruction, Configurations 4.2 (1996) 215-232.
9. Jackson Tony E., Chaos, Complexity and Sociology- Myths, Models and Theories: Ed., Raymond A. Eve, Sara Horsfall and Mary E. Lee, Sage Publication, International Educational and Professional Publisher, Thousand Oaks, London, New Delhi, 1997.
10. Kwiatkowska Teresa, "Beyond Uncertainties-Some open Questions about Chaos and Ethics", Ethics and Environment 6(1)2001, 96-115.
11. Jackson Tony E., Clopartora's Sister and Post modern Historiography: The Consequences of Chaos, Modern Fiction Studies 42.2 (1996) 397-417.
12. Sprott J.C., Chaos and Time Series Analysis, Oxford University Press, Oxford, 2003.
13. Lorenz E.N., (1963), J. Atmos Sci., 20, 130.
14. Rössler O., (1976) Phys. Lett. A57; 397.
15. Sharma Subhash, Governance and Corruption, Management Reviews, 4(3), (2008), 23.

16. Schuster, Heinz George (1998), Deterministic Chaos, Second Revised Edition, VCH Verlagsgesellschaft Publishers, Weinheim.

17. Grassberger, P. and Procaccia, I. (1983), Physica D 9:198-208.

18. Rastogi R.P and Mathur P., Proc. Ind. Nat. Sci. Acad., 75 No. 3 (2009) 127-130.

19. Rastogi R.P and Mathur P., Proc. Ind. Nat. Sci. Acad., 75 No. 4 (2009) 159-165.

CHAPTER 18

Diagnosis of Epilepsy and Alzheimer's Diseases Using EEG: A Clinical Review

[1]Sanjeev Kendre, [2]Vishal Waghmare and [2]Ganesh Janvale
[1]Government Medical Hospital, Pune (MS) India,
[2]Dept. CS&IT, Dr B.A.M. University, Aurangabad (MS) India
E-mail: sanjeevkendre@gmail.com, vishal_pri1@yahoo.co.in, ganesh.janvale@gmail.com

ABSTRACT

Epilepsy and Alzheimer's diseases are key diseases which are associated with the electrical activity changes in human brain and so they need to be evaluated through Electroencephalogram (EEG), Digital Signal Processing and Statistical Methods. EEG is basic non invasive brain computer interface (BCI) beside the Magneto-encephalography (MEG) and functional Magnetic Resonance Imaging (fMRI). In this paper, the diagnostic value of the EEG is reviewed and the clinically ease been verified. The paper reviews the technical diagnostic value and ease of EEG.

Keywords: Epilepsy and Alzheimer's disease, EEG, BCI, fMRI

1. INTRODUCTION

This instruction file for Word users (there is a separate instruction file for LaTeX users) may be used as a template. Kindly send the final and checked Word and PDF files of your paper to the Contact Volume Editor. This is usually one of the organizers of the conference. You should make sure that the Word and the PDF files are identical and correct and that only one version of your paper is sent. It is not possible to update files at a later stage. Please note that we do not need the printed paper.

EEG is the recording of electrical activity on the surface of the scalp produced by the firing of neurons within the brain. The Neurons, or nerve cells, are electrically active cells that are primarily responsible for carrying out the brain's functions. Neurons create action potentials, which are discrete electrical signals that travel down axons and cause the release of chemical neurotransmitters at the synapse, which is an area of near contact between two neurons EEG reflects correlated synaptic activity caused by post-synaptic potentials of cortical neurons. The electric potentials generated by single neurons are far too small to be picked by EEG or MEG [1]. EEG activity always reflects the summation of the synchronous activity of thousands or millions of neurons that have similar spatial orientation. Because voltage fields fall off with the square of the distance, activity from deep sources is more difficult to detect than currents near the skull. The epilepsy and Alzheimer's disease are associated with the electrical change in grey matter and the key to the diagnosis is interpretation of the altered evoked or non evoked potentials of the neural cell i.e. neurons. The Section 2 describe about diagnosis methods for both the diseases. The classification of Epilepsy and Alzheimer's diseases are detailed in Section 3. The section 4 clears the syndromes of the brain diseases. Last section of the paper concludes the works.

2. DIAGNOSIS METHODS

Conventionally the various diagnostic methods for both epilepsy and AD are common which include following modalities

1. Brain scan: The following methods are used to brain scan for Diagnosis of Alzheimer's Diseases.
    (a) CT scan
    (b) MRI
    (c) SPECT (single photo emission computed tomography)
    (d) PET (positron emission tomography)
    (e) PiB PET (Pittsburgh compound B PET to image beta amyloid plaques in grey matter)
2. BCI (effective for epilepsy diagnosis)
    (a) Invasive BCI (have little diagnostic value)
    (b) Partially invasive BCI – Electrocoticography (the electrodes are implanted through bur hole and is important for more higher spatial resolution, better signal-to-noise ratio, wider frequency range of epileptic foci and usually advised for preoperative evaluation of foci.
    (c) Non invasive BCI – (i) EEG (ii) magneto encephalography (iii) functional magnetic resonance imaging (fMRI)
3. Histopathology (AD)
    Brain metabolites as biomarker for the AD
    Cerebrospinal fluid analysis for the beta amyloid for AD through spinal tap [2] [3] [4] [5]

(A) Classification of Epilepsy and Alzheimer's disease

(B) Alzheimer's Disease (AD)

AD is most common age-related dementia (out of one's mind) and is associated with biochemical, genetic and environmental causes. First described by German psychiatrist and neuropathologist Alois Alzheimer in 1906. According to the Diagnostic and Statistical Manual of Mental Disorders, fourth edition text revision (DSM-IV-TR), dementia is the development of multiple cognitive deficits manifested by both memory impairment and impairment in at least one other cognitive domain including language, praxis, gnosis, and executive functioning [6]. AD is mainly characterized by degeneration of basal forebrain cholinergic neurons and cerebral deposition of amyloidal beta-peptide (Aâ)-laden plaques and tau proteins in the form of neurofibrillary tangles. Inflammatory processes, oxidative stress and synaptic loss are other neurochemical attributes of AD.

Most genetic (familial) Alzheimer's disease is due to mutations on the genes coding for the Aâ precursor protein (APP) and presenilins (PS) 1 and 2 located on chromosome no 21 and 14 respectively that is why the association of AD with trisomy 21 is well established. Current understanding of the exact sequence of these events in the disease process is slowly emerging, and so are the drug targets that can be successfully used for AD. Apoptosis or programmed cell death (PCD) is a normal event under genetic control. However, misregulation of apoptosis plays a pivotal role in the development AD.

Slowly progressive decline in memory and orientation, normal results on laboratory tests, and an MRI or CT scan showing only diffuse or posteriorly predominant cortical and hippocampal atrophy is highly suggestive of AD

The disease is classified as per the severity of the clinical signs and symptoms.

Mild cognitive impairment is considered preclinical AD and may or may not be considered for Clinical classification as such. Following are the clinical stages in development of AD as per severity of the symptoms [7].

(A) Pre dementia (B) Early dementia (C) Moderate dementia and (D) Advanced dementia.

(B) Epilepsy

Epileptic seizures are sudden, involuntary behavioral events associated with excessive or hypersynchronous electrical discharges in the brain.

Using the definition of epilepsy as two or more unprovoked seizures, the incidence of epilepsy is ~0.3–0.5% in different populations throughout the world, and the prevalence of epilepsy has been estimated at 5–10 persons per 1000.

In 1981, the International League against Epilepsy (ILAE) published a modified version of the International Classification of Epileptic Seizures that has continued to be a useful classification system. This system is based on the clinical features of seizures and associated electroencephalographic findings as shown in the Table 1[4][5].

Table 1   International Classification of Epileptic Seizures and symptoms

Sr. No.	Epilepsies	Subtypes / Symptoms
1	Simple partial seizures	Motor, Somatosensory, Autonomic, or Psychic symptoms
2	Complex partial seizures	Begin with symptoms of simple partial seizure but progress to impairment of consciousness, Begin with impairment of consciousness.
3	Partial seizures with	Begin with simple partial seizure, Begin with complex partial secondary generalization seizure (including those with symptoms of simple partial seizures at onset)
4	Generalized seizures	Absence (typical and atypical), Myoclonus, Clonic, Tonic, (convulsive or non Tonic-clonic, Atonic/akinetic convulsive)

Although there is no general epileptic personality, a group of traits termed the Gastaut-Geschwind syndrome occurs in a subset of patients with complex partial seizures.

3. EPILEPSY AND ALZHEIMER'S SYNDROMES

The electroencephalogram (EEG) recorded during the seizure (i.e., an ictal EEG) may show abnormal discharges in a very limited region over the appropriate area of cerebral cortex if the seizure focus involves the cerebral convexity. Seizure activity occurring within deeper brain structures is often not recorded by the standard EEG, however, and may require intracranial electrodes for its detection. The routine interictal (i.e., between seizures) EEG in patients with complex partial seizures is often normal or may show brief discharges termed epileptiform spikes, or sharp waves. Interictal EEG shows a normal background with frequent generalized polyspike and wave discharges that may be anteriorly dominant or diffuse. Polyspike and wave discharges by definition have at least 3 spikelike components as shown in Figure 1.

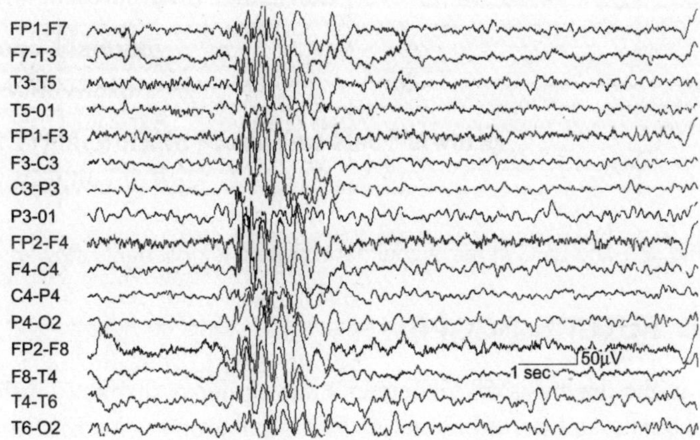

Fig. 1   EEG waves of Polyspike and discharges seen in juvenile myoclonic epilepsy

The electrophysiologic hallmark of typical absence seizures is a generalized, symmetric, 3-Hz spike-and-wave discharge that begins and ends suddenly, superimposed on a normal EEG background. Hyperventilation tends to provoke these electrographic discharges and even the seizures themselves and is routinely used when recording the EEG.

The EEG during the tonic phase of the seizure shows a progressive increase in generalized low-voltage fast activity, followed by generalized high-amplitude, polyspike discharges. In the clonic phase, the high-amplitude activity is typically interrupted by slow waves to create a spike-and-wave pattern. The postictal EEG shows diffuse slowing that gradually recovers as the patient awakens.

Medical diagnosis of Alzheimer's disease is hard, and symptoms are often dismissed as normal consequences of aging. Diagnosis is usually performed through a combination of extensive testing and eliminations of other possible causes. Psychological tests such as Mini Mental State Examinations (MMSE), blood tests, neurological examination, and increasingly, imaging techniques are used to help diagnose the disease [8].The brainwaves of patients demonstrated that they have slower EEG readings as shown in Figure 2. For people in the pre-clinical stage of dementia, that is before the diagnosis was made, the EEG showed almost no indication of any disturbance.

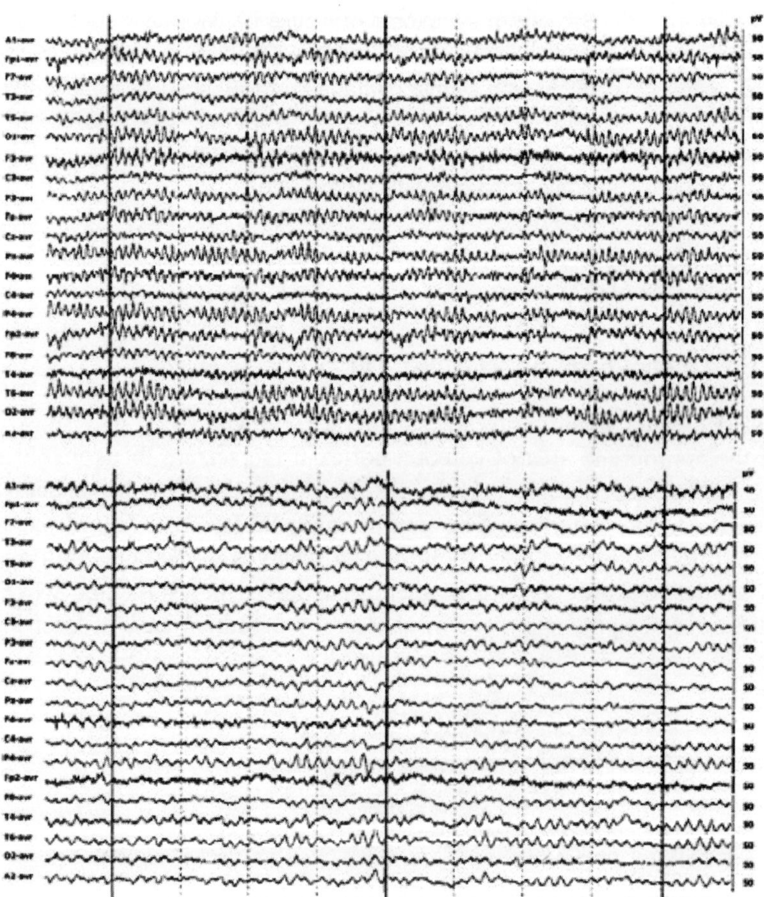

Fig. 2 The EEG in the Alzheimer's patient is noticeably slower.

4. CONCLUSION AND FUTURE SCOPE:

Use of electroencephalograph in the diagnosis of Alzheimer's and Epilepsy distinctly differentiate the conditions with reduced complexity of EEG signals and perturbations in EEG synchrony. The Electroencephalography is simple, noninvasive, basic, portable and technically effective BCI for diagnosis of the Epilepsy and Alzheimer's diseases.

References

1. Anthony Fauci, Eugene Braunwald, Dennis Kasper, Stephen Hauser, Dan Longo, Larry Jameson and Joseph Loscalzo, "Harrisons Principles of Internal Medicine 17th edition", The Mc Graw-Hill, ISBN-978-0-07-146633-2

2. Waldemar G, Dubois B, Emre M, et al. (January 2007). "Recommendations for the Diagnosis and Management of Alzheimer's Disease and other Disorders Associated with Dementia: EFNS Guideline". Eur J Neurol 14 (1): e1–26

3. Cognitive reserve hypothesis: Pittsburgh Compound B and fluorodeoxyglucose positron emission tomography in relation to education in mild Alzheimer's disease". Ann. Neurol. 63 (1): 112–8.

4. Rupsingh R, Borrie M, Smith M, Wells JL, Bartha R (June 2009). "Reduced hippocampal glutamate in Alzheimer disease

5. De Meyer G, Shapiro F, Vanderstichele H, Vanmechelen E, Engelborghs S, De Deyn PP, Coart E, Hansson O, Minthon L, Zetterberg H, Blennow K, Shaw L, Trojanowski JQ (August 2010). "Diagnosis-Independent Alzheimer Disease Biomarker Signature in Cognitively Normal Elderly People". Arch Neurol. 67 (8): 949–56

6. Benjamin Sadock, Virginia Sadock, and Ruiz Pedro, "Kaplan & Sadock's comprehensive text book of psychiatry", 2009, 0781768993

7. Eva Arnaiz, Ove Almkuist, "Neuropsychological features of mild cognitive impairment and preclinical Alzheimer's disease" Volum 107, page 34-41, February 2003.

8. Palmer K., Berger AK., Monastero R., Winblad B., B£ckman L. and Fratiglioni L., "Predictors of progression from mild cognitive impairment to Alzheimer disease", Neurology 68 (19): 1596–1602, 2007.

CHAPTER 19

Human-Computer Interaction in Computer Aided Learning

[1]Rupali Patil, [2]Hansraj Patil and [3]Ramesh Manza

[1]Department of Computer Science, S.S.V.P.S. Sansatha's, P.R. Ghogare Science College, Dhule-05(MS) India,
[2]Department of Computer Management, Systel Institute of Management & Research, Dhule-02(MS) India,
[3]Department of Computer Science and I.T., Dr. B.A.M. University, Aurangabad-04(MS) India,
E-mail: rupalihpatil@yahoo.com, hmpatil.systel@gmail.com, manzaramesh@gmail.com

ABSTRACT

Human Computer Interaction as it may apply specifically to educational environment. The study of Computer Aided learning (CAL) for primary school children in rural area has been done to improve the quality of education by looking, into the specific learning need of children to track the progress of each child. This research is valuable because it concentrates on the need for new thinking on design & deployment of computer based learning techniques for primary schools in developing region. The goal is to introduce children to the use of computers & to develop the positive attitude in children for coming to school for getting education without creating the pressure to learn but to let them play with the computer. The main aim is to improve the quality of education by exploring various tools, teaching learning methods & materials that can change the paradigm of the way children learn in these schools.

Keywords: CAL- Computer Aided learning, HCI- Human Computer Interaction

1. INTRODUCTION

Today computer is used in different areas like business, education, government, medical development etc. Now a day's education is very fast and complex and there are so many competitions. So students required a technique by which they can learn more in short span of time. As pictures are thousands times better than words so just instead of reading books they would like to learn from pictures in which there may be animations. By which they can enjoy learning.

We observed that students from rural area are week and shy as compared to students from urban area. There is needed to feel the gap between them. For that we have to improve the quality of education of rural area from primary level.

Computer Aided Learning (CAL) is based on the integrated approach whereby the computer programme does not replace a lecturer or an instructor but it is introduced during the course as a learning resource.

Objective: The main objective of the CAL is to attract the children, retain them in the school and to improve the quality of the education through animated multimedia based educational content.

Our main aim in the use of CAL is to enhance learning in primary schools.

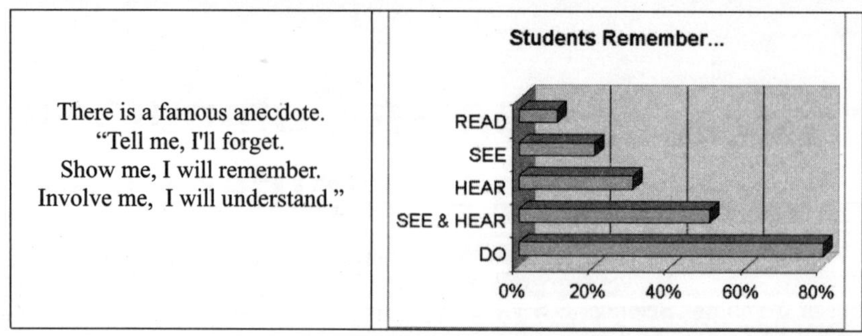

Pal J.(2005) The social and organizational factors affecting CAL, and behavioral aspects of children learning in sheared access scenario. Prasad S.(2008) "Computer-aided learning has the power to transform education in a fundamental way," Parth Sarwate from Azim Premji Foundation. Meiting Bai (2008) describes programs to reduce the gap between big-city and rural education in primary and secondary schools. At the turn of the millennium the Indian government launch universal education program known as Sarva Shiksha Abhiyan (SSA) aims to achieve relevant elementary education for all Indian children by 2010.Linden L and et al (2003) Present the result obtained after the first year of two year randomized evolution of a computer assisted learning (CAL) program in Vadodara, India. They find the program to be quite effective. It increased math scores by 0.37 standard deviation

From the literature CAL may be an effective method of teaching well defined concept concerning one aspect of the curriculum.

Research Design

For the case study 1st Std. students of two schools listed below were chosen

Name of School	Total No. of Students	Group A	Group B
Raje Sambhaji Miltry School	35	18	17
Z.P. Primary School, Dhamane	56	28	28

Subjects Mathematics, Science and Language were selected for the implementation of CAL. We used different multimedia S/W that is available in the market. Also we gave own developed S/W for practice.

Implementation Process

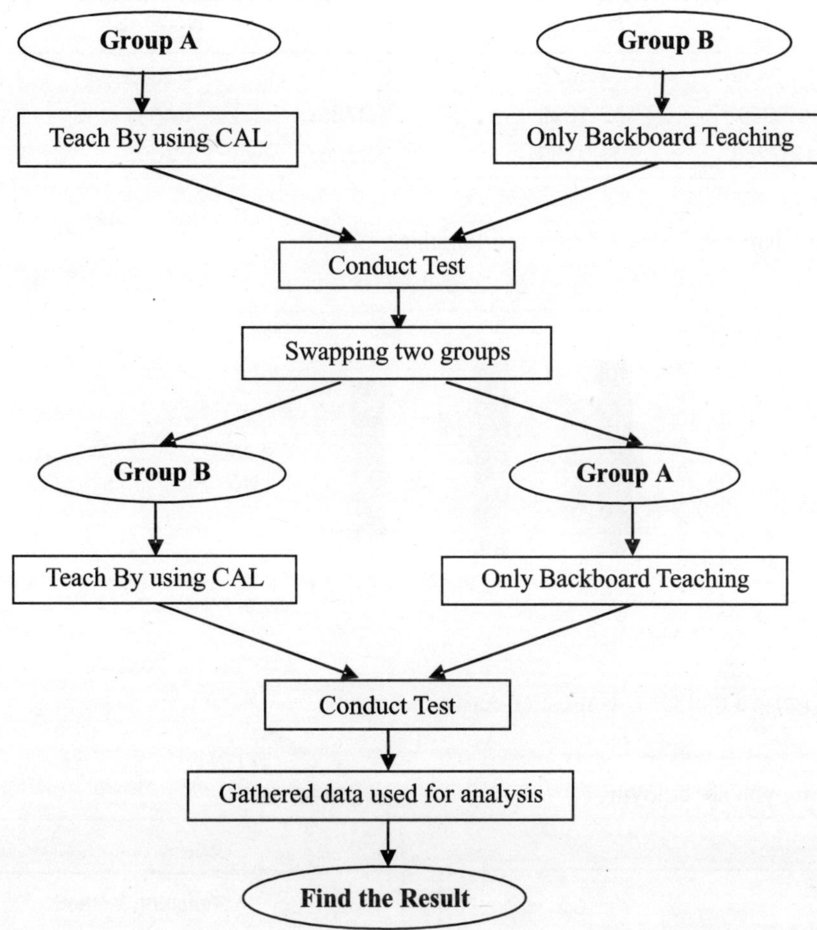

Same process was repeated for each subjects and the result of student test report was prepared.

Method of Generation of Data and Collection

We collected data from 91 students and 11 teachers. Data generation methods are used questionnaires, observations and some time oral interviews. For analysis visual aid used are tables and charts.

Frequency distribution table of students test performance

Range of Marks	Science		Math		English	
	CAL	NO CAL	CAL	NO CAL	CAL	NO CAL
0-4	1	4	2	3	2	5
4-8	5	18	4	15	10	17
8-12	13	26	17	25	22	31
12-16	45	29	38	27	38	26
16-20	27	14	30	21	19	12

From above table we calculate Mean, Standard Deviation and 't' value.

Subject	Mean		Standard Deviation		t-test R
	CAL	NO CAL	CAL	NO CAL	
Science	14.0439	11.3626	3.4828	4.3665	4.5795
Math	13.956	12.1099	3.7735	4.4511	3.0179
Language	12.7253	11.0109	3.9726	4.3005	2.7932

Student performance Chart for Science, Math and language

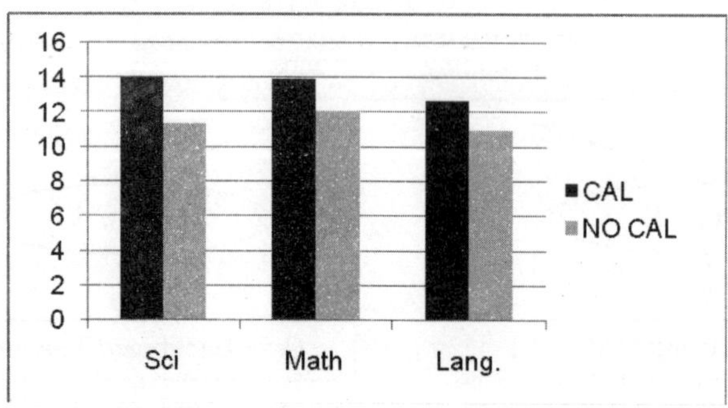

Using 'T' test, we observed that CAL is most effective in Science

Which type of teaching you are enjoying?

Teaching Method	Frequency	Percentage
Classroom teaching	3	3
Computer teaching	6	7
Combination of classroom and computer teaching	82	91

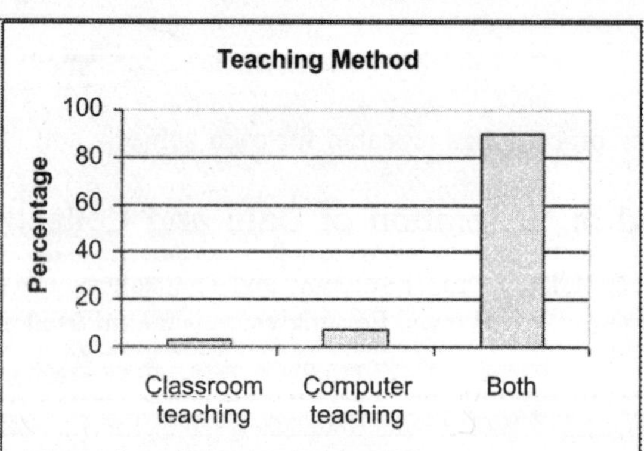

As students are small & they are not fully aware of computer they need teacher's help, so most of the students prefer both classroom and computer teaching.

From Questionnaires Opinion of Maximum Teachers

Sr.No.	Questions	Opinion of Most of teachers
1.	Which are the different teaching aids you are using to teach?	Blackboard, charts and Maps
2.	Which method is suitable for students?	Textual, picture, sound & animation.
3.	Which method is suitable for revision	Combination of Classroom & Computer teaching
4.	The quality of the materials	Excellent
5.	What you think about CAL?	Excellent
6.	For which subject CAL is effective?	Math and science
7.	Computer aided learning is	Time Saving

RESULTS

For 0.05 level of significance 't' value is 1.96 and for o.o1 level of significance 't' value is 2.58. Obtained 't' values are greater than even 0.01 level of significance for each subject, so CAL is most effective for teaching. Out of three subject CAL is most suitable for science.

There is positive impact of computer aided learning on the learning achievement levels among students in Raje Sambhaji Military School, Morane and Z.P. primary school, Dhamane. While these finding are encouraging we realize the need for more research on this subject.

INTERPRETATION

- Most of students are from rural area and their parents are farmer and labour. They are not educated. Students are not aware of computer.
- Students in rural areas suffer from lack of sufficient materials and tools and many families have difficulty in providing such tools for their children.
- State government provides the computers and required software in schools.
- When teacher uses computer for teaching, student can view the reality, they no need to do imagination while learning. Teacher's headache for controlling the class became less.

CONCLUSION

Computer presentation is particularly suited to subjects that are visually intensive, detail oriented, and difficult to conceptualize. The children are attracted and retained in the schools and improved the quality of the education through animated multimedia based educational content and better performance in examinations. Good quality content enhance the quality of learning in joyful manner.

RECOMMENDATIONS

- The effective use of a computer in primary schools depends on the availability of a wide range of suitable compatible educational software.
- To effectively implement computer aided learning in schools, financial support is needed for: - Adequate teacher training, Extra hours for teachers to design assignments and questions, Computers and software, Pedagogical support.
- Children need to learn how to use and control computers.
- Expansion of computer aided learning requires cultural change as well as careful strategic planning, resource sharing, staff incentives, active promotion of multidisciplinary working, and effective quality control.

LIMITATIONS

There is a need of continuous enhancement of the quality of the content to meet ever change needs of the children.

References

- Pal, J 'Early-stage practicalities of implementing computer aided education: Experience from India, 'Technology for Education in Developing Countries, 2006. Fourth IEEE International Workshop on Date: 24 July 2006 pp. 26-30
- Prasad, S.(2008) "Education takes off in rural India, helped by PCS, ZDNet Asia Friday July 18 2008 04: 50 pm
- Linden, L., Banerisee, A., Duflo, E. (2003) Computer – Assisted learning: Evidence from a Randomized Experiment [Online] poverty Action Lab Paper No. 5
- Meiting, B. 2008 "The Rural Distance Education in Primary and Secondary Schools in Gansu, China" [online] Available from http://www.itdl.org/Journal /Jul_08 /article02.htm
- Sanjawani Mahale(2006) "Sankhiki Tantrache upyojan", Y.C.M.O.U.(Nasik) M.Ed. Shishankram.
- Bhatt, M. (2008) 'Computer-aided learning programme to get a boost this fiscal'[online] date 17 Feb 2008 Available From: http://www.expressindia.com/latest-news/Computer-aided-learning-programme-to-get-a-boost-this-fiscal

CHAPTER 20

Diverse Classifier for Face Recognition

S.N. Kakarwal[1], V.R. Ratnaparkhi[2] and R.R. Deshmukh[3]

PES Engineering College, Aurangabad (MS) India, [2]Department CS&IT, Dr. B.A.M. University, Aurangabad (MS) India

E-mail: s_kakarwal@yahoo.com, var_ravi@yahoo.com, ratnadeep_deshmukh@yahoo.co.in

ABSTRACT

This paper proposes a novel face recognition which exploits wavelet transform based feature extraction technique. Classification is performed using thresholding method. We evaluate the proposed method using two face databases: FERET and Indian Face database. The experiment is carried out over 320 faces. Experiment shows that the result of our method is impressively better than the best known results with the same evaluation protocol.

Keywords: Feature Extraction, Classification, Correlation, False Acceptance Ratio, False Rejection Ratio and Receiver Operating Characteristics

1. INTRODUCTION

Face recognition from still images and video sequence has been an active research area due to both its scientific challenges and wide range of potential applications such as biometric identity authentication, human-computer interaction, and video surveillance. Within the past two decades, numerous face recognition algorithms have been proposed as reviewed in the literature survey. Even though we human beings can detect and identify faces in a cluttered scene with little effort, building an automated system that accomplishes such objective is very challenging. The challenges mainly come from the large variations in the visual stimulus due to illumination conditions, viewing directions, facial expressions, aging, and disguises such as facial hair, glasses, or cosmetics [1]. Face Recognition focuses on recognizing the identity of a person from a database of known individuals. Face Recognition will find countless unobtrusive applications such as airport security and access control, building surveillance and monitoring Human-Computer Intelligent interaction and perceptual interfaces and Smart Environments at home, office and cars [2]. Within the last decade, face recognition (FR) has found a wide range of applications, from identity authentication, access control, and face-based video indexing/browsing, to human-computer interaction/communication. Two issues are central to all these algorithms: 1) feature selection for face representation and 2) classification of a new face image based on the chosen feature representation. This work focuses on the issue of feature selection. Among various solutions to the problem, the most successful are those appearance-based approaches, which generally operate directly on images or appearances of face objects and process the images as two-dimensional (2-D) holistic patterns, to avoid difficulties associated with three-dimensional (3-D) modeling, and shape or landmark detection [3]. The initial idea and early work of this research have been published in part as conference papers in [4], [5]. This paper is an extension for future work. A recognition process involves a suitable representation, which should make the subsequent processing not only computationally feasible but also robust to certain variations in images. One method of face representation attempts to capture and define the face as a whole and exploit the statistical regularities of pixel intensity variations [7]. We have used Wavelet transform to decompose face images and classified it with correlation and different threshold values.

The remaining part of this paper is organized as follows. Section II extends to the feature mapping, which also introduces and discusses the Wavelet Transform in detail. In Section III, extensive experiments on FERET and Indian databases are conducted to evaluate the performance of the proposed method on face recognition. Finally, conclusions are drawn in Section IV with some discussions.

2. PATTERN MATCHING

2.1 Pattern Recognition Methods

During the past 30 years, pattern recognition has had a considerable growth. Applications of pattern recognition now include: character recognition; target detection; medical diagnosis; biomedical signal and image analysis; remote sensing; identification of human faces and of fingerprints; machine part recognition; automatic inspection; and many others.

In communication with the outer world, one of the most important goals for human beings is to recognize objects. For example, from an image, image set, or image sequence of objects, we need to recognize the object orientation, location, arrangement, size and shape they have.

Pattern recognition is, in general, a complex procedure requiring a variety of techniques that successively transform the iconic data to information directly useable for recognition. Traditionally, these methods are grouped into two categories: structural methods and feature space methods. Structural methods are useful in situation where the different classes of entity can be distinguished from each other by structural information, e.g. in character recognition different letters of the alphabet are structurally different from each other. The earliest-developed structural methods were the syntactic methods, based on using formal grammars to describe the structure of an entity. Some other methods, which may be structural, are machine vision methods such as those based on point distribution models, active contours, etc [8].

In feature-space methods, a set of measurements (typically numerical) is made on each real-world entity (pattern), and from the measurement, feature set is extracted. This characterizes the class of patterns.

The traditional approach to feature-space pattern recognition is the statistical approach, where the boundaries between the regions representing pattern classes in feature space are found by statistical inference based on a design set of sample patterns of known class membership [8]. Feature-space methods are useful in situations where the distinction between different pattern classes is readily expressible in terms of numerical measurements of this kind. The traditional goal of feature extraction is to characterize the object to be recognized by measurements whose values are very similar for objects in the same category, and very different for objects in different categories. This leads to the idea of seeking distinguishing features that are invariant to irrelevant transformations of the input. The task of the classifier component proper of a full system is to use the feature vector provided by the feature extractor to assign the object to a category [9]. Image classification is implemented by computing the similarity score between a target discriminating feature vector and a query discriminating feature vector [10].

2.2. Wavelet Transform

Wavelet is an increasingly popular tool in image processing and computer vision. Many applications, such as compression, detection, recognition, image retrieval have been investigated. Wavelet transform has nice features of space-frequency localization and multiresolutions. The main reasons for Wavelet transforms popularity lie in its complete theoretical framework, the great flexibility for choosing bases and the low computational complexity [7].

Wavelets decompose complex signals into sums of basis functions – in this respect they are similar to other discrete image transforms. However, wavelets are local in both frequency and time and are able to analyze data at different scales or resolutions much better than simple sine and cosine can [11].

Wavelets are an extension of Fourier analysis. The goal is to turn the information of a signal into numbers –

coefficients – that can be manipulated, stored, transmitted, analyzed, or used to reconstruct the original signal. There are not only two big classes of wavelet transforms - continuous and discrete - but discrete transforms can be redundant, orthogonal, or biorthogonal. Each category contains innumerable possibilities, Daubechies wavelets alone constituting a very big class [12].

DWT for an image as a 2-D signal can be derived from 1-D DWT. The easiest way for obtaining scaling and wavelet functions for two dimensions is by multiplying two 1-D functions. The scaling functions for 2-D DWT can be obtained by multiplying two 1-D scaling functions: $\phi(x, y) = \phi(x)\ \phi(y)$. Wavelet functions for 2-D DWT can be obtained by multiplying two wavelet functions. For the 2-D case, there exist three wavelet functions that scan details in horizontal ψ (I)$(x, y) = \varphi(x)\psi(y)$ vertical ψ(II)$(x, y) = \psi(x)\phi(y)$, and diagonal directions: ψ(III)$(x, y) = \psi(x)\psi(y)$ [13]

As in any pattern classification task, feature extraction plays a key role in face recognition process. In feature extraction stage, a proper face representation is chosen to make the subsequent face processing not only computationally feasible but also robust to possible intrinsic and extrinsic facial variations [14]. In this paper, 2D Discrete Wavelet Transform is used to extract the features from the faces.

2.3 Correlation

Here we consider it as basis for finding matches of a sub image $w(x, y)$ of size J X K within an image $f(x, y)$ of size M X N, where we assume that $J<=M$ and $K<=N$.

In its simplest form, the correlation between $f(x, y)$ and $w(x, y)$ is

$$c(x, y) = \sum_{s} \sum_{t} f(s, t) w(x + s, y + t) \tag{1}$$

For $x = 0, 1, 2, …, M – 1, y = 0, 1, 2, .., N – 1$ and the summation is taken over the image region where w and f overlap. Figure 1 illustrates the procedure, where we assume that the origin of f is at its top left and the origin of w is at its center. For one value of (x, y), say, (x_0, y_0) inside f, application of Eq. (1) yields one value of c. As x and y are varied, w moves around the image area, giving the function $c(x, y)$. The maximum value (s) of c indicate the position (s) where w best matches f. Note that accuracy is lost for values of x and y near the edges of f, with the amount of error being in the correlation proportional to the size of w. The correlation function given in equation (2) has disadvantage of being sensitive to changes in the amplitude of f and w. For example, doubling all values of f doubles the value of $c(x, y)$.

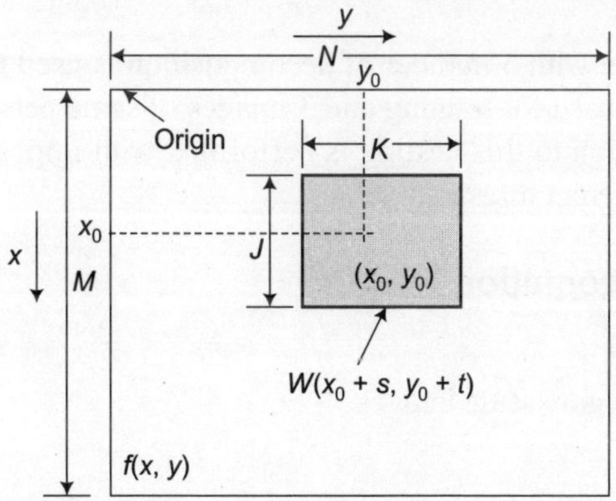

Fig.1 Arrangement for obtaining the correlation of f and w at point (x_0, y_0)

An approach frequently used to overcome this difficulty is to perform matching via the correlation coefficient, which is defined as specified in Eq. (2)

$$\gamma(x, y) = \frac{\displaystyle\sum_s \sum_t [f(s,t) - \bar{f}(s,t)][\, w(x, +s, y+t) - \overline{w}\,]}{\{\displaystyle\sum_s \sum_t [f(s,t) - \bar{f}(s,t)]^2 \sum_s \sum_t [\, w(x+s, y+t) - \overline{w}\,]^2\}^{1/2}} \tag{2}$$

where $x = 0, 1, 2, , .., M-1$, $y = 0, 1, 2, .., N-1$, w' is the average value of the pixel in w (computed only once), f' is the average value in the region coincident with the current location of w, and the summations are taken over the coordinates common to both f and w. The correlation coefficient $\gamma(x, y)$ is scaled in the range -1 to 1, independent of scale changes in the amplitude of f and w[15].

3. EXPERIMENTS

3.1 Facial Database

There are many facial databases available for evaluating face recognition algorithms. The FERET facial database consists of 13539 facial images corresponding to 1,565 subjects. Since images are acquired during different photo sessions, the illumination conditions and the size of the face may vary. The diversity of the FERET database is across gender, ethnicity, and age. The images are acquired without any restrictions imposed on facial expression and with at least two frontal images shot at different times during the same photo session. The FERET database has become the de facto standard for evaluating face recognition technologies [2]. The FERET dataset used in our experiments includes 160 face images corresponding to 8 different subjects. In order to extract the facial region, the images are normalized to the size 512×512. All images are gray-scale images.

3.2 INDIAN FACE DATABASE

The database contains a set of face images taken in February, 2002 in the IIT Kanpur campus. There are eleven different images of each of 40 distinct subjects. For some subjects, some additional photographs are included. All the images were taken against a bright homogeneous background with the subjects in an upright, frontal position. The files are in JPEG format. The size of each image is 640×480 pixels, with 256 grey levels per pixel. In this paper we have used 180 images with 8 different subjects. To extract the features from the faces the images are normalized to the size 480×480 pixels. All images are gray-scale images [16].

In our experiment, 'Haar' wavelet with 5 number of decomposition is used to compress and decompress the facial images.10 persons with 5 images are used for training and 3 images of same persons are used for testing. It is the set of images used during training. In addition to this, testing is performed with impostor faces. Results of classification are obtained by using correlation and different threshold values.

3.3 Steps used in Face Recognition

1. Read the Images
2. Convert the color images into gray scale images
3. Normalize the images

1. Apply Haar Wavelet to extract the features
2. Obtain Correlation of the image feature space
3. Classify the images by using different values of thresholding
4. Analyse the performance by computing FAR and FRR at different values of threshold

3.4   Performance Evaluation

A typical biometric verification system commits two types of errors: *false match* and false *non-match*. Note that these two types of errors are also often denoted as *false acceptance* and *false rejection*; a distinction has to be made between positive and negative recognition; in positive recognition systems (e.g., an access control system) a false match determines the false acceptance of an impostor, whereas a false non-match causes the false rejection of a genuine user. On the other hand, in a negative recognition application (e.g., preventing users from obtaining welfare benefits under false identities), a false match results in rejecting a genuine request, whereas a false non-match results in falsely accepting an impostor attempt. The notation "false match/false non-match" is not application dependent and therefore, in principle, is preferable to "false acceptance/false rejection." However, the use of false acceptance rate (FAR) and false rejection rate (FRR) is more popular and largely used in the commercial environment [17]. Traditional methods of evaluation focus on collective error statistics such as EERs and ROC curves. These statistics are useful for evaluating systems as a whole. *Equal-Error Rate* (EER) denotes the error rate at the threshold t for which false match rate and false non-match rate are identical: $FAR(t)= FRR(t)$ [18]. FRR is False Rejection Ratio, which means the fault when someone which registered in the system was refused by system [19]. Table I presents the FRR values of genuine person faces. FAR is False Acceptance Rate, which is the fault where someone of user which does not enlist will be held true by the system. FAR values for impostor persons are presented in Table II.

Finally, Table III presents the FAR and FRR values for all persons with different threshold values. The FRR and FAR for number of participants (N) are calculated as specified in Eq. (3) and in equation Eq. (4)[19].

$$\text{FRR} = \frac{1}{N} \sum_{n=1}^{N} \text{FRR}\,(n) \tag{3}$$

$$\text{FAR} = \frac{1}{N} \sum_{n=1}^{N} \text{FAR}\,(n) \tag{4}$$

Table 1   Recognition Performance of Indian Face Database and FERET Database

Threshold	Indian Face Database		FERET Database	
	FRR	FAR	FRR	FAR
0.5	0.06	1	0.26	0.23
0.55	0.06	1	0.23	0.2
0.6	0.06	1	0.33	0.12
0.65	0.06	1	0.33	0.06
0.7	0.06	0.83	0.23	0.02
0.75	0.06	0.52	0.33	0.0
0.8	0.06	0.19	0.46	0.0
0.85	0.03	0	0.59	0.0
0.9	0.19	0	0.8	0.0
0.95	0.96	0	1	0.0

The FAR-FRR values of Indian Face Database shown in Fig. 2.

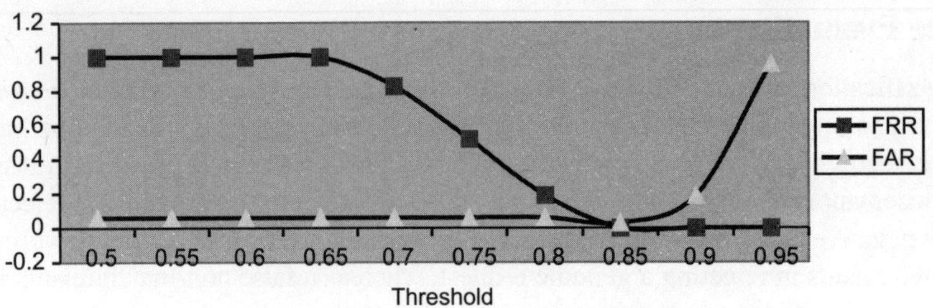

Fig. 2   FAR-FRR Diagram of Indian Face Database

The FAR-FRR values of FERET Database are shown in Fig. 3.

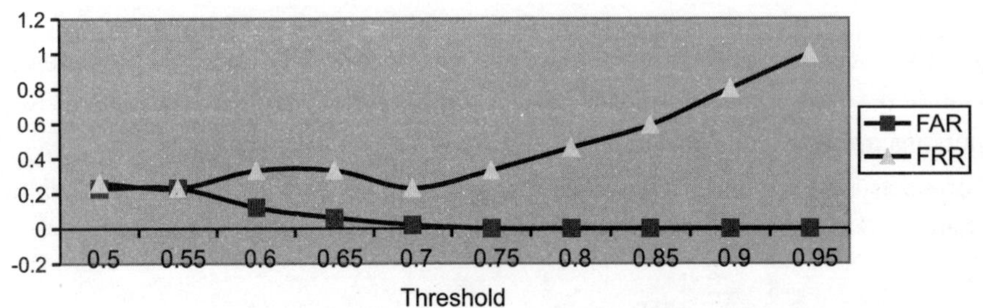

Fig. 3   FAR-FRR Diagram of FERET Database

4.   CONCLUSIONS

This paper investigates the feasibility and effectiveness of using correlation and threshold values for face description and recognition. A 2D Discrete Wavelet Transform is proposed to capture the variations in faces. Face recognition based on correlation can be performed by using thresholding. Experimental results on Indian Face database and FERET database demonstrate that the proposed Correlation and thresholding outperforms in recognition. Experiments have been conducted on various face conditions, including different angles, expressions etc. It is shown that the proposed method of face recognition gives satisfying results for threshold-0.85(Indian face database) and threshold-0.55 (FERET database).. At $t = 0.85$, the value obtained for FAR is 0.0 and FRR is 0.03. In case of FERET database FAR = FRR, when $t = 0.55$, the value obtained for FAR is 0.23and FRR is 0.2. There is a trade-off between FAR and FRR values. The optimum thresholds value i.e. the value where FAR = FRR, is 0.85(Indian face database) and 0.55 (FERET face database) as shown in Graph 1 and Graph 2.

Acknowledgements

The authors would like to thank the anonymous reviewers for their critical and constructive comments and suggestions.

References

1. Yu Su, Shiguang Shan, Xilin Chen, and Wen Gao: Hierarchical Ensemble of Global and local Classifiers for Face Recognition, IEEE Transactions On Image Processing, Vol. 18, No. 8, August 2009, pp 1885 – 1896

2. Chengjun Liu, Harry Wechsler: Independent Componenet Analysis of Gabor Features for Face Recognition, IEEE Transactions on Neural Networks, Vol. 14, July 2003, pp 919-928

3. Juwei Lu, Konstantinos N. Plataniotis,, Anastasios N. Venetsanopoulos: Face Recognition Using Kernel Direct Discriminant Analysis Algorithms, IEEE Transactions On Neural Networks, Vol. 14, No. 1, January 2003, pp 117-126

4. S.N. Kakarwal, S.D. Sapkal, P.J.Ahire, Dr. D.S. Bormane: Analysis of Facial Image Classification using Discrete Wavelet Transform, Proc. International Conference ICSCI, 2007, pp 700-705

5. S.N. Kakarwal, Mahananda Malkauthekar, Shubhangi Sapkal, Dr. Ratnadeep Deshmukh: Face Recognition using Fourier Descriptor and FFNN, Proc. IEEE International Advance Computing Conference, 2009, pp 2740-2742

6. S.N. Kakarwal, Dr. R.R. Deshmukh: Wavelet Transform based Feature Extraction for Face Recognition, pp 100-104, IJCSA Issue-I June 2010, ISSN 0974-0767

7. Bai-Ling Zhang, Haihong Zhang and Shuzhi Sam Je: Face Recognition by Applying Subband Representation and Kernel Associative Memory, IEEE Transaction on Neural Networks, Vol. 15, Jan 2004, pp 166-177

8. Daisheng Luo: Pattern Recognition and Image Processing (Horwood Publishing Limited 1998), pp 2-3

9. Richard O. Duda, Peter E. Hart, David G. Stork: Pattern Classification (John Wiley 2001), pp 11-12

10. Chengjun Liu: Learning the Uncorrelated, Independent, and Discriminating Color Spaces for Face Recognition, IEEE Transactions On Information Forensics And Security, Vol. 3, No. 2, June 2008, pp 213-222

11. Milan Sonka: Image Processing, Analysis, and Machine Vision (Thomson Learning 2001), pp 617

12. Barbara: The World According to Wavelets, pp 30

13. Sonja Grgic, Mislav Grgic, Branka Zovko-Cihlar: Performance Analysis of Image Compression Using Wavlets, IEEE Transactions on Indutrial Electronics, Vol. 48, No. 3, June 2001, pp 682-695

14. Yu Su, Shiguang Shan, Xilin Chen, and Wen Gao: Hierarchical Ensemble of Global and Local Classifiers for Face Recognition, IEEE Transactions On Image Processing, Vol.18, No. 8, August 2009, pp 1885 -1896

15. Rafel C. Gonzalez, Richard E. Woods: Digital Image Processing (Pearson Education), pp703-704

16. Website:/http://vis-www.cs.umass.edu/~vidit/IndianFaceDatabase

17. Davide Maltoni, Dario Maio, Anil K. Jain, Salil Prabhakar: Handbook of Fingerprint Recognition(Springer), pp 3

18. Neil Yager and Ted Dunstone: The Biometric Menagerie, IEEE Transactions On Pattern Analysis And Machine Intelligence, VOL. 32, NO. 2, FEBRUARY 2010, 220-230

19. Website: http://www.bromba.com/faq/biofaqe

CHAPTER 21

A Comparative Study Using Wavelet and SVM for Devanagri Characters Recognition

Anilkumar Holambe
College of Engineering, Osmanabad (MS) India
E-mail: anholambe@yahoo.com

ABSTRACT

This paper presents a wavelet-based approach for recognizing handwritten and printed Devnagari characters. In this paper we have used wavelet for feature extraction of the character. We have developed six handwritten data feature sets and six printed data feature set ,each dataset is divided in four part for our experimentation. We have also used wavelet kernels and regular kernels in SVM classification. Each SVM kernel is applied on total 12 x4=48 feature datasets.

Keywords: Wavelet, MAT, Complex Wavelet, Autocorrelation.

1. INTRODUCTION

Handwritten and printed character & digit recognition is an important topic in OCR applications and pattern classification . There are so many techniques of Pattern Recognition such as Template Matching, Neural Networks, Syntactical Analyses, Wavelet Theory, Hidden Markov Models, Bayesian theory etc have been used to develop efficient OCRs for different languages. OCR work on printed Devanagri script started in early 1970s. Some of the efforts on Devanagri character recognition are due to Sinha [1,7,8] and Mahabala [1]. Sethi and Chatterjee [5] also have done some earlier studies on Devanagri script and presented a Devanagri hand-printed numeral recognition system based on binary decision tree classifier. They [6] also used a similar technique for constrained hand-printed Devanagri character recognition. The first complete OCR system development of printed Devanagri is perhaps due to Palit and Chaudhuri [4] as well as Pal and Chaudhuri [3]. A survey for hand-written recognition of character is proposed [2]. In this paper we are using wavelet theory based feature extraction methods.

2. DATASET

In the present work we have developed printed and handwritten database. For printed we have used different ISM office fonts. and for handwritten we have collect dat from people of different age groups and from different profession. This data were scanned at 600 dpi using a HP flatbed scanner and stored as gray-level images. A few samples from this database are shown in Figure 1.

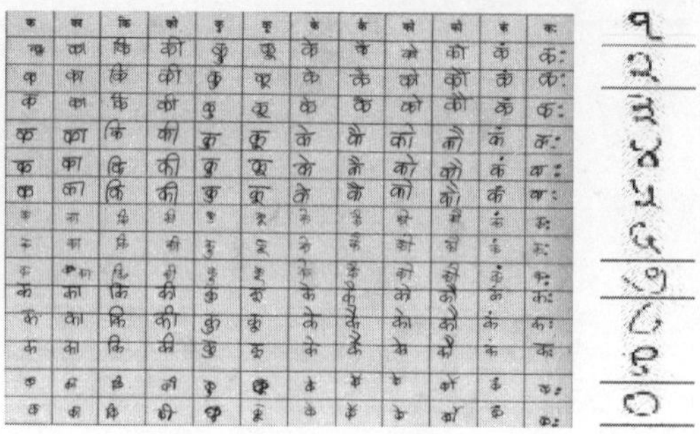

Fig. 1 Samples from database of handwritten Devanagari characters and numerial.

The database is exclusively divided into training and test sets. The distribution of samples in these training and test sets over 10 digit classes for numerical data. For Devnagari character has about 11 vowels ('svar') and 33 consonants or ('vyanjan'), and 11 modifiers so we organized data in 55 character classes. The handwritten database is collected from marathi peoples.

3. FEATURE EXTRACTION

3.1 Wavelet Theory

A character image of size N × N can be decompose into its wavelet cofficents by using Mallat's pyramid

$$*\bar{H}]_{2\downarrow1} * \bar{G}]_{1\downarrow3}, \; m = N/2^k + 1,...,N|2^{k-1}; \; n = 1,...$$

$$\bar{H}]_{2\downarrow1} * \bar{H}]_{1\downarrow2}, \; m = 1,...,N/2^k; \; n = N/2^k, \; n = N/2^k + 1,...,\Lambda$$

Here LL, LH, HL, and HH represent four subimages of the image being decomposed. After wavelet decomposition, the object image energy is distributed in different subbands, each subband image contains one feature.

3.2 Feature Set S1: Directional – Based Wavelet Features

Kirsch nonlinear edge enhancement algorithm is used to extract statistical features from the characters and then wavelet transform is applied on these statistical features to form original features. Kirsch nonlinear edge enhancement algorithm is applied to an N × N character Image to extract horizontal, Vertical, Right-diagonal and left-diagonal directional features and global features; then 2-D wavelet transform is used to filter out the high frequency components of each directional Feature image and character image, respectively, and to convert the feature matrix into a 4 × 4 matrix. Apply Daubechies-4 wavelets to four directional feature matrices and the character image, and only keep 4 × 4 low frequency components of each as features. Total, 16 × 5 = 80 features can be extracted from each character, detail can be found in [10] [11] [12] [13] [14].

3.3 Feature Set S2: MAT based Gradient Features

$$\pi/4 \; |1.0,|$$

Medial Axial Transformation Algorithm is used to finding a binary image centre skeleton and to converts a binary image into a grayscale image with maximum values on the central skeleton of the character. we can extract MAT Gradient-based features by Normalize the MAT image with its pixel values from we use sobel operator to convolute the normalized image to generate the amplitudes and phases of the gradient image. we count the gradient direction of each pixel of the convoluted image with nonzero gradient magnitude values as a direction feature. Finally to get the features each gradient direction is quantized into one of eight directions at intervals. Each normalized gradient image is divided into 16 sub-images. The number in each direction of each sub-image is counted as a feature. The total number of features are 4 × 4 × 8 = 128 detail can be found in [10] [11] [12] [13] [14].

3.4 Feature Set S3: Complex Wavelet Features

$$\frac{N}{2} \times \frac{N}{2}.$$

A character image of size 28(N) × 28(N) is divided into four sub band images: LL, LH, HL,HH at the first level of tree and each of the sub band images has a size of At each higher level, the decompositions are based on the LL sub band image at the previous level. The feature extraction is conducted at the third level. The number of features = 4 × 4(for each sub band image) *3 (high frequency sub band image for each tree) *2 (trees) + 4 × 4(for each sub band image) *2(trees)*2(parts: real and imaginary) =160 detail can be found in [10] [11] [12] [13] [14].

3.5 Feature Set S4: Median Filter Gradient Features

For this feature extraction set we convolute a character image by a 2D median filter; we use Robert operators on the median – filtered image to generate the amplitudes and phases; and finally count the gradient direction of each pixel with nonzero gradient magnitude values as a direction feature. So the total number of features is 128 detail can be found in [10] [11] [12] [13] [14].

3.6 Feature Set S5: Image Thinning Distance Features

In this feature set, the distance features in both horizontal and vertical directions are extracted firstly, an N × N character image is thinned and the thinned image is scaled into an 8 × 8 array. The thinned image is scanned both horizontally and vertically respectively. In the horizontal scanning, for each pixel in the 8 × 8 thinned image, if the value of the pixel is 0 (black), then the distance is 0; otherwise, the distance is set to the distance from that pixel to the nearest black pixel in both horizontal directions on the scanning line. For any pixel, if there are no nearest black pixels in both directions, the distance of the pixel is set to the distance from the pixel to one of two edges, whichever has longer distance to the edge. In the vertical scanning, the same algorithm is applied. In total there are 128 features detail can be found in [10] [11] [12] [13] [14].

3.7 Feature set S6: DCT – Based Wavelet Features

The discrete wavelet transform (DWT), which is based on sub-band coding is found to yield fast computation of wavelet transform. Binarize the image using Otsu method apply morphological thinning, operation.In order to extract local features compute the standard Deviation of the image block. In order to get image bock Apply DCT and divide the magnitude (image) of DCT into 4 equal non-overlapping block, perform Wavelet (Daubechies 4) decomposition for the magnitude (image) of DCT to obtain approximation, vertical, horizontal and diagonal coefficients.Compute the Standard Deviation for each frequency bands separately. Store all the computed features in a vector detail can be found in[14][15].

4. SUPPORT VECTOR MACHINE

where $\qquad\qquad\qquad X \in R^N, y \in \{-1, 1\},$

The support vector machine (SVM) was first developed by Vapnik and used for classification in many applications such as handwritten digit recognition, image classification, face detection, object detection, text classification etc. [16-20]. Given an training example set The kernel function can map the training examples in input space into a feature space such that the mapped training examples are linearly

$$W(\alpha) = \sum_{i=1}^{n} \alpha_2 - \frac{1}{2} \sum_{i=1}^{n} \sum_{j=1}^{n} \alpha_i\, y_i,\, \alpha_i,\, v_j\, K(X_j, X_j), \qquad\qquad (5)$$

Subject to

$$\sum_{i=1}^{n} \alpha_i y_i = 0$$

$$\alpha_i \in [0, C]$$

for $\qquad i \in [1, n]$

The decision function becomes

$$f(x) = \text{sign}\left(\sum_{i=1}^{n} \alpha_1 y_i K(X_i, X_j) + b\right), \tag{6}$$

$$b = Y, -\left(\sum_{i=1}^{n} \alpha_1 y_i K(X_r, X_i) + b\right), \tag{7}$$

$$(X_r, y_r)$$

where is any training example. We are using following SVM kernels.

4.1 Polynomial

$$K(X, X') = \langle X, X'\rangle^d \tag{7}$$

where d is the degree of the polynomial

4.2 Gaussian Radial Basis Function

$$|K(X, X') = \exp\left(-\frac{\|X - X'\|^2}{2\sigma^2}\right) \tag{8}$$

4.3 Exponential Radial Basis Function

$$|K(X, X') = \exp\left(-\frac{\|X - X'\|^2}{2\sigma^2}\right) \tag{9}$$

It produces a piecewise linear solution that is attractive when discontinuities are acceptable.

4.4 Spline

A spline kernel is defined as

$$+ \langle X, X'\rangle + \frac{1}{2}\langle X, X'\rangle \min(X, X') - \frac{1}{6}1 \tag{10}$$

4.5 Wavelet

The Wavelet kernel is defined as

$$|K(X, X') = \prod_{i=1}^{N}\left(\psi\left(\frac{x_1 - x_1'}{a}\right)\right)$$

where is the dimension of the input feature vector, and a is the scale factor.

4.6 Autocorrelation Wavelet kernel

$$K(X, X') = K(X - X')$$

A Translation invariant kernel is an admissible support vector (SV) kernel if and only if its Fourier transform is non-negative [21]. This can be satisfied by defining the following auto-correlation wavelet kernel [22]:

$$K(X, X') = \prod_{i=1}^{N}\left(\psi\left(\frac{x_1 - x_1'}{a}\right)\right) \tag{12}$$

where N is the dimension of the input feature vector and a is the scale factor. It should be mentioned that we can choose any compactly supported wavelet function to construct auto correlation waveletkernel $K(x, x')$.Details can be found in [23].

5. RESULT AND OBSERVATIONS

Data used for the present work were collected from different individuals. We considered 15000 basic characters (vowels as well as consonants) and 10000 numerical samples of Devnagari for the experiment of the proposed work. We have collected this data from different writer. The age group of writter is from 5years child to 60 years old man. We have also consider the profession of the writer i.e. student, clerk, officer, lecturer ect.We also formed printed database of ISM office fonts, in which we have used font size of 16 and different fonts. Here we have developed the six feature sets from our data collected and six for printed characters. Each feature set is divided in four parts i.e. vowels ('svar'), consonants ('vyanjan')without modifiers, consonants ('vyanjan') with modifiers, Number. Then we have used SVM with six different kernels. The results are given in following tables for different kernels used with SVM classifier.

Table 1 Result polynomial kernel

polynomial kernel	Feature Set	vowels ('svar') (%)	consonants ('vyanjan') without modifiers (%)	consonants ('vyanjan') with modifiers (%)	Number
Handwritten	S1	85	83	80	89
	S2	84	81	78	90
	S3	82	79	81	87
	S4	81	84	82	88
	S5	83	85	79	90
	S6	84	85	81	89
Printed	S1	90	88	89	89
	S2	89	89	88	91
	S3	91	87	88	92
	S4	90	89	87	90
	S5	92	86	90	91
	S6	90	88	91	92

Table 2 Result Gaussian Radial

Gaussia n radial	Feature Set	vowels ('svar') (%)	consonants ('vyanjan') without modifiers(%)	consonants ('vyanjan') with modifiers (%)	Number
Handwritten	S1	82	79	81	87
	S2	87	80	80	8 6
	S3	85	81	83	8 5
	S4	83	85	79	9 0

Contd...

	S5	82	84	81	8 9
	S6	84	85	84	9 0
Printed	S1	90	88	87	8 8
	S2	92	90	85	8 9
	S3	93	85	86	9 0
	S4	90	84	88	8 6
	S5	89	90	82	8 4
	S6	84	83	85	8 9

Table 3 Result Exponential Radial Basis

Expone ntial basis radial	Feature Set	vowels ('svar') (%)	consonants ('vyanjan') without modifiers (%)	consonants ('vyanjan') with modifiers (%)	Number
Handwritten	S1	80	78	81	8 9
	S2	79	82	87	8 8
	S3	81	85	84	8 7
	S4	78	88	85	8 4
	S5	85	87	82	8 4
	S6	89	86	81	8 6
Printed	S1	89	89	83	8 1
	S2	90	87	86	8 2
	S3	87	89	87	8 3
	S4	91	88	85	8 4
	S5	90	89	88	8 1
	S6	87	88	84	8 6

Table 4 Result Spline kernel

spline kernel	Feature Set	vowels ('svar') (%)	consonants ('vyanjan') without modifiers (%)	consonants ('vyanjan') with modifiers (%)	Number
Handwritten	S1	87	85	85	89
	S2	88	84	86	87
	S3	85	86	82	88
	S4	87	82	83	87
	S5	85	83	82	89
	S6	87	89	81	90
Printed	S1	90	90	89	90
	S2	88	94	92	91
	S3	89	93	91	92
	S4	91	92	93	93
	S5	92	91	94	94
	S6	89	83	86	87

Table 5   Result wavelet kernel

wavelet kernel	Feature Set	vowels ('svar') (%)	consonants ('vyanjan') without modifiers(%)	consonants ('vyanjan') with modifiers (%)	Number
Handwritten	S1	89	89	88	90
	S2	87	88	87	91
	S3	89	85	86	89
	S4	85	86	85	92
	S5	86	87	84	91
	S6	87	87	88	92
Printed	S1	90	91	89	93
	S2	89	89	87	94
	S3	88	91	89	89
	S4	91	88	90	91
	S5	90	92	91	90
	S6	89	88	84	89

Table 6   Result Autocorrelation Wavelet kernel

Auto correlation Wavelet kernel	Feature Set	vowels ('svar') (%)	consonants ('vyanjan') without modifiers(%)	consonants ('vyanjan') with modifiers (%)	Number
Handwritten	S1	88	87	86	8 1
	S2	85	86	82	8 0
	S3	87	84	84	8 3
	S4	86	82	83	7 9
	S5	87	85	86	8 1
	S6	87	81	81	8 4
Printed	S1	90	90	90	8 1
	S2	92	93	89	8 2
	S3	91	91	92	8 3
	S4	89	92	94	8 4
	S5	88	89	88	8 1
	S6	87	87	81	8 6

6. CONCLUSION

we can conclude from above result is that wavelets serve as a good feature set for the character images. The result obtained for recognition of Devnagari characters show that reliable classification is possible using SVMs kernels.

References

1. R.M.K. Sinha, H. Mahabala,,"Machine recognition of Devanagri script", IEEE Trans. System, Man Cybern. 9(1979) 435-441.
2. Plamondon, R. Srihari, S.N., Ecole Polytech, Montreal, Que.; Online and Offline HandwritingRecognition: A comprehensive Survey, 1EEE Transactions on Pattern Analysis and Machine Intelligence. Vol. 22, No. 1. JANUARY 2000 63
3. U. Pal , B.B. Chaudhuri , "Printed Devanagri script OCR system", Vivek 10 (1997) 12-24
4. S. Palit, B.B. Chaudhuri,,"A feature-based scheme for the machine recognition of printed Devanagri script", P.P. Das,
5. B.N. Chatterjee (Eda.) Pattern Recognition, Image Processing and Computer Vision, Narosa Publishing House: New

Delhi, India 1995, pp. 163-168

6. I.K. Sethi, B. Chatterjee, "Machine recognition of constrained hand-printed Devanagri numerals", J. Inst.Electron. Telecom. Eng. 22 (1976) 532-535.

7. I.K. Sethi, B. Chatterjee,"Machine recognition of constrained hand-printed Devanagri characters", Pattern Recognition 9 (1977) 69-76

8. R.M..K. Sinha, "A syntactic pattern analysis system and its application to Devanagri script recognition", Ph.D. Thesis, Electrical Engineering Department, Indian Institute of Technology, India, 1973.

9. K. Jain, P. W. Duin, and J. Mao, "Statistical Pattern Recognition: A Review," IEEE Trans. on Pattern Analysis and Machine Intelligence, Vol. 22, no. 2, pp. 5-37, 2000.

10. S. G. Mallat, "A Theory for Multiresolution Signal Decomposition: the Wavelet Representation," IEEE Trans. on Pattern Analysis and Machine Intelligence, vol. 11, no. 7, pp. 674-693, 1989

11. W.K. Pratt, Digital Image Processing. New York Wiley, 1978.

12. Ping Zhang, Reliable recognition of handwritten digits using a cascade ensemble classifier system and hybrid features, Ph.D. thesis, Concordia University, Montreal, P.Q., Canada, 2006.

13. N.G. Kingsbury, Image Processing with Complex Wavelets, Phil. Trans. R. Soc. Lond, A 357, 1999, pp. 2543-2560.

14. C.K. Chu, Wavelets: A Mathematical Tool for Signal Processing, Philadelphia: Society for Industrial and Applied Mathematics, 1997.

15. S. Mallat, A Wavelet Tour of Signal Processing, Second Edition, Academic Press, 1999.

16. Kannada, English, and Hindi Handwritten Script Recognition using multiple features, Proc. of National Seminar on Recent Trends in Image Processing and Pattern Recognition (RTIPPR-10), Editors: Dr. P.S. Hiremath et. al., Excel India Pub., New Delhi, ISBN: 93-80043-74-0, pp 149-152.

17. V.N. Vapnik, The Nature of Statistical Learning, Springer-Verlag, New York, 1995.

18. V.N. Vapnik, Statistical Learning Theory, Wiley, New York, 1998.

19. C. Cortes, V.N. Vapnik, Support vector networks, Machine Learning 20 (1995) 273–297.

20. Q. Song, W.J. Hu, W.F. Xie, Robust support vector machine for bullet hole image classification, IEEE Transactions on Systems, Man and Cybernetics – Part C 32 (4) (2002) 440–448.

21. L. Zhang, W. Zhou, L. Jiao, Wavelet support vector machine, IEEE Transactions on Systems, Man, and Cybernetics – Part B 34 (1) (2004) 34–39.

22. Smola, B. Scholkopf, K.-R. Muller, The connection between regulation operators and support vector kernels, Neural Network 11 (1998) 637–649.

23. G.Y. Chen, G. Dudek, Auto-correlation wavelet support vector machine and its applications to regression, in: Proceedings of the 2nd Canadian Conference on Computer and Robot Vision, May 9–11, British Columbia, 2005.

24. G.Y. Chen, W.F. Xie,Pattern recognition with SVM and dual-tree complex wavelets, Image and Vision Computing 25 (2007) 960–966

CHAPTER 22

Designing and Development of Speech Database: The Technical Review

Aaron M. Oirere, Vishal Waghmare, Ganesh Janvale and Ratnadeep Deshmukh
Department of Computer Science & IT, Dr. Babasaheb Ambedkar Marathwada University, Aurangabad-431004 (MS) India
E-mail: vishal_pri1@yahoo.co.in; ganesh.janvale@gmail.com; ratnadeep_deshmukh@yahoo.co.in

ABSTRACT

The speech database is one of the crucial items used for the automatic speech recognition system (ASR System). The paper reviews numerous techniques to design and development speech databases for different purpose. The paper presents here compression of four different language databases which are Marathi, Telugu, Tamil, Hindi and Spanish. It also gives the proposal to design and development of Swahili language database for automatic recognition system.

1. INTRODUCTION

Language technologies can provide solutions in the form of natural interfaces so that digital content can reach to the masses and facilitate the exchange of information across different people speaking different languages. Our overall goal is to develop speech recognition and speech recognition systems for most of Swahili language. Swahili is a Bantu language that serves as a second language to various groups traditionally inhabiting parts of the East African coast. About 35% of the Swahili vocabulary derives from the Arabic language, gained through more than twelve centuries of contact with Arabic-speaking inhabitants of the coast of Zanj. It also has incorporated Persian, German, Portuguese, English and French words into its vocabulary through contact during the last five centuries. Swahili has become a second language spoken by tens of millions in three countries, Tanzania, Kenya, and Congo (DRC), where it is an official or national language.

In this paper, we discuss the comparatives of different language database and Swahili language database for building large vocabulary speech recognition systems. The work could also be of great interest and significance to a large number of speech scientists as languages have certain properties that make them a special case. Most of the Indian languages are phonetic in nature. This is to say that there exists a one-to-one correspondence between the orthography and pronunciation in these languages. There are a number of phones present in the Indian languages, like the retroflexes, aspirated stops etc, which English and most European languages don t possess. At the same time, there are not many differences between the phone sets of individual Indian languages. This paper is organized as follows: Section 2 describes the comparison of techniques to design and development speech databases. Section 3 describes the ideas to design and develop Swahili language database. The concluding remarks and future work are stated in the Section 4.

2. DATABASE COLLECTION IN VARIOUS LANGUAGES

2.1 Mandarin – English

2.1.1 Data collection

The data was taken and categorized in three categories: native mandarin corpus, native English corpus and mandarin accented English and were recording through telephone line and digitalized at 8 KHz sampling rate with 18 bits resolutions. Mandarin was taken from the native Chinese, English were recorded in higher rate and were band limited to 4 KHz by down sampling and was collected in the house labeled as GTC (general Telephone conversation corpus) speech data was from 60 males and 60 females speakers each with 200 utterances for every day conversations.. The data was taken in restaurants, streets and other noisy places with different background noises, speaker fluency an accent.

2.1.2 Data base

It was chosen from taking single set of bilingual acoustic set of bilingual acoustic model derived by phone clustering. It was developed instead of using two separate monolingual models for each language. The novel two-pass phone clustering method based on confusion matrix (TCM) was presented and compared with the log-likelihood method and it was found that TCM had better results than log-likelihood.

The data was taken in two approaches that is: pronunciation and acoustic. Acoustic dealt with the utterance; which were collected in a region where the matrix language was spoken. It was categorized in three stages: a single set of acoustic to handle both inter- and intra-sentence language switching, a two- pass cross language phone clustering approach based on confusion matrix, optimal way of merging the phone sets of English and mandarin. By merging and clustering the phone set of these two languages, anew set of mono-phones covering both language are determine. The data consist the names of the singers and titles of the songs, they had total of 10179 utterances: 8183 mono-mandarin, 1650 mono-English and 346 bilingual

2.2 Hindi Database

2.2.1 Data collection

In the sound unit the sentence were represented as sequence of phonemes. The units were acoustically homogeneous and fairly distinct from each other. Acoustic-phonetic features of Hindi language differ from that of European language. Aspiration is a phone in Hindi unlike in English. Rectroflexion features were occurring in prominent places in Hindi. The list all the acoustic –phonemic in complete closure of oral tract i.e. plosives, affricates and nasals labeling was done by special symbols which represented devoicing of the voiced closure, voicing of a unvoiced closure, voiced glottal fricative, tongue, click, glottal stops, voiced segmentations, vowel and silence.

2.2.2 Designing of sentences

Designing of the sentence was done in three format i.e. one contain all the phonemes, another rich in phonemic context and final used the identification of dialect/accent. The sentences were syntactically valid and meaningful. 10 sentences were taken in two parts: 2 sentences containing dialects and 8 sentences containing as much of phonetic context as possible. The sentences were made to be syntactically valid, meaningful, natural, simple and short for easy understanding and feature extraction. Designed that each subject was to speak 10 sentences containing of two parts first consist two dialects which contain all the phonemes of the language and secondly they cover the large set of diverse phoneme context.

2.2.3 Designed strategy

100 sets of Hindi sentences were spoken by 100 speakers and were chosen from a corpus of machine readable Hindi text from diverse source. The short sentences were represented by less than 80 ASCII character were retrained. A text to phoneme was used after taking in account the micro-phonemic rule in Hindi. Dialect sentences were selected which

contained maximum number of dialect Hindi phonemes and speed sounds of manner and place of articulation were minimized.

2.2.4 Data collection

The data was collected in two ways; in the room and the field.

The speaker was 100 and each of them read 10 sets phonetically rich sentences which were digitally recorded. In the room there was a close talk of a distance of 5 cm from the mouth and another which was in the field mounted in the desk at a distance of 1 meter and it was collected in the simple shift of the time indices. Then the data was segmentation and labeling. The sampling was done at 16 KHz and digitalized with 16 bits. Vowel duration was also done for it was useful for understanding and capturing systematic variations occurring in natural speech. Occurrences of vowels were more than consonants. The durations were differing from one to another. This was done by the mean and standard deviation. The durations were checked on native Hindi speakers and non-native speakers and it was found that systematic behaviors were distinct.

2.2.5 Database

The database was developed well to capture phonetic, acoustic, intra-speaker and inter-speaker variability in Hindi. The database contains 500 sentences taken from 50 speakers. Vowels duration was done synthesis in high quality speech which was done by the help of mean and standard variation of the vowels from the native Hindi and non-native. The database was well done to capture phonetic, acoustic, intra-speaker and intra-speaker.

3. PROPOSAL FOR DEVELOPMENT OF SWAHILI LANGUAGE DATABASE

In this section, the various steps involved in building the speech corpora are detailed. Firstly, the recording media will be chosen so as to capture the effects due to channel and microphone variations. For the databases that will be built for the Swahili language ASRs, the speech data will be recorded over calculated number of landline and cellular phones using a multi-channel computer telephony interface card.

3.1 Speaker Selection

Speech data is collected from the native speakers of the language who will comfortable in speaking and reading the language. The speakers will be chosen such that all the diversities attributing to the gender, age and dialect are sufficiently captured. The recording is clean and has minimal background disturbance. Any mistakes made while recording will be by re-recording or by making the corresponding changes in the transcription set.

3.2 Data Statistics

Speakers from various parts of the respective states (regions) will carefully recorded in order to cover all possible dialectic variations of the language. Each speaker will be recorded 52 sentences of the optimal text. To capture different microphonic variations, four different cellphones or landline will be used while recording the speakers.

4. CONCLUSION

In this paper, we discussed the optimal design and development of speech databases for the English and Hindi language. We hope the simple methodology of database creation presented will serve as catalyst for the creation of speech databases in all other languages. We also proposed the methodology to design and develop Swahili language speech database for automatic recognition system. We hope the ASRs created will be served as baseline systems for further research on improving the accuracies in each of the languages. Our future work is focused in tuning these models and test them using language models built using a larger corpus and to develop large vocabulary speech database recognition system.

References

1. http://tdil.mit.gov.in/corpora/ach-corpora.htm#tech
2. L.Rabiner, A Tutorial on Hidden Markov models and Selected Applications in Speech Recognition, Proc. Of IEEE, Vol. 77 No. 2, 1989.
3. Samudravijaya K, P.V.S.Rao, and S.S.Agrawal, Hindi Speech Database, Proc. Int. Conf. on Spoken Language processing (ICSLP00), Beijing, China, October 2000, CDROM paper: 00192.
4. Singh, S.P., et al Building Large Vocabulary Speech Recognition Systems for Indian Languages, International Conference on Natural Language Processing, 1:245-254, 2004.
5. Richard Winsky. 1997. "Definition of Corpus, scripts and standards for Fixed Networks", SpeechDat project, doc ref LE2-4001-SD1.1.3, 22.

CHAPTER 23

Automatic Clustering and User Profiling of Web Users Using Web Usage Mining Techniques and Its Comparative Study

Sachin Deshpande, Anand Khandare and Megharani Patil
Computer Engineering Department, Mumbai University, Mumbai (MS) India
E-mail: sachin.deshpande@vit.edu.in, anand.khandare@thakureducation.org, megharani.patil@thakureducation.org

ABSTRACT

This paper present a implementation of tool for automatic clustering and user profiling of web site user using a concepts of web Uses mining Techniques and the comparison of various data mining techniques with respect to web site for various products. The input for this tool web usage patterns from Web log or click stream of a web site which is collected from the web server and applied web usage mining for clustering users and discovering user profiles. In this paper we have developed web site for various products that is managed by the nonprofits organization that does not sell any products but only collects analysis of users that are using web site. This analysis include, what are the users, what they have looked at our web site and their interests, needs and preferences. This analysis can help the business to improve the profit by selling only required products to customers. Hence, we present an approach for discovering user profiles. A tool in this paper uses the clustering algorithms. This approach is useful for clustering and user profiling. This application can be used for web personalization.

Keywords: clustering, click stream, user profiles, web mining.

1. INTRODUCTION

This Customer Relationship Management (CRM) can use data from inside and outside of the organization to understand its customers by clustering users of same requirements and making customer profiles. Understanding of the customer preferences, needs, and interests can increase the profit of company by selling the required products to its customers. Hence, accurate knowledge about the customer requirements, preferences and needs can helps in making effective CRM. Today the goal of every businesses are to move online, and increase the competition level between businesses ,to keep the old customers and increasing new customers for making good profits .So for that businesses should understand the exact requirements needs and preferences of .So collecting such type of information manually is difficult because it is large amounts of data available in these online. There are considerable advances in Web usage mining. This paper presents approach to mine Web site with the challenging characteristics of today's Web sites, such as evolving profiles, dynamic content using knowledge discovery techniques to discover Web user profiles. These user profiles can be discovered using Web usage mining techniques that can automatically extract frequent access patterns from the user click streams stored in

Web log files. These profiles can later be harnessed toward personalizing web site. In this paper, we present a complete framework and results of mining Web usage patterns with real-world challenges such as evolving access patterns, dynamic pages from the web log of web sites. For this tool we have implemented the web site for various types of products. The Web site is managed by a nonprofit organization that does not sell anything but only provides accurate and complete information. Hence to collect and understand the different modes of usage and to know what kind of information the visitors seek and read on the Web site and how this information evolves with time. For this reason, we perform clustering of the user. This tool can collect huge amounts of information and generate large useful analysis of web site users. This analysis can tell us What are the users, What type of products they are looking, their needs interests and. Then businesses can use this analysis to improve the profits of business by selling the required products to their customers. This work also compares the various data mining clustering techniques with themselves and conventional methods using various matrices. We have applied two clustering techniques such as K-Mean clustering and Agglomerative clustering to cluster the users. Results of these two methods are compared based on two matrices Such as time complexity and Squared Sum Error of a partition (SSE) and Accuracy of a clustering (ACC).

2. BACKGROUND AND RELATED WORK

There are several existing approaches for collected and discovering the user profiles from the web.

The Mining Web Access Logs Using Relational Competitive Fuzzy Clustering [3] define the notion of a "user session" as being a temporally compact sequence of web accesses by a user. It also defines a new distance measure between two web sessions that captures the organization of a web site. The Competitive Agglomeration clustering algorithm which can automatically cluster data into the optimal number of components is extended so that it can work on relational data. The resulting Competitive Agglomeration for Relational Data algorithm can deal with complex, non-Euclidean, distance/ similarity measures. This algorithm was used to successfully analyze server access logs and obtain typical session profiles of users. This algorithm can not deal with noisy data and can discover the evolving user profiles. Most fuzzy clustering techniques have the disadvantage that they either assume that the number of clusters is known. For these reasons, we have simple Agglomerative algorithm which can automatically cluster data into the optimal number of components using Euclidean distance. Agglomerative is reliable, computationally attractive, and practically insensitive to initialization.

The Web Usage Mining for Semantic Web Personalization [5], propose a web usage mining approach for semantic web personalization. The proposed approach first incorporates fuzzy logic into Formal Concept Analysis to mine user access data for automatic ontology generation, and then applies approximate reasoning to generate personalized usage knowledge from the ontology for providing personalized services. To provide semantic web personalization, we need to tackle the technical issues on how to define web access activities, discover hierarchical relationships from web access activities, transform them into ontology automatically, and deduce personalized usage knowledge from the ontology.

The Mining Evolving User Profiles in Noisy Web Click stream Data with a Scalable Immune System Clustering Algorithm[4] propose a new scalable clustering methodology that gleams inspiration from the natural immune system to be able to continuously learn and adapt to new incoming patterns. The Web server plays the role of the human body, and the incoming requests play the role of foreign antigens/bacteria/viruses that need to be detected by the proposed immune based clustering technique. In our approach we are directly collecting click steams from the web site and performing the clustering. In this paper we are implementing concepts of web usage mining to cluster the web user and then making profiles of both individual and group of users. Our web mining process for clustering and profiling consists of following steps

1. Collecting the click streams
2. Applying Data mining techniques
3. User profiling

Figure 1 shows the process of our mining. This process consists of collecting and storing the click streams in data base. Now we have applied the data mining clustering algorithms to cluster the users of similar behaviour and then discover their profiles.

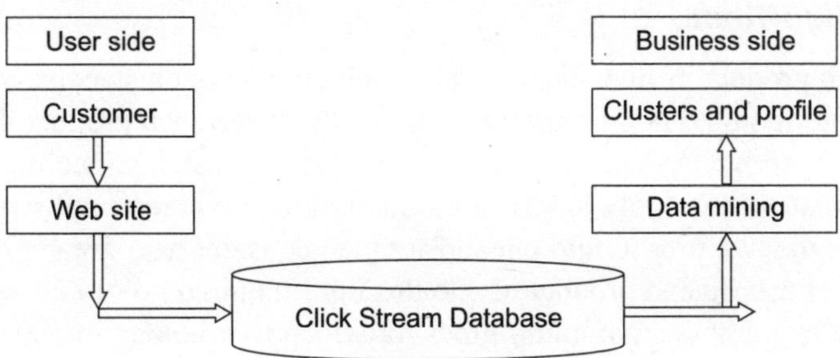

Fig. 1 Web Mining process

3. METHODOLOGY USED

3.1 Method of Data Collection

A tool presented in this paper uses the as a click streams of web site. For that we have developed the web site for different products of different categories. To access the products users have to log in first. After login user can see the various the products, give the ratings to products. Following is snapshot after login and selecting a particular product. When user performs any activity such as click/buy and given rating for product on web site, then automatically clickstreams is stored in data base. In database we are collecting user ID, userAction and user Rating. Following are the tables in data base.

1. User Information: It stores the information about user such as username, user id
2. Product Information: It stores the product information such as product name, product id and product categories.
3. User Browsing: It stores User id, product id and action perform by user (Click/Buy)
4. Product Rating: It stores product id, user id and rating given by user to that product

3.2 Criteria for Data Mining

Product Click: Product click means the number of time that product is clicked by the users. One user can click that product only once.

Product Rating: The average of rating given to single product. Rating is from 1-5. if 15 user has access the single product with rating between 1-5 then rating is average of all rating.

Category Click: Each product has category like mobile is category and nokia is product. Number of time the user have click to that category of product.

3.3 Techniques to Cluster the User

From the click stream database, we have consider Userid, Category id(CI), No. of clicks(CL), Product Rating(PR).We form the matrix of N X 3 by taking Userid as rows and CI, CL and PR as columns of matrix then we compare the each user with each column and based on these three attributes we put the each user in particular cluster.

3.3.1 K Mean Algorithm

(1) For all user first select centroid from all three column and Assign user to one of the columns.
(2) Assign each item from column to the cluster which has the closest mean using Euclidian distance.
(3) Calculate new mean for each cluster
(4) Repeat step (2) and step (3) until mean for each cluster doesn't change
(5) At the end we have to count the maximum times user for which user belongs to one cluster that is it's destination cluster.

3.3.2 *Agglomerative Algorithm*

This algorithm starts with each product its own cluster and iteratively merge clusters based on difference between item values such as click, rating until required no of clustered formed. (1) Place each product in its own cluster. (2) For first user find the adjacency matrix showing distance between self products and remaining (3) Find the minimum and maximum distance from this matrix. (4) Apply loop from minimum to maximum until required no of cluster will form. For minimum distance, Merge the two user id into one cluster then consider next greater distance and merge the above clusters which consist of pair of user id and product id. Do this until required no of cluster formed. (5) Repeat step 1-4 for all users (6) Then we have to count the maximum times for which user belong to one cluster that is its final cluster.

3.4 Comparison of Data Mining Techniques

1. Matrices to compare clustering algorithm

Squared sum error of a partition (SSE)

Formula:

$\Sigma\Sigma$square (d (mean, item (product id and user id) from that cluster)) For each cluster, I) Find difference between mean and item. Find the square of difference. Add all distances for that cluster. II) Repeat step I for all clusters III) Add those all sum of distances of all the clustersFor Agglomerative Algorithm difference is the distance between the cluster element with itself and other in the resultant cluster.

Percentage of analyzed methods for a partition (PAM)

Formula:

$PAM = \Sigma$ *(from 1 to q) pam(Cluster i)/q*

Pam (Cluster (i) = (no of item values which are grater than mean value in i th cluster)/(total no of items in that cluster) q = total no of clusters in which some item values are grater than mean value For Agglomerative Algorithm, q = total no of clusters in which Minimum distance that is greater than some threshold i.e. (e.g. assumed threshold value is two).

Accuracy of clustering (ACC)

Formula:ACC = ?(from 1 to q) acc(Cluster i)/q.

Acc (Cluster i) = (no of item values which are not grater than mean value in ith cluster)/(no of item values which are grater than mean value in ith cluster). q = total no of clusters in which some item values are grater than mean value. For Agglomerative Algorithm = total no of clusters in which Minimum distance that is greater than some threshold i.e. (e.g. assumed threshold value is two)

3.5 Implementations Details

This tool is totally implemented using open source software. For this tool we have developed the web site for products of different categories using java server pages (jsp) and java language and deployed in tomcat server. To store the clickstreams we have developed the database in mysql server with navcat as a GUI for tables .Finally all algorithms are implemented in java .GUI for project is implemented in JSP.

4. RESULTS OBTAINED

4.1 Clustering Results

To cluster the user we have applied the K mean and agglomerative algorithms with two types of cluster one is product clustering and another is user product clustering, both produces same results. In product clustering we have clustered the products based on clicks of product. In user product clustering we clustered the products and user based on both rating and click. We have applied the algorithms for the data of 20-25 users.

Results of k means(k = 4)

1. Product clustering
2. User Product Clustering

Table 1 Result of Product clustering

Product Clustering	
Cluster Number	*Product Name*
Cluster 1	TITAN Raga Diva Watch SELENE 9747YM04B
Cluster 2	Stylish Bio magnetic Wrist Watch, 13 Diamond Fancy Ring
Cluster 3	Royal Enfield Electra 5 S, Nokia 5800 XpressMusic, Bajaj Avenger, Nokia N97 GSM,
Cluster 4	Honda stunner CBF Self Drum, Nikon Coolpix L22, Canon Powershot A495, Art Silk Kurta Suit,Sony Cyber-shot DSC-H20,D&G Mens Rugby Chronograph Watch DW 0374,Nokia 7610s,Acer Aspire 4736Z, Sony NWZS543 4GB, Canon PowerShot SX120 IS, LG Cookie Pep GD510, MAHEK COLLECTION KURTA (J), Genius Kurta Suit Collection 01 Rotating Dial Watch Kinetic sym flyte, Sony Cyber-shot DSC-S930, TITAN Nebula Watch 5004DL01,

Table 2 Result of User Product

Cluster Number	User Id	UseProduct Clustering Product Name
Cluster 1	1	[Nokia 5800 XpressMusic, Nokia N97 GSM, Royal Enfield Electra 5 S, Bajaj Avenger]
	6	[Nokia 5800 XpressMusic]
	12	[Nokia 5800 XpressMusic, Royal Enfield Electra 5 S]
	15	[Nokia 5800 XpressMusic]
	2	[Nokia 5800 XpressMusic, Nokia N97 GSM, Royal Enfield Electra 5 S, Bajaj Avenger]
Cluster 2	3	[TITAN Raga Diva Watch SELENE 9747YM04B]
	14	[TITAN Raga Diva Watch SELENE 9747YM04B]
	17	[TITAN Raga Diva Watch SELENE 9747YM04B]
Cluster 3	8	[Nikon Coolpix L20, Nokia E71]
	11	[Nikon Coolpix L20, Baywatch Mens Watch Model Number 908]
Cluster 4	10	[Stylish Bio magnetic Wrist Watch, 13 Diamond Fancy Ring]
	9	[13 Diamond Fancy Ring]
	17	[13 Diamond Fancy Ring]

4.2 Comparison Results

We compared K-Mean clustering, and Agglomerative clustering with respect to matrices SSE. *K*-Mean clustering and Agglomerative clustering are also compared with respect to matrices PAM, ACC. Smaller values SSE indicate better partition meaning that SSE has to be minimized. Smaller values for PAM indicate short time for analysis meaning that PAM has to be minimized. Lager values for ACC indicate better partitions meaning that ACC has to be maximized. Comparison of conventional method, clustering methods is given in following table.

Table 3 Result of Comparison

Clustering Method	SSE	PAM	ACC
K-Mean Clustering	1053	0.417	1.125
Agglomerative Clustering	8300	1.0	0.0

K-Mean clustering has minimum SSE value, minimum PAM and maximum ACC value, means it is better method than agglomerative clustering.

5. CONCLUSIONS AND FUTURE WORK

5.1 Conclusion

In this study we found that clustering is useful for characterizing the behaviour of the both individual and group of users on web site Based on this project business can improve the profits by selling the different products based on user preferences, needs and interests .We applied two clustering algorithms, results of both algorithms are almost similar .But we compare these algorithms with respect to SSE, PAM and ACC and we found that values for the parameters are different. Hence we conclude that a k mean algorithm is better than agglomerative.

5.2 Future Work

In this paper we have clustered the user of web site in to different clusters based on click streams. We can use this clusters for various purpose

1. Web personalization
2. Targeted marketing

References

1. R. Cooley, B. Mobasher, and J. Srivastava, "Web Mining: Information and Pattern Discovery on the World Wide Web,"Proc. Ninth IEEE Int'l Conf. Tools with AI (ICTAI '97), pp. 558-567,1997.

2. O. Nasraoui, R. Krishnapuram, and A. Joshi, "Mining Web Access Logs Using a Relational Clustering Algorithm Based on a Robust Estimator," Proc. Eighth Int'l World Wide Web Conf. (WWW '99), pp. 40-41, 1999.

3. O. Nasraoui, R. Krishnapuram, H. Frigui, and A. Joshi, "Extracting Web User Profiles Using Relational Competitive Fuzzy Clustering," Int'l J. Artificial Intelligence Tools, vol. 9, no. 4,pp. 509-526, 2000.

4. Olfa Nasraoui, Cesar Cardona, Carlos Rojas, Fabio Gonzalez" Mining Evolving User Profiles in NoisyWeb Clickstream Data with a Scalable Immune System Clustering Algorithm" Proce of 5th WEBKDD Aug 03.

5. Baoyao Zhou1, Siu Cheung Hui, and Alvis C. M. Fong" Web Usage Mining for Semantic Web Personalization"

4. J. Srivastava, R. Cooley, M. Deshpande, and P.-N. Tan, "Web Usage Mining: Discovery and Applications of Usage Patterns from Web Data," SIGKDD Explorations, vol. 1, no. 2, pp. 1-12, Jan.200

6. M. Spiliopoulou and L.C. Faulstich, "WUM: A Web Utilization Miner," Proc. First Int'l Workshop Web and Databases (WebDB '98), 1998

Design an Algorithm for Weblogs Analysis: An Application of Business Intelligence

V.P. Mahatme, Aman Kumar, Jyoti Prakash and Shruti Nimbalkar
Department of Computer Technology, Kavikulguru Institute of Technology & Science, Ramtek (Nagpur) (MS), India-441106,
E-mail: mahatme.vilas@gmail.com, aman.raja6@gmail.com

ABSTRACT

Analysis of weblogs for business intelligence is the web mining activity that involves the automatic discovery of user access patterns. As more organizations rely on the internet and the World Wide Web. Organizations often generate and collect large volumes of data in their daily operations. Other sources of user information include referrer logs which contains information about the referring pages for each page reference and user registration. Weblogs provide online platform for discussion and keep track of comment gives by public for consumer product. It provides an opportunity for companies to understand and responds to the consumer by analysis this consolidated feedback. This paper presents the applications for mining large volumes of textual data for business intelligence. This propose such a system that gathers and annotates discussion relating to consumer products using a wide variety of state-of-the-art techniques like crawling, wrapping, search, computational linguistics for deriving Business intelligence from analysis of Weblogs.
Keywords: Text mining, Content systems, Computational linguistics, Machine learning, Business intelligence, Weblogs.

1. INTRODUCTION

Weblogs are frequently modified web pages, with entries usually organized in reverse chronological order. Blogosphere doubling in size about once every five months and about 30-40,000 new weblogs are being created each day [1]. Weblogs are places into three main categories: filters, personal journals, and notebooks [2]. Filters reflect important developments, such as news about world events. Personal journals are similar to diaries. Notebooks are hybrids of filters and personal journals. Personal journals and filters together take up over 80%. Filters are usually maintained in archives [3]. In the simplest terms, weblog is a website similar to that of a personal journal that is updated with individual entries or postings. The entries of the blog can also be dated and even assigned headings and keywords. Weblog is equivalent of e-mail, news-groups, message boards and chat-groups. Weblogs are seen as a form of individualistic expression, providing "personal protected space" where a weblog author can communicate with others while retaining control. Weblogs stand between the public and the private.

This paper describes an end-to-end commercial system that is used to support a number of business intelligence applications. In short, we describe system which analyses online data to help to make informed and timely decisions with respect to brands, products and strategies in the corporate space. The applications of these data are noted below such as

User trends - Informing subscriber about the recent trends in business field.

Early alerting - Informing subscribers when a rare but critical, or even fatal, condition occurs.

Buzz tracking – Informing about the trends in topics of discussion and understanding. What new topics are forming?

Sentiment mining - Extracting aggregate measures of positive vs. negative opinion.

For implementation of this system, weblogs is taken as a raw-data on which further operation like extraction of information from web page takes place.

2. LITERATURE REVIEW

According to Natalie Glance & et.al.[1] Weblogs and message boards provide online forums for discussion that record the voice of the public. Woven into this mass of discussion is a wide range of opinion and commentary about consumer products. This paper argues that applications for mining large volumes of textual data for marketing intelligence should provide two key elements: a suite of powerful mining and visualization technologies and an interactive analysis environment.

Kosuke Numa & et.al [4] proposed a weblog system called *ActionLog*, which can associate weblog entries to real world contexts. In this, it is not only useful for Weblog authors themselves, but also beneficial to communication among people, because people with the same or a similar context can easily find each other. ActionLog collects user actions from both Web-based and other real-world systems. Weblog contents are generated automatically from these user actions with related information. Users can browse and edit these entries as their personal action records and in addition can publish them for experience sharing. Its main objective is to help people to learn about presentations and to effectively meet other people in a limited amount of time and the least amount of user commitment. There are three main features, i.e., Personalization both in information capturing from users and in information providing to users, and persistent assistance throughout the conference.

According to Andreas Juffinger & et.al. [5] as people use weblogs to express thoughts, present ideas and share knowledge, weblogs are extraordinarily valuable resources, among others, for trend analysis. Trends are derived from the chronological sequence of blog post count per topic. The comparison with a reference corpus allows qualitative statements over identified trends. They proposed a cross language blog mining and trend visualization system to analyze blogs across languages and topics. The trend visualization facilitates the identification of trends and the comparison with the reference news article corpus.

Nikhil Belsare & et.al [6] proposed that Blog Harvest uses classification, linkage & topic similarity based clustering based opinion mining. Novel search interface they built to provide related blogs for queries along with the usual result ranking. Analysis of linkage between blogs has indicated that community forming in blogosphere is not a random process but is a result of shared interests binding bloggers together. Learning, analysis and usage of the user's interest and social linkage from the blog is therefore necessary to provide useful search faculty on the blogosphere to bloggers and revenue generation opportunities like advertising to the blog service providers.

3. PROPOSED APPROACH

In proposed model, internet discussion is considered as raw-data. With the help of this discussion, user classifies number of domain-specific topic like brand, price, and feature and performs base analysis of the sentiment regarding the topic. Thousands of messages can be analyzed. Messages are through a top-down methodology that starts with broad aggregate findings. The Comparatives analysis is done which is a simple way of breaking down the messages and generating a variety of metrics over each segment. Proposed work architecture is explained in Figure 1.

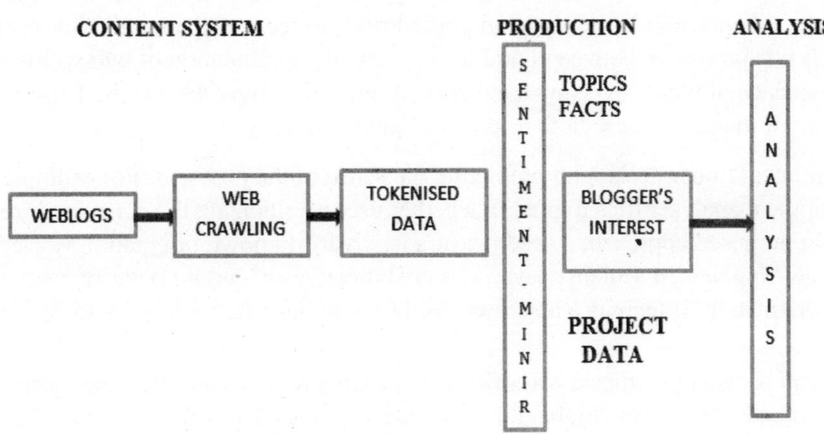

Fig. 1 System Architecture

3.1 System Architecture

Architecture contains sample weblogs as a raw-data for performing operation on it, web crawler for extraction of topic, other post of weblogs and parts of text tagger, tokenizer for separating the tokens, sentiment miner for sentiment analysis of user etc. Functions of each block are explained in later section.

Content System Discovery and harvesting of message data is the first component of our system. We have modules for extracting information from weblogs. Discovery and harvesting from 'Usenet' newsgroups is straight forward because 'Usenet' posts are well-defined structures. On the other hand in weblogs both discovery and harvesting are difficult. Discovery entails finding weblogs pertinent to a particular domain. Harvesting consists of extracting weblog posts from semi-structured web pages. The first step is designing a crawling strategy. The second step entails a kind of reverse engineering weblogs to reconstruct weblog posts. The solutions devised depend on the data source.

Weblogs The use of weblogs primarily for publishing as opposed to discussion. Blogs differentiates from other online community forums, such as newsgroups and message boards. Here, our goal is to extract structured data from the semi-structured weblog home page: the title, date, author, link and content of each newly published post. We call this task as weblog segmentation. We use a model-based approach to segment weblogs into posts. We complement our approach to model-based segmentation using weblog feeds when available. The weblog feed contains the updated content of the weblog in standardized XML format. A number of weblog hosting systems, such as live journal and Xanga, automatically provide a full-content feed for each hosted weblog. For achieving this goal, we use web crawler.

Web Crawler A web crawler is a relatively simple automated program or script that methodically scans or "crawls" through internet pages to create an index of the data it's looking for. There are many different uses for a web crawler. The most common use associated with the term is related to search engines. Search engines use web crawlers to collect information about what is available on public web pages. Their primary purpose is to collect data so that when internet surfers enter a search term on their site, they can quickly provide the surfer with relevant web sites. When a search engine's web crawler visits a web page, it "reads" the visible text, the hyperlinks, and the content of the various tags used in the site, such as keyword rich meta tags. Using the information gathered from the crawler, a search engine will then determine what the site is about and index the information. Every blog host has a different structure for all the blogs published on it. But in this system, crawler extracts posts from blogs and attributes of those posts (Title, Timestamp, Body, Permalink etc.). Since our analysis relies on the blogger network analysis, we have separate crawlers per blog host to extract this information.

Tokenizer Tokenizer is used to tokenize the weblog a content where each word of weblog is separated by the space behaves like a token. These token are tagged with the part of text using tagger. In developing the text tagger, we encountered two significant issues. Firstly, we are working with off-line data. The standard training sets given in the literature are used for training.

The second issue is to tokenization based on hand crafted rules to recover the words. For example, in the sentence ill buy a new car, there is no apostrophe between I and ll. It is actually combination of two words I and will. Our goal is to tag this underlying sequence of words by using hand crafted rules to recover the words. This information is then used for sentiment analysis and formation of association rules for query expansion.

Sentiment Miner   Sentiment miner deals with predicting the sense of the post text. For example, if user has written a product review then sentiment analyzer tries to predict whether user is criticizing the consumer product or he is praising the consumer product. In proposed approach, a seed list of adjectives of known orientation is used. The list is prepared manually with the help of WordNet. At sentence level, if more adjectives of certain polarity are used then sentence have that polarity (favoring) orientation. If there is a negation word (not, neither etc.) left to an adjective then current polarity is negated.

Another approach can be used to indicate classifier with product review data. Reviews with low rating are used to indicate negative classifier and reviews with higher rating are used to indicate positive classifier. Then these classifiers are used to determine sentiments.

Fact extraction is the culmination of the content system and the production system configured for a specific domain. Retrieved relevant messages are tagged with topics and then analyzed for sentiment and combination of brand topics with other topics. At this point, these extracted facts could be exported to a traditional data mining system. However, since each fact is backed by a segment of text, advanced text data mining algorithms are more appropriate for analysis.

Blogger's Interest   To predict the state of mind with which a blogger was posting an article, blog article are classified to some predefined emotional categories. Informative articles do not express personal emotions. Recognition of human emotion has long been a hot research topic. In recent years, with the dramatic increase of blog data, plentiful of free textual data with people's emotions or feelings can be obtained that attract many researchers to the domain of blogger's emotion recognition. Therefore extracting the affective articles from the whole textual data is important step of proposed work. By this emotion recognition can easily be applied to the whole blog space.

Who appears most number of times in the weblogs, then find out the area from which this word belongs and on the basis of that field, we could find out the interest of blogger. Consider any blogger write article in the weblog, this weblog as a sample for performing analysis .During analysis, if movie word is repeated most of times and on the basis of this analysis, we can easily predict that this word movie is related to the entertainment field. So, we can easily find that the blogger is much more interested in entertainment field and he is expressing his view about any particular movie. This is the method, we are using for getting the information about the blogger's interest.

Analysis   The numbers of metrics can be created to facilitate exploration of data that provide summary of discussion across number of dimension. The key base metrics we provide are as follows.

Buzz Count. A simple count of the number of messages, alternately expressed as a percentage.

Polarity. A 1-10 score representing the overall sentiment can be expressed about a topic or intersection of topics. The score is based on the posterior estimate of the ratio of the frequency of positive to negative comments.

Author Dispersion. A measure of how spread out the discussion of a particular topic is? High values indicate that many people are talking about a particular topic, where low values indicate that discussion is centered on a small group of people. This measure is more indicative than just counting of unique authors for a topic, as error in the topic classifications dilutes the understanding of the spread of discussion.

Board Dispersion. Similar to author dispersion, this measures how many different places are seeing discussion about a particular topic. Topics that have a board dispersion that grows rapidly over time indicates a viral issue. If such a viral issue is negative, prompt attention is often recommended.

These metrics serve two purposes. First, they give a starting point for top-down exploration. Second, they provide dashboard-style summary statistics that can be disseminated.

3.2 Flow Graph of the Proposed Work

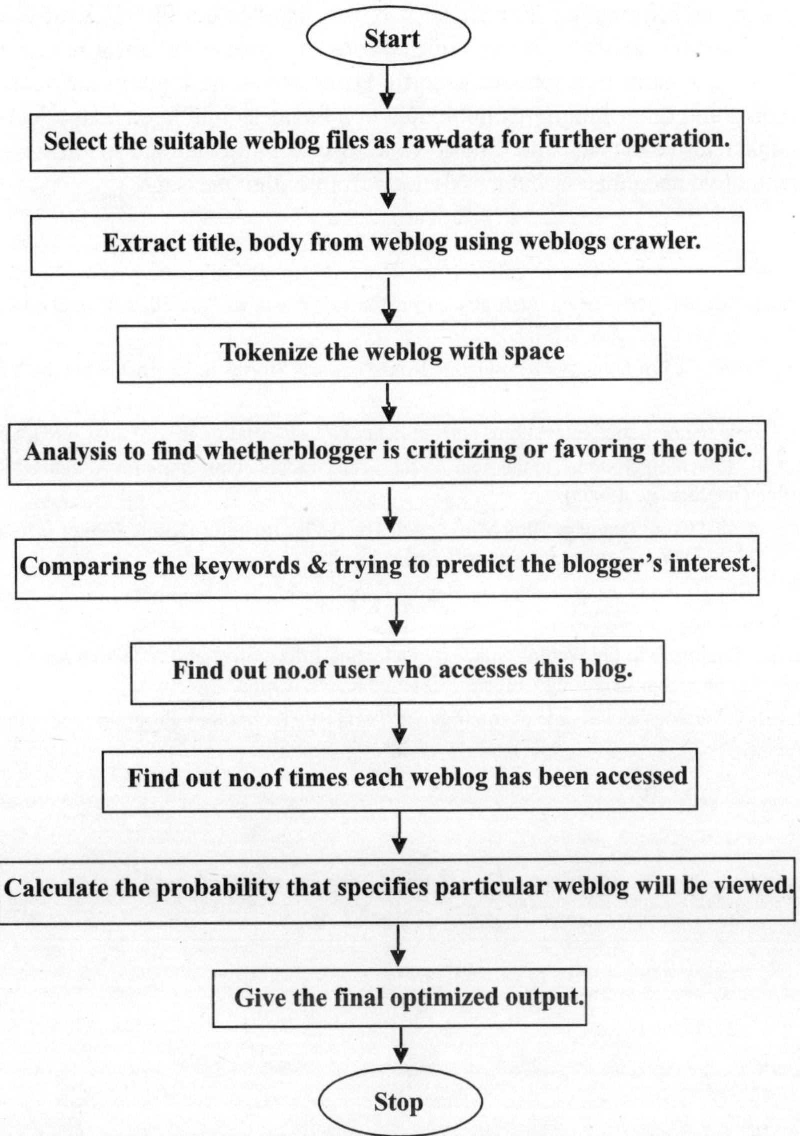

Snapshots

Sample blog and corresponding tokenized data is shown as partial result of the work.

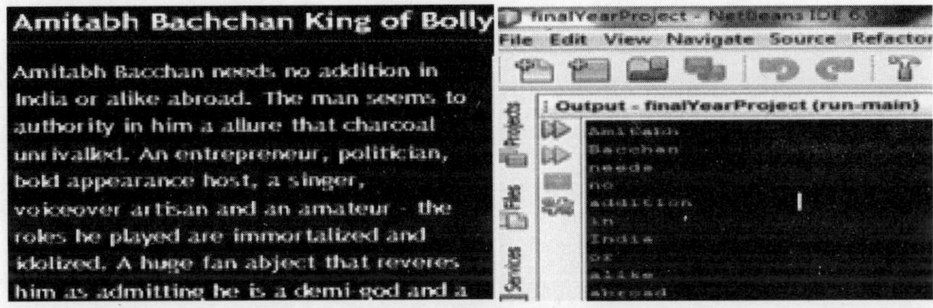

Fig. 3   Weblog and its tokenized data.

4. CONCLUSION

Blogs are a source of enormous information. For a user it is very hard to get the relevant information from this huge network. Proposed work is weblogs analysis that provides means to correlate the information found on different blogs. This described an end-to-end system that gathers specific types of online content and delivers analytics based on classification, phrase finding and other mining technologies in a business intelligence application. The analysis system allows a user to rapidly characterize the data and drill down to discover and validate specific issues. The system delivers both qualitative and quantitative accounts of features derived from online messages.

References

1. Natalie Glance & et. al., "Deriving Marketing Intelligence from Online Discussion", Intelliseek Applied Research center, Pittsburgh, PA 15217, KDD'05, Chicago, illilois, USA, (2005).

2. Andrew S. Gordon, "Mining Commonsense Knowledge from Personal Stories in Internet Weblogs", Institute for Creative Techno University of California, USA.

3. Jeffrey C_ Reynar, "Topic segmentation- algorithms and applications", dissertation in computer science & information technology.

4. Kosuke Numaa &et al, "A Weblog grounded to the Real World", The Graduate University for Advanced Studies (Sokendai), American association for artificial intelligence, (2005).

5. Andreas Juffinger & et. al., "Cross language Blog Mining and Trend Visualization" Know-Center Inffeldgasse 21A/II Graz, Austria, 18th International World Wide Web Conference, Madrid, Spain, (2009).

6. Nikhil Belsare &et al, "BlogHarvest: Blog Mining and Search Framework", Tech Mahindra Ltd. Pune India, International Conference on Management of Data, Delhi, India,(2006).

7. Xiaochuan Ni &et al," Exploring in the Weblog Space by Detecting Informative and Affective Articles", Department of Computer Science and Engineering Shanghai Jiao-Tong University, Shanghai, P.R. China.

8. John Griffith, "BlogINT: Weblogs as a Source of Intelligence", MITRE, Technology Program access from www.mitire.org.

CHAPTER 25

Web Index Recommendations

M. Sree Vani[1], Aruna Malapati[2] and O. Yaswanth Babu[3]
[1]Associate Professor, Department of CSE, MGIT, Gandipet, Hyderabad -500079,
[2]Assistant Professor, Computer Science and Information Science Group, Bits-Pilani, Hyderabad Campus,
Hyderabad (AP)-500079, India
[3]Senior IT Engineer, TCS, Gachibowli, Hyderabad (MS)-500079, India
E-mail: osreevani@gmail.com; aruna.ranganath@gmail.com; oyaswanth@gmail.com

ABSTRACT

Web usage mining is the automatic discovery of user access patterns from Web servers. Analyzing server's data can help organizations determine the life time of customers, cross marketing strategies across products, and effectiveness of promotional campaigns, among other things. Web index pages are pages that contain references or brief summaries of other pages. The goal is to identify whether a new web index page will interest a user or not through analyzing the web index pages that the user has browsed. We designed a new system called Web Index Recommendations for discovery and analysis of user patterns. User patterns (i.e. Entry/Exit times) are successfully identified and are recorded in a database. Upon analyzing the user's behaviour a fresh web index page is derived. We derive this by calculating the difference between the Entry/Exit times of all the pages the user has visited. The next time the user login's the user is presented with a revised web index page.

Keywords: Web Mining, Web Indexing, User Patterns.

1. INTRODUCTION

With the explosive growth of information sources available on the World Wide Web, it has become increasingly necessary for users to utilize recommender systems to track and analyze their usage patterns. Recommender systems have enhanced e-business by converting browsers to buyers, increasing cross-sell by identifying related products, and building loyalty. These systems primarily use association rule mining for pattern detection. In an e- business scenario, a recommender system uses user's /customer's web logs as data sources. In this paper, we designed a new system called Web Index Recommendations for discovery and analysis of user patterns. Web index pages are pages that contain references or brief summaries of other pages. These pages contain plentiful information by means of references, leaving the detailed presentation to their linked pages. A example of a web index pages is the health entry of Yahoo (http://health.yahoo.com), it is shown in Fig. 1.

The goal is to identify whether a new web index page will interest a user or not through analyzing the web index pages that the user has browsed. A positive web index page is such a page that the user is interested in at least one of its linked pages. [18]. A negative web index page is such a page that none of its linked pages interested the user. The difficulty added in this learning lies in that the available information about the user is whether he or she is interested in an index page, instead of specifying the concrete links that he or she is really interested in. There are many web index pages

Fig. 1 Web index page

on Internet. Some of these pages may contain issues interesting to the web user while some may not. It would be interesting to analyze automatically these pages and to show to the user only the pages which contain issues interesting for him or her. The web index recommendation problem consists of building a model to establish exactly which web page index it is that interests a given user from among the contents of a myriad of web index pages that have already been labelled as being "of interest" or "not of interest" for this particular user.

The rest of this paper is organized as follows. Section 2 presents Literature Survey. Section 3 describes the problem definition and Methodology. Section 4 describes Pseudo code of Application. Section 5 presents Conclusion and Future work.

2. LITERATURE SURVEY

2.1. Web Mining

Since the advent of the Internet, many studies have investigated the possibility of extracting knowledge and patterns from the Web, because it is publicly available and contains a rich set of resources. Many Web mining techniques are adopted from data mining, text mining, and information retrieval research [1], [2]. Most of these studies aimed to discover resources, patterns, and knowledge from the Web and Web-related data (such as Web server logs). Web mining research can be classified into three categories: Web content mining, Web structure mining, and Web usage Mining [6].

2.1.1. Web Usage Mining

Web usage mining focuses on using data mining techniques to analyze search logs or other activity logs to find interesting patterns. A Web server log contains information about every visit to the pages hosted on the server, such as files requested, user's IP address, and timestamp. By performing analysis on Web usage log data, Web mining systems can discover knowledge about a system's usage characteristics and the users' interests. Such knowledge can be used for personalized Web applications, marketing, Website evaluation, and decision support [4], [16], [17].

2.1.2 Web Structure Mining

Web structure mining studies the model underlying the link structures of the Web. Such models have been widely used to infer important information about Web pages. Hyperlinks among Web pages are usually indicators of high relevance or good quality. Web structure mining has been used for search engine result ranking, with Page Rank [13] and HITS [14] being the most widely used, and has also been applied to analyze online activities of different social groups [15].

2.1.3 Web Content Mining

Web content mining refers to the discovery of useful information from Web contents, including text, images, audio, video, etc. Resource discovery from the Web [7]–[9], Web document categorization and clustering [10], [11] and information extraction from Web pages [12] are important Web content mining topics.

2.2. Survey of existing systems

Most web browsers today come with a start page that contain a GUI consisting of a set of tabs which contain links to all the pages the user has visited. The start page also contains the recently closed web pages and also history [5]. But a web browser will restrict a user from accessing highly confidential or restricted information. A web browser will lose user's information once the cookies are deleted and the session expires, the user's information is no longer with the web browser.

2.2.1. Auditing and User Accountability

Do you know who is accessing your sensitive database data? Business mandates and compliance requirements are driving organizations to audit all database activity. Database audit trails must include the individual SQL query, the database response, the timestamp, and, most importantly, he individual user that accessed or changed database data. Unfortunately, for many multi-tier applications, it can be difficult—if not impossible—to identify the end user from database transactions alone [23]. Universal User Tracking tracks end users without requiring any changes existing databases, applications, or network. Universal User Tracking supports enterprise applications, such as Oracle E-Business Suite, SAP, PeopleSoft, J.D. Edwards, and Siebel, as well as custom and internally-developed applications. With Universal User Tracking, organizations can identify the actual end users that accessed their most sensitive information: customer, employee, and financial data. By tracking application and database users, Secure-Sphere can display user IDs in security alerts, audit logs, and reports. Web Application User Tracking leverages Imperva's expertise of Web technology to recognize when users login to an application. By associating a session ID, such as a cookie or session parameter, with a user name, Secure-Sphere can track all Web activity by user name. Web Application User Tracking enables Secure-Sphere to recognize the individual application users that perpetrated malicious attacks. In addition, Secure-Sphere can be configured to monitor or block individual application users.

2.2.2. Universal User Tracking

Keywords on the login page, keywords on the successful or failed results page, and when an application sets a session cookie. Secure-Sphere customers can verify that the automatically learned information is correct or edit the User Tracking settings. Once the learning process is complete, Secure-Sphere will dynamically track every user login. Secure-Sphere will bind the user ID with the corresponding HTTP session token. This allows Secure-Sphere to track the application user throughout the HTTP session.

Direct User Tracking is the most basic type of user tracking, relying on the native database authentication mechanisms. Direct User Tracking records the database user ID, hostname, IP address, and operating system name of the user directly accessing the database. When users login directly to a database through a dedicated connection, Secure-Sphere associates the user ID, hostname, IP and system name with all subsequent SQL transactions performed by the user [23].

Database User ID is the user name that a user supplies when authenticating to the database. For multi-tier applications, the Database User ID is the name of the application server that connects to the database. Client Device Hostname is the name of the machine from which database transactions originate. Client IP Address is the IP address of the machine from which database transactions originate.

2.2.3 Enhances Auditing and Security Using Universal User Tracking

Universal User Tracking is an important element of Secure-Sphere's database and web application security and auditing capabilities.

2.2.3.1 Monitoring and Alerts

Because of Universal User Tracking, Secure-Sphere can display the end user ID in all security alerts. User-specific alerts augment understanding of security events and facilitate forensics efforts.

2.2.3.2 Audit Logs

Secure-Sphere records user information in audit trails. Each SQL transaction is accurately associated with an application user. Universal user tracking not only increases the business relevance of audit log messages, but it helps organizations meet today's stringent compliance requirements.

2.2.3.3 Reports

User information included in many pre-defined reports and administrators can generate security and activity reports by user. Universal User Tracking enables granular reports of user access even in connection pooling environments.

2.2.3.4 Access Policies

Because Secure-Sphere tracks both database and application users, Administrators can enforce access policies by user ID. Administrators can create custom rules that specify what URLs can be accessed or what SQL queries can be executed. In addition, if a specific security event occurs, Secure-Sphere can be configured to monitor or block the user responsible for a given period of time.

2.2.3.5 User Profiling of Direct Database Users

By positively identifying users, Secure-Sphere can profile legitimate user activity and, as a result, detect usage anomalies. Secure-Sphere tracks user names, IP addresses, hostnames and operating system names in its user profile. If a database user performs an unusual database transaction or if a user logs in from an atypical IP address, Secure-Sphere can generate an alert or block the transaction

3. PROBLEM DEFINITION

Upon visiting a certain website the user is confronted with an index that consists of links to other pages. The user may find one or two pages in the index page to his liking and hence spends more time on those webpages. When he visits the same website he might end up doing the same process all over again. This process may consume time and lead to frustration.

3.1 Mod ules

Our Project is based on the client server architecture and for that we have a module that performs the functions of a client i.e. USER and the role of server is handled by the ADMINISTRATOR. Thus the modules involved in our project are.

3.1.1 User Module

A user is given a login id and a password and with those two credentials the user performs a login operation that is similar to typing in a URL in the address bar of a browser and then the user is presented with a simple web page that consists of links to other pages, This page is termed as a Web Index Page. The user clicks on only those links that interest him and browses the web site and then performs the logout operation that is very synonymous to closing the webpage.

3.1.2 Administrator Module

The Administrator plays the role of a server in handling User (client) requests, the responsibility of the administrator is record the user actions i.e. the amount of time spent on each page by the user by calculating the entry/exit time of the user. The Administrator is invisible in the context of the website.

On Analyzing the entry/exit times of user the administrator will provide the user with a fresh web index page the next time the user visits the same website. For carrying out this task the administrator records the entry/exit times in a secure database.

3.2 Methodology

The design of the entire system is done using UML which is a standard way to write a system's blueprints, covering conceptual things, such as business processes and system functions, as well as concrete things, such as classes written in a specific programming language, database schemas and reusable software components.

The class diagrams use case diagrams and interaction diagrams are provided to get an overall idea of the internal happenings and also the relations between various entities. Refer to Fig. 2, which depicts the overall sequence diagram of the application.

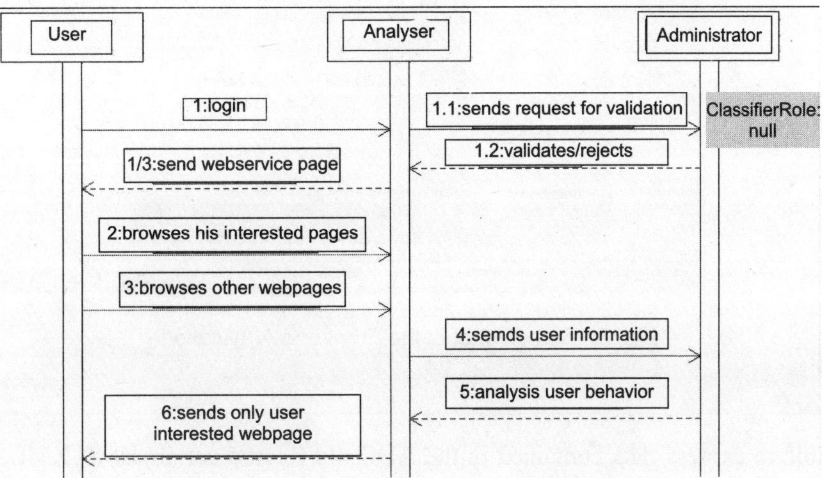

Fig. 2   Sequence Diagram of the application

The above sequence diagram houses three objects user, analyzer, and administrator and depicts the flow of control between them.

3.2.1 Client Application Development

Client applications are the closest to a traditional style of application in Windows-based programming. These are the types of applications that display windows or forms on the desktop, enabling a user to perform a task. Client applications include applications such as word processors and spreadsheets, as well as custom business applications such as data-entry tools, reporting tools, and so on. Client applications usually employ windows, menus, buttons, and other GUI elements, and they likely access local resources such as the file system and peripherals such as printers.

3.2.2 Server Application Development

Server-side applications in the managed world are implemented through runtime hosts. Unmanaged applications host the common language runtime, which allows your custom managed code to control the behaviour of the server. This model provides you with all the features of the common language runtime and class library while gaining the performance and scalability of the host server.

3.2.3 Server-side managed code

ASP.NET is the hosting environment that enables developers to use the .NET Framework to target Web-based applications. XML Web services, an important evolution in Web-based technology, are distributed, server-side application components similar to common Web sites. However, unlike Web-based applications, XML Web services components have no UI and are not targeted for browsers such as Internet Explorer and Netscape Navigator. Instead, XML Web services consist of reusable software components designed to be consumed by other applications, such as traditional client applications, Web-based applications, or even other XML Web services. As a result, XML Web services technology is rapidly moving application development and deployment into the highly distributed environment of the Internet. Finally, like Web Forms pages in the managed environment, your XML Web service will run with the speed of native machine language using the scalable communication of IIS. Refer to Fig. 3 which shows the screen shot of the front end application.

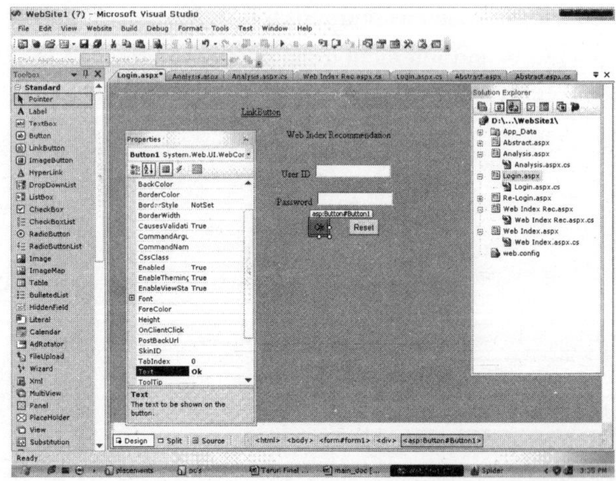

Fig. 3 Screen shot of the Front end Application

3.2.4 XML Support

Although it was possible to express data contained in the ADO.old Record-set object as XML, the process wasn't as straightforward as it might have been. Support for XML was added as an afterthought in ADO.old, and it was supported in an extremely clunky way; in fact, you could argue that ADO.old's XML support was so convoluted that it made sense to use it only in the context of data operability with other ADO data sources.

XML support in ADO.NET is provided through the DataSet object. The DataSet can always be rendered as XML with a single method call, and the XML that it renders is structured in a way that's easy to work with, whether you're working within the .NET framework or on some other platform.

3.2.5 Factored Data Access API

Developers liked ADO. Old because the number of objects it provided was small and easy to understand. In fact, it was possible to perform most common data operations with a limited knowledge of only two objects: the Recordset and Connection objects.

The architects of ADO.NET have attempted to divide its functionality in a more granular fashion. The objective behind this is to give you more lightweight objects.

3.2.6 No Support for Server-Side Cursors

A cursor is a software construct that enables your code to step though rows in a result set one row at a time. There are different types of cursors; some cursors enable you to jump around from one record to another in the result-set with impunity (so-called scrolling cursors). In the Microsoft database cosmology, there are also "forward-only" or "firehose" cursors, which permit you only to move from the beginning of the recordset to the end without moving backward; some database programming purists argue that a cursor that does not scroll is not really a cursor at all.

3.2.7 Scenarios for Using ADO.NET

One of the most common questions developers ask when attacking a new API is how to do the most basic operations that they are accustomed to performing with the perfectly good API that they already use it.

4. INDEX PAGE REPRESENTATION

4.1. Pseudo Code of the Application

```
protected void Page_Load(object sender, EventArgs e)
{
Label1 .Text = "welcome" + " " + Session["user_id"]; }

protected void LinkButton1_Click1(object sender, EventArgs e)
{
Response.Redirect("Technology.aspx");
}

protected void LinkButton2_Click1(object sender, EventArgs e)
{
Response.Redirect("Sports.aspx");
}

protected void LinkButton3_Click(object sender, EventArgs e)
{
Response.Redirect("page3.aspx");
}

protected void LinkButton3_Click1(object sender, EventArgs e)
{
Response.Redirect("page3.aspx");
}
protected void LinkButton3_Click2(object sender, EventArgs e)
{
Response.Redirect("Finance.aspx");
}
protected void LinkButton4_Click(object sender, EventArgs e)
{
Response.Redirect("astrology.aspx");
}
```

4.2 Statistical Representation of Application

The Fig. 4 illustrates our application. It contains Technology, Sports, Movies and Finance web pages. A particular user total time spent in Technology page is 20 sec , total time spent in sports page is 25 sec , total time spent in movies page is 55 sec and total time spent in finance page is 10 sec. User spent more time in Movies web page. So, our system will recommend Movies web page, when the same user relogins. Fig 5 illustrates Accuracy of our application. We are succeeded up to 90% to recommend more interested web pages, when user relogins.

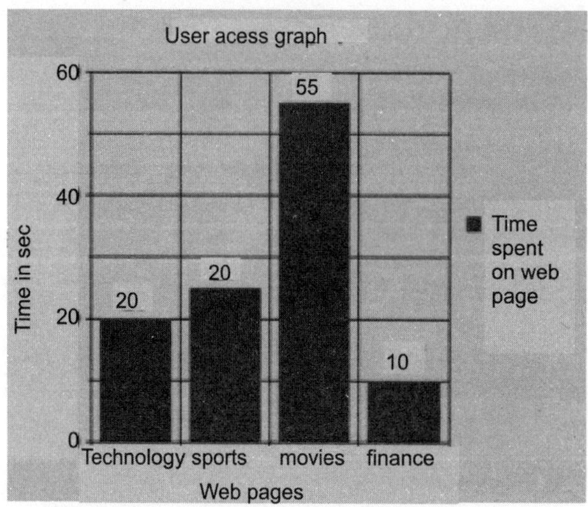

Fig. 4   Access graph of Application

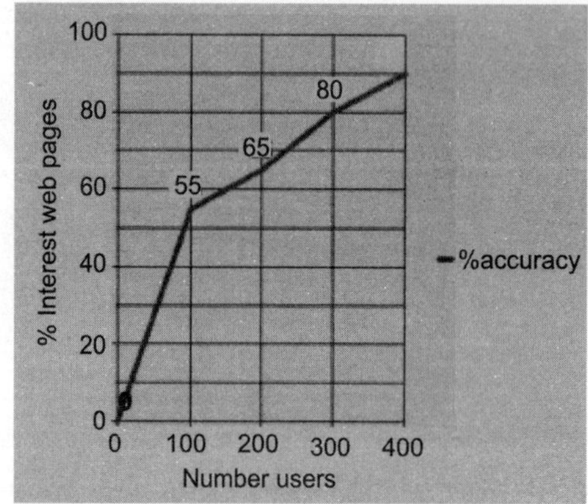

Fig. 5   Accuracy graph of application

5.   CONCLUSION AND FUTURE WORK

We have included all requirements while developing this package. The system has been implemented and tested successfully. It meets the information requirements specified to a great extent. The next time the user login's the user is presented with a revised web index page. We are succeeded up to 90% to recommend more user interested web pages to the users. There is always room for improvement in software, however efficient it may be. And throughout the development of the system, proper consideration has been given for a wide range of new enrichments in the future. We can classify users based on their interests. The classification is carried out with the help of a simple rule based qualifier. We can enhance security of a website by restricting the user access to new/unseen Web Pages. Merging our project with Google analytics will help creating a faster and automated version of analyzing user patterns.

References

1. O. Etzioni, "The World-Wide Web: Quagmire or gold mine?," Commun. ACM, vol. 39, no. 11, pp. 65–68, 996.

2. H. Chen and M. Chau, "Web mining: Machine learning for Web applications," Anu. Rev. Inf. Sci., vol. 38, pp. 289–329, 2004.

3. M. Chau, B. Shiu, I. Chan, and H. Chen, "Redips: Backlink search and analysis on the Web for business intelligence analysis," J. Amer. Soc. Inf. Sci. Technol., vol. 58, no. 3, pp. 351–365, 2007.

4. X. Fang, M. Chau, P.J. Hu, Z. Yang, and O.R.L. Sheng, "Web mining based objective metrics for measuring Website navigability," in Proc. Int. Conf. Inf. Syst., Milwaukee, WI, 2006.

5. B. Liu, M. Hu, and J. Cheng, "Opinion observer: Analyzing and comparing opinions on the Web," in Proc. 2005 WWW Conf., Chiba, Japan, 2005.

6. R. Kosala and H. Blockeel, "Web mining research: A survey," ACM SIGKDD Explor., vol. 2, no. 1, pp. 1–15, 2000.

7. J. Cho, H. Garcia-Molina, and L. Page, "Efficient crawling through URL ordering," in Proc. 1998 WWW Conf., Brisbane, Australia, 1998.

8. S. Chakrabarti, M.V.D. Berg, and B. Dom, "Focused crawling: A new approach to topic-specific Web resource discovery," in Proc. 1999 WWW Conf., Toronto, Canada, 1999.

9. M. Chau and H. Chen, "Comparison of three vertical search spiders," IEEE Computer, vol. 36, no. 5, pp. 56–62, 2003.

10. O. Zamir and O. Etzioni, "Grouper: A dynamic clustering interface to Web search results," in Proc. 1999 WWW Conf., Toronto, Canada, 1999.

11. W.Y. Chung, G. Lai, A. Bonillas, W. Xi, and H. Chen, "Organizing domain- specific information on the Web: An experiment on the Spanish business Web directory," Int. J. Hum.-Comput. St., vol. 66, no. 2, pp. 51–66, 2008.

12. M. Hurst, "Layout and language: Challenges for table understanding on the Web," in Proc. 1st Int. Workshop Web Document Analysis, Seattle, WA, 2001.

13. S. Brin and L. Page, "The anatomy of a large-scale hypertextual Web search engine," in Proc. 1998 WWW Conf., Brisbane, Australia, 1998.

14. J. Kleinberg, "Authoritative sources in a hyperlinked environment," in Proc. 9th ACM-SIAM Symp. Discrete Algorithms, San Francisco, CA, 1998.

15. M. Chau and J. Xu, "Mining communities and their relationships in blogs: A study of online hate groups," Int. J. Hum.-Comput. St., vol. 65, no. 1, pp. 57–70, 2007.

16. H. M. Chen and M. D. Cooper, "Using clustering techniques to detect usage patterns in a Web-based information system," J. Amer. Soc. Inf. Sci. Tech., vol. 52, no. 11, pp. 888–904, 2001.

17. G. Marchionini, "Co-evolution of user and organizational interfaces: A longitudinal case study of WWW dissemination of national statistics.

18. Multiple Instances Learning with Multi Objective Genetic Programming for Web Mining IEEE 2008 Hybrid Intelligent Systems. "Amelia Zafra and Eva Gibaja and Sebastian Ventura, Department of Computer Science and Numerical Analysis.University of C'ordoba".

CHAPTER 26

Freshness Tuning in Focused Crawler

Swati Mali, Suman Ninoroya, Kirtikumar Dupare and B.B. Meshram

VJTI, Mumbai (MS) India

E-mail: swati_mali@yahoo.co.in, sumanninoria1@gmail.com, kirtikumard@rediffmail.com, bbmeshram@vjti.org.in

ABSTRACT

The dynamic web keeps on changing and unnoticing an important event makes the result incomplete. All of the web pages do not change. Even if some of them change, they do not do the same with same frequency. So, having the same revisit frequency for all earlier visited pages merely creates overheads and does not contribute positively to the result. Here's a proposal of a focused crawler that talks about the strategy of how and when to revisit the earlier visited sites.

Keywords: Web Mining, Focused Crawling, Change Detection, Freshness Tuning, Page Age.

1. INTRODUCTION

A crawler is an automated script, which independently browses the World Wide Web. It starts with a seed URL and then follows the links on each page in a Breadth First or a Depth First method [1]. A Web Crawler searches through all the Web Servers to find information about a particular topic. However, searching all the Web Servers and the pages, are not realistic, because of the growth of the Web and their refresh rates. To traverse the web quickly and entirely is an expensive, unrealistic goal because of the required hardware and network resources [1, 2].

The web page has a structure and contains text, audio, video and images. Several algorithms have been proposed to store these pages and detect the page change. Saving the pages in tree structure is more difficult to store, modify and compare too. This paper tries to address the issue of how the web page should be stored and when it should be reassessed. This scheme assures that no important webpage that can influence the result is missed.

The paper starts with the introduction to the topic and is followed by literature review in Section 2. Section 3 details the proposed system architecture. The implementation details are illustrated in Section 4. The experimental evaluation and references are given in last two Sections 5 and 6.

2. LITERATURE REVIEW

Crawlers are widely used today. Crawlers for the major search engines (e.g., Altavista, InfoSeek, Excite, and Lycos) attempt to visit most text Web pages, in order to build content indexes. Other crawlers may also visit many pages, but may look only for certain types of information (e.g., email addresses). At the other end of the spectrum, we have personal crawlers that scan for pages of interest to a particular user, in order to build a fast access cache.

The design of a good crawler presents many challenges. Externally, the crawler must avoid overloading Web sites or network links as it goes about its business. Internally, the crawler must deal with huge volumes of data. Unless it has unlimited computing resources and unlimited time, it must carefully decide what URLs to scan and in what order. The crawler must also decide how frequently to revisit pages it has already seen, in order to keep its client informed of changes on the Web. In spite of all these challenges, and the importance of crawlers on the Internet, very little research has been done on crawlers.

2.1 Focused Crawler

Roughly, a crawler starts with the URL for an initial page P0. It retrieves P0, extracts any URLs in it, and adds them to a queue of URLs to be scanned. Then the crawler gets URLs from the queue (in some order), and repeats the process. Every page that is scanned is given to a client that saves the pages, creates an index for the pages, or summarizes or analyzes the content of the pages[1] [3] [5]. Focused crawler is a special kind of web crawlers those do not try to cover the entire web but then too give all the relevant search results.

Definition: A focused crawler is a program used for searching information related to some interested topics from the Internet [1] [2].

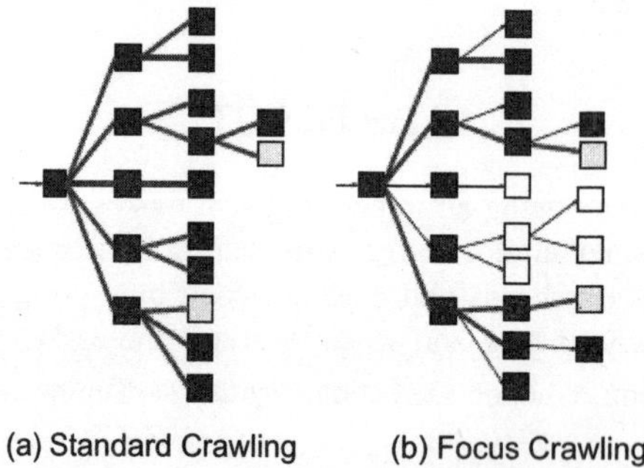

Fig. 1 Difference between focused crawler and universal crawler

A standard crawler follows each link, typically applying a breadth first strategy. If the crawler starts from a document which is i steps from a target document, all the documents that are up to $i - 1$ steps from the starting document must be downloaded before the crawler hits the target. A focused crawler tries to identify the most promising links, and ignores off-topic documents. If the crawler starts from a document which is i steps from a target document, it downloads a small subset of all the documents that are up to $i - 1$ steps from the starting document. If the search strategy is optimal the crawler takes only i steps to discover the target. A focused crawler efficiently seeks out documents about a specific topic and guides the search based on both the content and link structure of the web [2]. Figure 1 graphically illustrates the difference between an exhaustive breadth-first crawler and a typical focused crawler. A focused crawler implements a strategy that associates a score with each link in the pages it has downloaded [8, 9, 10]. The links are sorted according to the scores and inserted in a queue. A best first search is performed by popping the next page to analyze from the head of the queue. This strategy ensures that the crawler preferentially pursues promising crawl paths.

2.2 Crawling Policies

The behavior of a Web crawler is the outcome of a combination of policies [1] [3]:
- A *selection policy* that states which pages to download,
- A *re-visit policy* that states when to check for changes to the pages,
- A *politeness policy* that states how to avoid overloading Web sites, and
- A *parallelization policy* that states how to coordinate distributed Web crawlers.

Every crawler follows the Selection policy as it marks the most relevant pages to download. Moreover, the Web has a very dynamic nature. By the time a Web crawler has finished its crawl, many events could have happened. These events can include creations, updates and deletions. From the search engine's point of view, there is a cost associated with not detecting an event, and thus having an outdated copy of a resource. This makes the implementation of revisit policy an important matter. the question of whether the page should be recrawled or not can be answered by two properties of the page viz, freshness and age.

2.3.1 Freshness

This is a binary measure that indicates whether the local copy is accurate or not. The freshness of a page p in the repository at time t is defined as:

$$Fp\ (t) = 1 \quad \text{if } p \text{ is equal to local copy at time } t. \text{ Otherwise,}$$
$$Fp\ (t) = 0$$

2.3.2 Age

This is a measure that indicates how outdated the local copy is. The age of a page p in the repository, at time t is defined as:

$$AP\ (t) = 0 \quad \text{if } p \text{ is not modified at time } t. \text{ Otherwise,}$$
$$Ap\ (t) = (t - \text{modification time of } t)$$

3. SYSTEM ARCHITECTURE

The following diagram provides an overview of the following major crawling processes:
- Starting the crawl and populating the crawl queue
- Attempting to fetch a URL and index the document
- Following links within the document

The sections following the diagram provide details about each of the these major processes.

By crawling URLs in this priority, the crawler ensures that the freshest, most relevant content appears in the index. After configuring the crawl path and preparing content for crawling, the crawler can be started as a continuous or full crawl. When crawling begins, the crawler populates the crawl queue with URLs. The following diagram provides an overview of starting the crawl and populating the crawl queue.

Source of URL	Basis for Priority
Start URLs (highest)	Fixed priority
New URLs that have never been crawled	Page relevance by link and topic analysis
Newly discovered URLs	For a new crawl, estimated Page relevance by link and topic analysis
	For a recrawl, estimated Page relevance by link and topic analysis and a factor that ensures that new documents are crawled before previously indexed content
URLs that are already in the index (lowest)	Page relevance by link and topic analysis, the last time it was crawled, and estimated change frequency

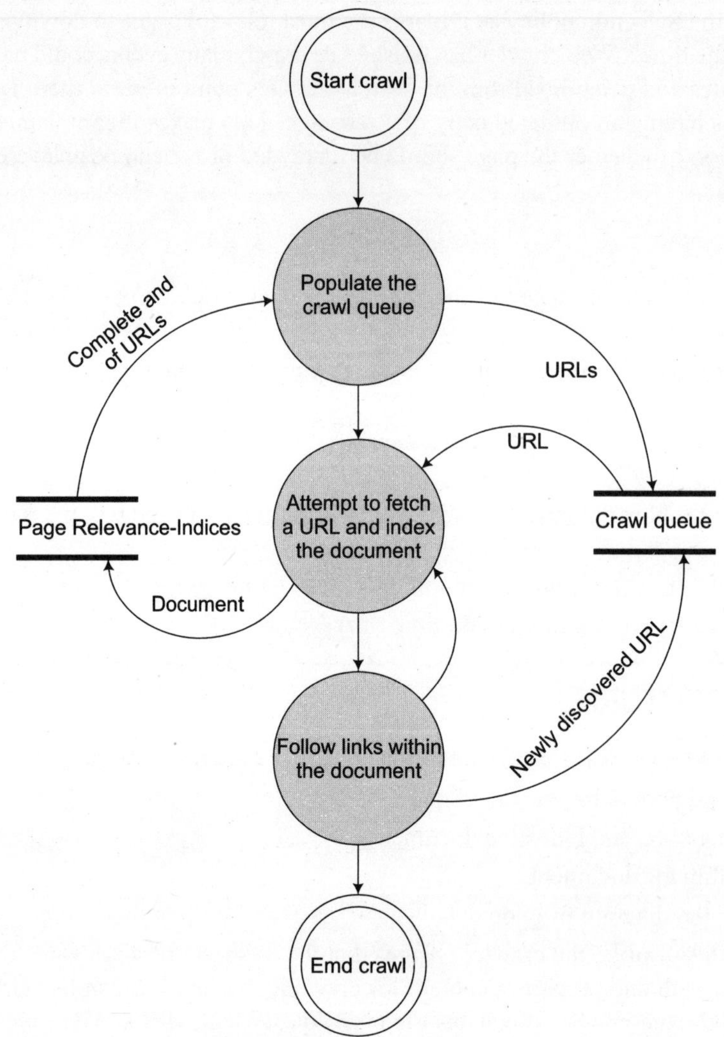

The crawler attempts to fetch the URL with the highest priority in the crawl queue. The following diagram provides an overview of this process.

If the crawler successfully fetches a URL, it downloads the document and caches it for indexing. Generally, if the crawler fails to fetch a URL, it deletes the URL from the crawl queue. Depending on several factors, the crawler may take further action when it fails to fetch a URL. When fetching documents from a slow server, the crawler paces the process so that it does not cause server problems. The crawler administrator can also adjust the number of concurrent connections to a server by configuring the web server host load schedule.

Cached Documents

When the crawler successfully fetches a document, it caches a copy of the document. To detect changes to cached documents when recrawling it, the crawler:

1. Downloads the document.
2. Computes a checksum of the file.
3. Compares the checksum to the checksum that was stored in the index the last time the document was indexed.
4. If the checksum has changed since the last modification time, the crawler replaces the document in cache. If the checksum has not changed, the crawler retains the cached document.

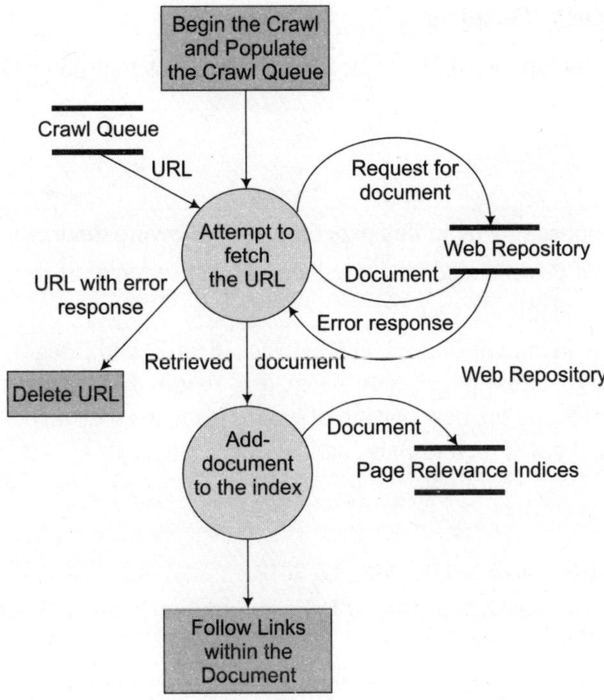

4. FRESHNESS TUNING

One can improve the performance of a continuous crawl using URL patterns on the **Crawl and Index and Freshness Tuning.** The **Crawl and Index combined with Freshness Tuning** page provides four categories of crawl behaviors. To apply a crawl behavior, specify URL patterns for the behavior.

1. Behavior Crawl Frequently

Use Crawl Frequently patterns for URLs that are dynamic and change frequently. One can use the Crawl Frequently patterns to give hints to the crawler during the early stages of crawling, before the crawler has a history of how frequently URLs actually change.

Any URL that matches one of the Crawl Frequently patterns is scheduled to be recrawled at least once every day. The maximum rate at which a URL can be scheduled to be recrawled is once every 15 minutes. In other words, the minimum wait time is 15 minutes. For this to happen, the URL's content must change at least every 30 minutes. If you have too many URLs in Crawl Frequently patterns, wait time will increase.

Behavior Crawl Infrequently

Use Crawl Infrequently Patterns for URLs that are relatively static and do not change frequently. Any URL that matches one of the Crawl Infrequently patterns is not crawled more than once every 90 days, regardless of its page relevance or how frequently it changes. One can use this feature for Web pages that do not change and do not need to be recrawled. One can also use it for Web pages where a small part of their content changes frequently, but the important parts of their content does not change.

Behavior Always Force Recrawl

Use Always Force Recrawl patterns to prevent the crawler from crawling a URL from cache.

Behavior   Recrawl   these   URL   Patterns

Use Recrawl these URL Patterns to submit a URL to be recrawled. URLs that you enter here are recrawled as soon as possible.

5.   CONCLUSION

The architecture that has been proposed by us in this paper has the following distinct advantages:

- The centralized database of downloaded URLs reduces the dependency of the system.
- The architecture is easily scalable.
- It understands the dynamic feature of the web and helps us identify and categorize frequently updated pages and the other categories. It revisits the pages only when it is required and thus, it strikes the perfect balance in revisiting old pages and crawling the new portion of web. This helps the crawler to clearly determine whether or not a page has changed and saves memory and bandwidth overheads.

References

1. www.wikipedia.org/web_crawler, accessed last May 12, 2010.
2. Mukhopadhyay et al, "A New Approach to Design Domain Specific Ontology Based Web Crawler", ICIT 2007, 10th International Conference on Information Technology, 289 – 291, Dec. 2007
3. Cui Xiaoqing Yan Chun, "An evolutionary relevance calculation measure in topic crawler" CCCM 2009, ISECS International Colloquium on Computing, Communication, Control, and Management, 267 – 270, Aug 2009
4. Zheng, Chen, "HAWK: a Focused crawler with content and link analysis", E-business engineering, 2008, ICEBE'08, IEEE international conference, pages 677-680, Oct 2008.
5. Zheng, Zhaou ET el, "URL Rule based focused crawler", E-business engineering, ICEBE'08, IEEE international conference, Oct 2008, pages 147-154, 2008.
6. Bidoki, Yazdani et el, "FICA: A fast intelligent crawling algorithm", Web Intelligence, IEEE/ACM/WIC International conference on Intelligent agent technology, Pages 635-641, 2007.
7. Peisu, Ke et el, "A Framework of deep web crawler", 27th Chinese Proceedings of the 27th Chinese Control Conference, Pages 582-586, July 16-18, 2008.
8. Yadav, Sharma et el, "Architecture for parallel crawling and algorithm for change detection in web pages", 10th International Conference on Information Technology, Pages 258-264, ICIT 2007.
9. Junghoo Cho, Hector Garcia-Molina, Lawrence Page, |Efficient crawling through URL ordering", 7th International WWW Conference, April 14-18, Brisbane, 1998.
10. Yuan, Yin et el, "Improvement of pagerank for focused crawler", 8th ACIS International Conference on Software Engineering, Artificial Intelligence, Networking, and Parallel/Distributed Computing, Pages 797-802, SNPD 2007.

CHAPTER 27

Link Mining: A Grand Challenge of Data Mining

Dhanashri Wategaonkar and Jyoti Gadekar
MIT College of Engineering, Paud Road Pune (MS) India
E-mail: wdhanashri20; jyo.gadekar@gmail.com

ABSTRACT

A newly emerging research area at the intersection of research in social network and link analysis, hypertext and web mining, relational learning and inductive logic programming and graph mining. It is an important challenge for data mining to tackling the problem of mining richly structured datasets, where the objects are linked in some way. Links among the objects may demonstrate certain patterns, which can be helpful for many data mining tasks and are usually hard to capture with traditional statistical models. It discusses some ongoing challenges and suggests ideas that could be opportunities for solutions.

1. INTRODUCTION

A key emerging challenge for data mining is tackling the problem of mining richly structured, heterogeneous, multirelational datasets. These kinds of datasets are best described as networks or graphs. Here nodes are objects and edges are links [2]. Link mining encompasses a range of tasks including descriptive and predictive modeling. Link mining is a convergence of research in social network, link analysis, hyper text and web mining, graph mining, relational learning and inductive logic programming. We use the term link mining to put a special emphasis on the links moving them up to first-class citizens in the data analysis endeavor. However, and perhaps more important, it also represents an important and essential set of techniques for constructing useful applications of data mining in a wide variety of real and important domains. Link mining presents both challenges and opportunities [4]. It presents challenges because data mining techniques for non-linked data are inadequate for similar problems with linked data and because the combinatory of linked domains typically far exceed those of domains characterized by non-linked data. It presents opportunities because the structure of linked data provides both constraints on what can be inferred and additional information for inference than can be obtained from non-linked data. But with the introduction of links, new tasks also come to light. Examples include predicting the numbers of links, predicting the type of link between two objects, inferring the existence of a link, inferring the identity of an object, finding co-references, and discovering sub graph patterns. We define these tasks and describe them in more detail in section 3.

2. LINK MINING DOMAINS

As mentioned in the introduction, link mining puts a new twist on some classic data mining tasks. Here we provide a list of possible tasks [5].We illustrate each of them using first three domains as motivations:

- web data (**web**)
- bibliographic data (**cite**)
- epidemiological data (**epi**)
- communication data (**comm**)
- customer networks (**cust**)
- collaborative filtering problems (**cf**)
- trust networks (**trust**)
- biological data (**bio**)

Web Data domain: In it the objects are web pages, and links are in-links, out-links and co-citation links. Attributes include HTML tags, word appearances and anchor text [1].

Bibliographic Data domain: In a bibliographic domain, the objects include papers, authors, institutions, journals and conferences. Links include the paper citations, authorship and co-authorship, affiliations, and the appears-in relation between a paper and a journal or conference [1].

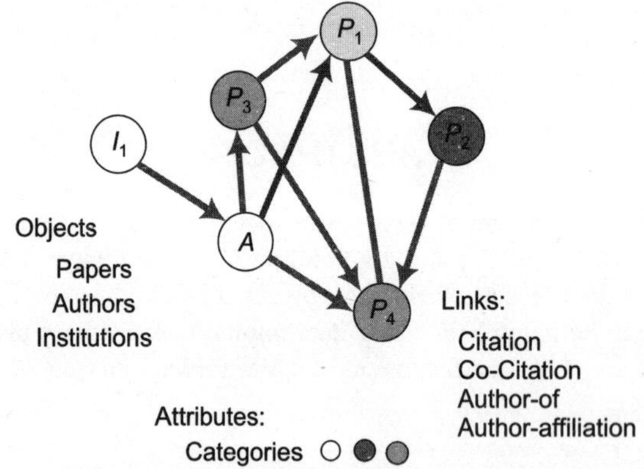

between people and which disease strain a person is infected with it.

3.   LINK MINING TASKS

Link mining embodies descriptive and predictive modeling. By considering links (the relationships between objects), more information is made available to the mining process. This brings about several new tasks. Here, some tasks are listed with examples from various domains.

Table 1   Classification of common link mining tasks.

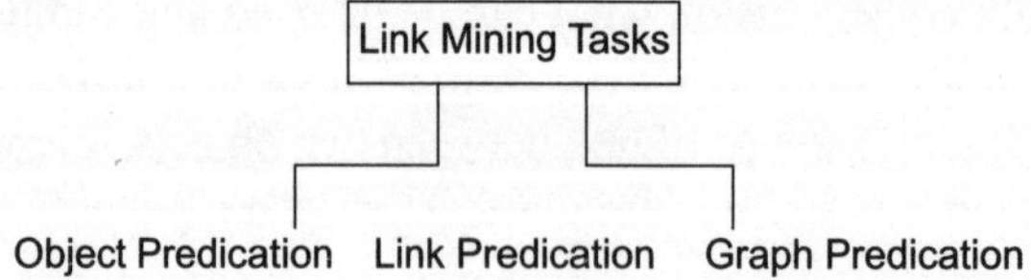

3.1   Object Prediction

Object Prediction is again classify into four different categories. We will see each and every deeply.

3.1.1 Object Classification

This predicts the category of an object based on its attributes and its links and attributes of linked object [6].

In Bibliographic domain it predicts the topic of a paper based on the words used in the paper, the topics of papers it cites, the research interests of the author [Figure 2.1].

3.1.2 Object Type Prediction

This predicting the type of an object based on its attributes and its links and attributes of linked objects[6]. In the bibliographic domain, an example of object type prediction is that it predict the venue type of a publication (conference, journal, and workshop) based on properties of the paper [Figure 2.1].

3.1.3 Object Identity

It also called as Object Reconciliation or Entity Resolution. It predicts when two objects are the same, based on their attributes and their links. This task is common in record linkage, duplicate elimination and information extraction [6]. In web domain, it predicts when two sites are mirrors of each other. In Bibliographic domain it predicts when two citations are referring to the same paper [Figure 2.1]. In epidemiology domain it predicts when two disease strains are the same.

3.1.4 Group Detection

Predicting when a set of entities belong to the same group based on clustering both object attribute values and link structuring. Identifying research communities [6]. An area of application is the identification of web communities where a web community is a collection of web pages that focus on a particular theme of topic. In Bibliographic domain similar example is the identification of research communities [Figure 2.1].

3.2 Link Prediction

In Link prediction, measures for analyzing the proximity of network nodes can be used to predict and rank new links. It classify into four categories as:

3.2.1 Link Classification

In Traditional classification methods, objects are classified based on the attribute that describe them [6]. It predicts type or purpose of link based on properties of the participating objects. In the web domain example of link-based classification that has received a fair amount of attention in web-page classification. In this problem, the goal is predict the category of a web page based onwards on the page, links between pages, anchor text and other attributes of the pages and the links. In the bibliographic domain, an example of link-based classification is predicting the category of a paper, based on its citations, the papers that cite it and cocitations (papers that are cited with this paper) [Figure 2.1]. In the epidemiology domain, an example is the task of predicting the disease type based on characteristics of the people (note the arbitrary possible prediction direction) or predicting the person's age, based on the disease they are infected with and the ages of the people they have been in contact with.

3.2.2 Link type Prediction

This predicts the type or purpose of a link, based on properties of the objects involved [6]. In the epidemiology domain, an example is the task of predicts whether two people who know each other are family members, coworkers. In the bibliographic domain, an example of this is predicting whether a paper will cite another paper or an advisor-advisee relationship between two coauthors [Figure 2.1]. Given Web page data, it try to predict whether a link on a page is an advertising link or a navigational link.

3.2.3 Link Cardinality Estimation

Link cardinality estimation has two forms. In first, it predicts the number of links to an object. In web domain, it predicts the authoritativeness of a page based on the number of in-links; identifying hubs based on the number of out-links, In Bibliographic domain it predicts the impact of a paper based on the number of citations [Figure 2.1]. In epidemiology domain it predicts the infectiousness of a disease based on the number of people diagnosed [6]. In second, it predicts the number of objects reached along a path from an objecting. It is important for estimating the number of objects that will be returned by a query. In web domain, it predicts number of pages retrieved by crawling a site. In Bibliographic domain it predicts the number of citations of a particular author in a specific journal. In epidemiology domain it predicts the number of elderly contacts for a particular patient.

3.2.4 Predicting Link Existence

This predicting whether a link exists between two objects. In the web domain it predicts whether there will be a link between two pages. In the bibliographic domain it predicts whether a paper will cite another paper [Figure 2.1]. In the epidemiology domain it predicting whom a patient came in contact.

3.3 Graph Prediction

Graph Prediction having different categories as:

3.3.1 Sub graph Identification

It finds characteristic sub graphs within networks. It is focus of graph-based data mining.In the bibliographic domain it is discovery of sub graphs corresponding to protein structures [Figure 2.1].

3.3.2 Predicate Invention

It induces a new general relation/link from existing links and paths. In the bibliographic domain it explain propose concept of advisor from co-author and financial support [Figure 2.1].

3.3.3 Metadata Mapping

Metadata mining can be used for schema mapping, schema discovery and schema reformulation. In the bibliographic domain it matching between two bibliographic sources [Figure 2.1].In web domain it predicts discovering schema from unstructured or semi structured data.

4. LINK–BASED STATISTICAL MODEL

The exploitation of link information between objects brings on additional tasks for link mining comparison with traditional mining approaches. The implementation of these tasks, however invokes many challenges. In this section some of them are listed:

Challenge 1: Logical vs. Statistical Dependences

The first challenge in link mining and multi-relational data mining is coherently handling two different types of dependence structures:

Link structure -the logical relationships between objects.

Probabilistic dependency -the statistical relationship between attributes of objects. The coherent handling of these dependences is also a challenge for multirelational data mining where the data to be mined exist in multiple tables [8]. We must search over the different possible logical relationship between objects. Model search is complicated by the fact that attributes can depend on arbitrarily linked attributes. This takes huge search space which further complicates finding a possible mathematical model. Methods developed in inductive logic programming may be applied here, which focus on search over logical relationship. Figure 4.1 object '?' creates its own paper from its neighbor.

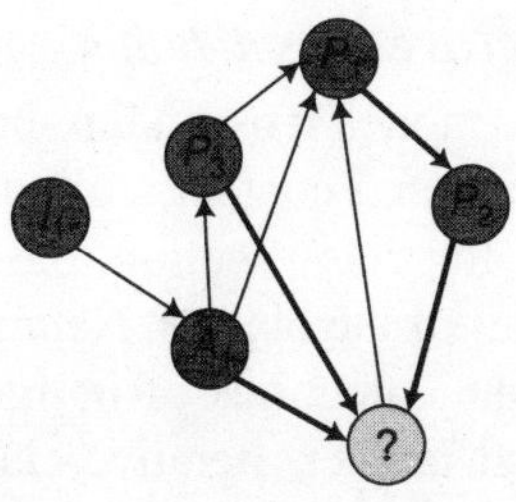

Challenge 2: Feature Construction

A second challenge is feature construction in the multi-relational setting. The attributes of an object provide a basic description of the object [8]. Traditional classification algorithms are based on these types of object features. In a link-based approach, it may also make sense to use attributes of linked objects [3]. In addition, the links may also have attributes. The goal of this is to construct a single feature representing these attributes .In many cases, objects are linked to a set of objects [1]. To construct a single feature from this set of objects, we may either use:

1. Aggregation: It takes a multi set of values over the set of related objects and returns a summary of it. In this example in mode object all the related information is store from P1, P2 and P3 and summery of it is store in P.

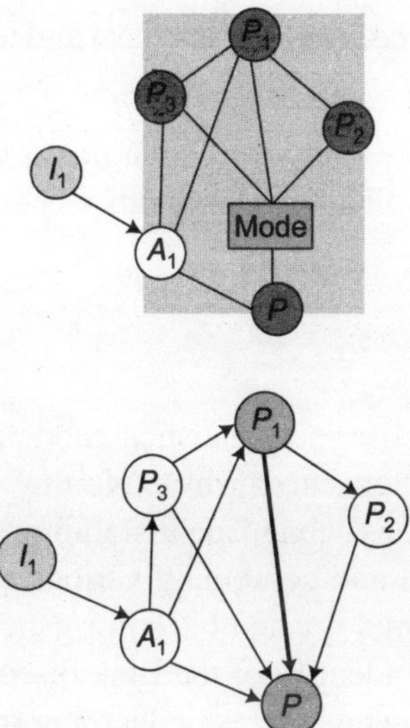

Challenge 3: Individuals vs. Classes Dependencies

A third challenge checks whether the model refers explicitly to individuals and classes or generic categories of individuals.

1. Instance-based Dependencies or Former model like to be model that a connection to a particular individual may be highly predictive [8]. Papers that cite P3 are likely to be from other.

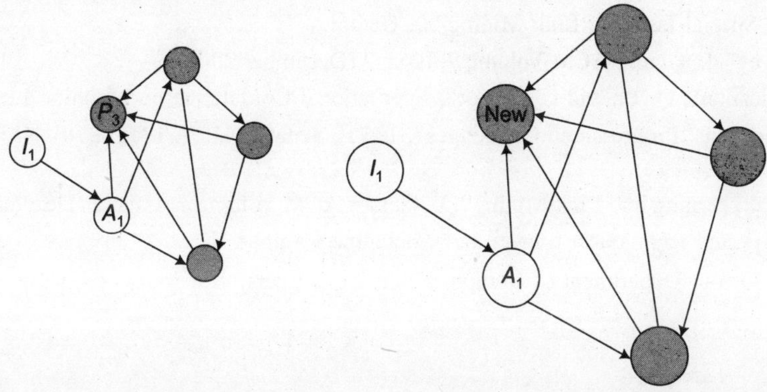

Challenge 4: Collective Classification and collective consolidation

A fourth challenge is classification using a learned model. It uses a link-based statistical model for classification. A learned link-based model specifies a distribution over link and content attributes, which may be correlated based on the links between them [8]. Consider training a model for classification, based on a set of class-label objects. Traditional classification methods consider only the attributes of the objects. Naturally, for linked objects, updating the category of one object can influence our inference about the categories of its linked neighbors. This requires a more complex classification algorithm than for a propositional learner. Iterative classification algorithms have been proposed for hypertext. The general approach of iterative classification has been studied in numerous fields, including relaxation-labeling in computer vision .Some approaches make assumptions about the influence of the neighbor's categories (such as that linked objects have similar categories); we believe it is important to *learn* how the link distribution affects the category[7].

Challenge 5: Effective Use of Labeled and Unlabeled Data

A fifth challenge is combination of label and unlabeled data [8]. Unlabeled data can help infer the object attribute distribution. In link-based domains, unlabeled data provide three sources of information:

- Helps us infer object attribute distribution.
- Links between unlabeled data allow us to make use of attributes of linked objects [7].
- Links between labeled data and unlabeled data (training data and test data) help us make more accurate inferences.

Challenge 6: Link Prediction

A sixth challenge in it is that the prior probability of any particular link is typically extraordinarily low. For medium-sized data sets, we have had success with building explicit models of link existence [7]. It may be more effective to model links at higher level required for large data sets.

5. CONCLUSION

Link mining is exciting new research area and poses new statistical modeling challenges .Link mining is an emerging area within data mining that is focused on finding patterns in data by exploiting and explicitly modeling the links among the data instances. In recent years, significant progress has been made in defining and addressing the core link mining challenges, yet much work remains to be done in refining and combining various approaches and solutions. Domains include the world-wide web, bibliographic citations, criminology and bio-informatics, to name just a few. There are other different data mining challenges in link mining such as identify of the Link discovery, common relational patterns, where these topics lie in research area .There has been a growing interest in learning from linked data, which are described by a graph in which the nodes in the graph are objects and the edges/hyperedges in the graph are links or relations between objects. We have given a brief summary of some of the work in this area, and some of the challenges in link mining.

References

1. "Link Mining: A New Data Mining Challenge", L. Getoor. SIGKDD Explorations, volume 4, issue 2, 2003.
2. "Introduction to the Special Issue on Link Mining",L. Getoor.
3. "Link mining: a survey", L. Getoor ACM Volume 7, Issue 2 (December 2005).
4. "Link-based Classification", Q. Lu and L. Getoor", International Conference on Machine Learning, August, 2003.
5. "Link Mining Applications: Progress and Challenges", Ted E. Senator ARPA/IPTO 3701 N. Fairfax Drive Arlington, VA 22203
6. "Statistical Relational Learning and Link Mining", L. Getoor ACM Volume 7, Issue 2 (December 2005).
7. "Data mining"concept and techniques, Liawei and Micheline Kamber.
8. "Link Mining" Lise Getoor Department of Computer Science University of Maryland, College Park.

CHAPTER 28

Design of Student Classification Algorithm Using Decision Tree

V.P. Mahatme, Satendra Kumar, Prince Raj, Amit Kumar Bisen and Supriya Sinha
Department of Computer Technology, Kavikulguru Institute of Technology and Science, Ramtek, Nagpur (MS), India-441106.
E-mail: mahatme.vilas@gmail.com, satendra.k7412}@gmail.com

ABSTRACT

Today's educational system provides vast research scope to study how students learn and what approaches to learning leads to success. What are their merits, skills and strength. Where they lack and which skill need to be improved or inculcated in order to achieve their goal and avoid failure. This paper proposes data mining technique to classify students in order to predict their final grade using decision tree based on curricular, co-curricular and extracurricular activities of student. It explains an automated process of decision tree development using attributes and classes specified after deciding their priorities and compute the accuracy of classification and generalization. It proposes design, implementation, and evaluation of a series of decision tree and compares their performance. This method may be of considerably useful in grouping students with similar merits and demerits. Thus identifying students at risk early, especially in very large classes and allow the teacher to provide appropriate advising in a timely manner. Thus reducing the failure percentage to a significant level and improve the performance of students.

Keywords: Data Mining, Classification, Clustering, Decision Tree.

1. INTRODUCTION

Data mining is the nontrivial extraction of implicit, previously unknown and potentially useful information from the data. It encompasses a number of technical approaches, such as clustering, data summarization, classification, finding dependency networks, analyzing changes and detecting anomalies [4]. In order to get required benefits from such large data and to find hidden relationships between variables, different data mining techniques are developed and used. Clustering and decision tree are most widely used techniques for future prediction. The main objective of clustering is to partition students into homogeneous groups according to their abilities. These applications can help both teacher and student to enhance the quality education. This study aims to analyze how different factors affect a student's performance during academic career using decision tree. The attributes provided for decision tree implementation will be prioritized first according to their importance of generating appropriate classification and then these prioritized attributes will be used to implement decision tree for classification of the students. The parameters used at different levels of tree for decision making may be changed. Thus, number of trees can be developed. Efficiency of each tree will be evaluated and finally the best tree will be found out. Clustering is one of the basic techniques often used in analyzing data sets. This study makes use of cluster analysis to segment students into groups according to their abilities.

2. BACKGROUND

2.1 Data Mining Techniques

There are two fundamental goals of data mining: prediction and description. Prediction makes use of existing variables in the database in order to predict unknown and other values of interest, and description focuses on finding patterns describing the data and the subsequent presentation for user interpretation. There are several data mining techniques fulfilling these objectives. Some of these are association, classification, sequential patterns and clustering.

Clustering Clustering is a method of grouping data into groups, so that the data in each group share similar trends and pattern. The clustering algorithms attempts to automatically partition the data space into a set of regions or cluster.

Classification Classification involves finding rules that partitions the data into disjoint groups. Classification analyses the training data set and constructs a model based on the class level, and aims to assign a class level to the future unlabelled records. Since the class field is known, this type of learning is known as supervised learning. A set of classification rules are generated by such a classification process, which can be used to classify future data. These are several classification discovery models. They are: decision trees, neural network, genetic algorithms and the statically models like linear/ geometric discriminates.

Association Rules An association rule is an expression of the form X ? Y, where X and Y are sets of items. The intuitive meaning of such a rule is that the transaction of database which contains X tends to Y. Given a database the goal is to discover all the rules that have the support and greater than or equal to the minimum confidence and support respectively.

Deviation Detection Deviation detection is to identify outlining points in a particular data set, and explain whether they are due to noise or other impurities being present in the data or due to trivial reasons.

3. RELATED WORK

One of the most useful data mining tasks is classification. There are different educational objectives for using data mining techiniques. Shaeela Ayesha et.al applied a data mining technique named k-means clustering to analyze student's learning behavior [3]. Chen et.al discovered potential student groups with similar characteristics and reactions to a particular pedagogical strategy [12]. Cocea et.al identifies learners with low motivation and find remedial actions to lower drop-out rates [15]. S.J.d. Baker et.al uses text replays, a method for generating labels that can be used to train classifiers of student behavior [11]. Prediction of student academic success (classes that are successful or not) using discriminant function analysis is done by Martínez, D. [16]. Minaei-Bidgoli et.al predicts a student's marks (pass and fail classes) using regression techniques in Hellenic Open University data [18]. Behrouz Minaei-Bidgoli .et.al presents an approach to classifying students in order to predict their final grade based on features extracted from logged data in an education web-based system [1]. Educational data mining is used by Erdogan and Timor to identify and enhance educational process which can improve their decision making process [8]. Comparison of different data mining methods and techniques for classifying students based on their Moodle usage data and the final marks obtained in their respective courses is performed by Cristobal romero et.al [2]. Henrik concluded that clustering was effective in finding hidden relationships and associations between different categories of students [10]. A case study that uses student's data to analyze their learning behavior to predict the results and to warn students at risk before their final exams was given by Galit et. al [9]. An attempt to use the data mining processes, particularly classification, to help in enhancing the quality of the higher educational system by evaluating student data to study the main attributes that may affect the student performance in coursesis made by Qasem A et.al. [20].

4. PROPOSED APPROACH

R.T.M Nagpur University result of B.E 6th semester Computer Technology Summer-2010 is considered as test data along with this, internal assessments of students which depends on certain criteria such as midterm marks, class test, practical work etc, will be selected.

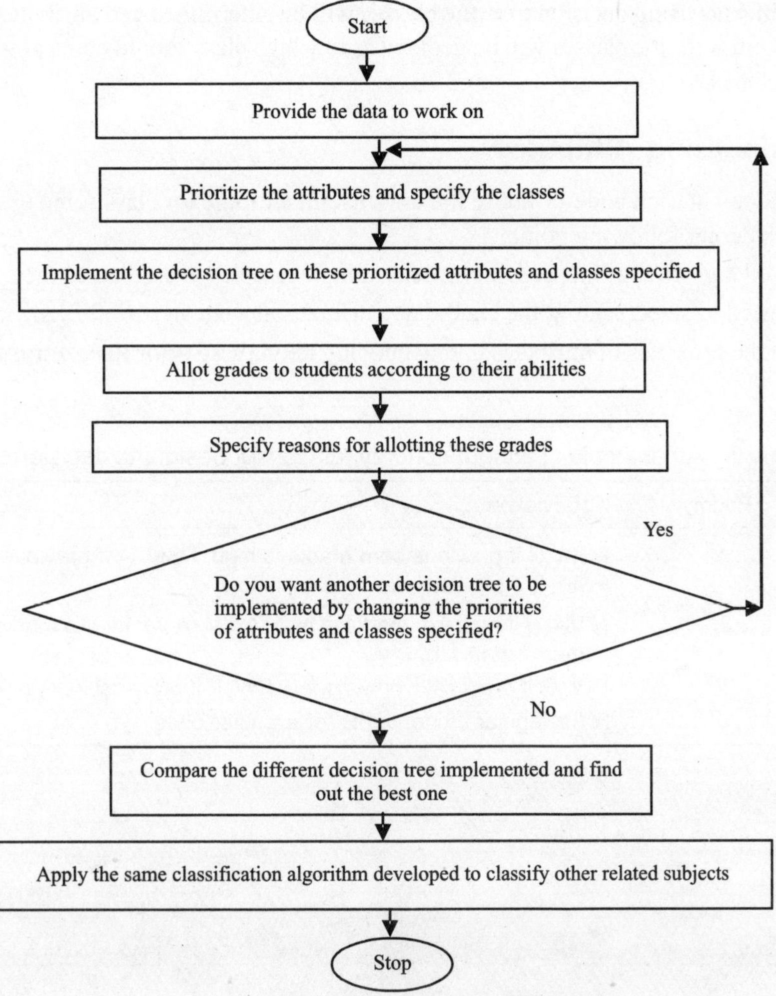

Fig. 1   Flow graps of the proposed approach.

The key attributes which are required for decision tree implementation are as follows:

(i) Attribute-value description - It encompasses object or cases which are expressible in terms of a fixed collection of properties or attributes, such as previous semester marks, midterm marks, practical work, attendance, class quiz, assignments etc.

(ii) Predefined classes (target values) - These are target function which has discrete output values (Boolean or multiclass). i.e. the attributes will be used to classify the students into various classes.

(iii) Sufficient data - Enough training cases should be provided to understand and design the model. So, data of sufficient number of students will be required to design a perfect decision tree.

The students can be grouped regarding their final grades in several ways, three of which are:

(i) There are 36 possible grades which can be considered as students final grades; e.g. $A++$, $A+$, A, $AB++$, $AB+$, AB, $B++$ up to FG.

(ii) We can group them into three classes, "*high*" representing grades from $A++$ to BC, "*middle*" representing grades from $C++$ to DE, and "*low*" representing grades below DE.

(iii) We can also categorize students with one of two class labels: "*Passed*" for grades above EF, and "*Failed*" for grades below or equal to $F++$.

For classifying the students using decision tree, the classes will be determined and attributes for these classes will be determined. Then the priorities for the classes will be decided as to which class should come at which level of the tree and then the tree will be developed.

4.1 Criteria for Prioritizing Attributes

Selection of an attribute to test at each node - Choose the most useful attribute for classifying examples. Information gain can be calculated by considering following points

(a) Measures how well a given attribute separates the training examples according to their target classification.

(b) This measure is used to select among the candidate attributes at each step while growing the tree.

The user can specify the priorities of attributes and depending upon these prioritized attributes, decision tree will be designed.

Table 1 An example of attribute priority relation for designing decision tree

Attributes	Priority	Abbriviation
Previous semester marks	1st	PSM_H if previous sem marks is high, PSM_A if previous sem marks is average, PSM_L if previous sem marks is low
Midterm marks	2nd	MTM_H if midterm marks is high, MTM_A if midterm marks is average, MTM_L if midterm marks is low
Practical work	3rd	PW_G if practical work is good, PW_L if practical work is low.
Attendance	4th	R for regular students, IR for irregular ones

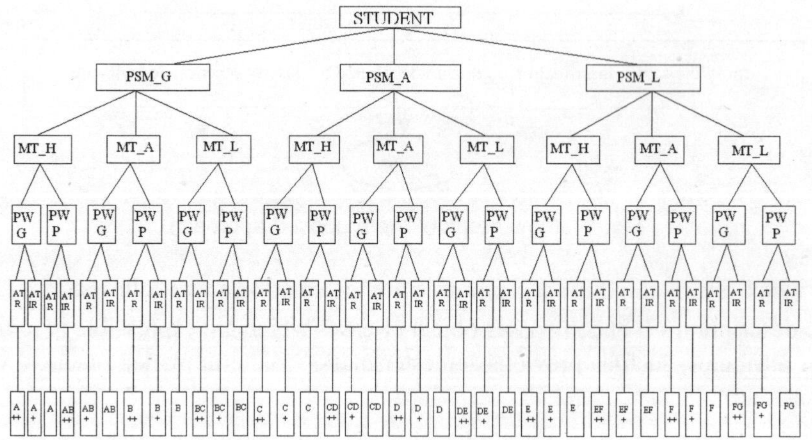

Fig. 2 Decision tree developed by proposed model

For deciding the priorities of attributes the above prioritizing criteria must be considered because if the priorities of attributes and classes are changed then the design of tree will also changed It may be possible that the priorities decided by the user may not be perfect so, once the tree is developed its training accuracy and testing accuracy is found by determining its entropy and gain.

4.2 Entropy

Entropy is a measure of homogeneity of the set of examples. Given a set S of positive and negative examples of some target concept (a 2-class problem), the entropy of set S relative to this binary classification is

$$E(S) = - p(P) \, log \, 2 \, p(P) - p(N) \, log \, 2 \, p(N) \tag{1}$$

4.3 Information Gain

Information gain measures the expected reduction in entropy, or uncertainty.

$$\text{Gain}\ (S, A) = \text{Entropy}\ (S) - \sum_{v\ \in^*\ \text{values}\ (A)} |S_v|/|S| * \text{Entropy}\ (S_v) \tag{2}$$

Values (A) is the set of all possible values for attribute A, and S_v the subset of S for which attribute A has value v. $S_v = \{s\ \text{in}\ S\ |\ A\ (s) = v\}$.

The first term in the equation for *Gain* is just the entropy of the original collection S.

The second term is the expected value of the entropy after S is partitioned using attribut A. It is simply the expected reduction in entropy caused by partitioning the examples according to this attribute. It is the number of bits saved when encoding the target value of an arbitrary member of S, by knowing the value of attribute A. As, higher training accuracy does not mean good generalization. So the priorities may need to be changed and the classes may be redefined. On theses modified data, new decision tree will be created and compared with previous tree. So, provision will be provided to the user that he can himself decide the priorities of class and attributes or leave it on to the system to prioritized attributes and classes in an automated way. Once the prioritized attributes have been decided the tree is developed. Thus, there will be number of trees for classification of students available from which the best can be chosen depending upon the combination of higher training and good generalization, which suits the classification most. Having done with classification the reason for classifying a student to a particular grade will be provided on demand. So that students at risk may be identified early, especially in very large classes. Proposed work will provide suggestions to the teacher which will be adopted by the students to improve their grades. So that they can best utilize their skills. The module allows the teacher to provide appropriate advising in a timely manner. This model identifies the weak students before final exam in order to save them from serious harm. Instructor can take appropriate steps at right time to improve the performance of student in final exam. It deals with both kind of assessments especially internal assessment in order to predict students whose performance is low. This model check the performance of student at different levels before final exam in order to predict weak students and take appropriate steps to save them from failure thus reducing the drop out ratio to a significant level and improve the performance of students. The optimal classifier in every case is highly dependent on the student's attributes and classes. In practice, one might come across a case where no single decision tree can classify with an acceptable level of accuracy. In such cases it would be better to pool the results of different decision trees to achieve the optimal accuracy. Every decision tree operates well on different aspects of the training or test feature vector. As a result, assuming appropriate conditions, combining multiple decision tree may improve classification.

5. CONCLUSION

This study reveals various minute details of classification of students by briefing the extract of the study done so far, and proposes an automated method of decision tree implementation by deciding priorities of attributes and also comparing the various decision tree developed by changing the priorities of attributes so that not only classification is perfect but also a good generalization is achieved. This work may improve student's performance; reduce failing ratio by taking appropriate steps at right time to improve the quality of education.

References

1. Arun K Pujari "Data Mining Techniques", Universities Press (2007), pg 153-193.
2. Shaeela Ayesha, Tasleem Mustafa, Ahsan Raza Sattar, M. Inayat Khan" Data Mining Model for Higher Education Sys", European Journal of Scientific Research ISSN 1450-216X Vol. 43 No. 1 (2010), pp.24-29.
3. Chen, G., Liu, C., Ou, K., Liu, B. Discovering Decision Knowledge from Web Log Portfolio for Managing Classroom Processes by Applying Decision Tree and Data Cube Technology. Journal of Educational Computing Research 2000, 23(3), pp.305–332.

4. Cocea, M., Weibelzahl, S. Can Log Files Analysis Estimate Learners Level of Motivation? Workshop on Adaptivity and User Modeling in Interactive Systems, Hildesheim, 2006. pp.32-35.

5. Ryan S.J.d. Baker1, Adriana M.J.A. de Carvalhorsbaker, dikajoazeirodebaker " Labeling Student Behavior Faster and More Precisely with Text Replays", Human Computer Interaction Institute, Carnegie Mellon University.

6. Martínez, D. Predicting Student Outcomes Using Discriminant Function Analysis. Annual Meeting of the Research and Planning Group. California, 2001. pp.163-173.

7. Minaei-Bidgoli, B., Punch, W. Using Genetic Algorithms for Data Mining Optimization in an Educational Web-based System. Genetic and Evolutionary Computation, Part II. 2003. pp.2252–2263.

8. Behrouz Minaei-Bidgoli, Deborah A. Kashy, Gerd Kortemeyer, William F. Punch "predicting student performance: an application of data Mining methods with the educational web-based system Lon-capa", 33rd ASEE/IEEE Frontiers in Education Conference, November 5-8, 2003. pp.1-6

9. Cristobal romero, sebestian ventura, Pedro G. Espejo and Caser Hervas, "data mining algorithm to classify students", Computer Science Department, Cordoba University, Spain,2007.

10. Henrik (2001) Clustering as a Data Mining Method in a Web-based System for Thoracic Surgery, 2001.

11. Galit.et.al (2007) "Examining online learning processes based on log files analysis: a case study. Research, Refelection and Innovations in Integrating ICT in Education".

12. Qasem A. Al-Radaideh, Emad M. Al-Shawakfa, and Mustafa I. Al-Najjar" Mining Student Data Using Decision Trees", Department of Computer Information Systems Faculty of Information Technology and Computer Science Yarmouk University, Irbid 21163, Jordan

13. Barandela, R., Sánchez, J.S., García, V., Rangel, E. Strategies for Learning in Class Imbalance Problems. Pattern Recognition 2003, 36(3), pp.849-851.

14. Breiman, L. Friedman, J.H., Olshen, R.A., Stone, C.J. Classification and Regression Trees.Chapman & Hall, New York, 1984.

15. Alaa el-Halees (2009) Mining Students Data to Analyze e-Learning Behavior: A Case Study.

16. Erdogan and Timor (2005), "A data mining application in a student database", Journal of Aeronautic and Space Technologies July 2005 Volume 2 Number 2 (53-57).

17. Chi, Z., Yan, H., Pham, T. Fuzzy Algorithms: with Applications to Image Processing and Pattern Recognition. World Scientific, Singapore, 1996.

18. Martínez, F.J., Hervás, C., Gutiérrez, P.A., Martínez, A.C., Ventura, S. Evolutionary Product-Unit Neural Networks for Classification. Conference on Intelligent Data Engineering and Automated Learning. 2006. pp.1320-1328.

19. Superby, J.F., Vandamme, J.P., Meskens, N. Determination of Factors Influencing the Achievement of the First-year University Students using Data Mining Methods. Workshop on Educational Data Mining, 2006. pp. 37- 44.

CHAPTER 29

Efficient Mining of Association Rules Using Linked List and Tries Based Apriori Algorithm

Shailendra W. Shende[1] and Jitendra V. Tembhurne[2]

[1]Department of Information Technology, Yashwantrao Chavan College of Engineering, Nagpur (MS), India
[2]Department of Computer Technology, Kavikulguru Institute of Technology & Science, Ramtek, Nagpur (MS), India
E-mail: shailendra.shende, jitendratembhurne} @gmail.com

ABSTRACT

In this paper, we focused on APRIORI algorithm, a popular data mining technique and compared the performances of a linked list based APRIORI implementation as a basis and a tries-based implementation on it for mining frequent item sequences in a transactional database. We examined the data structure, implementation and algorithmic features mainly focusing on those that also arise in frequent item set mining. These algorithms have given us new capabilities to identify associations in large data sets.

Keywords: Frequent item-sets, Candidate item-sets, Pruning and Join.

1. INTRODUCTION

The rapid development of computer technology, especially increased capacities and decreased costs of storage media, has led businesses to store huge amounts of external and internal information in large databases at low cost. Mining useful information and helpful knowledge from these large databases has thus evolved into an important research area [5], [6], [7]. Among them association rule mining has been one of the most popular data-mining subjects, which can be simply defined as finding interesting rules from large collections of data. Association rule mining has a wide range of applicability such as Market basket analysis, Medical diagnosis/ research, Website navigation analysis, Homeland security and so on.

Association rules are used to identify relationships among a set of items in database. These relationships are not based on inherent properties of the data themselves, but rather based on co occurrence of the data items. Association rules first introduced in [1]. The subsequent paper [8] is considered as one of the most important contributions to the subject. Its main algorithm, Apriori, not only influenced the association rule mining community, but it affected other data mining fields as well. Association rule and frequent item-sets mining became a widely researched area, and hence faster and faster algorithms have been presented. Numerous of them are Apriori based algorithms or Apriori modifications.

The rest of this paper is organized as follows. In section (2) we give a formal definition of association rules and the problem definition. Section (3) introduces our development. Experimental results are shown in section (4). Section (5) contains conclusions.

2. ASSOCIATION RULE PROBLEM

In a database of transactions D with a set of n binary attributes (items) I, a *rule* is defined as an implication of the form

$$X \rightarrow Y \quad \text{where } X, Y \subseteq I \text{ and } X \cap Y = \emptyset.$$

The sets of items (for short *item sets*) X and Y are called *antecedent* (left-hand-side or LHS) and *consequent* (right-hand-side or RHS) of the rule respectively. The *support, supp(X),* of an item set X is defined as the proportion of transactions in the data set which contain the item set.

The *confidence* of a rule is defined

$$\text{conf } (X \rightarrow Y) = \text{supp}(X \cup Y) / \text{supp}(X).$$

Following the original definition given by *Agrawal* et al [1], *association rules (ARs)* are implication rules that inform the user about items most likely to occur in some transactions of a database. They are advantageous to use because they are simple, intuitive and do not make assumptions of any models. Their mining requires satisfying a user-specified *minimum support* and a user-specified *minimum confidence* from a given database at the same time. To achieve this, association rule generation is a two-step process. First, minimum support is applied to find all frequent item-sets in a database. In a second step, these frequent item-sets and the minimum confidence constraint are used to form rules. While the second step is straight forward, the first step needs more attention.

2.1 Steps in Finding the Association Rules

Suppose one of the large item-sets is L_k, $L_k = \{I_1, I_2, ..., I_k\}$, association rules with this item-set are generated in the following way: the first rule is $\{I_1, I_2, ... , I_{k-1}\} = \{I_k\}$, by checking the confidence this rule can be determined as interesting or not. Then other rule are generated by deleting the last items in the antecedent and inserting it to the consequent, further the confidences of the new rules are checked to determine their usefulness. Those processes iterated until the antecedent becomes empty. Since the second sub-problem is quite straight forward, most of the researches focus on the first sub-problem. In the contest for *Frequent Item-set Mining* Implementation, *Apriori* has proved to be one of the most versatile and successful algorithms ranking next only to more sophisticated algorithms like *éclat*[16], *nonordfp and lcm*. It has been proved by scholars that *Apriori* outperforms some of these algorithms in areas like space and database content.

2.2 Apriori Algorithm

Apriori [2] was proposed by Agrawal and Srikant in 1994. The algorithm finds the frequent set L in the database D. It makes use of the downward closure property. The algorithm is a bottom search, moving upward level by level, it prunes many of the sets which are unlikely to be frequent sets, thus saving any extra efforts.

Candidate Generation: Given the set of all frequent $(k-1)$ item-sets, we want to generate a superset of the set of all frequent k-item-sets. The intuition behind the apriori candidate generation procedure is that if an item-set X has minimum support, so do all subsets of X, after all the $(1+1)$- candidate sequences have been generated, a new scan of the transactions is started (they are read one-by-one) and the support of these new candidates is determined.

Pruning: The pruning step eliminates the extensions of $(k-1)$ item-sets which are not found to be frequent, from being considered for counting support. For each transaction t, the checks which candidates are contained in t and after the last transaction are processed; those with support less than the minimum support are discarded.

2.3 Linked Based APRIORI Algorithm

Pass 1

1. Generate the candidate items-sets in C_1
2. Save the frequent item-sets in L_1

Pass k

1. Generate the candidate item-sets in C_k from the frequent item-sets in L_{k-1}
   (a) Join $L_{k-1} p$ with $L_{k-1} q$, as follows:
       insert into C_k
       select *p.item 1, q.item 1, ..., p.itemk – 1, q.itemk – 1*
       from $L_{k-1} p, L_{k-1} q$
       where *p.item 1 = q.item 1, ... p.itemk – 2 = q.itemk – 2, p.itemk – 1 < q.itemk – 1*
   (b) Generate all $(k-1)$ subsets from the candidate item-sets in C_k
   (c) Prune all candidate item-sets from C_k where some $(k-1)$ subset of the candidate item-set is not in the frequent item-set L_{k-1}
2. Scan the transaction database to determine the support for each candidate item-set in C_k
3. Save the frequent item-sets in L_k

3. MOTIVATION

The efficiency of frequent item-sets mining algorithms is determined mainly by three factors: the way candidates are generated, the data structure that is used and the implementation details [4]. In this paper we proposed two different data structure techniques for the implementation of Apriori algorithm, to make it more efficient.

3.1 Data Structure Description

Linked List Representation. Here we use two kinds of structures—node
and an item-set.

```
struct node{
    int index ;
    struct item-set *item,*temp1;
    struct node *next;
};
```

```
    struct item-set{
    int *data;
    struct item-set *next1;
};
```

There are two separate linked lists one composed of nodes, where each node specifies the index, i.e., *k*. Each node will again have a second linked list composed of item-sets associated with it. This connected second linked list will contain the actual items from the transactional database.

The choice of the data-structure to store the candidates is the determining factor in calculating the efficiency of the algorithm. We present an analysis of our implementations using simple linked-lists and tries separately.

The Tries Implementation of Apriori. The *Tries* [3] data structure used here is similar to the one proposed by *Ferenc Bodon* [4]. A tries is a rooted and labeled tree. Though tries are generally used to store words, they are also useful in storing and retrieving any finite ordered sets. We utilize this property in building the tries for Apriori. The tries contains an item set if there exists a path where the nodes are labeled by the elements of the set, in increasing order. A candidate k-item set $C = \{i_1 < i_2 < .... < i_n\}$ is represented by the nodes $i_1, i_2 ......i_n$ order.

```
struct node{
    short int item, depth, sup;
    struct child *dp;
};

    struct child{
    struct node *next;
    struct child *nextc;
};
```

Support counting is done by reading transactions one-by-one and determining which candidates are contained in the actual transaction. We maintain two indices to count support, one for the items in the transaction and the other for the nodes, each being initialized to the first element. After that, we check if the elements pointed by the two indices are equal. If true, we call the process recursively, otherwise we increase the index that points to the smaller item. These steps are repeated until the end of the transaction or the last edge is reached. The support counters of the leaves in the path are increased if the nodes in one path are similar to the particular transaction. The time of finding supported candidates in a transaction can be reduced significantly by storing some extra information at the nodes. While counting support, we often have to make superfluous moves in tries search in the sense that there are no candidates in the direction we are about to explore. To avoid this superfluous traveling, at every node, we store the length of the longest directed path that starts from there. When searching for k-item set candidates at depth d, we move downward only if the maximal path length at this node is at least k-d. The most important function that we use is probably the intersection pruning method suggested by *Bodon* [4] with a slight modification of our own. We denote by u the parent of the node that has to be extended (say **u'**). Suppose that the node u is at a depth l, to determine the children of **u'**, we first consider the subsequences at depth l, compare with **u'** and one-by-one denote these nodes at depth l by v. The intersection of the children of u and each and every v is appended to **u'**. Thus the pruned candidate is obtained in a simple go, saving a lot of superfluous traversals and hence computation time.

This technique of pruning could however not be applied to 1-item-sets and 2-item-sets candidate generation and we had to write separate functions for them. Some other issues had to be taken special care of such as the adjustment of the depth of the nodes after deletion is performed. Our implementation differed from that of *Bodon* only slightly in that *Bodon* had computed the children (**v'**) of v having the same label as that of the node that had to be extended while we did not consider any **v'**, reason being, we did not label our edges as the values or the items of the item sets. We used nodes only for that purpose.

4. EXPERIMENTS AND ANALYSIS

In this section, we present a performance comparison of the implementation; The algorithms were executed on a workstation with AMD AthlonTM 64*2 Dual Core Processor, 2.81 GHz and 2.00 GB of RAM on Fedora OS.

4.1 Results of Linked List Based Implementation

Table 4.1 shows that; on constant support (50%) and with different database size, memory used by algorithm and running time of algorithm.

4.2 Results of Tries Based Implementation

Table 4.2 shows that; on constant support (7%) and with different database size, memory used by algorithm and running time of algorithm.

Table 4.1 Memory and Time Requirement of Linked List Based APRIORI Implementation.

Database Size	Support	Memory used (in bytes)	Time (in sec.)
18000	50	16496	0.05495
20000	50	16238	0.05495
50000	50	19082	0.10989
80000	50	22110	0.16484

Table 4.2 Memory and Time Requirement of Tries Based Implementation.

Database Size	Support	Memory used (in kilo bytes)	Time (in sec.)
10000	7	42	0.01
15000	7	221	0.02
20000	7	713	0.07
30000	7	3703	0.37
50000	7	29266	4
70000	7	113700	25
100000	7	477745	170

5. CONCLUSION

The following observations are made from the above results: Linked list based implementation is good only for a small database. As the database size increases, the implementation fails to give desired results. For small database the Linked-List implementation was better. The size and depth of the tries can be attributed to this observation. Memory uses is much better in the Tries implementation. The memory increases exponentially with increasing database because the depth of the Tries increases exponentially. The time required also follow the same trend as the memory as with increase with depth the search space is also increasing.

References

1. R. Agrawal, T. Imielinski, and A. Sawmi.: Mining Association Rules between Sets of Items in Large Databases. In proc. of the ACM SIGMOD Conference on Management of Data, (1993) 207-216

2. Rakesh Agrawal and Ramakrishnan Srikant.: Fast Algorithms for Mining Association Rules in Large Databases. In Jorge B. Bocca, Matthias Jarke, and Carlo Zaniolo, editors, Proc. of the 20th International Conference on Very Large DataBases, VLDB, Santiago,Chile, September (1994) 487-499

3. Edward Fredkin.: Trie Memory. Communications of the ACM, Vol. 3, No. 9. (1960) 490

4. Ferenc Bodon.: A Trie-based APRIORI Implementation for Mining Frequent Item sequences. ACM, New York, USA, August. (2005)

5. R. Agrawal, T. Imielinksi and A. Swami.: Database Mining: A Performance Perspective, IEEE Transactions on Knowledge and Data Engineering. (1993)

6. M.S. Chen, J. Han and P.S. Yu.: Data Mining: An Overview from a Database Perspective, IEEE Transactions on Knowledge and Data Engineering. (1996)

7. C.Y. Wang, T.P. Hong and S.S. Tseng.: Maintenance of Discovered Sequential Patterns for Record Deletion. Int. Data Anal, February. (2002) 399-410

8. R. Agrawal and R. Srikant.: Fast Algorithms for Mining Association Rules. In Proc. of Int. Conf. On Very Large Databases (VLDB), Sept. (1994)

9. A. Sarasere, E. Omiecinsky, and S. Navathe.: An Efficient Algorithm for Mining Association Rules in Large Databases. In Proc. 21St International Conference on Very Large Databases (VLDB), Zurich, Switzerland, Also Catch Technical Report No. GIT-CC-95-04. (1995)

10. B. Goethals.: Efficient Frequent Pattern Mining. PhD thesis, Transactional University of Limburg, Belgium. (2002)

11. B. Liu, W. Hsu, and Y. Ma.: Integrating classification and association rule mining. In Proc. 1998 Int. Conf. Knowledge Discovery and Data Mining (KDD'98), New York, NY, Aug. (1998) 80-86

12. C.Y. Wang, T.P. Hong and S.S. Tseng.: Maintenance of Discovered Sequential Patterns for Record Deletion. Int. Data Anal., February. (2002) 399-410

13. D.W.L. Cheung, J. Han, V. Ng, and C.Y. Wong.: Maintenance of Discovered Association Rules in Large Databases: An incremental updating technique. In ICDE. (1996) 106-114

14. D.W. L. Cheung, S.D. Lee, and B. Kao.: A General Incremental Technique for Maintaining Discovered Association Rules. In Database Systems for Advanced Applications, pages 185-194. (1997)

15. E.H. Han, G. Karpis, and V. Kumar.: Scalable Parallel Data Mining for Association Rules. July 15. (1997)

16. Y. Fu.: Discovery of multiple-level rules from large databases. (1996)

CHAPTER 30

Data Mining and Decision Support

Yogita S. Pagar*, Vishakha R. Mote, Rahul S. Bramhane***,**
Lecturer*, Lecturer** & Head and S.G. Lecturer***
Department of Information Technology, P.E.S. College of Engineering, Aurangabad, (MS) India
E-mail: yspagar@yahoo.com, vishakha.mote@yahoo.co.in, rahulbramhane@indiatimes.com

ABSTRACT

This paper provides some insights into the possible integrating aspects of two currently separate research areas Data mining (DM) and Decision Support (DS), and investigates the relation of DM and DS with Expert Systems (ES). In particular it investigates how DM can be used to support DS, and vice versa, how DS can be used to support DM. Finally, we investigate what future developments could lead to the integration of DM and DS.

INTRODUCTION

Data Mining (DM) is concerned with finding patterns in data which are interesting (according to some user- defined measure of interestingness, e.g., with coverage above the requested threshold) and valid (according to some user defined measure of validity, e.g., classification accuracy). Numerous data mining algorithms exist, including the predictive data mining algorithms, which result in classifiers that can be used for prediction and classification, and descriptive data mining algorithm that serve other purposes like finding of associations, clusters, etc. The area has recently gained much attention of industry, due to the existence of large collections of data in different formats (including large data warehouses), and the increasing need of data warehouses, e.g., in the form of relational data tables, there has recently been also increased interest in text and web mining. Decision Support (DS) is concerned with developing systems aimed at helping decision makers solve problems and make decision. Their main characteristics are that they incorporate both data and models, are designed to assist managers in semi structured or unstructured decision making processes; support, rather than replace, managerial judgment and are aimed at improving the effectiveness (rather than efficiency) of decision. Decision Support Systems (DSS) can be data or model oriented. Data oriented DS tools (modern data warehouse, data cubes and OLAP, together with data visualization) involve no models, but enables good data understanding through segmentation, slicing, dicing, drilling down, rolling up and other operations. On the other hand, model oriented DS tools support the development of decision models in the form of decision trees (notice that a decision tree as understand in decision support has a substantially different format from the decision trees used in data mining), influence diagrams and multi attribute models.

In this paper we reflect upon the relation between data mining, decision support and expert systems. In particular we explore means of combining data mining with decision support, involving joint data preprocessing, standards for model exchange, and meta learning provides decision support when choosing best data mining tools for a given problem.

1. DATA MINING, DECISION SUPPORT AND EXPERT SYSTEMS

Generally speaking, Decision Support Systems (DSS) are a broader notion than expert systems. There is a large intersection between the two, but some expert systems are not DSS. Expert systems that reproduce the reasoning process of a human decision maker can be categorized as process oriented DSS.

A narrower definition of DSS taken in this paper is a system that helps humans to choose the best among the available alternatives. A DSS will evaluate all the alternatives (for example, all the individuals applying for a bank loan), ranking them in accordance with the systems evaluation or utility function. On the other hand, when an expert system is used, for example, to diagnose patients, one is typically not interested in ranking patients according to some criterion, but rather in obtaining a prognostic/diagnostic outcome for an individual patient.

A typical expert system architecture consists of a knowledge base, an inference engine and a user interface, as shown in figure. A DSS architecture proposal by E.G. Mallach, on the other hand, consists of a data base, a model base, possibly a knowledge base, and a user interface. Notice a clear distinction between the two: an expert system does not involve a database, whereas the correspondence between an expert system knowledge base, and a model and a knowledge base in DSS, is not completely clear, since a DSS architecture should also explicitly include an analysis or inference engine. In comparison with a classical expert system architecture, a now a days architecture of a DSS could be as shown in figure, where the scheme is adapted for use in the field of medical decision making.

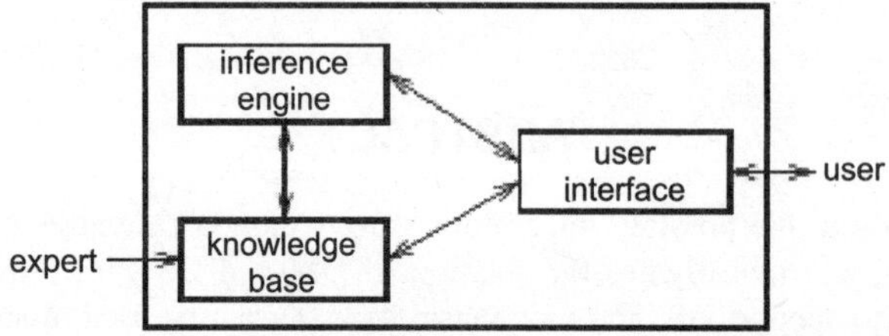

Fig. 1 A classical expert system schema

The figure indicates that current DSS need to deal also with large volumes of data, as well as data gathering and analysis via the Internet and intranet.

The main source of knowledge for DM is data from which knowledge is extracted. On the other hand, in DS the main source is human knowledge, formalized in a format requested by a selected DS tool. There are many examples where the knowledge of experts and knowledge extracted from data have been integrated, so that the results of data mining feed into a decision support system, complementing expert knowledge. It is worthwhile noticing that a set of rules or a decision tree induced by a machine learning system can be viewed as an automatically constructed expert system knowledge base, and that the inference engine is simply rule firing or path finding in a decision tree, resulting in a probability distribution of customers (for instance, patient diagnoses). In this way, predictive machine learning can largely replace the standard expert system development methodology, provided that there is a sufficient amount of data (solved problems) available.

There are important approaches integrating expert provided knowledge and induced knowledge. The entire paradigm of multi- relational data mining, and inductive logic programming (ILP) in particular, employs background knowledge provided by experts as input to a learning system. In ILP, for instance, background knowledge is crucial for the success of learning. Another approach to the integration of expert knowledge and induced knowledge has been proposed in the development of an expert system for ECG diagnosis of cardiac arrhythmias. The developed methodology proposes a semi automatic knowledge acquisition cycle, involving a qualitative model construction, simulation of the model to construct an exhaustive database of example, and inductive learning from examples to build a compact expert system knowledge base.

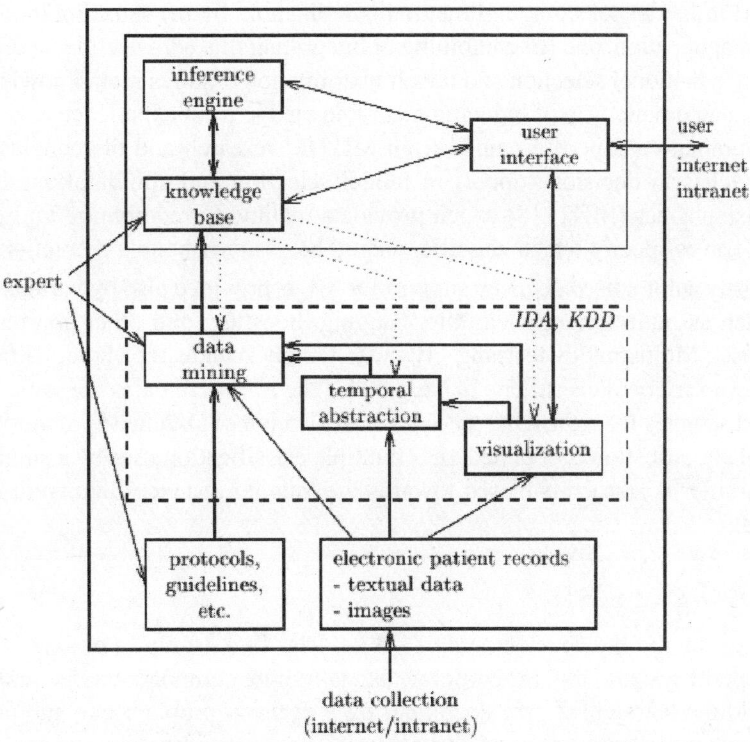

Fig. 2 A decision support system schema

2. INTEGRATING ASPECTS OF DM AND DS

2.1 DS for DM

This section presents selected decision support methods, providing support in model selection (where models are developed by different DM algorithms or a single DM algorithm using different parameter settings). Selection of the best algorithm for a given dataset, and model integration/combination. As outlined low, cost-sensitive classification supported by the ROC methodology can be used to find an optimal solution. Moreover, meta-learning can be applied to build rules or decision trees proposing the best classifier for a given classification task. Other meta-learning approaches to combine classifiers can be used. The well-known ROC (Receiver Operating Characteristic) methodology, initially used in medicine for cost-sensitive decision making, allows model selection using the ROC convex hull, indicating a tradeoff between specificity and sensitivity of classi_ers.4 A ROC curve indicates a tradeoff that one can achieve between the false alarm rate (1 - Specificity, plotted on the X-axis) that needs to be minimized, and the detection rate (Sensitivity, plotted on the Y -axis) that needs to be maximized. Improved performance in terms of sensitivity, specificity and classification accuracy can be achieved by the adaptation of selected data mining methods to dealing with misclassification costs in the estimation of probabilities. More importantly, an appropriate sensitivity-specificity tradeoff, determined by the expert, can be achieved by applying different algorithms, as well as by different parameter settings of a selected data mining algorithm. In the context of developing a method for decision support for DM, the ROC method allows, through the construction of a convex hull of a set of points (results of classifiers), to identify and select models/classifiers that are optimal for a given sensitivity-specificity tradeoff. ROC analysis thus provides an integrated set of solutions, together with their optimality conditions in terms of sensitivity and specificity. Consequently, ROC analysis can be viewed as a decision support method for model selection and combination. With increasingly many DM techniques to choose from, meta-learning seems to provide the means for successful industrial/commercial take-up of the DM technology. Meta-learning, e.g., as investigated in the EU funded project METAL (see http://www.metal-kdd.org/), aims at the development of methods and tools for providing support in model selection and method combination, by (a) selecting the best/most suitable model/algorithm to use on a given application, and (b) combining or integrating this with useful and effective transformations of the data. Automatic guidance in model selection and data transformation requires meta-knowledge. The use of inductive learning techniques offer an automatic way of inducing meta-knowledge from experience as well as revising prior meta-knowledge, retrieved as cumulative expertise gained from ML/DM research and the conclusions of past comparative studies. Successful approaches to decision support in model selection and combinations have been developed, an example being Meta Decision Trees (MDT) [8] which provide a method for combining multiple classifiers. Instead of giving a prediction, MDT leaves specify which classifier should be used to obtain a prediction for a given dataset.

A less explicit and mostly automatised decision support for ML is provided also by various approaches to combining of multiple classifiers, such as multi strategy learning, bagging, boosting, and other approaches to building optimal classifiers for a given dataset. Multistrategy learning [4] varies factors such as the choice of the learning method or the abstraction level to produce a variety of classifiers. In bagging [3] the learner remains the same but variety is achieved by learning from bootstrapped samples from the data; the final classification of obtained by majority voting. In boosting [8], on the other hand, the final classification is obtained after multiple classification runs by a single learner; in the next run, the data from which a classifier is learned is biased towards the training instances that were incorrectly classified in a previous classification run.

2.2 DM for DS

DM methods can be used to support the development of DS models. Two examples of sing DM for DS are outlined. A multi-attribute decision support system DEX [1] corporate a data-mining component in the knowledge acquisition phase to semi automatically build the hierarchical tree decomposing a decision problem into sub problems. This is done by asking the expert to evaluate a pre-defined set of partial decision making situations, and inducing or extrapolating a completed evaluation (utility) function from example solutions. The strongest link between data mining and decision support has been achieved by the system HINT [3] which enables the development of a DEX decision support model from data. HINT uses a function decomposition approach to develop a hierarchical composition of the decision problem into sub problems, thus automating part of the decision making process. For a given dataset, the constructive induction system HINT namely outputs a concept hierarchy, which needs to be developed manually in the standard DEX DS methodology. It was shown in a dozen of DS problems that HINT can indeed reconstruct experts' decision knowledge.

2.3 Current Trends in DM and DS Integration

Despite this new commercial development, many integrating issues remain to be solved, and DM and DS integration techniques proposed. In addition to the integration issues of DM and DS described in two previous sections, the Sol Eu-Net project (see http://soleunet.ijs.si) is exploring further means of combining data mining with decision support, involving joint data preprocessing, standards for model exchange, and meta-learning providing decision support when choosing best data mining tools for a given problem. Some of the project partners (Czech Technical University, Dialogues GmBH, Bristol University, Oxford University and J. Stefan Institute) have been involved in the development of the following tools, that can be used in integrating data mining and decision support: A pre-processing tool, based on the Sumatra scripting language [2], applicable for data pre-processing for both data mining and decision support. It allows access to various data sources, enabling simple definition of transformation tasks using a library of templates. A common representation language supporting the exchange of data mining and decision support models for different application and visualization tools. This development is built as an addition to the currently developing PMML (Predictive Model Markup Language) standard (see www.dmg.org). Its advantage is its independence of a selected application, platform and operating system.

Meta-learning tools for classifier selection, and ROC methodology for model selection (see the previous section). Shared ontology, using the developing Sol-Eu-Net On Line Glossary of Terms SOGOT. The RAMSYS methodology for solving data mining and decision support problems, requiring remote collaboration of project partners [9].

3. CONCLUSIONS

The two areas, data mining and decision support, are complementary, and there is also a strong link with expert systems. The most pressing integrating issue, however, is the integration of the database, data mining and decision support technology. Hopefully, OLE DB for Data Mining [10], to appear as part of the Microsoft SQL Server under the name Analysis Services, will provide a platform enabling cost and performance effective integration of data mining, decision support and information systems. Despite this new commercial development, many integrating issues remain to be solved, and integration techniques proposed in future work.

References

1. M. Bohanec and V. Rajkovi_c. DEX: An expert system shell for decision support. Sistemica 1(1), 145{157, 1990.

2. I. Bratko, I. Mozetic and N. Lavra_c. KARDIO: A Study in Deep and Qualitative Knowledge for Expert Systems, MIT Press, 1989.

3. L. Breiman. Bagging predictors. Machine Learning 24: 123{140, 1996.

4. T.G. Diettrich. Machine learning research: Four current directions. em AI Magazine 18: 97{136, 1997.

5. S. D_zeroski and N. Lavra_c (eds.) Relational Data Mining. Springer, 2001.

6. U. Fayyad, G. Piatetski-Shapiro, and P. Smith. From data mining to knowledge discover: an overview. In U. Fayyad, G. Piatetski-Shapiro, P. Smith, and R. Uthurusamy (eds.) Advances in Knowledge Discovery and Data Mining, 1{34. MIT Press, Cambridge, MA, 1996.

7. U. Fayyad, G. Piatetski-Shapiro, P. Smith, and R. Uthurusamy (eds.) Advances in Knowledge Discovery and Data Mining. MIT Press, Cambridge, MA, 1996.

8. Y. Freund and R.E. Shapire. A decision-theoretic generalisations of on-line learning and an application to boosting. Journal of Computer and System Sciences 55: 119{ 139, 1997.

9. J. Han and M. Kamber. Data Mining: Concepts and Techniques. Morgan Kauf- mann, San Francisco, CA , 2001.

CHAPTER 31

Assessing Water Pollutants Using GIS Based Data Analysis

Swati Vitkar[1] and Chaitali Gadekar[1]

[1]S.I.E.S. (Nerul) College of Arts, Science and Commerce (I.T. Dept.), Sri Chandrasekarendra Saraswati Vidyapuram,
Plot 1-C, Sector V, Nerul, Navi Mumbai (MS)– 400 706, India
E-mail: swativitkar@gmail.com

ABSTRACT

Since freshwater is available on the landscape and the community uses it for their sustenance, each habitation has particular history related to the quality attached with it and as it has a geographical context, study of its quality, variation of its quality in different seasons and the effects of the human activities on its quality is important. Any natural resource possessing multidimensional aspects is well understood if represented in the form of proper maps, are amenable to better insight so that development and management strategies could be derived. The conventional method of preparation of maps, keeping the records of chemical analysis and trying to relate to the analytical procedures like multi-layer integration, tabular / attribute data linkage needed for planning becomes laborious and time consuming.At the same time, the multi-dimensions of information if linked properly and provided with a synoptic view, creates a knowledge base that is essential for development and management oriented planning. In this regard, author decided to adopt a Geographic Information System (GIS) approach to develop a Spatial Information and Knowledge Base on the water quality of Navi Mumbai to establish its relationship with the influencing factors like geology, runoffs and anthropogenic activities. The software used for the present environmental study are SQL server 2005, VB .NET and GIS software GRAM++. The analysis of results drawn at various stages of work revealed that GIS is an effective tool for preparation of maps showing spatial distribution of various water quality parameters and the water quality problems could be identified and correlated with the activities taking place to interpret the reasons for deterioration of its quality. Thus survey and analysis of pollution pattern using GIS can become further useful for achieving sustainable management of these freshwater resources which is the main aim of this project. This model can be replicated in greater extent. This is an executable model and can be used by CIDCO or NMMC to demarcate the location distribution of water pollutants in a comprehensive manner and helps in suggesting the remedial measures to control freshwater pollution in a holistic way.

Keywords: VB, VB.NET, SQL server,GRAM++, dissolved oxygen, COD, Chlorides, Total dissolved solids, Total solids, Total suspended solids, pH, Temp. Conductivity

1. INTRODUCTION

Water is an important and the most abundant resource in the biosphere. The water molecule is represented as H_2O, with an oxygen atom in the central position, bound by two hydrogen atoms. Rapid urbanization, industrialization and certain agricultural practices have led to pollution and deterioration of natural water bodies. These water bodies are constantly being abused by activities, such as, washing and domestic/industrial waste loads. Indiscriminate use of pesticides and fertilizers, combined with inadequate training of farmers and workers, has led to highly contaminated agricultural runoffs being released in water bodies. In urban areas, the situation is worsened often by the direct discharge into the natural water bodies of untreated or partially treated sewage and industrial wastes. Water pollution can also result from natural processes, such as, surface runoffs due to rains or presence of dead organic matter, but these are slow processes, giving enough time for the water body to rejuvenate. Since freshwater body has a geographical context, study of its quality, variation of its quality in different seasons and the effects of the human activities on its quality is important.

Water pollution is the presence of foreign substances in water. Water pollution results into degradation of environment. Water quality maintenance required to avoid future degradation of water. Water analysis can be done at various study zones (industrial, residential areas) and in different seasons can be carried out. Water analyzing activity can be done by collecting water samples from various water bodies. Water samples can be further tested on the basis of their chemical and physical properties. Water analysis is one of the basic important activities of environmental studies. Water analysis tests the Water quality, Detect % of water pollution, Concentration of various pollutants in water. Thus spatial distribution maps of various pollution parameters are used to demarcate the location distribution of water pollutants in a comprehensive manner and helps in suggesting water pollution control and remedial measures in a holistic way.

GIS is geographic information system (GIS) is a computer-based tool for mapping and analyzing things that exist and events that happen on Earth. A geographic information system (GIS), also known as geospatial information system, is a system for capturing, storing, analyzing and displaying geospatial data. GIS is an effective tool for preparation of maps showing spatial distribution of various water quality parameters. In this way, the water quality problems could be identified and could be correlated with the activities taking place to interpret the reasons for deterioration of its quality. GIS study proves to be an important tool to evaluate the impacts of the anthropogenic/natural activities on the quality of water. A GIS model is being designed to work on any type of parameters that affect the water body. The impact of such water bodies on humans is assessed by their health conditions.

2. SCOPE OF THE PRESENT STUDY

This software will help end users such as Municipal Corporations, or any Environmental Department to store, maintain and update geographical information system. The present study was confined to Navi Mumbai (19° 2′ 2.20″ N, 73° 0′ 43.71″ E). This city lies across the Thane creek, north east of Mumbai and flanked by the Thane creek waters on its west, south-west and north-west contours. Navi Mumbai had been developed a s a planed city by City and Development Corporation of Maharashtra (CIDCO). There are 6 nodes and approximately 30-50 sectors in each node. In several nodes the city has fresh water lakes (ponds). The Navi Mumbai Municipal Corporation (NMMC) and CIDCO have also impounded creek water creating a series of water holding ponds. The study was carried in one of the nodes of Navi Mumbai viz Nerul Node (19° 2′ 2.20″ N, 73° 0′ 43.71″ E)

Earlier work by Dr. B.S. Mahajan was carried out through Health And Environment Action Based Learning (HEAL) project undertaken by Homi Bhabha Centre for Science Education (HBCSE), a branch of Tata Institute of Fundamental Research (TIFR), Mumbai.

This project was carried out with the assistance of National Service scheme (NSS) cell of University of Mumbai. One of the parts of the project that is present study area (Nerul node) was carried out under the supervision of the author and trained teachers of the SIES (South Indian Education Society), Nerul college.

In order to develop an approach, conceptualize the design and to examine the utility of the study it has been decided to consider Nerul (Navi Mumbai) area which is an extension of Mumbai.

3. DESCRIPTION OF STUDY AREA

The locations studied were in Navi Mumbai. In all four lakes and ponds were studied namely Ganesh Talab, Shiv Mandir Lake, Creek opposite Chanakya, Chincholi lake. All the lakes are located in a residential area near school, garden, temple, hospitals [1].

Table 1 Description of all the water bodies in the study area

Name	Type	Location	Address	Longitude (X)	Latitude (Y)
Ganesh Talab	Fresh Water	Residential	Karave *gaon*, Sector 32/38	19° 1′ 14.09″	73° 0′ 43.00″
Creek	Creek Water	Residential	opposite Chanakya Palm Beach Road	19° 1′ 42.25″	73° 0′ 27.01″
Chincholi lake	Fresh Water	Residential	Sec. 8	19° 2′ 48.90″	73° 1′ 7.20″

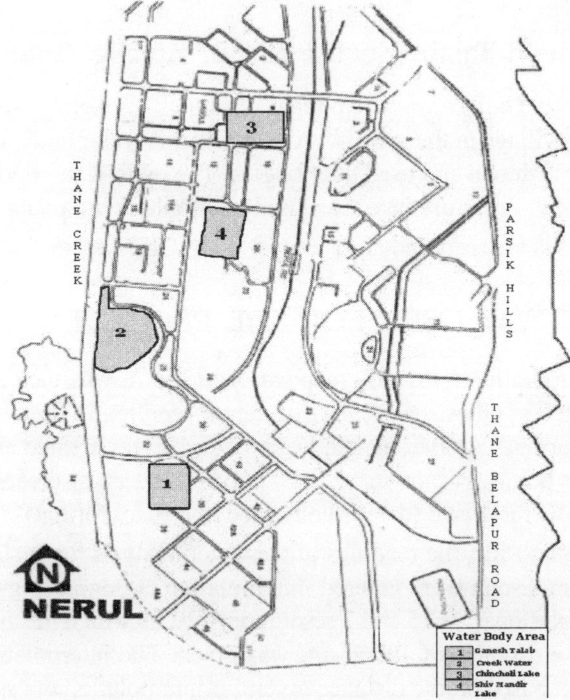

Fig. 1 Water Body area in Nerul (study area)

ShivMandir Lake	Fresh Water	Residential	Sec. 18A	19° 2′ 57.20″	73° 0′ 43.71″

4. METHODOLOGY

- Open water bodies, both fresh water and creek water, were checked in each of the study zones. Water samples were collected according to the standard protocol of procedures.

- These samples were collected at the four corners of the fresh water body, depending on the ease/accessibility of sample collection. The locations of sampling points and sampling method were mostly kept constant during the three seasons (Monsoon, Winter, and Summer). Water quality was determined by studying its physical and chemical properties.

- The water samples were first checked for physical properties on the site and then analyzed chemically at HBCSE laboratory on the next day. The samples were carefully stored in cold conditions during the interim period.

- The physical properties studied were: colour, odour, turbidity and temperature. The chemical properties studied were:. dissolved oxygen, COD, Chlorides, Total dissolved solids, Total solids, Total suspended solids, pH, Temp.

Conductivity.

- The water samples were analyzed for bacterial contamination (faecalcoliforms) as MPN (Most Probable Number) test.

- Due to the time factor, water analysis kits were used for chlorides, fluorides, ammonia and alkalinity.Chemical analysis of water samples was carried out by following the procedures given in *Standard Methods for the Examination of Water and Wastewater*; 20th edition, American Public Health Association (also given in HEAL Protocol Guide). For some chemicals (phosphates, copper, iron, chromium), colour grids were developed at HBCSE and hence the pollutant concentrations are expressed as Low (L), Permissible (P), High (H) and Critical (C). This fixed protocol was followed for the three seasons. The water samples were analyzed for bacterial contamination (faecal coliforms) as MPN (Most Probable Number) test, only during April 2005 [2]

4.1 Sampling Site I: Ganesh Talab, Sector 32/38, Karave Goan

Type of water body: Fresh water body *Outlets/Inlets:* No inlets or outlets. *General observations:* This is a big water body (sampling pts. 2, 3, 4) with Karave village in the vicinity. Along side this water body, there is a big well (sampling pt.1), relatively clean, from which water is drawn and used by villagers. The main water body is maintained by the NMMC; it had a boundary wall. Beyond point 4, the entire lake was highly eutrophic with pistia and typha plants. [2]

Like this all sampling site details are recorded and input is fed to GIS system.

5. HOW GIS SOFTWARE WAS USED FOR THE PROJECT

First Navi Mumbai Municipal Corporation (NMMC) map was scanned. It was then registered on 1:72165 scale using Map Edit module (vector data model) of GRAM++. Then different layers (roads, railways etc) were digitized (converting hard copy into GIS recognizable format). A layer named water body ID was created and the name of the locations were sampling was done were entered as points. For the same, even polygon layer was created showing the actual boundary of those lakes. Now the point layer was rasterised (data is converted into pixel format).

For interpolation purpose, in a text file, the readings of the water analysis for each location in different seasons like pre-monsoon, monsoon and post-monsoon were entered. Interpolation is done using the terrain module of GRAM++. Here a resolution is given i.e X resolution = 29.75 and Y resolution = 29.78 which means 1pixel = 29 mts. Columns = 500 and Rows = 375 was entered and a distance of 10000 mts was given. The interpolation result for each parameter was stored in separate files. In the result based on the distance given for interpolation the spread for each parameter could be found out.

By using ODBC connectivity between the backend (SQLServer-2005) and front end (Visual Basic 6.0) following reports are generated. We can integrate Map with the Database using 'Image' control of VB6. After connecting Database with VB form, an image has been stored in the Database, and that image will be displayed on the screen. Map is stored as an image which consists all four water bodies studied. After clicking on zoom tool only selected water body is popped up. Visual Basic forms and report generated contains the information about all parameters available in each water body in each season for a particular sample. Only on selection of the water body or season or parameter particular query is fired, information is retrieved from the database and displayed on the form and report is generated. [16]

6. VISUAL BASIC FORMS AND REPORTS

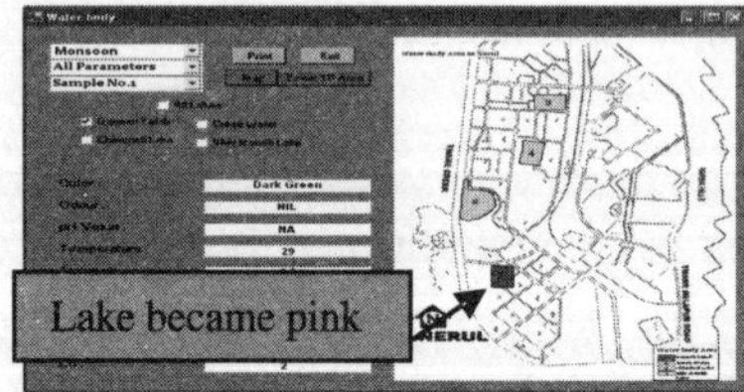

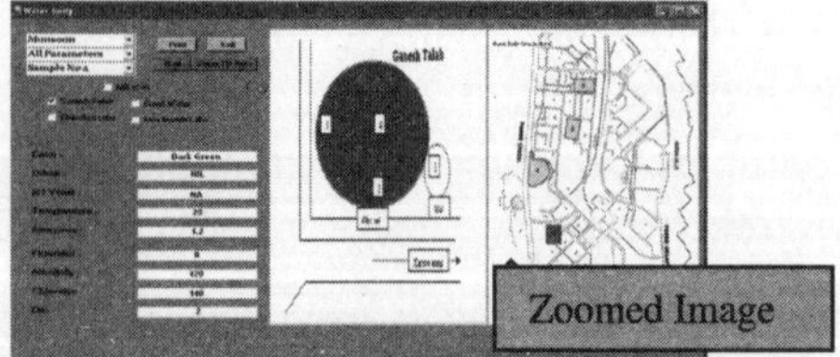

Fig. 2 VB forms of selected water body   **Fig. 3** Zoomed image of selected water body

Following maps will show the Map having all four water bodies in study area for a selected parameter for Monsoon and sample no. 1. Shades of the same colour has been used to show the density of that parameter contained in all water bodies. [7]

After selecting the water body from the check box and selecting other options available, only selected water body turned to pink. Now after selecting zoom to button the image stored in the database for that lake is popped as zoomed image and displayed on the VB form.

7. FINDINGS

With the help of the GIS system and its analysis module the following results were obtained for the Nerul water bodies.

7.1 Nerul (Results) Summer

1. High turbidity was observed in most of the water bodies.
2. High phosphate levels were observed in the creek water samples.
3. High iron content was observed in the Chincholi water Ganesh lake at Karave.
4. High chloride levels were observed in Chincholi water body.
5. Low levels of DO were observed in all water bodies though Ganesh *talab* samples recorded comparatively higher DO levels (2 to 3.2 mg/l vis-a-vis 0.4 to 1.6 mg/l at other sampling points).

Like this Wnter and Monsoon results are also recorded.

8. CONCLUSION

Thus survey and analysis of pollution pattern using GIS can become further useful for achieving sustainable management of these freshwater resources which is the main aim of this project. Thus GIS study proves to be an important tool to evaluate the impacts of the anthropogenic/ natural activities on the quality of freshwater. Thus spatial distribution maps of various pollution parameters are used to demarcate the location distribution of water pollutants in a comprehensive manner and helps in suggesting freshwater pollution control and remedial measures in a holistic way. For instance, at the primary level, emphasis can be put on general observations. This entire exercise can be carried out on a small or large scale. It is hoped that this project, can help in the efforts to prevent further deterioration of our environment and reduce the related disease burden.

It will also help in fast retrieval of the data as this model is using very strong model developed in SQL Server 2005 (RDBMS) as back end and Visual Basic 6.0 as front end as well as GIS software for getting map as an output. Such type of water monitoring can be followed in various area at different scales of operation has become a strong possibility today. Hence if same type of data is collected which will fit in this model, then this model can be executed

The observed environmental quality trends also highlight the need for steps to be taken to clean up the environment and thus improve the environment and health status of citizens of Navi Mumbai. This could be done by committed involvement of individuals, educational institutions, NGO's and by the NMMC. The Maharashtra Pollution Control Board (MPCB), scientists, along with the industries in the area, also have an important role to play in making Navi Mumbai a better place to live in. The proposed system brings automation, sharing and exchange of information, team work and dynamism. Making comparison gets easier by seeing the analyses and the syntheses. Implementation of legal action and regulations for preventing the water quality from further getting deteriorated some Remedial measures can be imposed.

As traditional RDBMS or SQL-DBMS products focused on the efficient management of data drawn from a limited set of data-types (defined by the relevant language standards), an object-relational DBMS allows software-developers to integrate their own types and the methods that apply to them into the DBMS. [4] This model can be improvised by including neighborhood analysis using higher version of GIS software and by using multimedia database with VB.NET or Java as a front end. The existing model is best suitable for the same type of data.

References

1. Dr. B.S.Mahajan, Ms. Suma Nair.: Protocol guide Health and Environment : Action based Learning. Homi Bhabha Centre for Science Education, Mumbai, 2004-05

2. Dr. B.S.Mahajan, Ms. Suma Nair.: Technical Report Health and Environment Action based Learning. Homi Bhabha Centre for Science Education, Mumbai, 2004-05.

3. Silberschatz, Korth, Sudarshan.: Database System Concepts. McGraw Hill

4. Ramkrishanan,Gehrke.: Database Management Systems. 3rd Edition. MGH

5. Chang.: Introduction to GIS. Tata McGraw Hill

6. Ian Heywood.: Introduction to GIS. Tata McGraw Hill

7. Julia case Bradley, Anita C. Millspaugh.: Programming in VB 6. TMH

8. http://en.wikipedia.org/wiki/Object-relational_database

9. www.esri.arcview, www.gisday.com

10. ArcNews.:A magazine featuring GIS success stories of organizations .

11. ArcUser.:A magazine for ESRI software users.

12. ArcWatch.:An e-magazine for GIS news, views, and insights.

13. GRAM++ User Manual, IIT Mumbai.

CHAPTER 32

The Evolution of the Association Rules

[1]Jitendra Agarwal and [2]Varshali Jaiswal
[1]Department Information Technology RGTU,
[2]School of Information Technology Rajiv Gandhi Technological University (State Technological University of MP)
E-mail: jitendra@rgtu.net, varshalijaiswal@gmail.com

ABSTRACT

Association rules are a popular and well researched method for discovering interesting relation between variables in large databases. And discovering association rules is one of the most important tasks in data mining. For generating strong association rules is depend on the association rule extraction by any algorithm for example Apriory algorithm or Fp-growth etc. The evolution of the rules by interestingness measure for example support/confidence, lift/interest, Correlation Coefficient, Statistical Correlation, Leverage, Conviction etc. The association rules mining are dependent on both steps equally. The classical model of association rules mining is support-confidence, the interestingness measure of which is the confidence measure. The classical Interestingness measure in Association Rules have existed some disadvantage. This paper present measurements (support/confidence, intrest/lift, Chi-square Test for Independency, Correlation Coefficient, Statistical Correlation) to calculate the strength of association rules. Besides Support and confidencet, there are other interestingness measures, which include generality, reliability, peculiarity, novelty, surprisingness, utility, and applicability. This paper investigates the evolution association rule mining.

Keywords: association rules; support/confidence; interest/lift; Chi-square Test for Independency; Correlation Coefficient; Statistical Correlation

INTRODUCTION

In the previous few years a lot of work is done in the field of data mining especially in finding association between items in a data base of customer transaction. Association rule mining, one of the most important and well researched techniques of data mining[1]. It aims to extract interesting correlations, frequent patterns, associations or casual structures among sets of items in the transaction databases or other data repositories. Nowadays, association rules mining from large databases is an active research field of data mining motivated by many application areas such as telecommunication networks, market and risk management, inventory control etc.

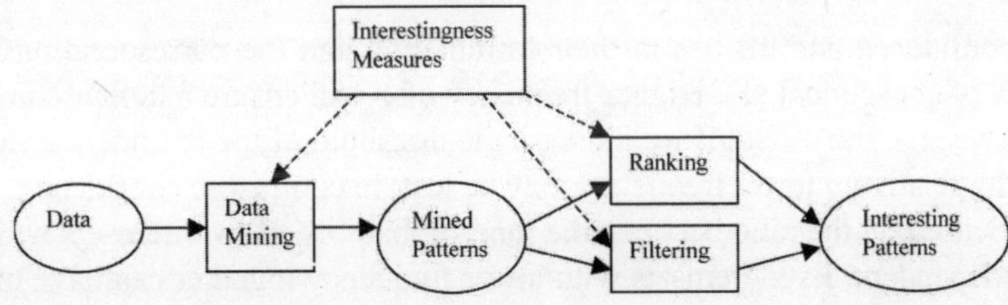

One challenge for the association rule mining is the rules measurement and selection. Since the data mining methods are mostly applied in the large datasets, the association mining is very likely to generate numerous rules from which it is difficult to build a model or summarize useful information. A simple but widely used approach to help mitigate this problem is to gradually increase the threshold value of support and confidence until a manageable size of rules is generated. It is an effective way to reduce the number of rules; however it may cause problems in the results as well. The major concern is that by increasing the minimum support and confidence value, some important information may be filtered out while the remaining rules may be obvious or already known. The data mining is a process involving interpretation and evaluation as well as analysis. For association rule mining, the evaluation is an even more important phase of the process.

This paper is divided in to three sections the first section gives the formal definition and some explanation of each measure. The second section gives us the calculation of each measure on our sample data and the last section contains our recommendation on using which measure for discovering the interesting rules.

1. Support/Confidence: *Support[1]* is defined as the percentage of transactions in the data that contain all items in both the antecedent and the consequent of the rule,

$S = P (X \cap Y) = \{X \cap Y\}/\{D\}$ Confidence is an estimate of the conditional probability of Given X, i.e. $P(X \cap Y)/P(X)$. $C = P (X \cap Y)/P(X)$ The support of a rule is also important since it indicates how frequent the rule is in the transactions. Rules that have very small support are often uninteresting since they do not describe significantly large populations

A rule that has a very high confidence (i.e., close to 1.0) is very important because it provides an accurate prediction on the association of the items in the rule. The disadvantage of this, it is not trivial to set good values for the minimum support and confidence thresholds.

Fundamental critique in so far that the same support threshold is being used for rules containing a different number of items

1. LIFT/INTEREST

A few years after the introduction of association rules, researchers [3] started to realize the disadvantages of the confidence measure by not taking into account the baseline frequency of the consequent. Therefore, Lift, originally called Interest, was first introduced by Motwani, et al., (1997), it measures the number of times X and Y occur together compared to the expected number of times if they were statistically independent. It is presented as:

$$I = P (X \cap Y)/P(X) \, P(Y)$$

Since $P(Y)$appears in the denominator of the interest measure, the interest can be seen as the confidence divided by the baseline frequency of Y. The interest measure is defined over $[0, \infty\,[$and its interpretation is as follows:

If $I < 1$, then X and Y appear less frequently together in the data than expected under the assumption of conditional independence. X and Y are said to be negatively interdependent.

If $I = 1$, then X and Y appear as frequently together as expected under the assumption of conditional independence. X and Y are said to be independent of each other.

If $I > 1$, then X and Y appear more frequently together in the data than expected under the assumption of conditional independence. X and Y are said to be positively interdependent.

Advantages

The difference between confidence and lift lies in their formulation and the corresponding limitations. Confidence is sensitive to the probability of consequent (Y). Higher frequency of Y will ensure a higher confidence value even if there is not true relationship between X and Y. But if we increase the threshold of the confidence value to avoid this situation, some important pattern with relatively lower frequency may be lost. In contrast to confidence, lift is not vulnerable to the rare items problem. It is focused on the ratio between the joint probability of two itemsets with respect to their expected probabilities if they are independent. Even itemsets with lower frequency together can have high lift values.

Disadvantages

The first one is related to the problem of sampling variability (see section Empirical Bayes Estimate). This means that for low absolute support values, the value of the interest measure may fluctuate heavily for small changes in the value of the absolute support of a rule. This problem is solved by introducing a Empirical Bayes estimate of the interest measure.

The second problem is that the interest measure should not be used to compare the interestingness of itemsets of different size. Indeed, the interest tends to be higher for large itemsets than for small itemsets.

3. Chi-square Test for Independency: A natural way to express the dependence between the antecedent and the consequent of an association Rule $X \cup Y$ is the correlation measure based on the Chi-square test for independence [3].

$$\chi^2 = \sum_x \sum_y \frac{(O_{xy} - E_{xy})^2}{E_{xy}}$$

The chi-square test for independence is calculated as follows, with Oxy the observed frequency in the contingency table and Exy the expected frequency (by multiplying the row and column total divided by the grand total) Therefore, the χ^2 is a summed normalized square deviation of the observed values from the expected values. It can then be used to calculate the p-value by comparing the value of statistics to a chi-square distribution to determine the significance level of the rule. For instance, if the p-value is higher than 0.05 (when χ^2 value is less than 3.84), we can tell X and Y are significantly independent, and therefore the rule $X \Rightarrow Y$ can be pruned from the results.

Advantages

The advantage of the chi-square measure, on the other hand, is that it takes into account all the available information in the data about the occurrence or non-occurrence of combinations of items, whereas the lift/interest measure only measures the co-occurrence of two itemsets, corresponding to the upper left cell in the contingency table.

Disadvantages

First of all, the Chi-square test rests on the normal approximation to the Binomial distribution. This approximation breaks down when the expected values (Exy) are small.

The Chi-square test should only beused when all cells in the contingency table have expected values greater than 1 and at least 80% of the cells have expected values greater than 5.

The Chi-squaretest will produce larger values when the data set grows to infinity. Therefore, more items will tend to become significantly interdependent if the size of the dataset increases. The reason is that the Chi-square value depends on the total number of transactions, whereas the critical cut off value only depends on the degrees of freedom (which is equal to 1 for binary variables) and the desired significance level. Therefore, whilst comparison of Chi-squared values within the same data set may be meaningful, it is certainly not advisable to compare Chi-squared values across different data sets.

4. Correlation Coefficient: The [7] correlation coefficient (also known as the Φ-coefficient) measures the degree of linear interdependency between a pair of random variables. It is defined by the covariance between the two variables divided by their standard deviations:

where $\rho XY = 0$ when X and Y are independent and ranges from $[-1, +1]$.

5. Statistical Correlation: To [8] get the association rules with real correlation, this measure put forward statistical correlation from the view point of statistics to compensate the deficiency of support-confidence. Statistical correlation is defined as equation, which is

$$\rho XY = \frac{P(X \cap Y) - P(X)P(Y)}{\sqrt{P(X)(1 - P(X))} \sqrt{P(Y)(1 - P(Y))}}$$

$$S_{\mathrm{corr}(x\,\cup\,y)} = \frac{|D|\,\mathrm{support}\,(x\cup y) - |D|\,\underset{i\varepsilon(x\cup y)}{\pi}\,\mathrm{support}\,(1)}{\sqrt{|D|\,\underset{i\varepsilon(x\cup y)}{\pi}\,\mathrm{sup}\,port\,(1)\,|D|\,(1 - \underset{i\varepsilon(x\cup v)}{\pi}\,\mathrm{sup}\,port\,(1))}}$$

If Scorrelation $\{X \cup Y\} < 0$, it denotes that theitems in antecedent X and the consequent Y of an association rule are negative correlation, and the items have a relationship of restricting each However, although the rule has promising other. confidence, it is totally misleading since If Scorrelation $\{X \cup Y\} = 0$, it means that the the baseline frequency of customers buyingitems in antecedent X and the consequent Y of an association rule are independent, and the item are not mutually influence.

Rules	Support	Confidence	Lift	Chi-square test	Corre ation	Statistical Corr elation
Cola → cheese	0.40	0.66	0.888	402.77	+ 0.23	− 0.100
Cheese → cola	0.40	0.533	0.888	402.77	+ 0.23	− 0.11

cheese is 75%. In other words, among all customers buying cola, the proportion of customers buying cheese is even lower than in the total group of customers.

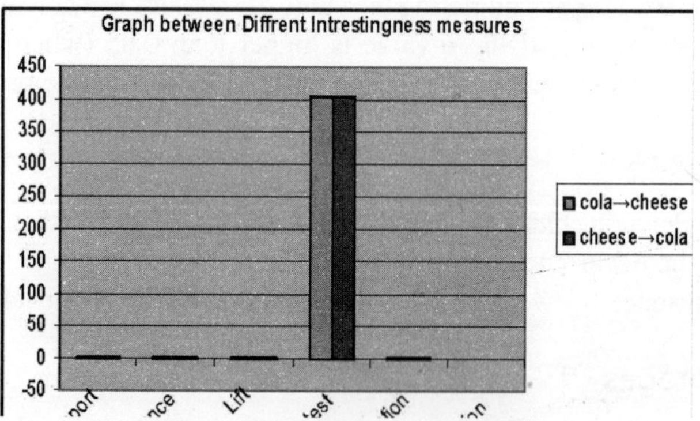

If Scorrelation $\{X \cup Y\} > 0$, it represents that the items in antecedent X and the consequent Y of an association rule have some degree correlation, and correlation is more and more strong with the Scorrelation increase.

Advantages

Scorrelation, which can enhance the correlation degree of items in association rule and cut negative correlation rules.

A example illustrates why confidence can be misleading to define interesting rules. Suppose the following situation. Among 5000 customers:

- 3000 buy cola
- 3750 buy cheese
- 2000 both purchase cola and cheese Example in table format

	Buy Cheese	Do not buy cheese	Total
Buy Cola	2000	1000	3000
Do not buy Cola	1750	250	2000
Total	3750	1250	5000

3. CONCLUSIONS

It is generally accepted that there is no single measure that is perfect and applicable to all problems. Usually different measures are complementary and can be applied at different

Then, the rule buys cola → buy cheese (40%, applications or phases. Tan et al., [2002] 66 %) could indicate a promising rule. conducted research on how to select the right measures for association patterns, and concluded that the best measures should be selected by matching the properties of the existing objective measures against the expectation of domain experts, which leads us to explore the subjective measures of the association rules. 20 The following suggestions can be formulated based on the analysis of the different interestingness measures discussed in the previously with example:

- Confidence is never the preferred method to compare association rules since it does not account for the baseline frequency of the consequent.
- The lift/interest value corrects for this baseline frequency but when the support threshold is very low, it may be instable due to sampling variability. However, when the data set is very large, even a low percentage support threshold will yield rather large absolute support values. In that case, we do not need to worry too much about sampling variability. A drawback of the interest measure is that it cannot be used to compare item sets or rules of different size since it tends to overestimate the interestingness for large item sets.
- When association rules need to be compared between data sets of different sizes, the Chi-square test for independence and Correlation analysis are not preferred since they are highly dependent on the dataset size. Both measures tend to overestimate the interestingness of item sets in large datasets.

References

1. Aggarwal & Yu, 1998 C.C. Aggarwal and P.S. Yu. A New Framework for Item Set Generation. In: Proceedings of the ACM PODS Symposium on Principles of Database Systems, Seattle, Washington (USA), 18-24, 1998.
2. Agresti, 1996 A. Agresti. An Introduction to Categorical Data Analysis. Wiley Series in Probability and Statistics, 1996.
3. Brijs et al., 1999 T. Brijs, G. Swinnen, K. Vanhoof and G. Wets. The use of association rules for product assortment decisions: a case study. In: Proceedings of the Fifth International Conference on Knowledge Discovery and Data Mining, San Diego (USA), August 15-18, 254260, 1999.
4. R. Agrawal, T. Imielinski, and A.N. Swami, Mining Association Rules between Sets of Items in Large Databases, in: Proceedings of the 1993 ACM SIGMOD Conference, pp.207–216, 1993.
5. Han J, Pei J, Yin Y, Mining frequent patterns without candidate generation[A], Proceeding of 2000 ACM-SIGMOD International Conference on Management of Data[C], pp.1–12, 2000.
6. R. Agrawal R S. "Fast Algorithms for Mining "Association Rules." Proc. 20th Int. Conf. on Very Large DataBases, 1994, pp: 487~499.
7. Jianhua Liu "A New Interestingness Measure of Association Rules" Second International Conference on Genetic and Evolutionary Computing,2008.
8. Jian Hu & Xiang Yang-Li "Association Rules Mining Based on Statistical Correlation 2008"
9. A.silberschatz AT. "What Makes pattern interesting in kownledge discovery systems." IEEE Transactions on Knowledge and Data Engineering, 1996, 8(6), pp: 970 974
10. T. Brijs, K. Vanhoof, G. Wets "Defining Interestingness For Association Rules" International Journal "Information Theories & Applications" Vol.10.

CHAPTER 33

Case Representation and Retrieval for Statistical Process Control

Morteza Behbahani, ABBAS Saghaei and Rassoul Noorossana
Department of Industrial Engineering, Islamic Azad University, Tehran, Iran
E-mail: mortezab77@gmail.com; a.saghaei@srbiau.ac.ir; norosana@eumst.edu

ABSTRACT

Statistical Process control (SPC) consists of methods for understanding, monitoring and improving process performance. So many cases are implemented in the field of SPC and similar past cases can be used as a guide to solve new problems of SPC Therefore, the main idea of this paper is the representation and retrieval of the cases of Statistical Process Control. The indexes have been chosen to represent the important aspects of the cases, and Nearest-neighbor retrieval is used to measure similarity between the current SPC case and past cases.

Keywords: Statistical Process Control; Case Representation; Case Retrieval; Nearest Neighbor Retrieval; Indexing; Similarity Relation; Knowledge Engineering

1. INTRODUCTION

Statistical Process control (SPC) consists of methods for understanding, monitoring and improving process performance over the time [16]. The successful results of SPC applications in various production and service industries have attracted attention of quality and statistic experts. Therefore, many investigations related to SPC have been done. But considering the broadness of SPC area, it is so hard to provide a comprehensive underlying model for SPC problem solving.

Knowledge engineering (KE) have been defined in 1983 by Edward Feigenbaum, and Pamela McCorduck as a discipline that involves integrating knowledge into computer systems by building, maintaining and developing knowledge-based systems(KBS) in order to solve complex problems.[5]

Case-based reasoning (CBR) systems are a type of Knowledge-Based Systems helpful for problem solving in domains without underlying model and comprehensive understanding [10]. The basic idea of CBR is that "The similar problems have similar solutions" [14]. In CBR, descriptions of past experience, represented as cases, are stored in a case base for later retrieval when the user encounters a new case with similar parameters.

So many cases are implemented in the field of SPC and they are accessible in article databases. Similar past cases can be used as a guide to solve new problems and implementation of SPC. Therefore, a framework for representation of SPC cases and retrieval of similar cases with current SPC problem has been proposed in this paper.

2. CASE REPRESENTATION

The cases of SPC are usually stored in databases in unstructured format. Indexes are used to represent cases and speed up retrieval. A flat case base is a common structure of case representation. In this method indexes are chosen to represent the important aspects of the case, and retrieval involves comparing the current case's features to each case in the case base. Case indexes should be predictive, address the purposes the case will be used for, be abstract enough to allow for widening the future use of the case base, and be concrete enough to be recognized in future. [10]

`The knowledge area of SPC is so broad therefore, the indexes are used to case retrieval are various and depending on the type of these indexes, they can get different values, such as: qualitative, quantitative, set of elements, string and etc.

A case may represent something different, but typically comprises a problem and solution. Thus, cases are usually represented as two sets of attribute–value pairs that represent the problem and solution features. So, a case base can be visualized in terms of problem space and solution space. The problem space of cases is used to case retrieval.

It's to difficult to make decision what features of a case must be represented and deciding on the indexing vocabulary generally requires knowing what are the important features of Statistical process control.

We have reviewed some important sources of SPC to extract main features of SPC problems and select some indexes to represent these important features.

2.1 An Overview of Statistical Process Control

The purpose of this article is not to describe all of SPC domain comprehensively, but to give an overview to detect some important features for case indexing.

Hardly any comprehensive descriptions of the SPC approach can be found, in literature. Some of these descriptions were found, focused on the methodological and organizational aspects of implementation (e.g [3], [4], [6], [11]). In these studies, some steps have been determined for implementation of SPC approach, such as: initial activities to develop a SPC system, process analysis, measurement system development, control charting, out of control action plan providing, process capability analysis and etc.

SPC is a practical approach to reduce variability of Processes. Therefore, understanding of the variation in values of a qualitative characteristic is of primary importance in SPC. Control charts are used to detect assignable cause variation. In many applications of control charting (e.g. [1], [16]) it's useful to distinguish between Phase I and Phase II methods and applications. In phase I, control chart limits are often calculated using parameter estimates from an in-control reference sample. In Phase II, new samples are compared with the estimated control limits to monitor for detecting assignable causes. If these causes can be eliminated from process, variability will be reduced and the process will be improved. Montgomery [9] described the process improvement activities using control charts.

By reviewing these sources and collecting the main topics have been discussed in them, the main parts of SPC approach can be briefly described in Fig. 1.

It has different parts and several issues about each part have been considered that may be effective in similar cases retrieval process. Main concepts and important features of these issues must be extracted to determine indexes for representing the cases of SPC.

Therefore, to extract these contents, we collected some important educational books about SPC (e.g.[8], [9], [12], [15] and etc) and used their materials especially their table of contents. Then, to avoid ignoring other important contents for indexing, we listed the keywords of top 1000 articles about SPC in terms of citation number and we investigated these materials and finally, by using these materials as well as comments of some quality experts, the indexes for representing cases related to SPC have been illustrated in Fig. 2.

2.2 Indexes for Case Representation

As shown in Fig. 2, in this system we use three different types of indexes to represent and retrieving the cases:

- Functional index describes the function of the case in the field of SPC and Functional Roles is the only sub-index of it.
- Functional roles: Each case, depending on the problem which is defined, goes through a path to address the problem. This path determines its functional roles. A case in the field of SPC can be taken one or more functional

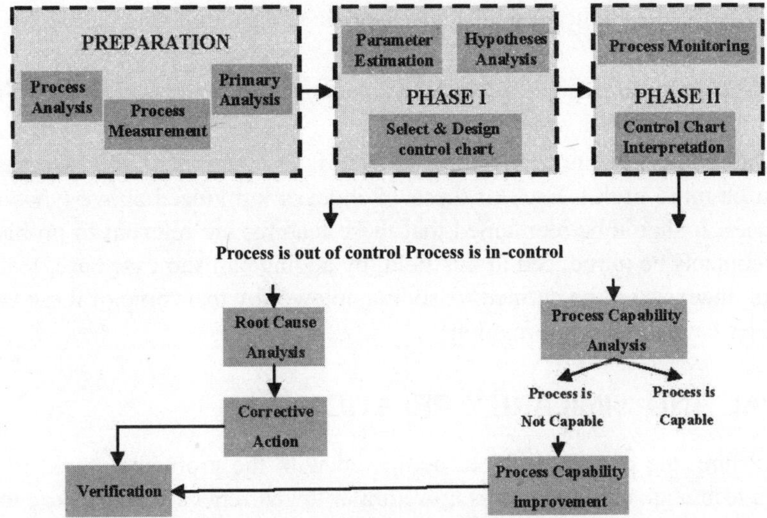

Fig. 1   The general approach of SPC

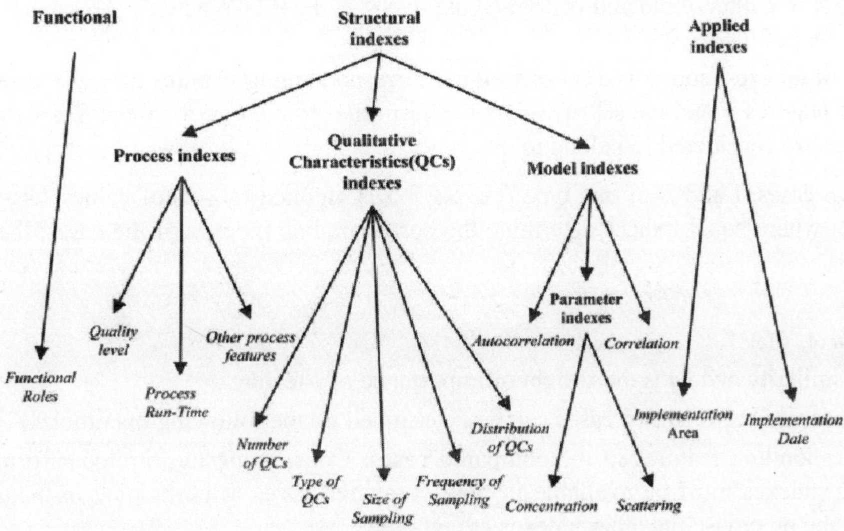

Fig. 2   The indexes for representing SPC

roles among following set that have been specified among the extracted materials of SPC mentioned above: Monitoring, Pattern recognition, Interpretation, Root Cause Analysis, Data Gathering, Data reduction, Data Clustering, Change point estimation, Parameter Estimation, Process Capability Analysis, Signal Analysis, Forecasting, Detect Assignable Cause, Chart Selection, Characteristic Selection, Model Selection, Accuracy Calculation, Fault Diagnosis, Chart Designing, Risk Analysis, Coast Analysis, Chart Designing, Specify Sampling method and etc.

- Structural indexes represent features which describe the structural components of the case. These indexes include: indexes of Process features that analyze the structure of the process that has been studied in the case (Quality level, Process Run-Time, Other Process features). indexes of Qualitative characteristics(QCs) which represent the features of the qualitative characteristics of the process that are controlled in the case (Number of QCs, Type of QCs, Sample size, Sample frequency, Distributions of QCs) and indexes of Model features which show some characteristics of the model of SPC have been applied in the case (Autocorrelation, Concentration parameter, Scattering Parameter, Correlation). Explaining all of these sub-indexes is beyond the scope of this paper.

- Applied indexes describe the application area and the date of case implementation. So, there are two following sub-indexes:
- Application area: SPC has been used in the various areas of Science and Technology. So, the application area of SPC cases can be useful in similar case retrieval.
- Implementation Date: Since the knowledge area of SPC is growing increasingly, retrieving the closer cases in terms of time can be more useful. Each of these 15 indexes introduced above (shown in Fig.2), represents a feature of SPC cases. It should be mentioned that these features are relevant to problem space not to solution space and if new contents be introduced in this field, by adding cases to case base, features can be updated and their corresponding indexes will be defined. Also, it's noteworthy that some of these case indexes can be given values because cases have limited information.

3. CASE RETRIEVAL AND SIMILARITY RELATION

During the retrieval procedure, the current problem compared with the problems stored in the case base. Nearest-neighbor retrieval [13] is a technique used to express how similar the current case is to a case in case base by measuring Degree of Similarity value. To determine how to measure the similarity between two cases of SPC we define some basic notions primarily:

Definition 1   A case A is a three-tuple and is defined as: $A = < F, V, W >$ Where F, a finite set of features of a case reflecting their nature (set of indexes);

V, a set of values of indexes; and W is a set of weights corresponding to features of acase reflecting the importance of indexes. The set of features F and the set of weights W form the structure S of case A $S = < F, W >$. The cases that have identical structure are considered to belong to one type.

Definition 2   For two cases A and B of one type (i.e. $SA = SB$), defined by sets of values $VA = \{a_1, a_2, ..., a_n\}$ and $VB = \{b1, b2, ..., bn\}$, where equal indices determine the corresponding indexes of the cases, the overall similarity is defines as:

$$**(,b),$$
$$sima\ w\ Sim\ A,\ B(,)**$$

$simi$ is the degree of similarity and wi is the weight of importance of i-feature .

Now, similarity measure between two cases can be determined by the following operations [7]:

- Find the corresponding features in the compared cases; Considering the limited information, the values of corresponding indexes must be available in both compared cases to participate in measuring the degree of similarity. On the otherwise the other indexes are ignored.
- for every feature, compute the degree of similarity between the corresponding indexes of the cases;
- Multiply the obtained values by the corresponding coefficient, reflecting the importance of the feature (weight of importance), that can be specified by the user in range of [0-10] for each feature, and sum them to get overall similarity value.

3.1   Computing the Degree of Similarity for Corresponding Features

The notion of similarity is opposite to the definition of difference. Therefore, a way of measuring degree of similarity is determination of the distance between two values. The partial similarity l for two corresponding features a and b is defined as:

$$sim\ (a,\ b) = l(a,\ b) = 1 - d(a,\ b) \tag{2}$$

where $d(a, b)$ is the distance function. The value of distance d is from the interval from 0 to 1. If the features are completely different then d equals 1.

3.2   Distance Measurements:

As mentioned previously, different types of indexes are used to represent the features of a case in SPC field. Depends on the type of these indexes, the distance measure may be different.

Avramenko and Kraslawski [2] collect some distance measures for different types of data that have applied in other investigations for Nearest-neighbor retrieval.

Some of these distance measures have been used in this research for computing the degree of similarity between two SPC cases. To learn more about these distance measures, see reference [2].

The type of introduced indexes is determined in Table 1. So, it is recognizable which distance measure (introduced in reference [2]) has been used to measure similarity between the corresponding indexes of two cases.

4.   CONCLUSIONS

We have developed a software based on the contents mentioned in this paper using *C #*.net 2008 and Access 2007. This software has 2 major modules, Case Registration and Case retrieving. In Case Registration module, the implemented cases can be indexed and stored in database and in Case Retrieving module, specifications of the current problems are entered by the user (assigning value to the indexes and determining the importance of each index); then, system searches the similar cases with current problem in database (case base) by measuring degree of similarity with each of the stored cases.

To check performance of this software, we have indexed 100 cases published in 3 major journals related to SPC (Journal of Quality Technology; Technometrics; Quality Engineering) and stored them in case base. Then, we used this case base to solve 50 hypothetical problems about SPC. In all efforts, the solutions of similar cases retrieved in database were helpful to solve new problems.

Results of implementing this representation and retrieval system include: This representation and retrieval system can be used as a virtual expert to solve SPC problems. Both types of knowledge can be used to solve SPC problems, since the cases can be simultaneously included tacit and explicit knowledge. High performance in searching similar cases, because of applying the similarity concept instead of exact matching.

Table 1   The type of indexes

INDEX	TYPE
Functional Roles Process Run	Set of elements
Time Quality Level of	Numeric
Process Other process	Numeric Vector
specifications Number of	Vector Set of
QCs Type of QCs Size of	elements Set of
Sampling Frequency of	elements
Sampling Distribution of QCs	Qualitative
Autocorrelation	Vector Set of
Concentration parameter	elements
Scattering parameter	Numeric Vector
Correlation Application area	Vector Vector
Implementation Date	Set of elements
	Numeric

References

1. ANSI/ASQ. B2-1996: Control Charts Method of Analyzing Data, American Society for Quality, Milwaukee, WI (1996)

2. Avramenko, Y.L., Kraslawski, A: Similarity Concept for Case-Based Design in Process Engineering. Computers and Chemical Engineering, Vol 30 (2006) 548-557

3. Berger, R.W. and Hart, Th. H: Statistical Process Control: A Guide for Implementation,Dekker, New York, NY. (1986)

4. Does, M.M., Schippers, W.A.J, Trip, A.: A Framework for Implementation of Statistical Process Control, International Journal of Quality Science, Vol. 2 No. 3, (1997) 181-198

5. Feigenbaum, E., McCorduck, P., and Nii, H.P: The Rise of the Expert Company, New York Times Books, (1988)

6. Gaafar, L.K. and Keats, J.B: Statistical process control: a guide for implementation, International Journal of Quality and Reliability Management, Vol. 9 No. 4, (1992) 9-20.

7. Kolodner, J: Case-Based Reasoning. Morgan Kaufman Publisher, Inc. San Mateo, CA (1993)

8. Montgomery, D.C: Introduction to Statistical Quality Control, sixth edition, John. Wiley & Sons, Hoboken, NJ (2009)

9. Oakland J S. Statisical process control. 5th ed. Oxford: Butterworth□]Heinemann, (2003)

10. Pal, S., Shiu, S: Faundations of Soft case Base Reasoning, Wiely & Sons, (2004)1-30

11. Parks, C.J: Statistical quality control: management's role, Manufacturing Engineering, Vol. 91 No. 6, (1983) 59-62.

12. Smith. G.M: Statistical Process Control and Quality Improvement. Prentice-Hall,(1998)

13. Watson, I. D: Applying Case-Based Reasoning: Techniques for Enterprise Systems. Morgan Kaufmann. San Francisco, California (1997) 23-47

14. Watson, L: Applying knowledge management, Morgan Kaufmann publication,(2003)20-27

15. Wheeler, D.J., Chambers, D.S: Understanding statistical process control (2ed.). Knoxville, Tennessee: SPC Press. (1992)

16. Woodall, W.H. 2000. Controversies and contradictions in statistical process control. Journal of Quality Technology, (2000) 341-378

CHAPTER 34

Density Based Approach for Discovering Intruders (Securing Database)

Rajurwar S.S.[1] and V.R. Ghorpade[2]

[1]Shivaji University, Kolhapur (MS), India, [2]D.Y. Patil College of Engineering and Technology, Kolhapur (MS), India

E-mail: balshetwar.satara@gmail.com, vijayghorpade@hotmail.com

ABSTRACT

The wealth of information embedded in huge databases belonging to corporations has encouraged a tremendous interest in the areas of knowledge discovery and data mining. Security of underlying data has become a major issue.

The approach proposed here discovers an intruder from the audit trails of the database by clustering them, these audit trails are large and dynamic in nature so an efficient clustering technique is proposed that makes proper use of main memory and also requires less I/Os.

Keywords: Intruder, Anomaly detection, Clustering, Audit log files

1. INTRODUCTION

The data and information embedded in huge database belonging to companies and organizations are their wealth and that is why they take great care of it from internal and external users. Therefore, development of DBMS with high security assurance is a central area of research. DBMS provides many mechanisms like: authentication, access control, encryption, auditing for security they alone does not assure data security. If they are used along with IDS they can protect data from malicious and unauthorized access (inside & outside users).

In order to discover intruders the audit log files are to be clustered .These audit log files are large & dynamic in nature so traditional clustering techniques cannot be efficient due to following problems:

1. They assume that there is sufficient main memory to hold the data to be clustered.
2. Requires more I/Os and performing continuously through the iterations of the algorithm are too expensive.
3. They also assume that the data is present all at once.

Because of the main memory restrictions the traditional algorithms do not scale up to large & dynamic database.

The algorithm proposed here creates clusters with minimum size & density that overcomes these problems.

Data mining refers to the process of semi-automatically analyzing large database and then finds useful patterns. Data mining technique called clustering is used here to create the profiles which are called as roles.

The important aspect of this paper is on proper utilization of main memory and less I/Os cycles while creating the profiles.

2. RELATED WORK

The NIST model defined in [1] shows the working of RBAC model. RBAC is a proven technology for large scale authorization but there is no standard model which results in uncertainty and confusion about its utility and meaning. It is vendor dependant system. Whereas in this paper a concrete algorithm for implementation has been proposed, which is not vendor dependant because profiles (roles) are created from the user behavior.

The mechanism proposed in [2] allows concurrent detection of malicious data access through online analysis of the DBMS audit trail and it is useful in detecting data attacks on database applications. In [2] if a wrong transaction happens to be a good transaction not yet learned, the DBA may add it to the profile this shows a tend toward supervised learning whereas the one which is proposed in this paper is unsupervised anomalous detection.

A.K.Majumdar and Abhinav Srivastav [3] focuses on intrusion detection in database by considering only those attributes of the database that are more sensitive to malicious modification compared to others and an algorithm is proposed that detect modification of sensitive attribute. Whereas the paper which is proposed here is for all sensitive or non-sensitive attributes so as to give security to all the attributes within the database.

The approach dealing with ID for operating system and networks have been developed [4][5] but they have no concrete algorithm and the ID designed for operating system and networks are not suitable for database security. Whereas the one proposed in this paper is totally for the security of data within the database.

Wenhui [6] has developed architecture for security of web based database system without proposing any specific ID mechanism. Anomaly detection of web based attacks has been proposed in [7].

A learning based approach for the detection of SQL attacks is proposed by Valuer .F. in [8]. The methodology used focuses on detection of attacks against backend databases used by web based applications. Whereas, the approach proposed in this paper tends towards general detection of anomalous access pattern in a database as represented by SQL queries submitted to the database.

A misuse detection system tailored for relational database systems is proposed in DEMIDS [9]. It uses audit log data to derive profiles. DEMIDS approach uses semantics encoded in a given database schema whereas the approach proposed in this paper build the profile using syntactic information from SQL queries appearing in the database log which makes this more general.

Martin Ester, [10] presents an approach for a density-based notion of clusters which is designed to discover clusters of arbitrary shape.

3. PROPOSED APPROACH

Many of the organizations define roles to the user for authorized access to the database but not all organizations follow the same. Under the condition where no roles are defined to users, every transaction is associated with the users who issued it. The raw approach would be to build a different profile for every user, but it is not efficient to create a profile for every user under a system where large number of users accesses the database. Many of the users are not particularly active and they submit a query occasionally to a database. Whereas in the case of active users, profiles would suffer from over fitting and in case of inactive users, they would be too general. This makes an adverse effect on the highly active users. This can be trounced by building user group profile (i.e.by clustering similar behaviors) that is solely based on the transactions that users submit to the database. This procedure is better for the highly active users and the same is used here in the paper.

3.1 Architecture of the System

Figure 1 shows the workflow of the proposed system. Every time a user fires a query it is then converted into an acceptable format (same as which is used to create profile). Then a match of this query and already created profiles is done and if found anomalous an alarm is raised to the administrator.

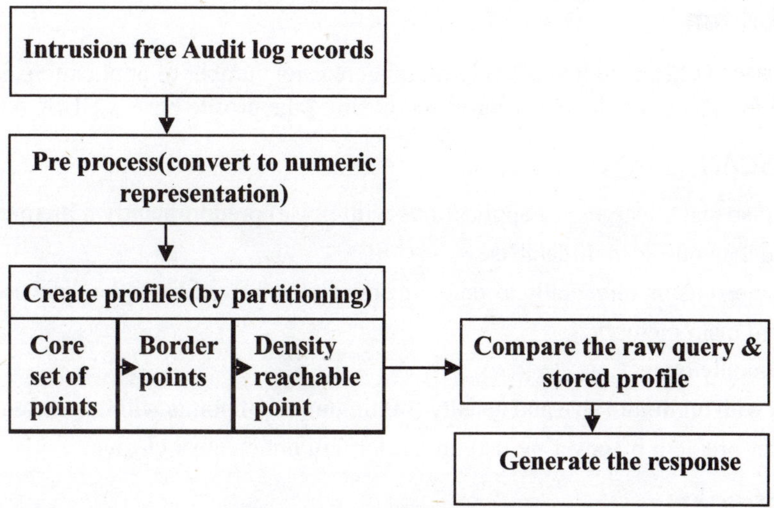

Fig. 1   Workflow of the system

3.2   Representation of Query

For extracting user actions from the database audit file assume that the database audit file has commands like select, insert, delete. To create profiles convert the database entries to a format that is acceptable by the algorithm which is used for clustering the user actions.

Let us represent each entry by five dimensional (5D) representation because it has five attributes (SQL command, projection related information, projected attribute, selection related information, selected attribute).

Thus 5D is the basic unit of data for viewing the log file and to create the profiles.

Definition   A 5D is representation of a log record of the database audit log file. Each entry consists of five fields: SQL command (SC), projection relation (PR), projection attribute (PA), selection relation (SR), selection attribute (SA).

The first field is symbol of SQL command issued by user remaining all are numeric fields showing the projection and selected relations and attribute

Table 1   How to construct a 5D

SQL command	5D
Select R1.A1, R1.C1, R2.B2, R2. D2 FROM R1, R2 WHERE R1.B1 = R2.B2	Select < 2 > < 4 > < 2 > < 2 >

3.3   Anomaly Detection

The method used for the intrusion detection is as follow:

1. Cluster the training set using DBSCAN algorithm.
2. Create a representation cluster for user. i.e. cluster which has maximum number of training set for user after clustering.
3. For every new query, its representation cluster is determined by mapping the user to cluster.
4. After a test to find the representative clusters if the result is positive, the query is marked as an anomaly and an alarm is raised.

3.4 DBSCAN Algorithm

Clustering on large database has been studied actively as an increasing number of applications involved huge amount of data. The algorithm used for clustering the log records and creating the profile here is DBSCAN algorithm.

3.4.1 Why use DBSCAN

DBSCAN (Density-based spatial clustering of applications with noise) predominantly a hierarchical technique.

1. Requires no more than one scan of database.
2. Able to update the results incrementally as data are added or removed from the database.
3. Works with limited main memory.
4. Process each tuple only once.
5. It creates clusters with minimum size and density (minimum no. of points within a certain distance of each other).
6. Handles the outlier problem by ensuring that an outlier will not create a cluster.

3.4.2 Working of DBSCAN

1. Obtain sample database.
2. Define two parameters mp & t-mp.mp indicates the minimum no. of points in any cluster [efficient use of main memory].t-mp indicates threshold i/p value, the distance of every point is less than t-mp [requires less I/Os & thus reduces the expenses of algorithm].
3. No. of clusters are determined by algorithm itself.
4. Firstly partition the point into core set of points that are all close to each other [core points are main portion of a cluster].
5. Then, partition to border points which are close to at least one of the core point.
6. Finally, partition the remaining points, which are not close to any core point [density reachable point].

Algorithm

```
Input:
    D={t₁,t₂,….,tₙ}//set of elements.
    mp                     // number of points in cluster
    t-mp //maxi distance for density measures
Output:
    K={K₁,K₂,K₃,….Kₖ} //set of cluster
DBSCAN algorithm:
K=0; //initially there are no clusters
for  i =1 to n do
if t ᵢ is not in a cluster, then
    X={t ⱼ|t ⱼ is density reachable from t ᵢ};
if X is a valid cluster, then
    K=K+1;
    Kₖ=X;
```

Algorithm 1

Example:

```
t-mp mp=4
```

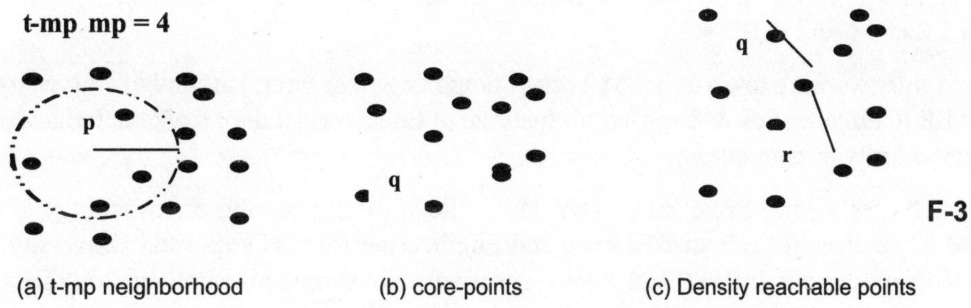

Fig. 3   DBSCN example

3.5   Time and Space Complexity

The time complexity of DBSCAN is $O\,(n\,lg\,n)$ while space is $O\,(n)$. This is worst case behavior. The time complexity can be reduced to $O\,(n)$.

4.   CONCLUSION

This paper shows an approach to discover an intruder by clustering the audit log file by using DBSCAN that uses main memory and I/O cycles efficiently.

5.   ACKNOWLEDGEMENT

 I would like to thank Prof.V.R.Gorphade for his encouragement and comments on earlier drafts of this paper. Without the support of my loving husband V.P. Balshetwar (B.E. Electronics) and our kids Siddhesh and Katyayani it would have been impossible to complete this work.

References

1. Sandhu, R., Ferraiolo, D., Kuhn, R. "The NIST model for role based access control: Towards a unified standard", In Proceedings of the 5th ACM Workshop on Role Based Access Control (2000)
2. Jose Fonseca, Marco Vieria and Henrique Maderia, "Online detection of malicious data access using DBMS auditing"
3. Abhinav Srivastva, Shamik Sural and A.K. Majumdar,"Database intrusion detection using weighted sequence mining", Journal of computer, Vol 1.1, no.4, July 2006.
4. Axelsson, S." Intrusion detection systems: a survey and taxonomy.",Technical Report 99–15, Chalmers Univ., (2000)
5. Hoglund, K.H.A., Sorvari, A." A computer host-based user anomaly detection using the self-organizing map."In Proceedings of the IEEE-INNS-ENNS International Joint Conference on Neural Networks (IJCNN) (2000)
6. Wenhui, S., Tan, T."A novel intrusion detection system modelfor securing web-based database systems." In Proceedings of the 25th Annual International Computer Software and Applications Conference (COMPSAC) (2001)
7. Kruegel, C., Vigna, G." Anomaly detection of web-based attacks."In Proceedings of the ACM Conference on Computer and Communications Security (CCS) (2003)
8. Valeur, F., Mutz, D., Vigna, G." A learning-based approach to the detection of sql attacks." In Proceedings of the International Conference on detection of intrusions and malware, and vulnerability assessment (DIMVA) (2003)

9. Chung, C., Gertz, M., Levitt, K." Demids: a misuse detection system for database systems." In Integrity and Internal Control in Information Systems: Strategic Views on the Need for Control. IFIP TC11 WG11.5 Third Working Conference (2000)

10. Martin Ester, Hans-Peter Kriegel, Jörg Sander, Xiaowei Xu "A Density-Based Algorithm for Discovering Clusters in Large Spatial Databases with Noise" In KDD-96: Published in Proceedings of 2nd International Conference on Knowledge Discovery and Data Mining (KDD-96)

Rajurwar S.S. is currently working towards her M.Tech (Computer Sci. & Engg.) at Shivaji University, Kolhapur, India. She received her AMIE (Computer Sci. & Engg.) from Institute of Engineers (India), Kolkata, India in 2007. Her research interest includes data security & data mining.

V. R. Ghorpade is a Professor and Principal of D.Y.Patil college of engineering & technology Kolhapur, India. He received B.E. and M.E. degrees in Computer Science and Engineering from Marathwada University, Aurangabad, and Shivaji University, Kolhapur, India, in 1990 and 2001 respectively. He earned his Ph. D. in 2008. His research interests include network security and ad hoc networks.

CHAPTER 35

Data Mining-Based Intrusion Detection Systems in Oracle Database 10g

Sonkar S.K., Wakchaure M.A. and Ubale V.S

Computer Engineering Department Electronic & Tel. Comm. Engineering Department AVCOE College of Engineering, Sangamner (MS)-422608, India

E-mail: sonkar_shrinivas@yahoo.co.in, manoj13apr@gmail.com, vilas_ubale@rediffmail.com

ABSTRACT

Network security technology has become crucial in protecting government and industry computing infrastructure. Modern intrusion detection applications face complex requirements – they need to be reliable, extensible, easy to manage, and have low maintenance cost. In recent years, data mining-based intrusion detection systems (IDSs) have demonstrated high accuracy, good generalization to novel types of intrusion, and robust behavior in a changing environment. Still, significant challenges exist in the design and implementation of production quality IDSs. Instrumenting components such as data transformations, model deployment, and cooperative distributed detection remain a labor intensive and complex engineering endeavor. This paper describes DAID, a database-centric architecture that leverages data mining within the Oracle RDBMS to address these challenges. DAID also offers numerous advantages in terms of scheduling capabilities, alert. Infrastructure, data analysis tools, security, scalability, and reliability. DAID is illustrated with an Intrusion Detection Center application prototype that leverages existing functionality in Oracle Database 10g

Keywords: IDS, Oracle database, RDBMS

1. INTRODUCTION

Intrusion detection is an area growing in relevance as more and more sensitive data are stored and processed in networked systems. An intrusion detection system (IDS) monitors networked devices and looks for anomalous or malicious behavior in the patterns of activity in the audit stream. A comprehensive IDS requires a significant amount of human expertise and time for development. Data mining-based IDSs require less expert knowledge yet provide good performance. These systems are also capable of generalizing to new and unknown attacks. Data mining-based intrusion detection systems can be classified according to their detection strategy. There are two main strategies : misuse detection and anomaly detection. Misuse detection attempts to match observed activity to known intrusion patterns. This is typically a classification problem. Anomaly detection attempts to identify behavior that does not conform to normal behavior. This approach has a better chance of detecting novel attacks. IDSs can also be distinguished on the basis of the audit data source (e.g., network-based, host-based). Successful detection of different types of attacks typically requires a variety of audit data sources. Building an IDS is a complex task of knowledge engineering that requires an elaborate infrastructure. An effective contemporary production-quality IDS need an array of diverse components and features, including:

- Centralized view of the data
- Data transformation capabilities
- Analytic and data mining methods
- Flexible detector deployment, including scheduling that enables periodic model creation and distribution
- Real-time detection and alert infrastructure
- Reporting capabilities
- Distributed processing
- High system availability
- Scalability with system load

Recent proposals have highlighted the need for an architecture and framework specification for IDSs. While these proposals provide a good foundation, they are somewhat general in nature and focus either on a methodology specification that alleviates the knowledge engineering effort or on component interaction specification (e.g., XML metadata). The details of the infrastructure required to support these feature-rich complex frameworks are not provided, instead such details are proposed to be handled by the system engineers responsible for the implementation. This paper demonstrates that the Oracle Database, with its capabilities for supporting mission critical applications, distributed processing, and integration of analytics, can be an appropriate platform for an IDS implementation. Given the data-centric nature of the intrusion detection process, leveraging existing RDBMS infrastructure can be both efficient and effective. The current paper presents DAID (Database-centric Architecture for Intrusion Detection) for the Oracle Database. This RDBMS-centric framework can be used to build, manage, deploy, score, and analyze data mining-based intrusion detection models. The described approach is adopted in the Intrusion Detection Center (IDC) prototype – an application implemented using the capabilities of Oracle Database 10g Release 2.

The paper is organized as follows. Section 2 outlines the proposed architecture. The individual components are described and illustrated with references to the IDC prototype and functionality available in the Oracle Database. Section 3 presents the conclusions and directions for future work.

2. A DATABASE-CENTRIC ARCHITECTURE

DAID (Figure 1) shares many aspects of the AMG (Adaptive Model Generation) architecture. As in AMG, a database component plays a key role in the architecture. Unlike AMG, where the database is only a centralized data repository, in DAID, all major operations take place in the database itself. DAID also explicitly addresses data transformations, an essential component in analytics. DAID has the following major components:

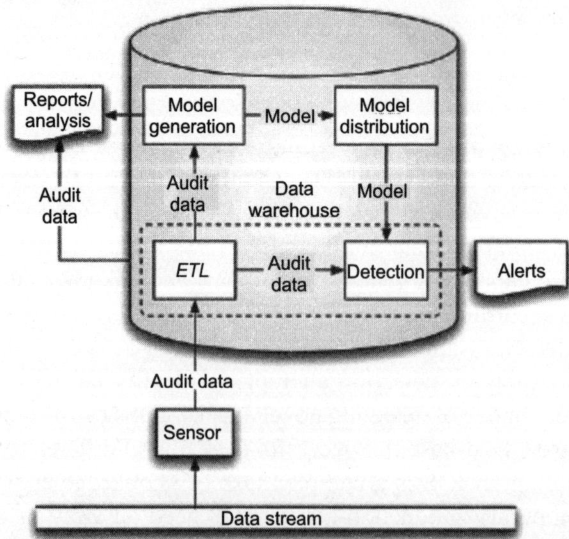

Fig. 1 Database-centric architecture for intrusion detection

- Sensors
- Extraction, transformation and load (ETL)
- Centralized data warehousing
- Automated model generation
- Automated model distribution
- Real-time and offline detection
- Report and analysis
- Automated alerts

The activity in a computer network is monitored by an array of sensors producing a stream of audit data. The audit data are processed and loaded in a centralized data repository (ETL). The stored data are used for model generation. The model generation data mining methods are integrated in the database infrastructure – no data movement is required. The generated intrusion detection models can undergo scheduled distribution and deployment across different database instances. These models monitor the incoming audit data. The database issues alerts when suspicious activity is detected. The models and the stored audit data can be also further investigated using database reporting and analysis tools. The key aspect to the described data flow is that processing is entirely contained within the database. With the exception of the sensor array, all other components can be found in modern RDBMS. Among the major benefits of using such an integrated approach are improved security, speed, data management and access, and ease of implementation. The following sections discuss and exemplify the functionality and usage of the individual components.

2.1 Sensors

A sensor is a system that collects audit information. Many types of audit streams can be used for detecting intrusions – examples include network traffic data, system logs on individual hosts, and system calls made by processes. Network sensors typically filter and reassemble TCP / IP packets in order to extract highlevel connection features (e.g., duration of connection, service, number of bytes transferred). A number of utilities exist to assist the user in this data extraction process Host sensors monitor system logs, CPU and memory usage on a machine. In a distributed architecture, an emphasis is placed on creating lightweight sensors since they are the only components that must run on the system that is being protected. DAID also favors a lightweight sensor approach since all computation intensive tasks (e.g., feature extraction, model generation, and detection) take place in the Oracle RDBMS. In the IDC prototype, we simulate a network environment by streaming previously collected network activity data. This dataset was originally created by DARPA and later used in the KDD'99 Cup. The same dataset has already been successfully used for demonstrating the capabilities of another intrusion detection framework.

2.2 ETL

Typically, sensor audit streams require further preprocessing and feature extraction before the data can be successfully used for data mining model generation. For example, temporal statistical features of connections and sessions have been found informative. Other more elaborate approaches (e.g., conceptual clustering) have also shown promise. In the RDBMS context, SQL and user-defined functions offer a high degree of flexibility and efficiency when extracting key pieces of information from the audit stream. Useful SQL capabilities include math, aggregate, and analytic functions. For example, windowing functions can be used to compute aggregates over time intervals or number of rows. The following query shows a windowing analytic function that computes the number of http connections to a given host during the last 5 seconds:

```
SELECT count (*) OVER
(ORDER BY time _ stamp
RANGE  INTERVAL '5'
SECOND PRECEDIN G) as http _ cnt
```

FROM connection _ data
WHERE dest _ host = 'myhost'
AND service = 'http';

The KDD'99 network activity data used in our study had already been suitably pre-processed. Therefore the current version of the IDC prototype does not include feature extraction or other raw data transformations at the processing ETL stage.

2.3 Data Warehouse

Using the Oracle database as a centralized data repository offers significant flexibility in terms of data manipulation. Inputs from different sources can be combined through joins. Without replicating data, database views or materialized views can capture different slices of the data (e.g., data over a given time interval, data for a specific host). Such views can be used directly for model generation and data analysis. The Oracle database has the additional benefits of data security, high availability and load support, and fast response time .

2.4 Model Generation

A number of data mining techniques have been found useful in the context of misuse and anomaly detection. Among the most popular techniques are association rules, clustering, support vector machines (S V M), and decision trees . The 10g version of the Oracle database offers robust and effective implementations of data mining techniques that are fully integrated with core database functionality. The incorporation of data mining eliminates the necessity of data export outside the database thus enhancing data security. The model representation is native to the database and no special treatment is required to ensure interoperability. In order to programmatically operationalize the model generation process, data mining capabilities can be accessed via APIs (e.g., JDM standard Java API, PL/S Q L data mining API [5]). Specialized GU Is as entry points can be also easily developed, building upon the available API infrastructure (e.g., Oracle Data Miner). Such GUI tools enable ad hoc data exploration and initial model investigation. The IDC prototype leverages the dbms _ data _ mining PL/SQL package to instrument the model build functionality. We train linear SVM anomaly and misuse detection models. S V M models have been shown to perform very well in intrusion detection tasks. The intrusion detection dataset includes examples of normal behavior and four high-level groups of attacks - probing, denial of service (dos), unauthorized access to local superuser/root (u2r), and unauthorized access from a remote machine (r2l). These four groups summarize 22 subclasses of attacks. The test dataset includes 37 subclasses of attacks under the same four generic categories. We use the test data to simulate the performance of the IDC prototype when operating in detection mode. For the misuse detection problem, the SVM model was used to classify the network activity as normal or as belonging to one of the four types of attack. The misuse classification results are summarized in Table 1. The overall accuracy of the system was 92.1%. Applying the cost matrix from the KDD'99 competition, the model had a misclassification cost of 0.248. These results are competitive with KDD'99 published results The poorer performance on the two rare classes (u2r and especially r2l) is a common problem for this dataset and is attributed to differences in data distribution between training and test data. For the anomaly detection problem, a one-class SVM model was used to identify the network activity as normal or anomalous. Since anomaly detection does not rely on instances of previous attacks, the one-class model was built on the subset of normal cases in the DARPA dataset. On the test dataset, the model had excellent discrimination with an ROC area of 0.989. Sliding the probability decision threshold allows trading-off the rate of true positives and false alarms – for example, in this model a true positive rate of 96% corresponded to a false alarm rate of 5%. Oracle's implementation of SVM is highly scalable Figure 2 depicts the build scalability of a linear SVM misuse model with increasing number of records. The datasets of smaller size represent random samples of the original intrusion detection data. Tests were run on a machine with the following hardware and software specifications: single 3GHz i86 processor, 2 GB RAM memory and Red Hat enterprise Linux OS 3.0.

Table 1 Confusion Matrix on DARPA Intrusion Detection Dataset (KDD'99 Competition)

actual/pred	normal	probe	dos	u2r	r21
normal	59332	1048	45	57	111
probe	603	3251	212	62	39
dos	7393	88	222288	75	9
U2r	178	1	8	33	8
r21	14683	41	7	31	14
					27

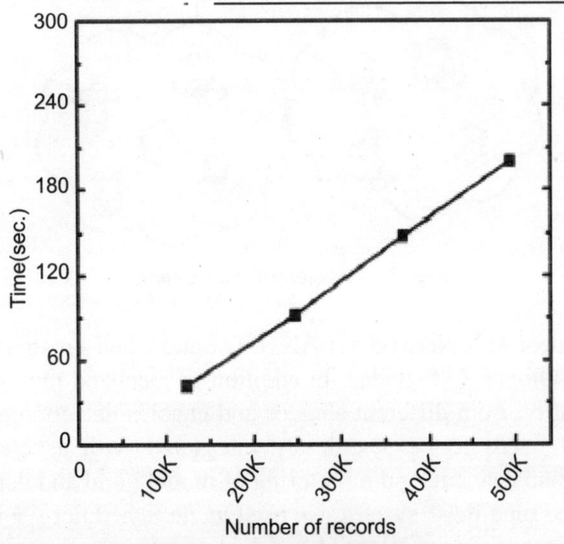

Fig. 2 SVM build scalability

The fast training times allow for frequent model rebuilds. In the IDC prototype, we schedule periodic model updates as new data is accumulated. A model rebuild is also triggered when the performance accuracy falls below a predefined level.

2.5 Model distribution

In DAID, model distribution is greatly simplified since models are not only stored in the database but are also executed in it as well. Models are periodically updated by scheduling automatic builds. The newly generated models are then automatically deployed to multiple database instances. Noel et al. point out a recent trend towards distributed intrusion detection systems where a single IDS monitors a number of network nodes and the monitored information is transferred to a centralized site. Examples of distributed architectures can be found in [26, 24, 23, 3]. IDSs implemented using a framework based on the Oracle RDBMS can transparently leverage Oracle's grid computing infrastructure – Real Application Clusters (RAC). Grids make possible pooling of available servers, storage, and networks into a flexible on-demand computing resource capable of achieving scalability and high availability. RAC allows a single Oracle database to be accessed by concurrent database instances running across a group of independent servers (nodes). The RAC nodes share a single view of the distributed cache memory for the entire database. An IDS built on top of RAC can successfully leverage server load balancing (distribution of workload across nodes) and client load balancing (distribution of new connections among nodes). Transparent application and connection failover mechanisms are also available, thus ensuring uninterruptible system uptime. Figure 3 illustrates the architecture of an IDS running on an Oracle RAC system.

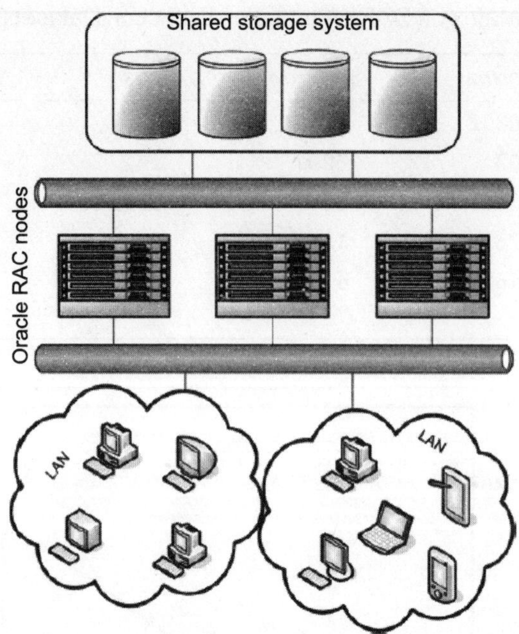

Fig. 3 Oracle grid computing

Audit data are collected from Local Area Networks (LANs). The audit data stream is monitored in one of the available database instances running on the Oracle RAC nodes. In addition to localized monitoring, the shared storage system allows pooling together of information from different sources and enables detection of system-wide attack patterns. A grid-enabled RDBMS-based IDS needs to be seamlessly integrated with a scheduling infrastructure. Such an infrastructure enables scheduling, management, and monitoring of model build and deployment jobs. Although the IDC prototype has not yet been deployed on a RAC system, we use Oracle Scheduler – a scheduling system that meets the above requirements – for management of the model build and deployment jobs.

2.6   Detection

Intrusion detection can be performed either realtime or offline. An IDS typically handles large volumes of streaming audit data. Real-time detection and alarm generation capabilities are critical for the instrumentation of an effective system. ADAM and MAIDS are examples of data mining IDSs addressing issues in real-time detection. In the context of DAID, an effective real-time detection mechanism can be implemented by leveraging the parallelism and scalability of the Oracle database. This removes the need for a system developer to design and implement such infrastructure. Figure 1 shows detection as a separate entity. However, inside the database, detection can be tightly integrated, through SQL, within the ETL process itself (indicated by the dashed box in Figure 1). The following example demonstrates how this integration was achieved in the IDC prototype. We make use of Oracle's 10g Release 2 PREDICTION SQL operator. The audit data are classified as attack or not by the misuse detection SVM model. The model scoring is part of a database INSERT statement:

```
INSERT INTO attack _ predictions
(id, prediction)
VALUES(10001,
PREDICTION
misuse _ model USING
'tcp' AS protocol _ type,
```

'ftp' AS service,

...

'SF' AS flag,

27 AS duration));

In addition to real-time detection, it is useful to perform offline scoring of stored audit data. This provides an assessment of model performance, characterizes the type and volume of malicious activity, and assists in the discovery of unusual patterns. Having detection cast as an SQL operator allows powerful database features to be leveraged. In our prototype, we create a functional index on the probability of a case being an attack. The following SQL code snippet shows the index creation statement:

```
CREATE INDEX attack _ prob _ idx
ON audit _ data
(PREDICTION _ PROBABILITY(
anomaly _ model,
0
USING *));
```

We use the anomaly detection S V M model. The 0 argument indicates that the probability of an anomaly / attack will be returned. Alternatively, a value of 1 would produce the probability of a connection being normal. The * symbol maps the audit _ data table columns to the list of predictors used during the model build. The functional index optimizes query performance on the audit data table when filtering or sorting on anomaly /attack probability is desired. The following query, which returns all cases in audit _ data with probability greater than 0.5 of being an attack, will have better performance if the attack _ prob _ idx index is used:

```
SELECT *
FROM audit _ data
WHERE PREDICTION _ PROBABILITY(
anomaly _ model,
0
USING *) > 0.5;
```

Processing high volumes of streaming audit data requires a system capable of scoring large datasets in real time. Figure 4 illustrates the PREDICTION operator's scalability. The scalability results were generated using a linear SVM misuse model built on 500,000 connection records. The same hardware was used as in the build timing tests.

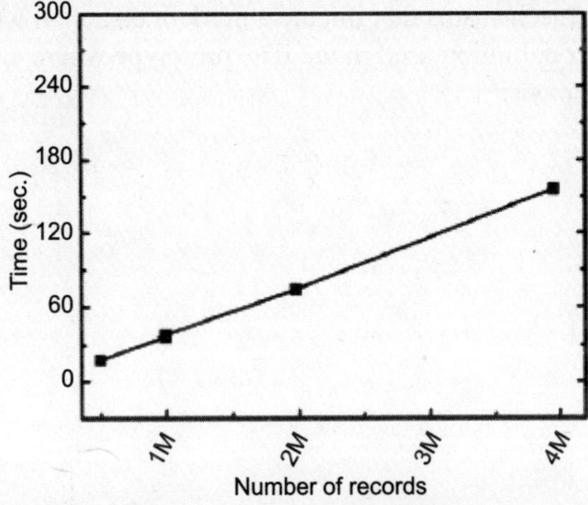

Fig. 4 Prediction scalability

The SQL PREDICTION operators also allow for the combination of multiple data mining models that are scored either serially or in parallel, thus enabling hierarchical and cooperative detection approaches. Models can be built on different types of audit data or different timeframes, can have different scope (localized vs. global detectors), and can use different data mining algorithms. The combination of multiple models and techniques has been found to be a key requirement for a successful data mining-based IDS. The next example shows a hypothetical use case where two models perform parallel cooperative detection. The query returns all cases where either model1 or model2 indicate an attack with probability higher than 0.4:

```
SELECT *
FROM audit _ data
WHERE PREDICTION _ PROBABILITY(
model1,
'attack'
USING *) > 0.4
OR PREDICTION _ PROBABILITY(
model2,
'attack'
USING *) > 0.4;
```

In the current IDC prototype, the misuse and anomaly detection models are scored independently. We plan on extending the IDC implementation with sequential (or "pipelined") cooperative detection, where the results of one model influence the predictions of another model. In this case, when the anomaly model classifies a case as an attack with probability greater than 0.5, the misuse model will attempt to identify the type of attack:

```
SELECT id, PREDICTION(
misuse _ model USING *)
FROM audit _ data
WHERE PREDICTION _ PROBABILITY(
anomaly _ model,
0 USING *) > 0.5;
```

2.7 Alerts

Upon detection of malicious or anomalous activity, an IDS needs to generate an alarm, notify interested parties, and possibly initiate a response. Such a requirement can be easily met by employing existing Oracle database infrastructure. Database triggers are powerful SQL mechanisms that initiate a predefined action when a specific condition is met. The following statement shows the trigger definition used in the IDC prototype where an attack results in posting a message in a queue for handling attack notifications:

```
CREATE TRIGGER alert _ trg
BEFORE INSERT ON
attack _ predictions
FOR EACH ROW
WHEN (new.prediction <> 'normal')
BEGIN
DBMS _ AQ.ENQUEUE(
'attack _ notify _ queue',
...);
END;
```

The IDC prototype uses Oracle's Publish-Subscribe messaging infrastructure (DBMS_AQ PL/SQL package). We chose Publish-Subscribe as the messaging approach since it handles well asynchronous communications in distributed systems that operate in a loosely-coupled and autonomous fashion and which require operational immunity from network failures. The detectors act as publishers who send alerts without explicitly specifying recipients. The subscribers (users/applications) receive only messages that they have registered an interest in. The decoupling of senders and receivers is achieved via a queuing mechanism. Each queue represents a subject or a channel. Active publication of information to end- users in an event-driven manner complements the more traditional pull-oriented approaches to accessing information that are also available in Oracle. IDS alerts can be also delivered via a diverse range of channels (e.g., e-mails, cell phone messages). In the IDC prototype, an Oracle Application Server Portal-based application – the Intrusion Detection Center dashboard – monitors the state of the network and displays relevant information. One of the tasks of the IDC dashboard is to monitor the alert queue and display alert notifications. The alert notification information includes the type of attack (based on the misused model prediction) and some of the important connection details.

2.8   Reports and Analysis

Using the database as the platform for IDS implementation facilitates the generation of data analysis results and reports. Collected audit data, detection predictions, as well as model contents, can be inspected either directly using queries or via higher level reporting and visualization tools (e.g., Discoverer, Oracle Reports). This allows circumvention of a lengthy application development process and provides a standardized and easily customized report generation and delivery mechanism. The IDC dashboard leverages the tools available in Oracle Portal to instrument a network activity reporting and analysis mechanism.

- Number of intrusion attempts during the past 24 hours (top left panel)
- Breakdown of the network activity into normal and specific types of attack (top center panel)
- Detector error rate over the last 7 days (top right panel)
- Log of recent alerts (bottom panel)

On the details page (Figure 6), users can review historic data. When a date is selected in the top left panel, the graphs are updated with the corresponding network activity information. The bottom left panel displays the breakdown of network activity into normal and specific types of attack for the selected date. The middle panels show the distribution of connection activity over different types of protocol, service, etc. Clicking on any of the bars produces a breakdown of the network activity (normal and types of attack) for this particular value. For example, in Figure 6 the top right panel shows the breakdown of activity for the tcp protocol for the selected date.

3.   CONCLUSIONS

Database-centric IDSs offer many advantages over alternative systems. These include tight integration of individual components, security, scalability, and high availability. Current trends in RDBMSs are moving towards providing all key components for delivering comprehensive state-of-the-art IDSs. As illustrated above, Oracle Database 10g Release 2 already incorporates these key functionality elements. By leveraging the existing technology stack, a full-fledged IDS can be developed in a reasonably short time-frame and at low development cost. The similarities between real-time intrusion detection and real-time fraud detection (e.g., credit-card fraud, e-commerce fraud) suggest that DAID could be also applicable to these types of applications. This will be investigated in a future work. We also plan to extend the IDC prototype to take advantage of RAC and sensor data preprocessing at the ETL stage.

References

1. Barbarà, D., Couto, J., Jajodia, S., Popyack, L., and Wu, N., ADAM: A Testbed for E xploring the Use of Data Mining in Intrusion Detection, *ACM SI GMOD Record*, 30(4), 2001, pp. 15-24.

2. Cai, Y. D., Clutter, D., Pape, G., Han, J., Welge, M., and Auvil, L., MAIDS: Mining Alarming Incidents from Data Streams, In *Proc. 2004 ACM-SIGMOD Int. Conf. Management of Data (SIGMOD'04)*, ACM Press, New York, NY, 2004, pp. 919-920.

3. Chatzigiannakis, V., Androulidakis, G., and Maglaris, B., A Distributed Intrusion Detection Prototype Using Security Agents, *Workshop of the HP OpenView University Association*, 2004.

4. DataDirect Technologies, Using Oracle Real Application Clusters (RAC), http://www.datadirect.com/techzone/odbc/docs/odbc_oracle_rac.pdf, 2004.

5. DBMS_DATA_MINING PL/SQL package, Oracle10g PL/SQL packages and types reference, Ch. 23, Oracle Corporation, 2003.

6. Eskin, E., Arnold, A., Prerau, M., Portnoy, L., and Stolfo, S.J., A Geometric Framework for Unsupervised Anomaly Detection: Detecting Intrusions in Unlabeled Data, In D. Barbarà and S. Jajodia (eds.), *Applications of Data Mining inComputer Security*, Kluwer Academic Publishers, Boston, MA, 2002, pp. 78-99.

7. Eskin, E., Miller, M., Zhong, Z.-D., Yi, G., Lee, W.-A., and Stolfo, S. J., Adaptive Model Generation for Intrusion Detection, In *Proc. ACMCCS Workshop on Intrusion Detection and Prevention*, 2000.

8. Honig, A., Howard, A., Eskin, E., and Stolfo, S.J., Adaptive Model Generation, an Architecture for the Deployment of Data Mining-Based Intrusion Detection Systems, In D. Barbarà and S. Jajodia (eds.), *Applications of Data Mining in Computer Security*, Kluwer Academic Publishers, Boston, MA, 2002, pp. 154-191.

9. Hornick, M. and JSR-73 Expert Group, JavaTM Specification Request 73: JavaTM Data Mining (JDM), http://jcp.org/en/jsr/detail ? id = 73, 2004.

10. Hu, W., Liao, Y., and Vemuri, V.R., Robust Support Vector Machines for Anomaly Detection in Computer Security, In *Proc. International Conference on Machine Learning and Applications*, 2003, pp. 168-174.

CHAPTER 36

DRIVE BY EYE: An Intuitive Approach Towards Providing Enhanced Security in Computers

Vandana Bhat and Bharath S Sirur
Department of ISE, SDM College of Engineering, Dharwad, India
E-mail: mimosapudica2009@gmail.com, vshreenivas@yahoo.com

ABSTRACT

In this paper we introduce a well synchronized eye gaze tracking system with voice confirmation, which aims at adding new dimensions to the present level of providing authentication. It is specifically modeled for those areas where computers demand very high security. We use an IRVS based human machine interaction system using head and eye co-ordination movement, narrow FOV cameras & use those algorithms which are highly efficient and improve the system response time, which indeed ensures synchronization. Existing systems restrict the use of eye gaze for controlling applications in the computer (mainly for disabled), but we propose a new process flow model (a flow chart) which aims at making continuous iris pattern matching with voice confirmation for the execution of each command thus providing authentication for every application we choose, ensuring higher level of security in sensitive areas.

Keywords: Eye gaze tracking system, infrared video system (IVRS), Human machine interaction, system response.

I. INTRODUCTION

Consider a scenario where you have a password set to your computer, so that in your absence no one else should access it. It may be any type of password namely text, graphical, finger impression, retinal authentication etc. In this situation if any intruder tries to access your computer, his attempt to access, fails at the start up since he is not able to enter the correct password. But consider those situations, where you have already logged in to your computer and due to some urgency you go away from the computer without shutting it down. This may not be a major issue of concern at this level, but what if the same happens in the areas which demand a very high level of security. It might cause a huge data theft and anyone can break into the defence strategies and secrets in the field of defence, which is considered the backbone of our country. Our business strategies will no longer be confidential.

In this paper we propose a way of ensuring continues authentication through a implementation flowchart, which makes use of eye gaze and voice authentication and hence tackling the breach in security problem in sensitive areas. Providing continues authentication, in this context refers that, there is a continuous check for retinal or iris pattern before execution of every command.

II. THEORY

By studying the eye-head coordination we find there is some correlation between the motion of the head and that of the eyes. Previous study shows that, for eighty five percent of the saccades motions, the angular amplitude of the eye is within the 15 degrees in the normal situation. Also, the motions of the eyes are usually correlated with the head motions. The accuracy of the gazing is higher if one's head is free to move rather then keep still, in this way; the speed of eye motion could be regarded as faster [1].

It is proved that in order to improve accuracy and speed while keep comfort usage, it is necessary to add parameters of state of the head movements. In order to inspect the state of the eye-head coordination, this system has two cameras on the helmet. One camera gets the position of the centre of pupil through the infrared video system (IVRS) method while the other inspects the screen and gets the screen's spatial position relative to the user's head through the calculation of the projection area of the screen. By calculating data of head and eyes we can get the point which the user gazes on the screen.

A. Hardware Configuration

In the eye-head coordination we need to calculate the angle of the eyeballs and the head's position relative to the display screen, as stated earlier, which needs two cameras, the first of which is used to observe an eye while the second to capture potential head motion, relative to the computer display. Thus the hardware consists of a helmet and two cameras, filters and the infrared source as shown in the Fig. 1.

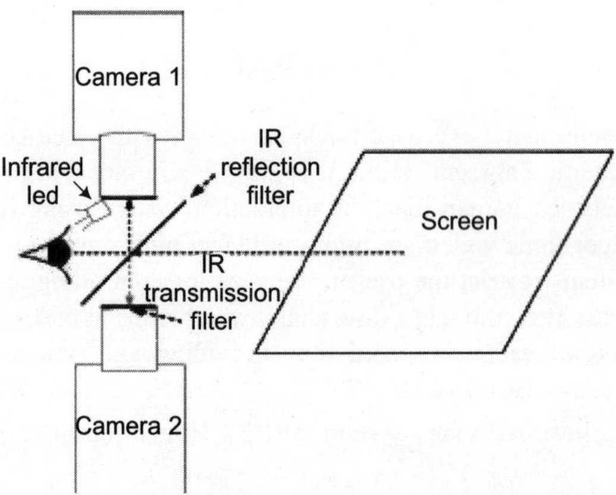

Fig. 1 Three paths of light in optic system

In order to calculate the angle of the eyeballs and the head's position relative to the computer screen, we propose a new optical system which can avoid complicated algorithms. We put two cameras up and down in one vertical line of the sight. Both cameras consist of an infrared (IR) transmission filter which could let 90% of the IR light pass but blocks the daylight. The reflection filter in front of the eyes should be positioned at an angle of 45 degrees. It can reflect the 90% of the IR light and let the day light pass. The system has 3 light paths. Path 1: the day light comes through the IR reflections filter and gets into the eyes. Path 2: the IR light comes from the IR light source, and is reflected by the eyeballs as well as the IR reflection filter, then it goes through the IR reflection filter and gets into the camera 1. In order to get a clear picture of the eyeball we need to use the telephoto lens. Path: the IR light which comes from the CRT and the LCD then reflected by the IR reflection filter, at last it gets into the camera 2. To ensure the user's head has enough space to move, this camera should use the wide angle lens as shown in Fig. 1.

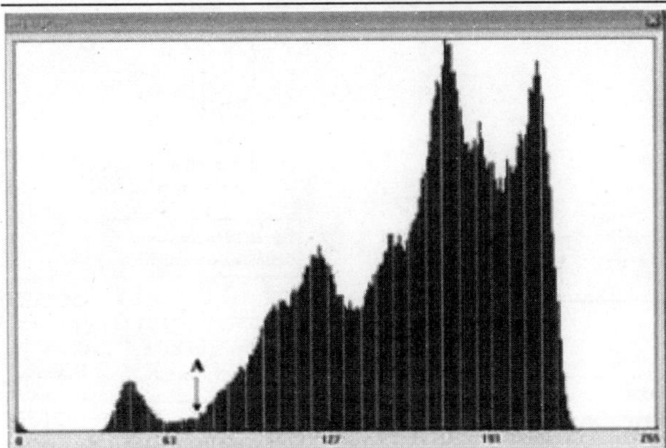

Fig. 2 Gray histogram of eye

B. System Implementation Algorithm

The algorithm contains eight parts

- Pupil identification and centre calculation;
- Pattern comparison with the feed;
- Screen identification and centre calculation;
- The correction of movement of pupil;
- Determining the point of gaze and transforming the pupil coordinates on to the screen;
- Eye wink detection and voice confirmation for execution of a command;

Pupil Identification and Centre Calculation

As we know the pupil and the iris have different reflectivity and absorptivity for the IR light. We can orient the brim of the pupil by using the gray histogram as shown in the figure.2. Considering that Asian people's upper eyelid always block part of the eyeball, the traditional algorithm has a huge fault. Based on the observation of the pupil's movement at the 15 degrees spatial angle from the camera, the contrail of the pupil is just like a circle. The new algorithm can locate centre of the pupil of yellow race. Here are the details:

We can get the adjacent segmentation of the pupil by analysing the colour image segmentation [2]. Then we get the brim of the pupil which is roughly a circle and locate a pair of points which has the largest distance between each other among all possible pairs. By using the 3s-rule we can eliminate the gross errors. By attaching those points we get the centre of the circle. Then we locate the sub-pixel coordinate centre of the pupil.

Pattern Comparison with the Feed

It consists of five major steps i.e., iris acquisition, localisation, normalisation, feature extraction and matching. The flow of process for pattern comparison is clearly depicted in Fig. 4.

After acquisition the inner pupil boundary is localized using Hough transformation. This technique performs better in the case of occlusions and images muddled by shadows and noise at the time of eye wink. The outer iris boundary is detected by circular summation of intensity approach from the determined pupil centre and radius. The localized iris image is transformed from Cartesian to polar co-ordinate system to handle different size, variation in illumination and pupil dilation. Corners in the transformed iris image are detected using covariance matrix of change in intensity along rows and columns. All detected corners are considered as features of the iris image. For recognition through iris, corners of both the iris images are detected and total number of corners that are matched between the two images are obtained. The two iris images belong to the same person if the number matched corners are greater than some threshold value. The Figure.5 pictorially represents the pattern matching process.

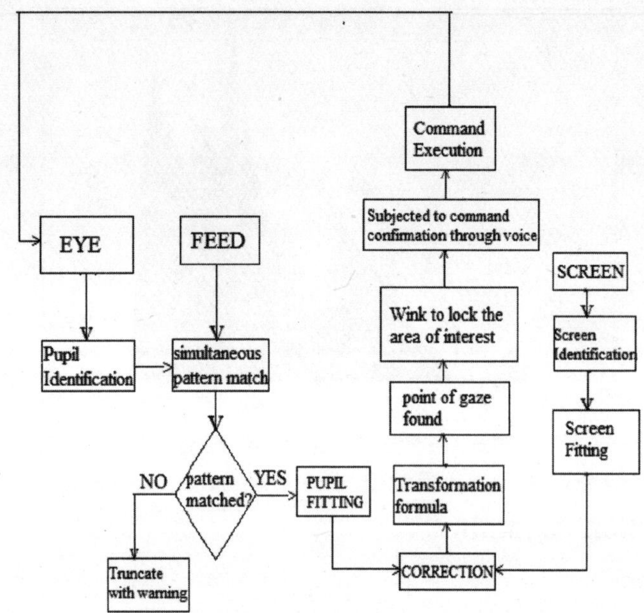

Fig. 3 Implementation Flowchart

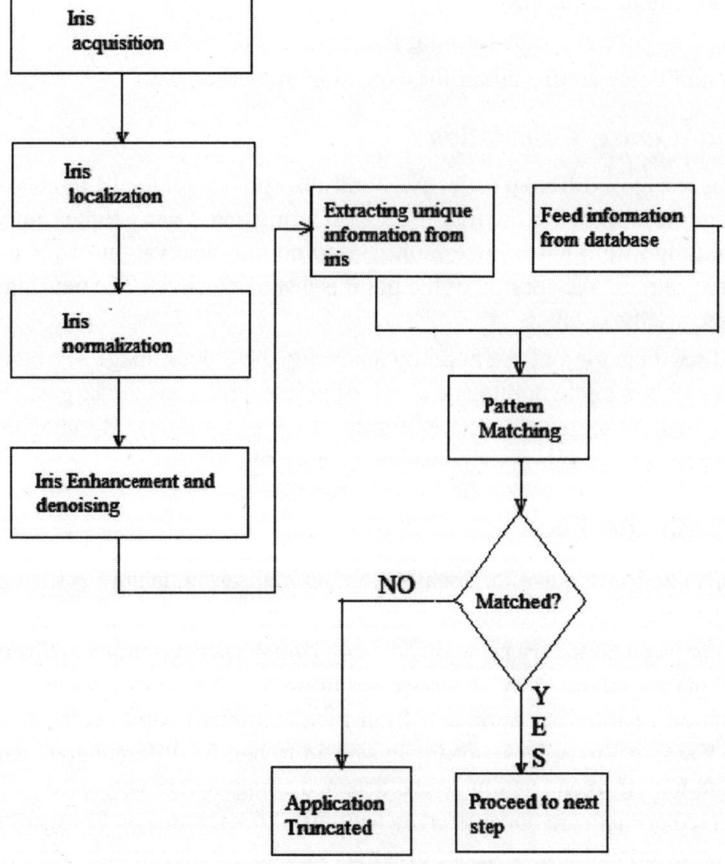

Fig. 4 Pattern matching flowchart

Screen Identification and Centre Calculation

Same as the pupil identification and fitting, by analysing the colour image segmentation, two points located farthest from each other can be identified. Then we can locate the four sides of the display by using one linear regression method and eventually locate the four angular points' coordinate as shown in Fig. 4.

Correction of the Movement of Pupil

From the equation 1, the projection of the item and its distance to the camera together can determine the size of this item.

$$z \begin{bmatrix} u \\ v \\ 1 \end{bmatrix} = \begin{bmatrix} f_x & 0 & u_0 & 0 \\ 0 & f_y & v_0 & 0 \\ 0 & 0 & 1 & 0 \end{bmatrix} \begin{bmatrix} R & T \\ 0^T & 1 \end{bmatrix} \begin{bmatrix} x_w \\ y_w \\ z_w \\ 1 \end{bmatrix} \tag{1}$$

fx, fy, $u0$, $v0$ are the inner parameters of the cameras. $u0$, $v0$ are the centre coordinate of the coordinate system, fx is the camera's telescope at the x-axis. fy is the telescope at y-axis.

$T = [tx, ty, tz]$ is the origin of the world coordinate system in the camera's coordinate system and matrix R is the coordinate transformation matrix.

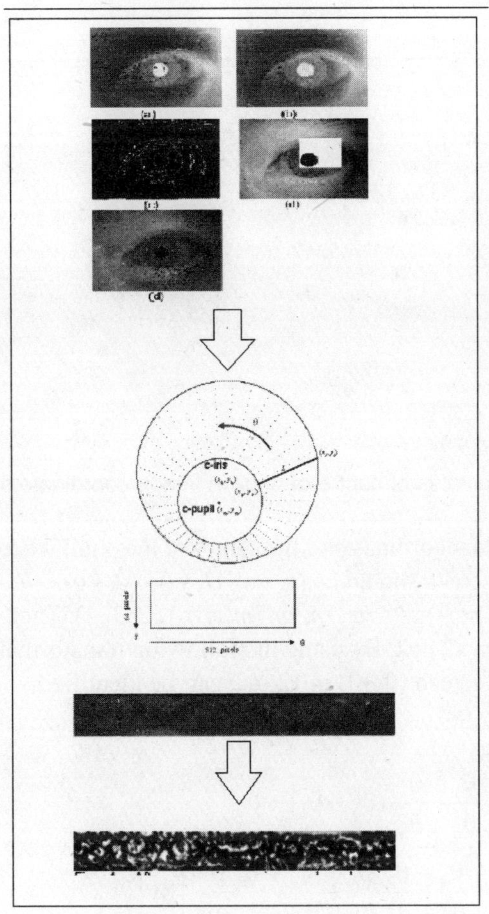

Fig. 5 Process flow in pattern matching

Here's the equation 2 supporting the matrix

$$\left.\begin{array}{l} r_{11}{}^2 + r_{12}{}^2\ r_{13}{}^2 = 1 \\ r_{21}{}^2 + r_{22}{}^2\ r_{23}{}^2 = 1 \\ r_{31}{}^2 + r_{32}{}^2\ r_{33}{}^2 = 1 \end{array}\right\} \tag{2}$$

From these equations above, it can be inferred that whatever the size of the display and the spatial location of the head, its projection is always in the image coordinate system $x2\ oy2$. Because of the speciality of the optical path, the fields of the eyes and the camera2 coincide with each other and have a linear relation. No matter which direction the head moves towards, the image of the screen will move opposite to those two fields in order to make sure the relation of the transformation doesn't change. Eventually when user gazes on some point on the screen, the line of sight can be projected to the coordinate system $x2\ oy2$, which makes this system target the right position on the screen.

Determining the Point of Gaze and Transforming it onto the Screen Coordinates

When the user is using this system for the first time, he needs to get the appropriate coordinate transformation by staring at the four corners of the screen clockwise from the top left-hand corner. After the calibration camera1 will relate the polar coordinates of the centre of the pupil ($p1, p2, p3, p4$) to its own image coordinate system $x1oy1$. And also, the image coordinate system $x2oy2$ will get the polar coordinates of the four corners of the screen (pa, pb, pc, pd), as shown in the Fig. 6 and Fig. 7.

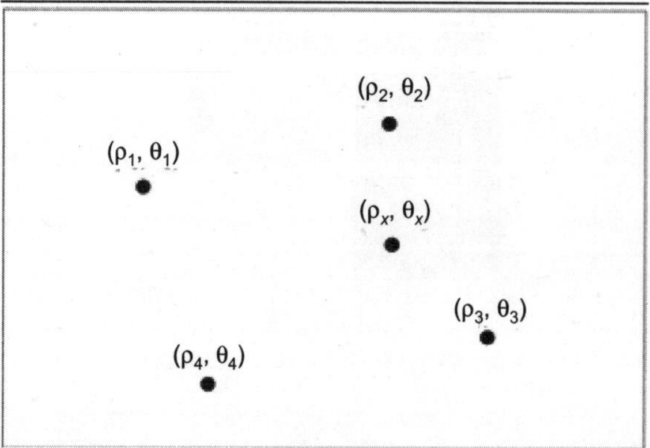

Fig. 6 Coordinates of centre of pupil in image coordinate system x1oy1

Consider the spot ($x, \bullet x$) is the polar coordinates of the centre of the pupil when the user stare at the screen , the polar coordinates of the four corners of the screen should be ($e, \bullet e$), ($f, \bullet f$), ($g, \bullet g$), ($h, \bullet h$). First, by checking $\bullet x$, calibration spots $\bullet n, \bullet m$ can be identified so that $\bullet n <= \bullet x <= \bullet m$, $\bullet n, \bullet m$ ($m, n = 1, 2, 3, 4$). Then calibration spots $\bullet j, \bullet i$ ($i, j = a, b, c, d$) relative to the image coordinate system $x2\ oy2$. By using the following transformation Equation 3, the polar coordinates of the spot which the eye gaze on the screen ($0, \bullet 0$) in $x2\ oy2$ can be identified.

After having transformed the coordinates onto the screen, the point of gaze can be calculated by the formula:

$$\left.\begin{array}{l} \theta_0 = \dfrac{\theta_x - \theta_m}{\theta_n - \theta_m}(\theta_j - \theta_i) + \theta_i \\[2em] \rho^0 = \left[\dfrac{\theta_x - \theta_m}{\theta_n - \theta_m}\dfrac{\rho j}{\rho n} + \dfrac{\theta_n - \theta_x}{\theta_n - \theta_m}\dfrac{\rho i}{\rho m}\right]\rho x \end{array}\right\}$$

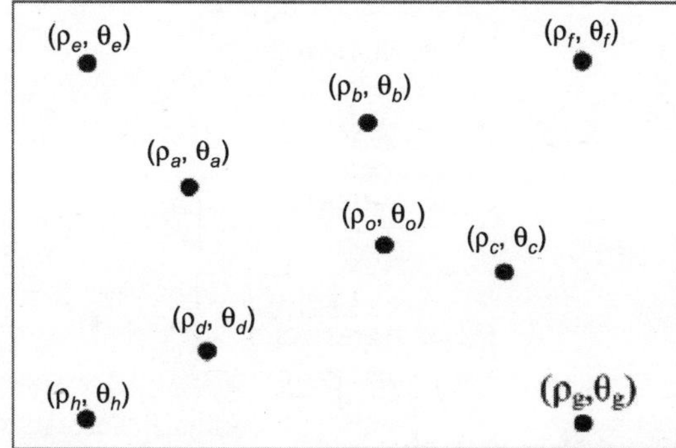

Fig. 7 Polar coordinates of the four corners of the screen in the image coordinate system *x2 oy2*

Wink Detection and Voice Confirmation for Execution of the Command

We are applying pupil image for getting the eye gaze point. The pupil image is obtained using infrared light sources. This is done by image difference method [3]. The pupil image is binaries with an appropriate threshold and the pixel number is counted every 1/60 s.

When the pupil area (pixel number) became less than a threshold for blink detection and then exceeded the threshold again, it was judged that the blink occurred. The signal of the blink was sent to the computer for menu presentation when the blink ended because the blink must have been distinguished from either the missing of the eye image from the camera frame or the closure of the eye for a short while.

An adaptive threshold setting method for blink detection was desired because the pupil area varies largely due to the environmental lighting. The threshold was determined as follows. Basically the threshold was set the level half of the pupil area one field before. During blink, to prevent the threshold level from decreasing accompanying with the pupil area, the following processes were executed. The pupil area waveform was always filtered by the 5-point moving average. When the blink was judged to occur, inputting the pupil area 3-fields before then into the arrays for moving average instead of the actual pupil area started, and continued until 3 fields after it was judged that the blink ended.

When one watches the menu screen, voluntary and involuntary blinks occur. In general, a voluntary blink is temporally longer than a involuntary one. The two types of blinks could be detected by setting the threshold a little higher than the maximum duration of the involuntary blinks. When a user blinked voluntarily as if clicking the computer mouse by finger, this blink was used for quick determination of the menu option selected by the eye-gaze.

Eye-gaze Compensation During Blink

The eye-gaze detection method was based on the relative positions between the centres of the glint (corneal reflection) and pupil image, which misses during a blink. In order to increase the precision of eye-gaze detection, we used the 10 point moving average method, which yields the phase delay in the eye-gaze point. The detected eye-gaze point coordinates were largely out of the actual eye-gaze point before or after the blink. This caused the shift of the option emphasized in colour in the menu screen near the blink in time. This makes the user feel uncomfortable as well as waste the time for the next menu selection. Furthermore, using the eye-gaze point coordinates immediate before the beginning of the blink, the shift of the emphasized option in the menu was removed by the following methods. When it was judged that the blink occurred, the inputs of the eye-gaze point 5 fields before then into the arrays for moving average instead of the actual eye-gaze points began. This process continued until when the blink was judged to have ended. By this procedure, the eye-gaze points were almost retained in the eye-gaze point immediately before the blink.

After the blink is being identified, the area of interest is locked. A voice confirmation "YES" would result in execution of the command and a "NO" would unlock the area of interest. The specific voice patterns to the feed would be input prior to the voice pattern comparison takes place.

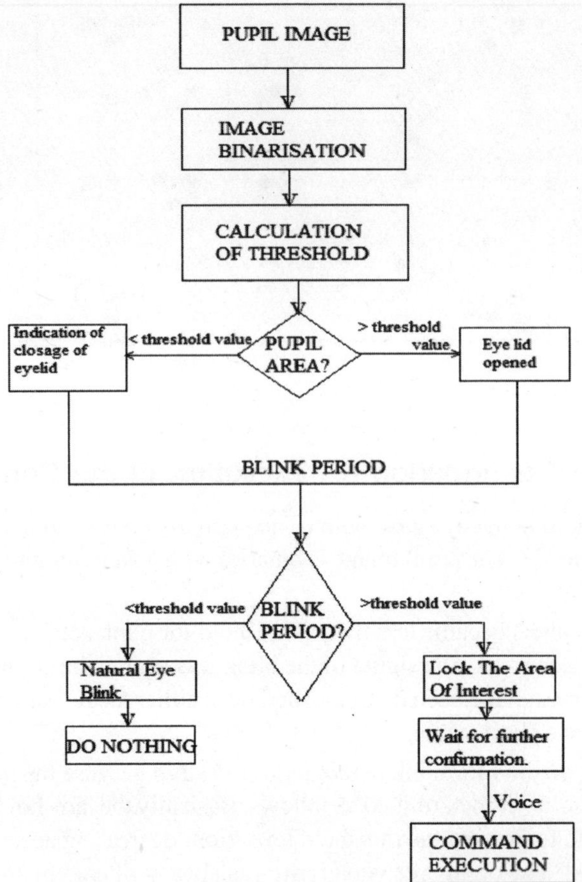

Fig. 8 Implementation Flowchart

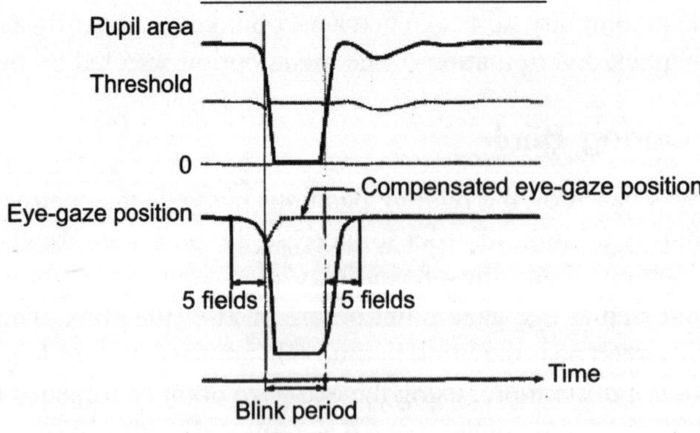

Fig. 9 Blink period calculation

III. CONCLUSION

In this paper, we proposed a simple and intuitive system through an implementation flowchart which ensures that there is continues authentication taking place before execution of every command in computers. The use of efficient algorithms for every basic step and good synchronisation between the subsystems results in an efficient system which can serve the purpose of providing very high security in sensitive areas.

References

1. FANG Lie-yi, SUN Fu-xing. Dual mode control of head movements during eye-head coordination [J]. Ac-ta Physiologica Sinica, 1995, 47(1): 45-53.

2. J. Bruce, T. Balch, M. Veloso. Fast and Inexpensive Color Image Segmentation for Interactive Robots[A]. IEEE Conference on Intelligent. Robot and Systems [C], 2000.

3. Y. Ebisawa and S. Satoh, "Effectiveness of pupil area detection technique using two light sources and image difference method", Proc. of 15th Ann. Int. Conf. of IEEE Eng. in Med. and Biol. Soc., 1268-1269 (1993).

4. FENG cheng-zhi, SHEN-wei, application of gaze tracking in human computer interaction – Journal of Zhehiang University, 2002, 29(9): 225-232.

5. ZHAO xin-can, ZUO hong-fu, XU xing-min, research on eye gaze tracking technology–J, optoelectronic engineering 2007,34(10):118-123.

CHAPTER 37

Cluster the Unlabeled Datasets Using Extended Dark Block Extraction

[1]Srinivasulu Asadi, [1]Ooruchintala Obulesu and [2]P Sunilkumar Reddy

[1]Department of IT, S.V.E.C, A. Rangampet, Tirupati-517 502, India, [2]Department of MCA, S.V.E.C, A.Rangampet, Tirupati (AP)-517 502, India

E-mail: srinu_asadi@yahoo.com, oobulesu681@gmail.com, pg.sunilkumar@gmail.com

ABSTRACT

Clustering analysis is the problem of partitioning a set of objects O = {o1... on} into c self-similar subsets based on available data. In general, clustering of unlabeled data poses three major problems: 1) assessing cluster tendency, i.e., how many clusters to seek? 2) Partitioning the data into c meaningful groups, and 3) validating the c clusters that are discovered. We address the first problem, i.e., determining the number of clusters c prior to clustering. Many clustering algorithms require number of clusters as an input parameter, so the quality of the clusters mainly depends on this value. Most methods are post clustering measures of cluster validity i.e., they attempt to choose the best partition from a set of alternative partitions.

In contrast, tendency assessment attempts to estimate c before clustering occurs. Here, we represent the structure of the unlabeled data sets as a Reordered Dissimilarity Image (RDI), where pair wise dissimilarity information about a data set including 'n' objects is represented as nxn image. RDI is generated using VAT (Visual Assessment of Cluster tendency), RDI highlights potential clusters as a set of "dark blocks" along the diagonal of the image. So, number of clusters can be easily estimated using the number of dark blocks across the diagonal. We develop a new method called "Extended Dark Block Extraction (EDBE) for counting the number of clusters formed along the diagonal of the RDI. EDBE method combines several image and signal processing techniques.

General Terms: Data Mining, Image Processing, Artificial Intelligence.

Keywords: Clustering, Cluster Tendency, Reordered Dissimilarity Image, VAT, C Means Clustering.

1. INTRODUCTION

The main Objective of our work "Estimating the number of clusters in unlabeled data sets" is to determine the number of clusters 'c' prior to clustering. Many clustering algorithms require number of clusters 'c' as an input parameter, so the quality of clusters is largely dependent on the estimation of the value 'c'. Most methods are post clustering measures of cluster validity i.e. they attempt to choose the best partition from a set of alternative partitions. In contrast, tendency assessment attempts to estimate c before clustering occurs. Our focus is on preclustering tendency assessment.

The existing technique for preclustering assessment of cluster tendency is Cluster Count Extraction (CCE). The results obtained from this are less accurate and less reliable. It does not concentrate on the perplexing and overlap issues. Its efficiency is also doubted. Hence we are introducing a new technique in our work. Our work mainly includes two algorithms, i.e. Visual Assessment of Cluster Tendency (VAT) and Extended Dark Block Extraction (EDBE). Here, we initially concentrate on representation of structure in unlabeled data in an image format. Then for that image VAT algorithm is applied, and then for the output of VAT, we apply EDBE algorithm, there by generating the valid number of peaks (i.e. number of clusters). Pair wise dissimilarity information of a dataset including 'n' objects is depicted as an n*n image, where the objects are potentially reordered so that the resultant image is better able to highlight the potential cluster structure of the data. The intensity of each pixel in the RDI corresponds to the dissimilarity between the pair of objects addressed by the row and column of the pixel. A "useful" RDI highlights potential clusters as a set of "dark blocks" along the diagonal of the image, corresponding to sets of objects with low dissimilarity.

This dissimilarity matrix generated will be provided as input to the VAT algorithm. RDI (Reordered Dissimilarity Image) that portrays a potential cluster structure from the pair wise dissimilarity matrix of the data is created using VAT. Then, sequential image processing operations (region segmentation, directional morphological filtering, and distance transformation) are used to segment the regions of interest in the RDI and to convert the filtered image into a distance-transformed image. Finally, we project the transformed image onto the diagonal axis of the RDI, which yields a one-dimensional signal, from which we can extract the (potential) number of clusters in the data set using sequential signal processing operations like average smoothing and peak detection. The peaks and valleys are found using peak detection techniques from the projected signal. These peaks and valleys are made to satisfy certain conditions. Only the peaks which satisfy the given condition will be considered as valid peaks. The number of valid peaks provides the number of clusters that can be formed from the unlabeled data sets. The proposed method is easy to understand and implement, and thereby encouraging results are achieved.

2. RELATED WORK

Visual methods for cluster tendency assessment for various data analysis problems have been widely studied [10], [5], [9]. For data that can be projected onto a 2D Euclidean space (which are commonly depicted with a scatter plot), direct observations can provide a good insight on the value of c. Apparently, Ling [1] first automated the creation of the RDI in 1973 with an algorithm called SHADE, which was used after the application of the complete linkage hierarchical clustering scheme and served as an alternative to visual displays of hierarchically nested clusters via the standard dendrogram. Since then, there have been many studies of the best method for reordering and for the use of RDIs in clustering. Two general approaches have emerged, depending on whether the RDI is viewed before or after clustering. Most RDIs built for viewing prior to clustering use algorithms very similar in flavor to single-linkage to reorder the input dissimilarities, and the RDI is viewed as a visual aid to tendency assessment. This is the problem addressed by our new DBE algorithm, which uses the VAT algorithm of Bezdek and Hathaway [2] to find RDIs. VAT is related but not identical to single-linkage clustering; see [11] for a detailed analysis of this aspect of VAT. Several algorithms extend VAT for related assessment problems. The bigVAT [3] and sVAT [4] offered different ways to approximate the VAT RDI for very large data sets. The coVAT [6] extended the idea of RDIs to rectangular dissimilarity data to enable tendency assessment for each of the four co-clustering problems associated with such data.

2.1 Review of VAT

The visual approach for assessing cluster tendency introduced here can be used in all cases involving numerical data. It is both convenient and expected that new methods in clustering have a catchy acronym. Consequently, we call this new tool VAT (visual assessment of tendency). The VAT approach presents pair wise dissimilarity information about the set of objects $O = \{o1 \ldots on\}$ as a square digital image with $n2$ pixels, after the objects are suitably reordered so that the image is better able to highlight potential cluster structure. To go further into the VAT approach requires some additional background on the types of data typically available to describe the set $O = \{o1 \ldots on\}$.

There are two common data representations of O upon which clustering can be based. When each object in O is represented by a (column) vector x in s, the set $X = \{x1 \ldots xn\}$? Rs is called an object data representation of O. The VAT tool is widely applicable because it displays a reordered form of dissimilarity data, which itself can always be obtained from the original data for O. If the original data consists of a matrix of pair wise (symmetric) similarities $S = [Sij]$, then dissimilarities can be obtained through several simple transformations.

For example, we can take $Rij = S\max - Sij$, where Smax denotes the largest similarity value. If the original data set consists of object data $X = \{x1 \dots xn\}$ s, then Rij can be computed as $Rij = xi - xj$, using any convenient norm on s, the VAT approach is applicable to virtually all numerical data sets

Figure 1(a) is a scatter plot of n ¼ 3,000 data points in $R2$, These data points were converted to a 3,000 * 3,000 dissimilarity matrix D by computing the Euclidean distance between each pair of points. The five visually apparent clusters in Fig. 1(a) are reflected by the five distinct dark blocks along the main diagonal in Fig. 1(c), which is the VAT image of the data after reordering. Compared with Fig. 1(b), which is the image of dissimilarities D in original input order, we can say that reordering is necessary to reveal the underlying cluster structure of the data. The reordering method of VAT is summarized in Table 1.

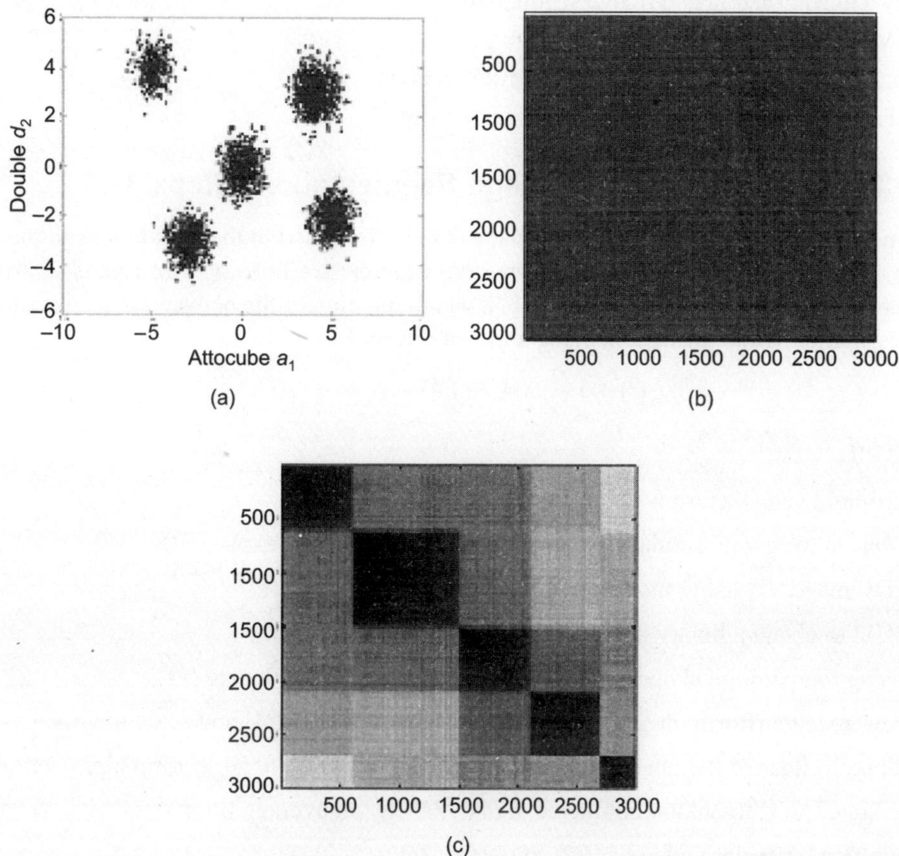

Fig. 1 (a) Scatter plot of a 3,000 point in data set with five cluster (b) Unordered image (c) Recordered VAT image I(D)

3. VAT ALGORITHM

Step 1: A dissimilarity matrix 'm' of size $n*n$ is generated from the input dataset 'S', where 'n' is the size of 'S'; // initialization

Step 2: set $K \bullet \{1, 2, 3 \dots n\}$, $I \bullet J \bullet \{ \}$, $P[\ ] \bullet \{0, 0, 0 \dots 0\}$;

Step 3: select $(i, \ j)^a$ argmax (mpq) such that $(p, q)^a K$ and set $P[1] \bullet i$; $I \bullet \{i\}$, $J \bullet K - \{i\}$;

Step 4: for $r \bullet 2, 3 \dots \dots n$ Select $(i, j)^a$ argmin (mpq) and set $P[r] < j, I < IU \{j\}, J < J - \{j\}$ Next r

Step 5: Obtain the ordered dissimilarity matrix 'R' using the ordering array P as $.Rij = mp \ (i) \ p \ (j)$ for $1 < = i, \ j < = n$.

Step 6: Display the Reordered Dissimilarity Image.

4. EDBE ALGORITHM

The existing system for automatically determining the number of clusters in unlabeled data sets is "cluster count extraction".

Because of its limitations like perplexing, and its inability in histogram overlapping, we are moving on to a new technique. The proposed system is "Extended Dark Block Extraction", which is nearly a parameter free method developed to automatically determine the number of clusters in unlabeled datasets. In short, EDBE is an algorithm that counts the dark blocks along the diagonal of a RDI.

EDBE algorithm mainly includes four major steps:

- Dissimilarity Transformation and Image segmentation.
- Directional Morphological filtering of binary image.
- Distance transform and diagonal projection of filtered image.
- Detection of major peaks and valleys in the projected signal

4.1 Dissimilarity Transformation and Image Segmentation (Steps 1-3)

Because information about possible cluster structure in the data is embodied in the dark blocks in the RDI, an important preprocessing step is image thresholding to extract the regions of interest. Choosing a threshold 'á' around the first mode is thus ideal for image segmentation. Otsu's algorithm [7], which maximizes the between class variance, has been widely used in image processing for automatically choosing a global threshold.

$$f(t) = 1 - \exp(-t / á)$$

EDBE ALGORITHM

Step 1: Find the threshold value 'á' from 'm' using otsu's algorithm.

Step 2: Transform 'm' in to new dissimilarity matrix '$m1$' with $m1\ ij = 1 - \exp(-m/á)$

Step 3: Form an RDI image '$I1$' using the previous module.

Step 4: Threshold '$I1$' to obtain a binary image '$I2$' using algorithm of otsu.

Step 5: Filter '$I2$'using morphological operations to obtain a filtered binary image '$I3$'.

Step 6: Perform a distance transform on '$I3$' to obtain a gray scale image '$I4$' and scale the pixel values to [0, 1].

Step 7: Project the pixel values of the image on to the main diagonal axis of '$I4$' to form a projection signal '$H1$'

Step 8: Smooth the signal '$H1$' to obtain the filtered signal '$H2$' by an average filter.

Step 9: Compute the first order derivative of '$H2$' to obtain '$H3$'.

Step 10: Find peak position 'pi' and valley positions 'vj' in '$H3$'.

Step 11: Select valid peaks by considering some conditions. Number of valid peaks gives number of clusters.

Step 12: Put the number of clusters into C-Means Clustering Algorithm and gives very good accuracy.

This does not affect the reordering by VAT but changes the histogram of dissimilarities. From the histogram of D0, we use Otsu's algorithm again to obtain a new threshold to convert the VAT image shown in Fig. 2(a) into a binary image shown in Fig. 2(b) by

$$I_{ij}{}^2 = 1, \quad \text{if } I_{ij}{}^2 > á$$
$$I_{ij}{}^2 = 0, \quad \text{otherwise.}$$

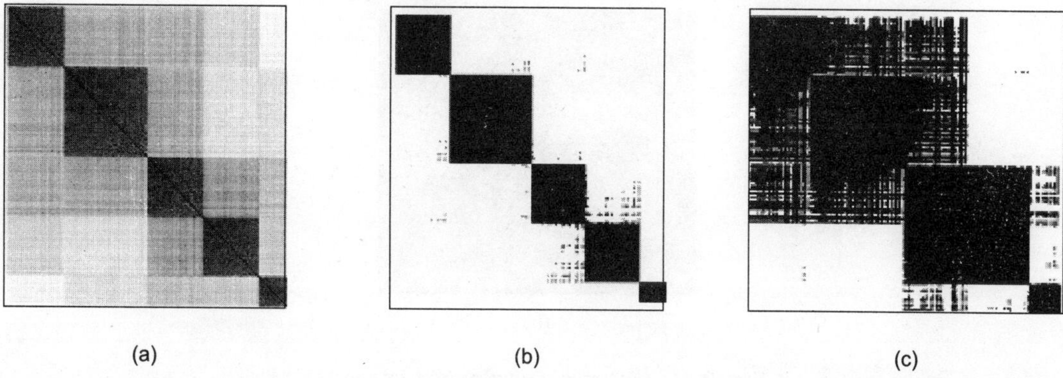

(a) (b) (c)

Fig. 2 (a) VAT image of I(D′) (b) Segmented image I(D′) (c) Segmented image before transformation

It can be seen that the segmentation result after transformation is far better than that before transformation.

Directional Morphological Filtering of Binary Image (Step 4)

To make the segmented image clearer, especially for the cases in which the degree of overlap between clusters is large, we use morphological operations [8] to perform binary image filtering. Morphological filtering is one type of processing in which the spatial form or structure of objects within an image is modified. Dilation and erosion are two fundamental morphological operations. The former usually causes objects to grow in size, while the latter causes objects to shrink. The morphologically filtered image is as shown in the Fig. 3(a)

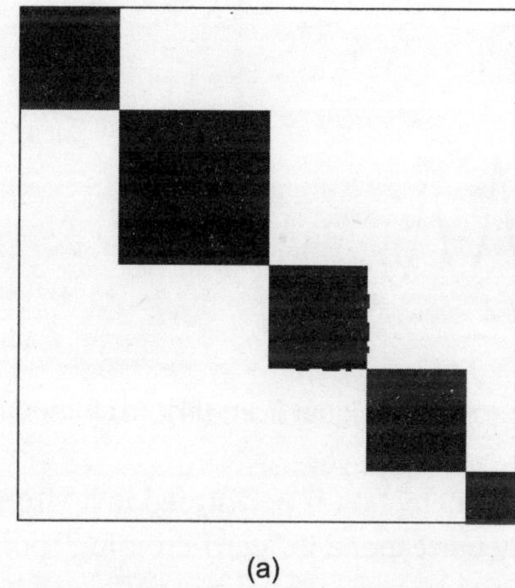

(a)

Fig. 3(a) Morphologically filtered Image

4.2 Distance Transform and Diagonal Projection of Image (Steps 5-6)

In order to convert the morphologically filtered image into an informative one that clearly shows the dark block structure information; we need to consider the values of pixels that are along or off the main diagonal axis of the image. First, we perform a DT of the binary image to obtain a new gray-scale image as shown in the Fig.3(b) A Distance Transform is a form of representation of a digital image, which converts a binary image to a gray-scale image in which the value of each pixel is the distance from the pixel to the nearest nonzero pixel in the binary image Fig.3(b).

There are several different DTs depending upon which distance metric is being used to determine the distance between pixels. We use the Euclidean distance. After the DT, we project "all" pixel values of the DT image onto the main diagonal axis to obtain a projection signal as shown in the Fig. 3(c).

(b)

Fig. 3(b)   Distance Transformed Image(I4)

4.3   Detection of Major Peaks and Valleys in the Projected Signal (Steps 7-10)

The number of dark blocks in any RDI is equivalent to the number of "major peaks" in the projection signal $H1$. We perform the detection of peaks and valleys to estimate the (cluster) number c, based on the "first-order derivative" of the projection signal. Although the projection signal $H1$ seems to be very smooth, we require further smoothing to reduce possible false detections due to noise in the signal. Here, we use a simple average filter 'h' to filter the projection signal, i.e., $H^{(2)} = h * H^{(1)}$, where '*' means linear convolution (see Fig. 3(c)), and the average filter h has length $l2 = 2*á*n$.

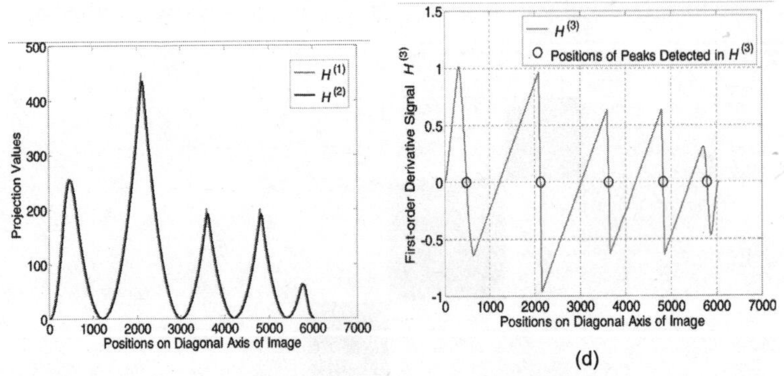

(d)

Fig. 3   (c) Diagonal projection signal from (I4); (d) First Order derivative signal

After that, the process of peak and valley detection is performed in a "from-rough-to-fine" manner. It is well known that the peaks and valleys of a signal usually correspond to "zero-crossing" points in its first-order derivative as shown in the Fig. 3d. Accordingly, we can find the initial sets of peaks pi and valleys vj by finding the corresponding from positive-to-negative zero-crossing points and from negative-to-positive zero-crossing points. To further remove minor false peaks, we use a size filter to remove relatively small valleys by validating the width between each two neighboring valleys.

That is, the peak pi within the two neighboring valleys will be kept as a meaningful major peak if $V(k+1) - V(k) >$ l3 $V(k) < P(i) < V(k+1)$, where l3 = 2án

Finally, we determine the number of dark blocks in the RDI (and, hopefully, the number of clusters c in the unlabeled data) as the number of resulting major peaks.

5.   CONCLUSION

This paper investigates a nearly parameter-free method for automatically estimating the number of clusters in unlabeled data sets. The only user defined parameter that must be chosen á controls the filter size. It is relatively easy to make a realistic (and useful) choice for á, since it essentially specifies the smallest cardinality of a cluster relative to the number of objects in the data. Cluster number should be EDBE that will probably reach its useful limit when the RDI formed by any reordering of D is not from a well structured dissimilarity matrix. In our experiments, we used the simple Euclidean distance to compute pair wise dissimilarities when the input data are feature vectors. The Euclidean distance may not be suitable for high dimensional or complex data valleys (such as wavelet-based multi-resolution analysis). EDBE provides an initial estimation of the cluster number, thus avoiding the requirement of repeatedly running a clustering algorithm multiple times over a wide range of c in an attempt to find useful clusters. In this way, EDBE compares favorably to post clustering validation methods in computational efficiency. It is noted that EDBE does not eliminate the need for cluster validity, but it simply improves the probability of success. A possible extension of this work concerns the initialization of the fuzzy post clustering algorithm for object data clustering. It should not be too hard to find an approximate center sample for each meaningful cluster from any well structured RDI.

References

1. R.F. Ling, Comm. ACM, vol. 16, pp. 355-361, 1973, "A Computer Generated Aid for Cluster Analysis,"
2. J. Huband, J.C. Bezdek, and R. Hathaway, Pattern Recognition, vol. 38, no. 11, pp. 1875-1886, 2005, "bigVAT: Visual Assessment of Cluster Tendency for Large Data Sets".
3. R. Hathaway, J.C. Bezdek, and J. Huband, Pattern Recognition, vol. 39, pp. 1315-1324, 2006, "Scalable Visual Assessment of Cluster Tendency".
4. W.S. Cleveland, Visualizing Data. Hobart Press, 1993. [6] J.C. Bezdek, R.J. Hathaway, and J. Huband, IEEE Trans. Fuzzy Systems, vol. 15, no. 5, pp. 890-903, 2007, "Visual Assessment of Clustering Tendency for Rectangular Dissimilarity Matrices".
5. R.C. Gonzalez and R.E. Woods, Prentice Hall, 2002, Digital Image Processing.
6. I. Dhillon, D. Modha, and W. Spangler, Proc. 30th Symp. Interface: Computing Science and Statistics, 1998, "Visualizing Class Structure of Multidimensional Data".
7. T. Tran-Luu, PhD dissertation, Univ. of Maryland, College Park, 1996, "Mathematical Concepts and Novel Heuristic Methods for Data Clustering and Visualization".
8. J.C. Bezdek and R. Hathaway, Proc. Int'l Joint Conf. Neural Networks (IJCNN '02), pp. 2225-2230, 2002, "VAT: A Tool for Visual Assessment of (Cluster) Tendency".
9. Liang Wang, Christopher Leckie, Kotagiri Ramamohanarao, and James Bezdek, Fellow, IEEE-MARCH 2009, Automatically Determining the Number of Clusters in Unlabeled Data Sets.

CHAPTER 38

Opinion Mining of Customer Reviews

Padmapani Tribhuvan[1] and Amrapali Tribhuvan[2]
[1]Marathwada Institute of Technology, Aurangabad (MS)-431028, India
[2]Department of Computer Science and IT, Deogiri College, Aurangabad (MS)-431005, India
E-mail: padmapani.prakash@gmail.com, amrapaliprakash512@gmail.com

ABSTRACT

The Web has become an excellent source for gathering consumer opinions. There are numerous Web sites containing such opinions. This paper focuses online customer reviews of products. This task is performed in three steps: 1)Mining features of product commented on (that is determining opinion features) 2)Identifying polarity of each opinion (that is deciding whether each opinion sentence is positive or negative 3)Summarizing the results using the discovered information. Finally, feature-based summaries of customer reviews are generated. Experiment results demonstrate the effectiveness of the proposed approach in opinion mining.

Keywords: Opinion mining, sentiment analysis, feature-based summaries.

1. INTRODUCTION

Opinion mining is a recent discipline of Information Retrieval and of Computational Linguistics which is concerned not with the topic a document is about, but with the opinion it expresses. It has a rich set of applications, ranging from tracking users' opinions about products or about political candidates as expressed in online forums, to customer relationship management. Opinion mining gathers and combines many concepts, ideas and methods of two disciplines Information Retrieval and of Computational Linguistics. Opinion Mining is concerned with the analysis of the opinions expressed in documents.

1.1 Development of Linguistic Resources of Opinion Mining

A common point in almost any work on Opinion Mining is the need to identify which elements of language contribute to express the subjectivity in text. Such identification if often accomplished by using a lexical resource. Linguistic resources of Opinion Mining are opinion words or phrases which are used as instruments for sentiment analysis. It also called polar words, opinion bearing words, subjective element, etc. This paper focus on sentence level sentiment analysis rather than document level sentiment analysis. Sentence level sentiment analysis uses Bootstrapping Process.

1.2 Feature-Based Opinion Extraction and Summarization

Since the number of reviews for an object can be large, a simple summary of opinions should be produced. The summary can be easily visualized and compared. There are three main tasks of producing opinion summaries: Identifying and extracting object features that have been commented on in each review; determining whether the opinions on the features are positive, negative or neutral; grouping synonyms of features.

2. RELATED WORK

Andrea Esuli [1] have shown an effective cross-language use of SentiWord-Net, by running experiments on opinion extraction on the Italian language,using an Italian "translation" of SentiWordNet scores based on aWordNet-aligned Italian lexical resource, MultiWordNet , obtaining again significant improvements.

Minqing Hu and Bing Liu[2] proposed a set of techniques for mining and summarizing product reviews based on data mining and natural language processing methods which provide a feature-based summary of a large number of customer reviews of a product sold online.

Shanmugandaram Hariharan, Ramachandran Srimathi, Murugan Sivasubramanian, Saranathan Pavithra have proposed that a technique that extracts the opinion words from the reviews. By using extraction algorithm proposed, they assign scores of each word of the review. This type of scoring may be unfair in some context and may lead to less accurate results.

Won Young Kim, Joon Suk Ryu, Kyu ll Kim, Ung Mo Kim[4] proposed method uses POS tagging that is one of natural language process techniques and proposed method that store feature and opinion of product in form of transaction and uses association rule mining method for analyzing transaction data and then uses PMI method for summarizing discovered association rules.

3. PROPOSED SYSTEM

Proposed System architecture is shown in following Fig. 1.

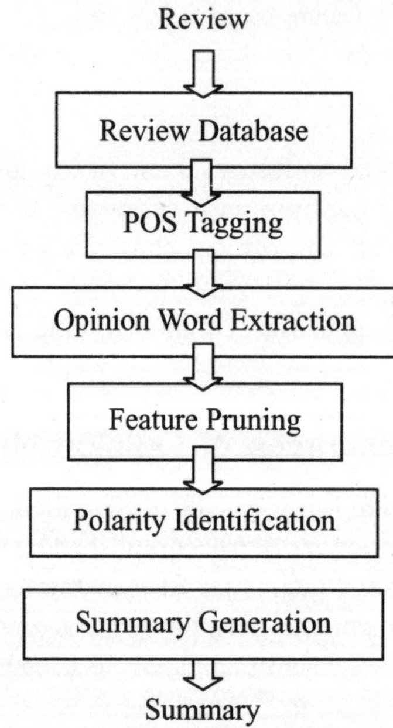

Fig. 1 Proposed System Architecture

3.1   POS (Part-of-Speech) Tagging

Part-of-Speech (POS) tagging is the process of assigning a part-of-speech like noun, verb, pronoun, adverb, adjective or other lexical class marker to each world in a sentence. The input to tagging algorithm is a string of words of a natural language sentence and finite list of part-of-speech tags. The output is a single best POS tag for each word. Stanford Tagger [5] is an application that analyze sentence for POS tagging. After POS tagging on a sentence, data structure form of phrase-structure tree [6]. Figure 2 shows the output of Stanford Tagger and Fig. 3 shows the output of Stanfold Parser. For the sentence- "The battery life is not long enough."

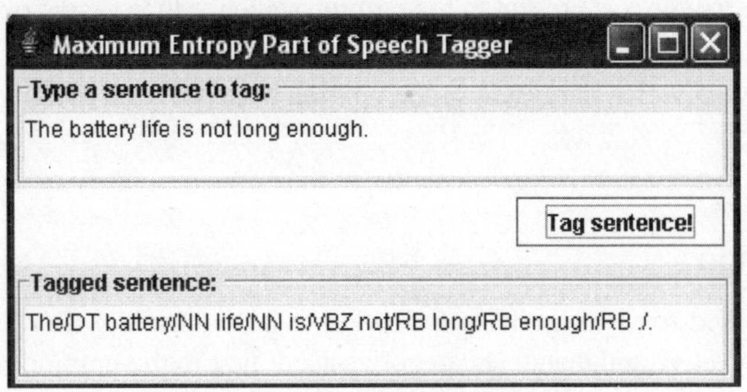

Fig. 2   Output of Stanford Tagger

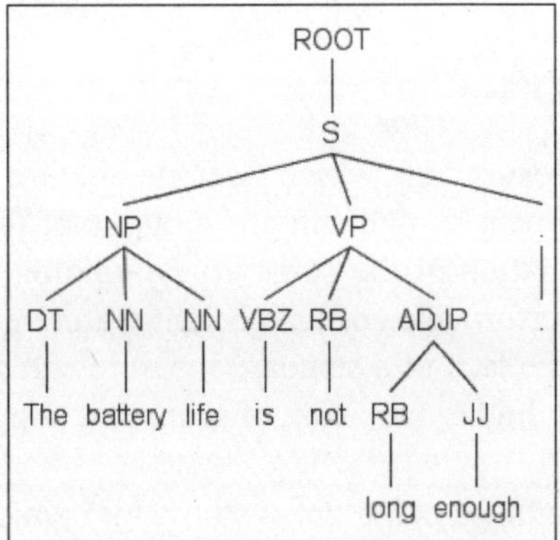

Fig. 3   Output of Stanford Parser

3.2   Opinion Word Extraction

If a sentence contains one or more product features and one or more opinion words, then the sentence is called an *opinion sentence*. Opinion words are extracted in the following manner

1. For each sentence in database, if sentence is opinion sentence then extract all the adjective words as opinion words.
2. For each feature consider each nearby adjective as its opinion word.

After opinion word extraction in feature pruning, redundancies are reduced from extracted opinion word.

3.3   Polarity Identification

In this step orientation of an opinion sentence, i.e., positive or negative is predicted. In general, the dominant orientation of the opinion words is used in the sentence to determine the orientation of the sentence. That is, if positive/negative opinion prevails, the opinion sentence is regarded as a positive/negative one.

For finding out opinion word polarity following steps are followed.

1. If opinion words are present in database then assign polarity stored in database.
2. If opinion words are not present in database then find its synonym. If synonym is present then assign polarity of that synonym to the opinion word and store it in database.
3. If opinion words are not present in database and its synonym is not present, then find its antonym. If antonym is present then assign opposite polarity of that antonym to the opinion word and store it in database.

For finding out opinion word polarity following steps are followed.

1. If odd number of negation words is present in the opinion sentence then assign opposite polarity of opinion word to that sentence.
2. If even number of negation words is present in the opinion sentence then assign polarity of opinion word to that sentence.
3. If negation word is not present in the opinion sentence then assign polarity of opinion word to that sentence.

3.3 Summary Generation

To generate the final feature-based review summary following steps are used: 1. For each discovered feature, related opinion sentences are put into positive and negative categories according to the opinion sentences' orientations. A count is computed to show how many reviews give positive /negative opinions to the feature. 2. All features are ranked according to the frequency of their appearances in the reviews. Feature phrases appear before single word features as phrases normally are more interesting to users. Other types of rankings are also possible.

4. EXPERIMENTAL EVALUATION

Opinion summarization methods were examined which include feature extraction, sentiment assignment, and visualization. Feature extraction and sentiment assignment are subtasks of feature-level sentiment classification while visualization is about the effective presentation of the summarized opinion. A total of six systems were introduced. Although each system demonstrated the performance of its inherent feature extraction and sentiment assignment, these cannot be compared to each other due to the lack of a standard measure and common test data set. However, the NLP-combining systems seems to show slightly higher precision of sentiment assignment.

Table 1 Characteristics of the six systems for opinion summarization.

System	Sentiment Resource	Extracting Opinion Expression	
		Feature Extraction	Sentiment Assignment
Review Seer(2003)	Thumbs up/down	Probabilistic model Naïve Bayes Classifier	
Red Opal (2007)	Star rating	Frequent noun and noun phrase	Average star rating
Opinion Observer (2004)	Linguistic Resource	CBA miner Infrequent feature selection	WordNet exploring Dominant polarity of each phrase
Kanayama's System (2004)	Linguistic Resource	Sentiment unit Modifying the machine translation framework	
WebFountain (2005)	Linguistic Resource	bBNP heuristic	Sentiment lexicon Sentiment pattern database
OPINE (2005)	Linguistic Resource	Web PMI	Relaxation labeling

5. CONCLUSION AND FUTURE WORKS

In this paper, a technique for mining and summarizing customer reviews based on data mining and natural language processing methods is proposed. The objective is to provide a feature-based summary of a large number of customer reviews of a product sold online. Our experimental results indicate that the proposed techniques are very promising in performing their tasks. Summarizing the reviews is not only useful to common shoppers, but also crucial to product manufacturers.

In future work, we plan to further improve and refine our techniques, and to deal with the outstanding problems identified above, i.e., pronoun resolution, determining the strength of opinions, and investigating opinions expressed with adverbs, verbs and nouns. Finally, we will also look into monitoring of customer reviews.

References

1. Andrea Esuli, 2008. Automatic Generation of Lexical Resources for Opinion Mining: Models, Algorithms and Applications.
2. Minqing Hu, Bing Liu, 2004 ACM. Mining and Summarizing Customer Reviews.
3. Shanmugandaram Hariharan, Ramachandran Srimathi, Murugan Sivasubramanian, Saranathan Pavithra, 2010 ACM. Opinion Mining and Summarization of Reviews in Web Forum.
4. Won Young Kim, Joon Suk Ryu, Kyu ll Kim, Ung Mo Kim 2009 ACM. A Method for Opinion Mining of Product Reviews using Association Rules.
5. Standard Tagger Version 3.0 (http://www-nlp.standfold.edu/software/tagger.html)
6. Standard Parser Version 6.3 (http://www-nlp.standfold.edu/software/lex-parser.html)
7. Agrawal, R. & Srikant, R. 1994. Fast algorithm for mining association rules. *VLDB'94*, 1994.
8. Boguraev, B., and Kennedy, C. 1997. Salience-Based Content Characterization of Text Documents. In *Proc. Of the ACL'97/EACL'97 Workshop on Intelligent Scalable Text Summarization*.
9. Bruce, R., and Wiebe, J. 2000. Recognizing Subjectivity: ACase Study of Manual Tagging. *Natural Language Engineering*.
10. Cardie, C., Wiebe, J., Wilson, T. and Litman, D. 2003. Combining Low-Level and Summary Representations of Opinions for Multi-Perspective Question Answering. *2003 AAAI Spring Symposium on New Directions in Question Answering*.

CHAPTER 39

SOA Governance and Planning

[1]**Ajit R. Pandey and [2]V.M. Thakare**
[1]MCA Department, Sinhgad Institute of Business Administration & Computer Applications, Lonavala, Pune (MS), India
[2]MCA Department, SGB Amravati University, Amravati (MS), India
E-mail: itajit@yahoo.co.in, vilthakare@yahoo.co.in

ABSTRACT

In the context of Service-Oriented Architecture (SOA), governance is an often-misunderstood term. Some people use the term SOA Governance to mean service lifecycle governance that is, governing the lifecycle of services from creation through deployment. Others take it to mean applying runtime policies to services. This paper defines and explains governance with SOA should ultimately be about delivering on your business and SOA objectives. It must link SOA investments to business goals and initiatives mitigate the risks associated with SOA, and fit into the context of an organization's overall IT Governance framework. The lack of working governance arrangements will be the most common reason for the failure of SOA projects (0.8 probabilities).

Keywords: SOA, EA, COBIT, TOGAF, OECD, ROI.

INTRODUCTION

The definition of governance implies that one need to have a SOA strategy, ensure that it is aligned with where your business is going and where you want to it to go, and develop a concrete idea of what you expect from your SOA investments. In order to deliver on these expectations, and as part of your SOA strategy, you need a plan that we refer to as the SOA Roadmap, which outlines the projects to be implemented with SOA and the capabilities that need to be put into place over a period of time (such as two to five years), to ensure that you deliver on your business and SOA strategy. The timeline and the roadmap both must have synchronization with updates in technology. By incrementally building the required capabilities over a period of time, you can increase your SOA maturity. The most important point to be kept in consideration is use of obsolete technology can lead to failure of SOA after certain few years.

SOA governance gives organizations the ability to track the life of each service from architectural inception, through design and development, and finally into its deployment environment. Effective SOA governance will be the primary way that companies can establish principles for the control of their organizations. So if governance with SOA is about decisions, processes, and policies, "What kinds of policies do you need to put into place? And to what do those policies need to be applied?" [1] [2] [3] [5] [7]

The Role of SOA Governance: [4] [6]

The definition of the word governance implies the action or manner of governing. SOA governance, introduces the notion of domain ownership, where domains are managed sets of Services sharing some common business context. In many cases these sets of Services are business Services, such as customer information, order processing, or product analysis. Each domain is responsible for maintaining the applications that support its Services and for maintaining the interfaces to its Services for other domains.

SOA governance is the set of solutions, policies and practices which enable companies to implement and manage an enterprise SOA. SOA governance addresses many challenges and makes it possible to realize ROI and the business benefits of loosely coupled services.

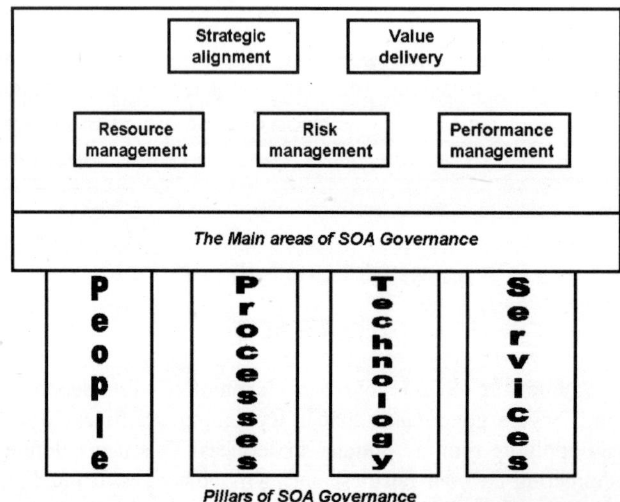

Fig. 1.1 SOA Governance Architecture

- **Strategic alignment** focuses on the imperative to align the business vision, goals and needs with the IT efforts.
- **Value delivery** focuses on how the value of IT can be proved through results like profitability, expense reduction, error reduction, improved company image, branding, and so on.
- **Risk management** focuses on business continuity and measures to be taken to protect the IT assets.
- **Resource management** focuses on optimizing infrastructure services that are a part of the On Demand Operating Environment (ODOE — see Resources) or other environment supporting the application services.
- **Performance management** focuses mainly on monitoring the services that run in a enterprise's ODOE or other environment. [7]

Any implementation of governance should be centered on the four pillars of enterprise architecture: people, processes, technology, and services. One mechanism to implement an enterprise IT and SOA governance is by establishing a center of excellence (COE) for IT and SOA governance that would enable a shared resource and capability center to function as a resource pool as new business application needs arise. A governance implementation needs to be supported by a hierarchical organizational reporting structure.

Soul of SOA Governance Strategy: [7]

Governance is the process of ensuring that whether the policies are enacting appropriately to meet the Business and SOA goals or not. Everything which is involved in business like, architecture, technology infrastructure, information, finance, portfolios, people, and projects must be choreographed with the policies to reach the goal of business and EA (Enterprise Architecture).

To address these challenges, organizations require a comprehensive and appropriately detailed SOA governance model that can be deployed in an iterative and incremental manner. A comprehensive SOA Governance model should cover all of the 3 main aspects, including:

- Processes – Including governing and governed processes
- Organizational structures – Including roles and responsibilities
- Enabling Technologies – Including tools and infrastructure

SOA Governance should be viewed as the application of Corporate Governance, IT Governance and EA Governance to Service Oriented Architecture. In effect, SOA Governance extends IT and EA Governance ensuring that the benefits that SOA extols are met. This requires governing not only the execution aspects of SOA but also the strategic planning activities. The term corporate governance can be viewed as a blend of IT, EA and SOA governance. The success of corporate governance policies are depends on the successful implementation of IT Governance and EA governance. Many industries still design their policies in reverse manner i.e. they begin with corporate governance policy and on that basis plan for their EA and SOA strategies.

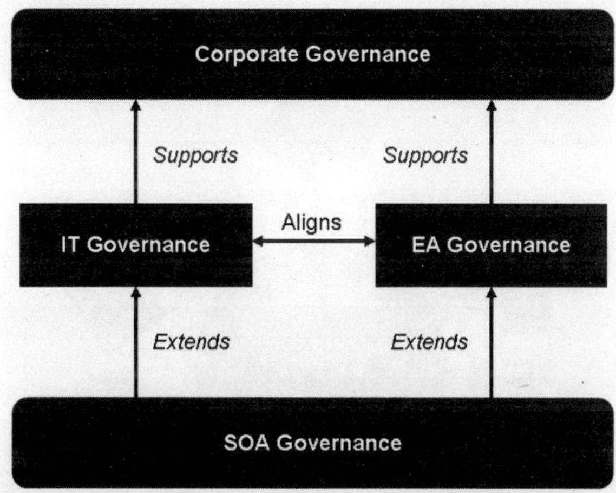

Fig. 1.2   SOA Governance Relationships

- Enterprise Architecture governance is the practice and orientation by which enterprise architectures and other architectures are managed and controlled at an enterprise-wide level. Source: TOGAF8.1.1(*The Open Group Architecture Framework)* [1]
- IT Governance includes the decision rights, accountability framework and processes, to encourage desirable behavior in the use of IT. Source: based on COBIT4.0 (*Control Objectives for Information and related Technology*) [2]
- Corporate Governance is the set of processes, customs, policies, laws and institutions affecting the way a corporation is directed, administered or controlled. Source: (Wikipedia based on OECD Principles of Corporate Governance).

SOA Governance Framework

The goal of the SOA Governance Framework is to enable organizations to define and deploy their own focused and customized SOA Governance model. [6] [7]

Since aspects of the SOA governance model require culture change, a SOA Governance regimen should never be deployed in a big bang approach. The framework defines an incremental deployment approach so that organizations can continue to meet their current demands while moving towards their long-term goals for SOA.

There is no single model of good SOA governance due to variants within an organization. Example of these variants includes the existing governance in place, the SOA maturity level, size of the organization, etc. In effect an organization's appropriate SOA Governance model is one that defines.

- What decisions need to be made in their organization to have effective SOA Governance?
- Who should make these SOA Governance decisions in their organization?
- How will these SOA Governance decisions be made and monitored in your organization?
- What organization structures, processes and tools should be deployed in your organization?

Organization should frankly assess their current governance regimen and practical governance goals. From this, an achievable roadmap for delivering governance can be created. The SOA Governance Framework consists of a SOA Governance Reference Model (SGRM) which is utilized as a starting point, and a SOA Governance Vitality Method (SGVM) which is a definition/improvement feedback process to define a focused and customized SOA Governance Regimen. [3]. [2] [7]

Proposed Five Step SOA Governance Model

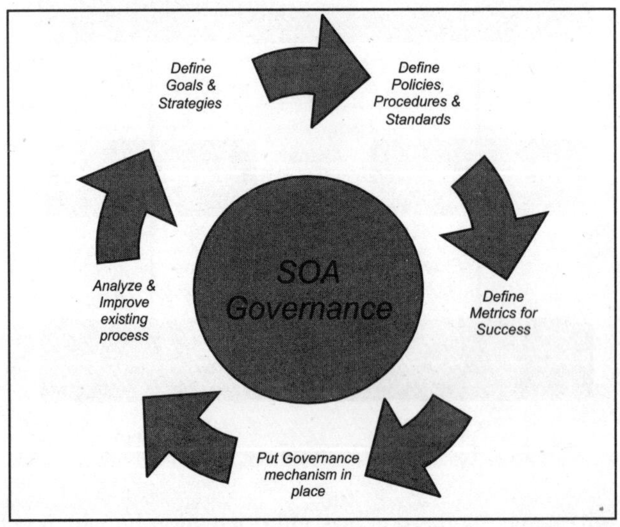

Fig. 1.3: 5   Step Governance Model

Step 1: Define Goals and Strategies

The first and most important step is defining the organization's SOA goals and strategies. These must be aligned with business goals and strategies for the SOA efforts to provide the greatest value. Most companies have goals around revenue, growth and maximum profit. The one overlooked thing is the change of business demands with respect to time. The design must be chalked out by considering the time required to implement the SOA governance and the changes which will occur in business during this period of time. As a part of this phase, it's also important to take into account applicable constraints, including resources, organizational readiness, budgeting, legacy and cultural issues.

Step 2: Define Policies, Procedures & Standards

Whatever SOA strategy your organization selects, in Step 2, you should clearly state who has decision and input rights in formulating specific governance policies, how the policies are communicated, how the execution of those policies is monitored, and how adjustments can be made to the policies based on real-life experience. Most companies begin their SOA journey using a project-based approach, meaning that the SOA efforts and tools are justified within the scope and budget of a development project. Many companies want to see success stories with SOA before expending the time and effort to fully align the various areas. Since the first SOA endeavors are project-based, these efforts typically leverage existing tools, such as application servers, Web service management platforms, portals, or other tools specific to the selected project. As subsequent projects are implemented, enterprises will add additional tools and infrastructures (such as BPEL process orchestration and business rules engines) based on project-level requirements. Governance begins with simple policies, procedures, and standards surrounding the use of these selected tools and doesn't venture much beyond the scope of projects.

Best Practice: Establish SOA goals, standards, policies, and procedures proportionate to your SOA maturity

Step 3: Define Metrecs for Success

Once you know what kinds of policies you need to focus on and where you are in the execution of your SOA strategy, you need to define the success factors and key performance indicators that will let you know you have achieved your goals and objectives. If you do not define metrics to measure the success of your SOA project, you are unlikely to establish the right governance mechanisms, and are equally unlikely to deliver on your SOA strategy. Your SOA metrics—which should be part of your EA metrics — may include the creation and use of reference architectures. These metrics should be communicated to the business and IT communities to clearly capture the business value of all the SOA activities and successes

Best Practice: Define clear metrics that are obtainable and can show your progress in maturing your SOA and EA efforts.

Step 4: Put Governance Mechanisms in Place

Step four of the SOA governance process involves the enactment of governance mechanisms, including how to obtain and evaluate metrics, how to enforce policies and procedures, and how to reward the architects and developers that create sharable services and the individuals or organizations that use them. While the process of collecting and measuring the metrics must be considered and planned in steps 2 and 3, this step represents the actual execution of those processes. For example, if one metric is the number of sharable services or the number of architectural assessments and their results, then actually putting in place the necessary policies to deliver the desired results is part of step 4. Some governance process must be automated and some manual, but we must ensure that they must be employed in same direction choreographed by step 2.

In order to make the procedures effective, you need endorsement from executives, to "encourage" the behavioral changes that SOA requires and to ensure the participation of the appropriate people. Also bear in mind that when you are setting up the governance mechanisms, governance overhead should be commensurate with the stage of SOA adoption and the size of your company. That is, you won't need much when you're starting out, but you should plan on progressively phasing in more policies as you increase your SOA maturity.

Best Practice: Put repeatable and well-defined governance processes in place and capture the metrics defined in steps 2 and 3

Step 5: Analyze & Improve Existing Process [7]

At this step, you should analyze the results of the governance policies that you put in place and gather metrics on the governance processes themselves, including their effectiveness. You should also measure the progress that you have made on your SOA Roadmap, relaxing overly restrictive policies where it makes sense and taking corrective action where necessary. A lot of companies separate "policies" (have to follow) from "guidelines" (should follow). Remember, you want to have an open environment in which people communicate their actions and experiences when they go off the beaten path.

As you keep improving your governance and overall EA practices, issues that had slipped through in the past including communication of the metrics and even the metrics themselves—will rise to the top and command attention until they can be fixed, automated, or in some way improved. This includes communication of the metrics and even the metrics themselves. Remember that feedback from the recipients of the metrics (typically the businesses) is vital to improving this process.

Conclusion

SOA is part of enterprise architecture, and should be driven by strategic and tactical business goals and objectives. To deliver on its business goals, a company should establish better alignment between architecture, technology infrastructure, information, portfolios, project execution, people, finance, and operations. As an organization matures in its EA and SOA efforts, these relationships need to become tighter. At the same time, the company can create a five-step governance process that starts simply and matures to become more effective and more efficient.

This article has described a framework and best practices for governing the SOA journey, and defined a five-step process that you can use to mature your enterprise SOA efforts, breaking down the barriers between businesses and maximizing the enterprise benefits from an SOA approach.

Reference

1. Mohamad Afshar, Contributing Authors: Michael Cincinatus, Dan Hynes, Kevin Clugage, Vishram Patwardhan SOA Governance: Framework and Best Practices, Version 1.1.

2. W.T. Tsai, X. Wei, Y. Chen, and R. Paul. A robust testing framework for verifying web services by completeness and consistency analysis. In *IEEE International Workshop on Service-Oriented System Engineering (SOSE)*, pages 159–166, Los Alamitos, CA, USA, 2005. IEEE Computer Society.

3. Rob Barry, "ENTERPRISE ARCHITECTURE IS MORE THAN A TECHNOLOGY", July 22, 2009.

4. David S. Linthicum, CEO of the Linthicum Group LLC, an SOA, consultancy, and former CEO of Bridgewerx Bringing Together Data Integration and SOA, Sep 23, 2009.

5. Mohammad, A.F.; Grant, E.S.; Goyal, S.; Bhatia, A.; Dept. of Comput. Sci., Univ. of North Dakota, GrandForks, ND, USA, *Issue Date: 25-27 Nov. 2009, On page(s): 287-292 Location: Athens, Print ISBN: 978-1-4244-5345-0.*

6. SOA Governance Tutorial http://searchsoa.techtarget.com/generic/0,295582,sid26_gci1363742_mem1,00.html

7. SOA Planning http://www.essaytown.com/paper/soa-abstract-although-service-oriented-architectures-become-popular-32415.

CHAPTER 40

Data Management Framework in Mobile Ad Hoc Networks

Rakesh S. Patil and Pratibha V. Waje
Sir Visvesvaraya Institute of Technology, Chincholi, Sinner-422101 Nashik (MS), India
E-mail: rakeshspatil@yahoo.com, wajepratibha85@rediffmail.com

ABSTRACT

A trust-based data management framework enabling mobile devices to access the distributed computation, storage, and sensory resources available in pervasive computing environments. Available resources include those in the fixed surrounding infrastructure as well as services offered by other nearby mobile devices. The authors have taken a holistic approach that considers data trust, security, and privacy and focus on the collaborative mechanisms providing a trustworthy data management platform in an ad-hoc network. The framework is based on a pack formation mechanism that enables collaborative peer interactions using context information and landmarks. A pack provides a routing substrate allowing devices to find reliable information sources and coordinated pro-active and reactive mechanisms to detect and respond to malicious activity. Consequently, a pack forms a foundation for distributed trust management and data intensive interactions. The focus is on building a trustworthy data management framework for personal mobile devices in pervasive environments, which utilize wireless connectivity to access resources provided by self-organizing networks. The approach to modeling trust is focused on risk management and coping with the inherent uncertainty arising from the serendipity in locating and communicating with other devices or resources. The approach focuses on enabling efficient resource location and trustworthy data management using pack formations. This paper describes data management framework with an emphasis on pack formation in mobile ad-hoc networks

Keywords: Ad Hoc Networks, MANET, Data Management, Framework

I. INTRODUCTION

(i) Motivation

Advances in technology and the growing demand for wireless connectivity are fueling a proliferation of wireless capabilities in everyday appliances. There is a large heterogeneity in the types of portable devices and their communication, computational, and storage capabilities. Moreover, computation capable embedded electronic devices equipped with sensors and actuators are transforming home, office and urban landscapes into resource-rich and data-intensive environments. Peer interactions that use local ad hoc connectivity are most suited in locating and consuming services available in vicinity, since infrastructure based continuous connectivity to the Internet is often unavailable or expensive. The focus of this paper is on building a trustworthy data management framework for personal mobile devices in pervasive environments, which utilize wireless connectivity to access resources provided by self-organizing networks. The authors have characterized such mobile ad hoc networks (MANETs) as having two kinds of nodes or actors:

Fixed assets businesses, including restaurants and stores, public service kiosks providing traffic, weather, road conditions; and Mobile devices, including mobile phones or car computers. Fixed assets can thus be associated with geographical locations, whereas mobile devices are assumed to have certain mobility profiles. Existing data management architectures assume that encountered devices and the information obtained from them are trustworthy. This assumption, however, is unrealistic in a pervasive environment. Therefore, assurances of the quality and accuracy of the retrieved information must be provided. Limited Internet connectivity makes it infeasible to use conventional security paradigms for determining the trustworthiness of other devices. For example, communicating with a trusted authority in order to verify the credentials of nearby entities may be impossible. Moreover, the nature of these environments requires these devices to function independently and be capable of making autonomous decisions about the trustworthiness of peers and accuracy of their information. Given the lack of centralized authorities in ad hoc networks, trust evaluation and reputation management are essential mechanisms that allow devices to function autonomously with minimal user intervention.

(ii) Approach Overview

Our approach to modeling trust is focused on risk management and coping with the inherent uncertainty rising from the serendipity in locating and communicating with other devices or resources. Also, it is necessary for devices to be able to dynamically respond to changes in the environment. In the context of MANETs, key factors in ascertaining situational trust include knowledge of the environment regarding mobility, network topology, and - proximity, reach ability, and availability of resources. Other factors include familiarity or knowledge of other node identities in the vicinity. Thus, we stress the need for devices to be aware of their context when making trusting decisions. A very basic form of trust is assumed to exist amongst all the participants in an ad hoc network-the expectation that other devices in the neighborhood will participate in the routing process and help relay data traffic. Without the existence of a basic communication mechanism to relay messages, no further interactions are possible. Higher degrees of trust can exist when devices seek to cooperate beyond provisioning the basic connectivity either for incentives or out of necessity. Reputations are used to estimate the risk of future cooperation based on past behavior. Recommendations are sought from other trusted peers when prior knowledge or reputation of the entity in question is not available. Our approach hinges on the use of normative behavior and activities monitoring in order to evolve trust relationships, maintain reputations, and detect malicious activity.

We define a pack as a dynamic grouping of individual devices which agree to collaborate in pursuit of individual, mutual and collective goals. In this paper, we describe a collaborative approach that addresses issues of trust and security in data management and present initial results from simulate on experiments on pack formation. Our approach is based on providing primitives for trust evolution and pack formation. A pack formation serves two purposes: A pack provides a routing substrate enabling devices to find reliable sources of information, and A pack supports a platform for coordinated pro-active and reactive mechanisms that can detect and respond to malicious activity. A pack, therefore, forms the basis for mobile devices to evolve, manage, and evaluate trust of their peers and information and services they offer.

II. BACKGROUND AND RELATED WORK

(i) Trust and Reputation Management in MANETS

Pervasive environments are in a constant state of flux. Routing mechanisms in self-organizing networks, which provide the communication mechanism, are necessarily of a collaborative nature. The inherent uncertainty in locating and accessing resources (services and data) further necessitate collaboration. Data reliability is also an important issue since prior trust relationships may not always exist. Moreover, finding reliable data on-demand in a serendipitous environment is another challenge. Collaboration on these various fronts requires various degrees of trust in potential collaborators. Using information from the surrounding pervasive environment introduces several trust and security issues. With a lack of security enforcing mechanisms or arbitrators, devices need to cope with the freedom of others and the possibility of malicious activity. Due to the potentially innumerable number of devices, it is unlikely to be able to individually cache all possible identities and their reputations. Moreover, it will be infeasible to maintain a consistent view on trustworthiness amongst all devices. We propose that it is sufficient to remember only devices that are of future potential value in forming social networks and those that will be most likely to cooperate, and maintain reputations regarding only those. Past research has provided insights into how a profile-driven agent can use notions of trust and reputations for query processing. However, several challenges remain, e.g., how to find reliable information, use active collaborations, leverage abundant storage - to collate and coordinate data search, and how to improve latency of simplistic discovery mechanisms.

(ii)   Data Management in Pervasive Environments

The concept of "data recharging," is likening to recharging a battery. Data recharging is the process of caching information relevant to the user's needs expressed in the user's profile. The profile is thus a form of long term query that continuously processes relevant data whenever it is available. When finding a resource of interest, the key is in finding the path of minimum cost and maximum benefit. Once data sources or other resources are located in the vicinity of the device (lack of prior arrangement or knowledge) the devices must have the option to either continuously monitor/use the resource (identified by its distinguishing source identity) or get updates of information of interest at a later time. This requires a close and continuous (minimal) interaction with surrounding nodes who provide assurance of trust about resources and volunteer or collaborate in availing the service. Since these devices are not continuously connected, such communication must be assumed to be intermittent at best. In Peer-to-Peer (P2P) networks data routing substrate enables resource pooling and scalability. In existing P2P deployments, connectivity is predominantly wire line. Motion of mobile devices is relative. From the perspective of a mobile device, the device can consider itself stationary and all available resources and device continuously moving. The following scenario presents a situation where some devices are relatively stationary with respect to the device. We use this scenario to exemplify and outline the characteristics of pervasive environments and the expected behavior of mobile devices. In the below scenario we expect the devices to utilize data and resource information from their local peers. Moreover, we assume that multiple devices will be able to cache information coming from the same source in the vicinity. Therefore, replication of the information is likely to increase data availability. Similarly, collaborative verification will help eliminate corrupt data. In the remaining sections of this paper, we explore the various possibilities and benefits of pack formation and the costs involved.

III.   TRUST-BASED FRAMEWORK

(i)   Assumptions

We assume that a mobile user is not continuously interacting with the device and making decisions. Instead the device is largely autonomous in its functioning and decision making while guided by the user's profile. The user is alerted if the device cannot make a crucial decision or if some event of interest occurs. The device is thus provided a specification of the kind of data it should be looking for. At certain intervals the user may refer to the device and available services the device can offer or locate within the environment. The device should then provide trustworthy services by ensuring fidelity of the services and the data they provide. Also it may cooperate with other devices in order to perform negotiated collective goals or tasks again based on the user profile or explicit notification from the user. The objective of the data management framework is to help locate specific resources or services and rate the quality and trustworthiness of those resources. It is usually not realistic to determine the correctness of data, as sensors may malfunction or be disabled. The data collection mechanisms must provide non-repudiation and indicate trustworthiness of the source. Data verification usually cannot be done unilaterally; instead, federated or distributed trust mechanisms are required. We assume that devices are able to sense their spatial and temporal contexts. We use a set of landmarks or beaconing devices that advertise themselves and can be used by mobile devices to identify context. We also assume that devices' identities are persistent. Therefore, reputations can be associated with them. Such identifiers are required to be unique and possess capabilities for non-repudiation. We qualify trust to be a temporary assessment, having an instantaneous value, computed based on the reputation of the identity in question, the context, and the current intent. By reputation we mean a tasteful quantity associated with an identity that stores information, for example, about past behavior, recommendations, accusations, or associated neighborhoods. Reputation of a device is used in computing its trustworthiness.

(ii)   Evolving, Managing, and Evaluating Trust

Social networks will play an important role in both the data management and trust evaluation aspects of pervasive computing. The context of a device is often used to guide its behavior. Additionally, we use associations of devices with the neighborhoods that they are seen in. For example, a student who frequently visits his University campus can notice other students on campus, and associate their identities with the context of the University campus. Given the finite number of potential neighborhoods that can be frequently visited, such a device can associate itself with particular neighborhoods of interest and time contexts - and also associate other devices with those neighborhoods.

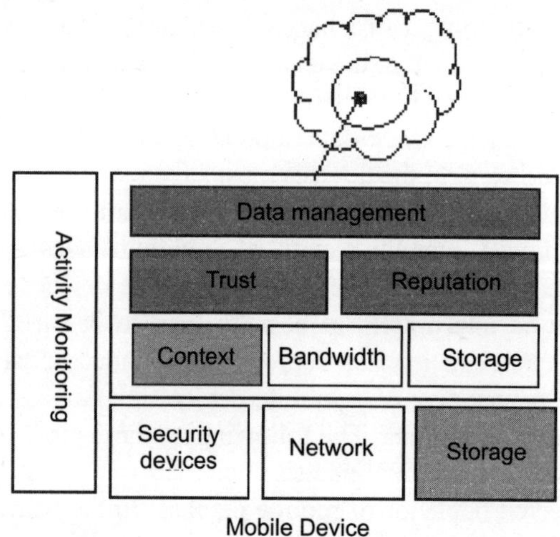

Fig. 2(a)

Figure 2(a) shows a hierarchy of the components involved in the data management framework on each individual device. Further each device is shown to be a pack member in some neighborhood, each part of a larger social network. Each device has its own view of the social network based on its own experiences and interactions. Figure 2 (b) illustrates a global view of the social network showing the individual mobile devices, packs, and neighborhoods in the social network. The trustworthiness of a peer or a resource in a neighborhood can be computed from the history of prior encounters or can be provided by other trusted devices in the same neighborhood. When trust opinion is sought from peers, it can be weighted by one's degree of trust in them. Assuming that devices can be associated with particular neighborhoods it is logical to assume that at least some such "resident" devices are present who can provide trust assessments about other devices. Consequently sufficient information about trustworthiness of devices in the neighborhood already exists within the neighborhood, distributed amongst its frequent visitors. Devices can be categorized into: trusted, offender and unknown.

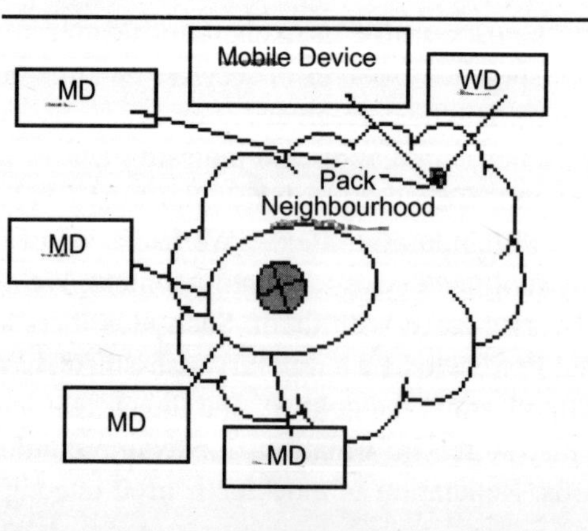

Fig. 2(b)

The necessity of cooperation in peer interactions is related to the current degree of resource and data availability. The need is higher when availability is low, i.e., when trustworthy resources who can provide the required data are unavailable or limited. Our approach relies on monitoring the availability of resources and levels of cooperation of other peers for adapting to current conditions and to reciprocate peer interactions. This serves as an encouragement for cooperation – a non-cooperating peer will get diminishing attention from its peers while cooperativeness is automatically rewarded. We consider two aspects of trust viz. the accuracy of data provided (validation/verification) and the degree of cooperation. A device which frequents a particular neighborhood will slowly build its reputation as a trustworthy resource. The degree of trust it enjoys in a particular neighborhood governs the level at which other devices and community resources are accessible or willing to cooperate. This knowledge of a device and its neighborhood associations thus serves as an enforcement for long term accountability. If a device exhibits malicious behavior, devices in the vicinity can effect an immediate response by denying further resources to the misbehaving entity. This response can be at all levels, from application to lower level networking layers. Furthermore, accusations of the recorded misbehavior are eventually propagated back to all its known home neighborhoods.

(iii)   Data Routing Substrate and Storage Management

Once social communities exist, it is possible for devices converging around a particular landmark to identify each other from their cached knowledge and trust relations. Pack formation is now possible from such a subset of entities willing to collaborate.

Due to the inherent nature of the recommendation system, there are several incentives for such devices to collaborate, viz.,

- increased scope of search faster data retrieval
- updates related to trust information
- faster updates to existing data sets
- increased awareness of trusted devices in the vicinity
- minimal effort in evaluating trustworthiness of providing source and accuracy of data, and re-assertion of their own membership in the pack.

Those devices that do not collaborate in these basic information exchanges risk losing their privileges by failing to reaffirm existing trust relationships. Since devices tend to cache the information related to the most recently encountered trustworthy and cooperative resources - uncooperative or passive devices stand to lose their established reputations by replacement in cache by other trusted sources. Moreover, this formation helps create a data routing substrate for distributed storage management amongst the pack members collaborating to achieve (individual or collective) goals. We are implementing such a data routing substrate that can provide pack members with an inexpensive and efficient mechanism for locating reliable information sources and collaborative queries.

CONCLUSIONS

Our approach focuses on enabling efficient resource location and trustworthy data management using pack formations. In order to enable pack formations we suggest the use of fixed landmarks in the pervasive environment to serve as nucleating points for social networks of frequent visitors. We presented scenarios to elucidate the context and identify the various crucial aspects, in evaluating trust in pervasive environments. Collaboration in routing and data management is key to the functioning of MANETs. Moreover, time is of essence in making trust decisions while locating resources and utilizing services as access is usually short-lived. While reputation management is essential in fostering cooperation and making trusting decisions, pack formations further simplify the decision making processes and provide added stability to resource location mechanisms in the highly dynamic MANET conditions, enabling an essential platform for trustworthy data management.

References

1. Anand Patwardhan: Querying in packs:Trustworthy data Management in Ad Hoc Networks

2. g2dn: Gnutella2 developer's network. http://www.gnutella2.com/ Open Source Napster Sever. http://sourceforge.net/projects/opennap/. Web Ontology Language (OWL).

3. T. Aura. Internet Draft: Cryptographically Generated Addresses (CGA).

4. J.B. Begole, J.C. Tang, R.B. Smith, and N. Yankelovich. Work rhythms: analyzing visualizations of awareness histories of distributed groups.

5. S. Buchegger and J.- L. Boudec. A robust reputation system for p2p and mobile ad-hoc networks, 2004.

6. M. Cherniak, M. Franklin, and S. Zdonik. Expressing User Profiles for Data Recharging.

7. M. Cherniak, E. Galvez, D. Brooks, M. Franklin, and S. Zdonik. Profile Driven Data Management.

8. M.J. Covington, W. Long, S. Srinivasan, A.K. Dey, M. Ahamad, and G.D. Abowd. Securing context- aware applications using environment roles.

CHAPTER 41

Developing Knowledge Engineering Framework for a Technical Higher Education Institute

Deepti Mehrotra[1] and Renuka Nagpal[2]
[1]Director, Amity School of Computer Science, Sector 44 Noida,
[2]Senior Lecturer, Amity School of Engineering and Technology, Sector 125 Noida
E-mail: director@ascs.amity.edu, rnapal1@amity.edu

ABSTRACT

Use of fully automated system for overall administration is need of today for all technical higher education institutes. These systems generate a huge data base which if fully exploited through proper knowledge engineering tools can be base for developing a decision support system. Like any other knowledge engineering environment here also the major concern is knowledge collection, measure relevance, i.e. evaluation and grading of the knowledge using knowledge audit. The key idea is to develop a framework named a knowledge base knowledge management system (KBKMS) that can identify problems that today's technical higher education are facing, propose a solution for it and evaluate it's implementation on overall system.

Keywords: Technical higher education (THE), knowledge engineering (KE), Knowledge base knowledge management system (KBKMS).

1. INTRODUCTION

Knowledge originates in individuals, but it is embodied in teams and organizations. Implying the Knowledge engineering principles one can develop a model that provide right information to right people at right time, using tools that analyze the information and give them power to respond to insight they glean from that information. Thus major role of such a system is to establish a proper coordination between people, process and technology and provide a framework for decision support system. In a technical educational institute, the people refer to students, faculty, staff and management. The processes include various processes like admission, examination, teaching, research and many more. The technology refers to the IT tools that are being used, like a fully automated system for the overall administration, the intranet and web portals that are frequently used to transferring the information like notice, tutorials, examination schedule etc. The role of KE framework is to align with these processes with a focuses on identifying the strength and weakness of them and provide solution to problems faced in implementing these process. As by the automated system a large amount of data is collected which is needed to be exploited through suitable technology and intelligent people to inference some decision. Decision making theory has strong roots in intelligence, design, choice, implementation sequence [1]. Thus there is a need to identify what information of the knowledge base can be qualified as intelligent and can be used for generating new knowledge for competitive advantage. Today all business organizations are using of Knowledge Management principles to develop a knowledge based decision system which can improve performance and generate profit for the organization. In this paper we will first discuss various modules of the technical higher education system and develop a knowledge repository by understanding why how and what of database and develop a knowledge engineering model that implements the philosophy of TQM where quality is continuous evolving process and is the responsibility of all entities involved in the system

2. KNOWLEDGE ENGINEERING FRAMEWORK

N Shadbolt[2] had proposed principles for developing a knowledge engineering system. The foremost requirement for creating such system is to recognize the different type of knowledge which exit in system. As per a popular framework for thinking there are two main types of knowledge: *explicit* and *tacit*[3]. Explicit knowledge is documented information that can facilitate action like strategies, methodologies, processes, patents, products, and services. It can be expressed in formal, shared language like formulas, equations, rules, and best practices. Tacit knowledge is know-how and learning embedded within the minds of the people in an organization. It involves perceptions, insights, experiences, and craftsmanship. A common initiative within the tacit knowledge approach is usually some effort to improve understanding of who knows about what in an organization. Examples of tacit knowledge in an organizational context are skills and competencies, experiences, relationships within and outside the organization, individual beliefs and values, and ideas. For an aim to endeavor the best to the student and society one need to understand the knowledge both analytically and tacitly. An important aspect of KE is to recognize different types of expert and expertise. The integration and balancing of leadership, organization, learning and technology in an enterprise-wide setting is a key requirement for developing KE framework along with actions performed to capture, store, distribute and analyze the information and convert it to knowledge. A lot of interest is shown in collecting the data but its conversion to information is not done in requisite manner. The key idea is to stress on the importance of organizational knowledge for creating activities rather than individual knowledge for creating knowledge. One of prime objective of this framework is convert tacit knowledge to explicit knowledge. As far as technical higher education is concern it is very complex system. Using explicit information one can tacitly generate knowledge in key areas of education system like teaching methodology, course content development, perquisite knowledge that student should have before opting the course and many more things for overall improvement student knowledge about that course and also the pedagogy and evaluation methodology adapted for that course.

Identifying the source of knowledge and its proper representation is important component of any knowledge system. An education institute is a pool of individual knowledge and there is need to create sharing culture to transfer individual knowledge into organization knowledge. There are various processes associated in technical higher education. Many automated systems that are used as the database for developing KE framework. The SAS, QAMS, ASM system described below produce a large amount of explicit knowledge. This explicit knowledge is exploited using appropriate tools of data mining and Statistics. However few systems like EVS, AMS, TIRDS use both explicit and tacit knowledge for concluding a decision.

Student administration system (SAS): This basically covers all student administration related information like admission, registration, attendance and examination result, placement and training status.

Quality and Academic monitoring system (QAMS): This system observe the performance of overall system is as per the quality guidelines framed by the organization by monitoring the performance of faculty, course development and deployment, feedback analysis, monitoring of student performance in evaluation system and placement.

Administration and staff management system (ASM): Overall administration of institute and staff members, their attendance, payroll management system, inventory control system.

Event Management System (EVS): As the technical institutes have to provide the technocrats for industry this is much required to understand the need of the industry. Thus the collaboration with various industry, other academic institutes and research organization for interdisplinary technology awareness among the students is required. It is almost mandatory for the technical institutes to conduct various events such a seminars, workshop, colloquium, industrial interaction sessions, and training for the students. Also it is required to provide some value added courses that can groom the student suitable for the industry. Institute has to conduct faculty development programs for updating faculty with latest technology, pedagogy techniques and research development.

Apex Management system (AMS): This is the management system to design the rules and policies for students, faculty and staff. The working of this system is basically governed by the tacit knowledge. While designing new policies the management has to anticipate the effect of any new designed policy and ensure that it comply the guidelines laid by the salutary body and mission of the institute

Technology Innovation and research development System (TIRDS): The quality of any organization is much rated by the research activities that are conducted and technology that are being developed, Patents and research publications, books that are in credit to it. Research has being always considered as source of tacit knowledge, but a lot of explicit knowledge is also required for its proper promotion:

- Funding opportunities which include government project and Consultancy of industry that are available.
- Pre-populated proposals, budgets, and protocols.
- Proposal-routing policies and procedures.
- Award notification, account setup, and negotiation policies and procedures.
- Contract and grant management policies and procedures.
- Technical and financial support available, report templates and policies.

Apart for it workshops and consultancy should be conducted to make the research scholars and faculty to aware them about intellectual property right act and encourage research activity in the institute.

3. DEVELOPING KNOWLEDGE ENGINEERING FRAMEWORK

Nissen et al [4,5] has developed a knowledge management life cycle model which makes flow time explicit and supports a multidimensional framework that enables a new approach to analysis and visualization of diverse knowledge-flow patterns in the organization. This model describes "a continuous cycle" with six phases of knowledge flowing through the organisation:

Creation: A new knowledge is generated within an organization by capturing and acquisition i.e, add new knowledge and settle existing knowledge. Various popular practices to generate knowledge are formal training, knowledge repositories, knowledge fairs, communities of practice, talk norms[6] our model has developed a knowledge repository using suitable agent.

Organization: The second phase involve development of knowledge map, building of knowledge, by employing systems such as taxonomies, ontology and repositories.

Formalization: The phase addresses mechanisms for making knowledge formal or explicit; it include storage techniques used in knowledge database and codify it using proper tools for conversion of tacit knowledge to explicit notation. The technical education KE framework has a distributed architecture, can be modeled as a multi-agent system, associating agents to all humans involved in the processes that run the institute (educational, research, institutional etc)[7,8] which are broadly classified as below:

Knowledge management agent: It takes care of management processes like storage, retrieval and inference of knowledge chunks according to the goal definition and includes (i) knowledge about knowledge, (ii) knowledge about processes, (iii) knowledge about users, and (iv) knowledge about goal definition and is responsible for activities like integration, validation, and utilization of different knowledge patterns acquired, like SAS is knowledge management agent which collect the information from which knowledge about student can be extracted.

Rule induction agent: It works on decision tree induction, classifies, and forwards the rules to other agents and used for framing the decision at process level.

Data filtering agent: Its prime objective is to filter data from the domain files, set parameters and suggestions of method.

Dynamic analysis agent: This agent uses dynamic analysis and statistical analysis methods for analyzing filtered data.

Distribution: The fourth phase concerns the ability to share or distribute knowledge in the enterprise through transfer and access, communication within the organization. Once the knowledge is being created it should be suitably distributed using tools such as portals for knowledge sharing and distribution.

Application : Utilization of knowledge application in problem solving or in decision making system

Evolution or maintenance phase: This phase involves evaluation of the KE process using knowledge audit. In order to measure a KE product we need design a metrics suite with several objectives including securing funding for KE implementation, providing targets and feedback on implementation, assessing implementation success, and deriving lessons for future implementation. Measures can assist in evaluating the initial investment decision and in developing benchmarks for future comparison. Thus this phase covers knowledge refinement and evolution, which reflects organizational learning, and thus a return to knowledge creation through time. It should be noted that the above models are generally iterative and involve feedback loops between stages.

4. DEVELOPMENT OF KNOWLEDGE BASE KNOWLEDGE MANAGEMENT SYSTEM (KBKMS)

After engineering the knowledge base we had designed and implemented the knowledge base knowledge management system (KBKMS) for a technical higher education institute. The steps taken to design this system are (Figure 1):

(a) Collect data from various systems.

(b) The management to set vision and design objective and quality guidelines. Knowledge Based Knowledge Management strategies has to designed which may include academic strategy, student strategy, management strategies and organizational strategies for which input from various sections are received

(c) Develop knowledge management road maps that establish relationship among various departments. It tell us where we can capture particular knowledge i.e., it points to where they can find certain expertise. This document helps us to design a framework for knowledge management system which reflects the current state of interrelationship among different departments and proposed future and overall milestones of the system.

(d) Identify the various knowledge processes and how various technology tools are used to implement it.

(e) Collect all type of knowledge.

(f) Determine the type of knowledge generated whether it is explicit or tacit. Utilize various tools like decision tree, production rules, frame, association rule data mining principles to extract explicit knowledge from the codified information. Data mining tools are extensively used for inferring information from the system and a lot of research is taking in area of educational data mining these tools helps us to codify the explicit information and also codify tacit knowledge to some extent [8,9].

(g) Identify tacit knowledge using what-how, what why principles.

(h) Distribute the knowledge to various system by identifying different agents.

(i) Coordinate various KM activities and there functions.

5. CONCLUSION

The given system provide organizational learning, the process of acquiring information; knowledge production, the process of transforming and integrating information into usable knowledge; and knowledge distribution; the process of disseminating knowledge throughout the organization. The above system helps us to develop decision support system that will be able answer the below most frequent faced questions in technical higher education:

- How can we better meet the needs of our student?
- How can we improve the student overall performance?
- What student interventions are most effective?

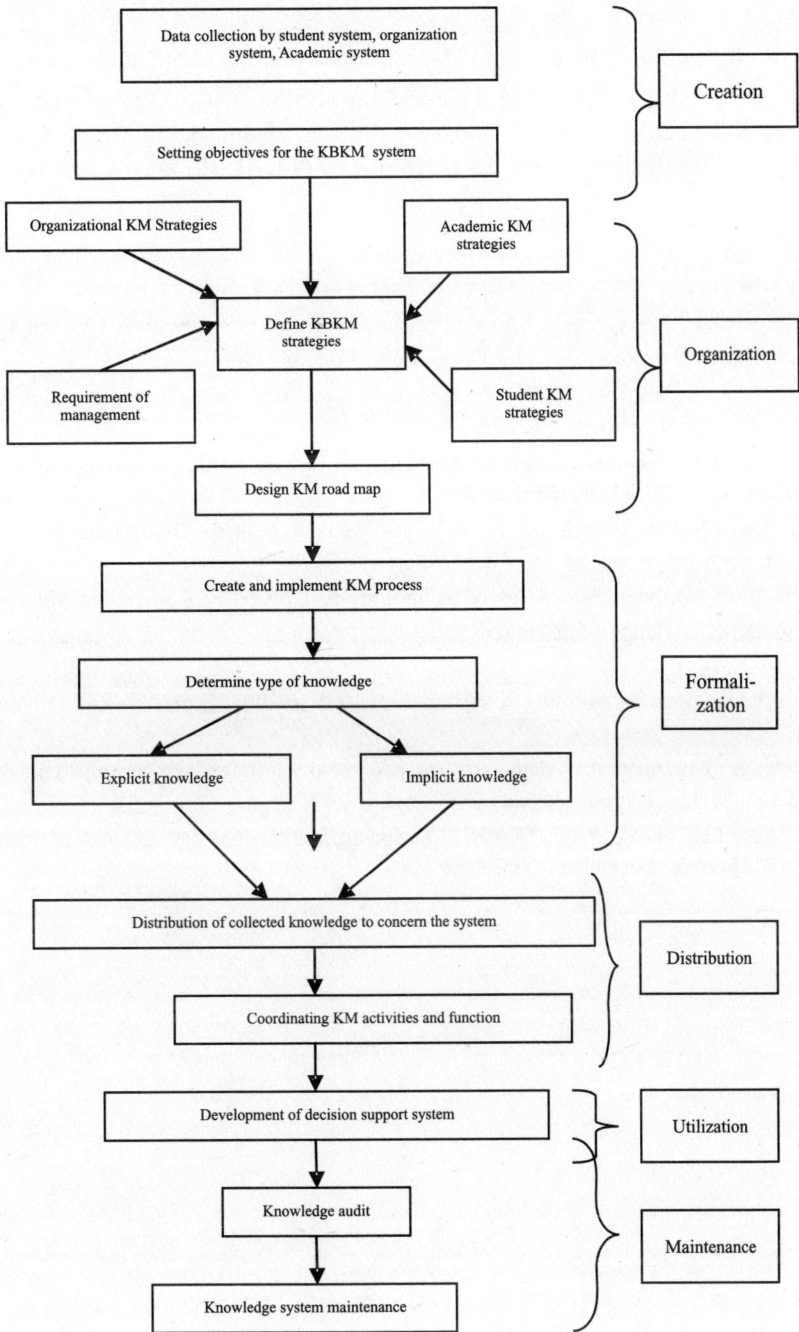

Fig.1 Implementation of Knowledge base knowledge management system

- How to seek greater administrative efficiency?
- How the curriculum and academic environment has improved the students learning ability?
- Which are programs of greater demand what new programs or courses should be introduced?
- How technology and other resources are utilized in cost effective and environment friendly manner?
- How innovative research and technology development can take place?
- What value added course should be conducted for overall development of student and fulfilling the mission and vision of institute?
- What student and faculty welfare scheme should be introduce to attract both student and qualified staff?

The quality as said is a continuous process and to achieve it one need to measure the effect of system at every stages. A large number of metrics had been proposed to measure the knowledge management system, e.g., knowledge performance index [10, 11] and for effective system the performance of KBKMS need to evaluate at different stages.

Reference

1. H.A. Simon, The New Science of Management Decision. Harper and Row, New York, 1960.
2. N. Shadbolt, From Knowledge Engineering to Knowledge Management, British Journal of Management, Vol 10, 309, 1999.
3. M. Polanyi, The Tacit Dimension. Routledge and Kegan Paul, London, 1966.
4. M. Nissen, M.N. Kamel, K.C. Sengupta, (2000). Integrated Analysis and Design of Knowledge Systems and Processes. Information Resources Management Journal 13 (1), 24-43.
5. Nissen, M., Levitt, R. (2002). Dynamic Models of Knowledge-Flow Dynamics, CIFE Working Paper No.76. Stanford University.Hoveida,978-1-4244-2917-2/08, IEEE, 2008
6. Priti Srinivas Sajja, Multi-Agent System for Knowledge-Based Access to Distributed Databases, Interdisciplinary Journal of Information, Knowledge, and Management Volume 3, 2008
7. Mihaela Oprea1, Elia Petre Applying Agent-Based Technology to University Knowledge Management
8. Luan, J. Data Mining and Knowledge Management in Higher Education – Potential Applications. AIR Forum, Toronto, Canada, 2002.
9. C. Romero, S. Ventra, Educational data mining: a survey from 1995 to 2005, expert system with applications vol 33, July 2007
10. S.M. Tseng, "Knowledge management system performance measure index" Expert Systems with Applications: An International Journal volume 34 , Issue 1 (January 2008) pp: 734-745
11. Kun Chang Lee, Sangjae Lee, Inwon Kang "KMPI: Measuring knowledge management performance" Information & Management Volume 42, Issue 8, December 2005, Page 1149

Knowledge-Based Simulation of Digital Transmission Lines: A Data Analysis Approach to Study Transmission Line Behavior

[1]Quazi Khabeer and [2]S.C. Mehrotra

[1]Tom Patrick Institute of Computer & Information Technology, Aurangabad (MS)-431001, India,
[2]Dr BAM University, Aurangabad (MS)-431001, India
E-mail: quazi.khabeer@gmail.com, mehrotra_suresh@yahoo.com

ABSTRACT

Data Analysis for Digital pulse representation with different frequency in GHz is carried out with centralized Knowledge based functions. A theoretical description of transmission model is used at high frequency. This paper describes implementation of the simulation by using Fourier Transform and also inverse Fourier transform techniques. At high frequency, wavelength of the waves becomes of the order of the length of the circuit. One needs to model all electrical parameters based on Maxwell's equations. The transmission of digital pulse in realistic conditions needs to be simulated by using the transmission line equation. Mathematical modeling of material is also given to include simulation of pulses in presence of materials.

1. INTRODUCTION

A Knowledge-based functions are defined for Data Analysis of Digital Transmission Lines. The Purpose is to study the Behavior of Transmission Lines at High Frequency in the range of GHz. (Fig.1).

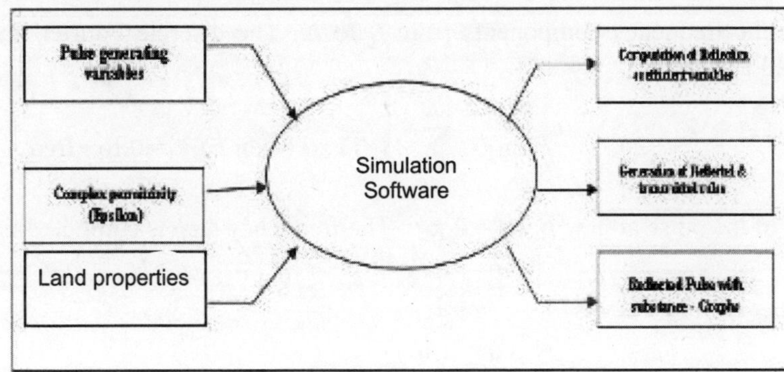

Fig.1 Knowledge - based function

In this paper the software can generate picoseconds pulses without or with noise. Its significant frequency components can be extracted by using the Fourier Transform technique. Thus time domain data is transformed into frequency domain. These frequency domain signals are reflected back with a material with known material properties. The mathematical description of the material is also included in the software. Then the software transforms back frequency domain signals into time domain. This illustrates that realistic information about the reflected pulses can be simulated.

2. DIGITAL SIMULATION OF PULSES IN TRANSMISSION LINES.

A Description of the Step Pulse

In our model, the step pulse is generated by the linear model. The sampling time is determined by the sampling frequency. The simulated pulse is shown in Figure 2.

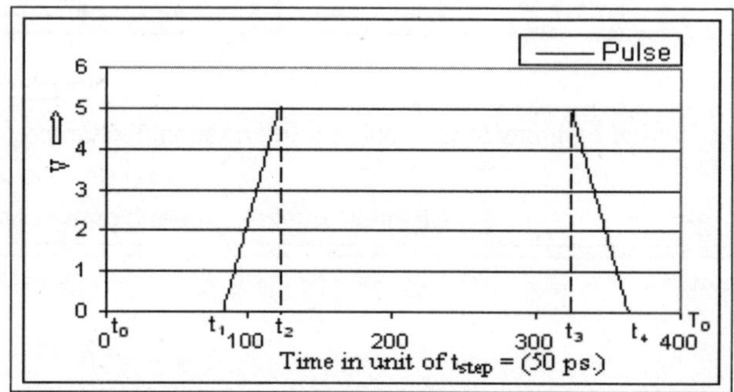

The sampling time can be determined by

$$tstep = 1/fs \tag{1}$$

where tstep is sampling time and *fs* is the sampling frequency. *T*0 is the total time of the pulse. $(t2 - t1)$ and $(t4 - t3)$ are rise time and fall time respectively. Total number of points, *np* can be computed as Fig. 2: Simulated Pulse.

$$np = (T0/tstep) + 1 \tag{2}$$

The upper frequency component fu present in the pulse is given by

$$fu = \tfrac{1}{2}\,fs \tag{3}$$

The lower frequency component can be computed as

$$f_L = 1/T_0 \tag{4}$$

The pulse contains the frequency components from f_L to *fu*. The discrete Fourier transform [1] of the pulse at frequency *fi* is computed as

$$F(\omega j) = \sum_{j=0}^{np} V(ti)\, \exp\,(-i\omega j\, ti),\, j = 0 \text{ to nfreq} \tag{5}$$

where $V(ti)$ is the value of the pulse at time *ti*, $\omega j = 2\,\pi\, fi$. The frequency step is computed from the duration of pulse as

$$fstep = 1/T_0 = f_L \tag{6}$$

Therefore the number of frequency is

$$\text{Nfreq} = (fu/f_L) \tag{7}$$

B. Pulse Reflection from the Load

When the pulse is reflected back from the load, its shape is dependent on the type of the load. The property of the load can be characterized by its frequency dependent permittivity. The model used in the work is described by the Havriliak-Negmi [2] model as follows.

$$\epsilon^* = \epsilon_\infty + (\epsilon_s - \epsilon_\infty)/[1 + (j\omega\tau)^\alpha]^{(1-\beta)} + \sigma/j\omega\epsilon_0 \tag{8}$$

where ϵ^* is complex permittivity, ϵ_s is static permittivity, ϵ_∞ is the permittivity at high frequency, t is the relaxation parameter, a and b are distribution parameters. s is the conductivity, ϵ_0 is permittivity in vacuum. The real part of (ϵ^*), ϵ', describes dispersion, where as imaginary part of (ϵ^*), ϵ'', describes absorpsation at angular frequency ω. The parameters for pure water at 200 C are, $\epsilon_s = 80$, $\epsilon_\infty = 4$, $\tau = 8$ ps, $? = 0$, $\alpha = 1$ and $\beta = 0$. The frequency dependent permittivity values are shown in Fig. 3 for the pure water system, at 300 C.

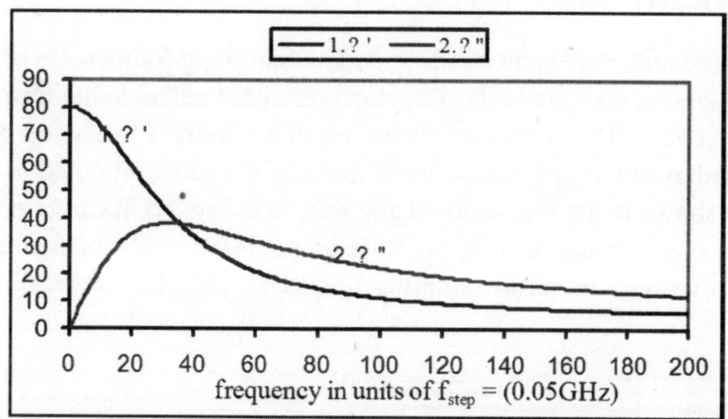

Fig. 3 Plot ª ' and ª" as function of frequency from the load for water.

The Fourier components will be reflected back

The reflection coefficient will also be complex which can be obtained by Transmission line theory [3] as follows.

$$\Gamma(\omega) = (\Gamma R - \Gamma I) = [(\gamma 0/\gamma 1)\ \tanh\ (\gamma 1 d) + 1]/[(\gamma 0/\gamma 1)\ \tanh(\gamma 1 d) - 1] \tag{9}$$

where ΓR and ΓI are real and complex parts of Γ, respectively. $\gamma 0$ is propagation constant in free space and $\gamma 1$ is propagation constant in the material under consideration, d is the length of the sample. The values of $\gamma 0$ and $\gamma 1$ are computed as follows.

$$\gamma_0 = \omega d/c \text{ and } \gamma_1 = \omega d/c\ \sqrt{\epsilon^*}$$

For different length of materials, the complex values of $\Gamma(w)$ is given in Figure (4) as function of frequency and for different pin length d. The quarter wave resonance can be seen very clearly from these figures.

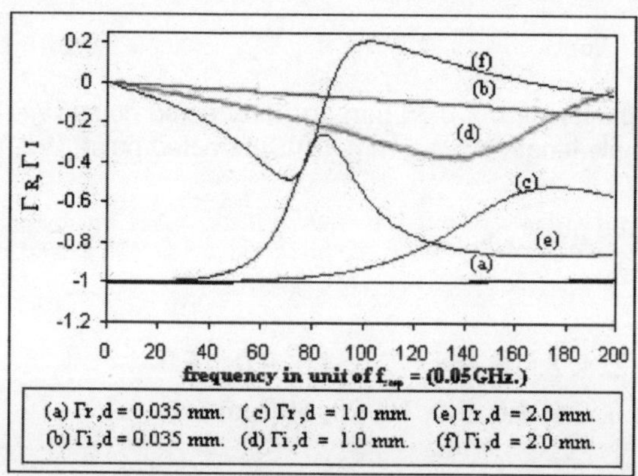

Fig. 4 ΓR and ΓI as function of frequency with $d = 0.35$, 1.0 & 2.0 mm.

C. Transformation of Reflected Pulse in Time Domain

The reflected Fourier components can be obtained from equation (5) and (9), as

$$F'(\omega j) = F'(\omega j) * \Gamma(\omega j) \tag{10}$$

where $F'(\omega j)$ is the fourier components of the reflected pulse at frequency fj. The reflected pulse, $V'p\,(ti)$ in time domain can be obtained by the Inverse Fourier transformation [4] as follows.

$$Vp'\,(ti) = \sum_{j=1}^{nfreq} f'(\omega j)\,\exp\,(-i\omega j\,ti),\ (i = 1\ \text{to}\ np.) \tag{11}$$

3. RESULTS OF SIMULATION

The reflected pulses are simulated under different conditions. The Sampling frequencies of 20GHz and 30GHz are set by the user. The amplitude of the pulse is given in volts. The step pulse parameters in the form of Rise time of pulse and fall time of pulse is given in nano seconds. The simulated results are in the form of following plotted graphs. The differences between the reflected pulses with material (Vx) and without material (Vr) are computed to see the effects of materials on the pulses. Some examples are shown in the Fig. 4a to 4d and Fig. 5a to Fig. 5d. It can be seen from the Figures, the pulse gets modified due to presence of the material. It is possible to get information of materials from the reflected pulse. Fig. 4a to 4d shows the results corresponding to sampling frequency 20GHz, whereas Fig. 5a to 5d corresponding to sampling frequency of 30 GHz.

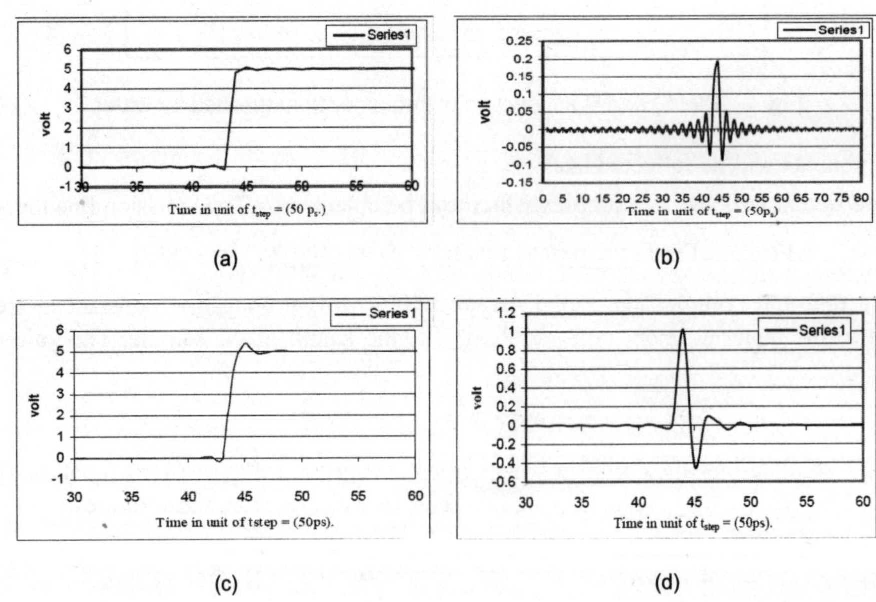

(a)   (b)

(c)   (d)

Fig. 4 (a) Reflected pulse with sample length d = 0.35 mm, (b) Subtracted pulse (Vx–Vr) with Sample length d = 0.35 mm, (c) Refelcted pulse with Sample length d = 1.0 mm, (d) Subtracted pulse (Vx–Vr) with Sample d = 1.0 mm

Transmission and Reflection of Digital pulse

    A. Sampling Frequency: 20 Ghz.

    B. Rise time: 10 Pico seconds.

    C. Substance Properties: $\in s$ = 2, 4, 8, 16 $\in \infty$ = 2.0, 4.0, 8.0, 16.0

    D. Diameter in mm: d = 0.1, 1.0, 2.5, 3.0, 5.0, 10, 20, 50 mm

E. Conductivity (sigma) = 0, 1

F. Noise: 0%, 10%

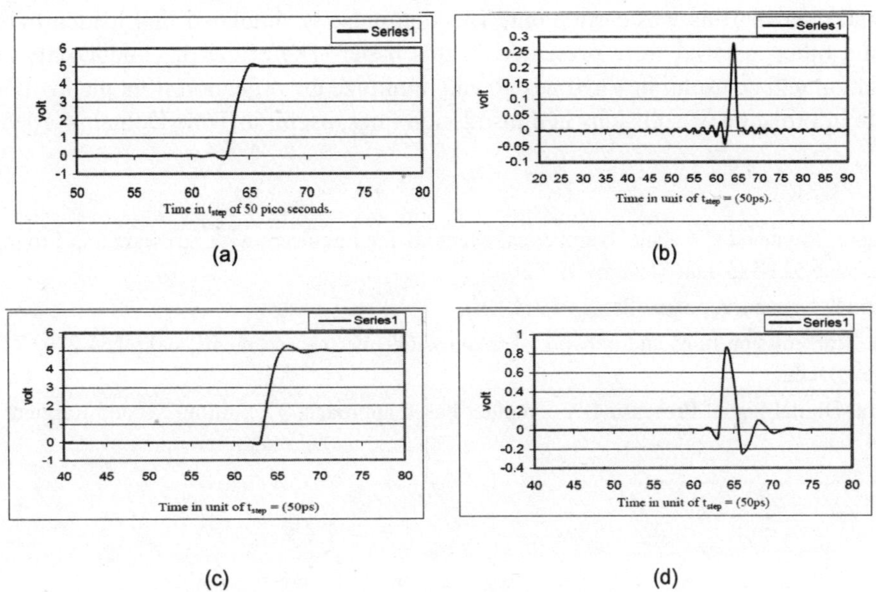

(a)   (b)

(c)   (d)

Fig. 5 (a) Reflected pulse with sample length d = 0.35 mm, (b) Subtracted pulse (Vx–Vr) with Sample length d = 0.35 mm, (c) Refelcted pulse with Sample length d = 1.0 mm, (d) Subtracted pulse (Vx–Vr) with Sample d = 1.0 mm

Substance Properties: ϵ_s = 2 & $\epsilon\infty$ = 2.0 Substance Properties: ϵ_s = 4 & $\epsilon\infty$ = 4.0

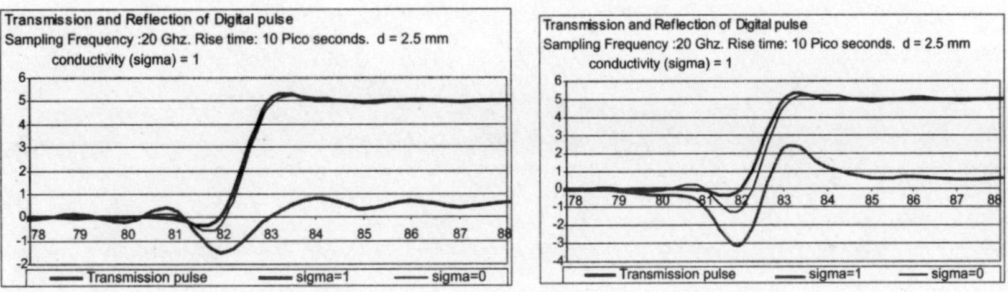

Substance Properties: ϵ_s = 8 & $\epsilon\infty$ = 8.0 Substance Properties: ϵ_s = 16 $\epsilon\infty$ = 16.0

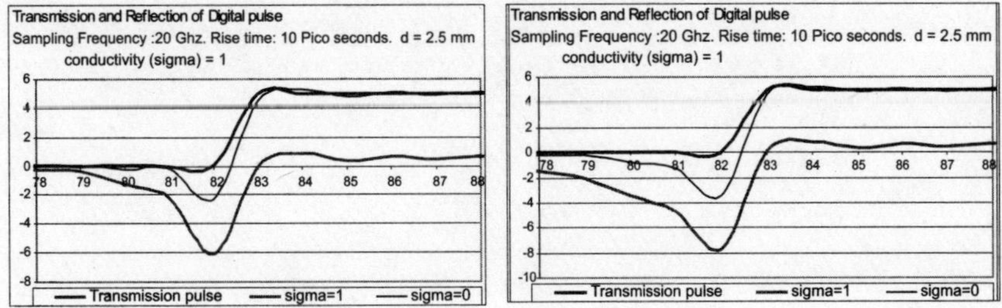

Observation

The effect of conductivity is also computed. The behavior of pulse changes with change in rise time and tau values. By changing different substance, the change is observed. The Simulation is also by introducing noise in the pulse.

4. CONCLUSION

Thus the simulation of Digital Transmission line was achieved. The Knowledge-based functions were defined based on Fourier Transform and data analysis was carried out. The step pulse is simulated in a loaded transmission lines. The example of water and other material were presented in this paper. The effect of conductivity and noise were also observed. The simulation will be useful in VLSI design and minimize the reflection from the load. This is also useful in getting more accurate information of collisions in transmission lines, useful in Time Domain Reflectometry (TDR).

References

1. Steven C Chapra, Raymond P. Canale. Numberical Methods for Engineers with Software and Programming Applications, fourth edition, page 523-535 Tata McGraw-Hill 2002

2. S. Havriliak and S. Negami, J. polyn., Sci.,14,99 (1966).

3. Umesh Sinha. Transmission lines and network. Transmission line measurements, page 263-279, 7th Edition, 2001, Satya Prakashan, New Delhi.

4. Sanjit K. Mitra. Digital Signal Processing-A computer based approach, 3rd Edition, Second Reprient 2006, Tata-McGraw-Hill Edition.

CHAPTER 43

Predicting the Data Congestion through Historical Points with the Innovation of Clustering in Seconds Based Time Series Analysis

Manikandan V, Sivasankar M, Karthikeyan S and Mohanapriya

Department of Computer Technology-PG, Kongu Engineering College, Perundurai, Erode, Tamilnadu, India

E-mail: maninihi@gmail.com, sivasankar043@gmail.com, karthikeyan50700hr@gmail.com, mohanapriyan08@gmail.com

ABSTRACT

In the case of data transfer in network and queuing theory, network congestion occurs when a link or node is carrying so much data that its quality of service is lacking. Typical effects include queuing delay, packet loss or the discard of new connections. A consequence of these latter two is that incremental increases in offered load lead either only to small increase in network throughput, or to an actual reduction in network throughput. In this paper we have given new approach to predict the congestion by historical data points. The seconds based time series analysis is done for solving the problem.

Keywords: prediction, time series analysis, congestion, traffic intensity

1. INTRODUCTION

The congestion is the resource allocation problem in the network. The congestion controlling, congestion detection, congestion avoidance algorithm is process of checking various factors across various layers of the network. The existing algorithms and approaches used are giving well performance across the various situations in the network. Analysis of the network congestion controlling algorithms is given in following section. Congestion control and resource allocations are two sides of the same coin. On the one hand, if the network takes a Active part in the resource allocation then congestion may be avoided. The congestion control is involves the both Hosts and network elements such as routers. When too many packets are contending for the same link, the queue overflows and packets have to be dropped. The resource allocation can be viewed as router centric versus host centric or reservation based versus feedback based or window based versus rate based solution.The TCP uses the Additive Increase Multiplicative Decrease (AIMD) with other schemes such as slow start for avoiding congestion. The concept of MSS and congestion Window is used in these algorithms TCP Tahoe and Reno are two variations to the basic AIMD scheme. High-speed TCP (HSTCP) is a new congestion control algorithm for TCP protocol. With TCP Vegas, timeouts were set and Round-trip delays were measured for every packet in the transmit buffer. In addition, TCP Vegas uses additive Increases and additive decreases in the congestion window. TCP New Reno improves retransmission during the fast Recovery phase of TCP Reno. During fast recovery, for every duplicate ACK that is returned to TCP New Reno, a Duplicate unacknowledged packet from the front of the transmit buffer is sent. In other words, several packets from the front of the transmit buffer may be retransmitted. For every ACK that makes progress in the sequence space, new unsent packets from the back of the transmit buffer are sent, to keep the halved congestion window full.TCP Hybla aims to eliminate penalization of TCP connections that incorporate a high-latency terrestrial or Satellite radio link, due to their longer round trip times. It stems from an analytical evaluation of the congestion. Window dynamics, which suggests the necessary modifications to remove the performance dependence on RTT.

Some other congestion avoidance algorithms are

- TCP Westwood
- TCP SACK
- H-TCP
- Scalable TCP
- HS-TCP
- BIC-TCP
- CUBIC TCP
- FAST TCP
- XCP
- LED

TCP Westwood + is a sender-side only modification of the TCP Reno protocol that optimizes the performance of TCP Congestion control over both wire line and wireless. TCPIllinois is a variant of TCP congestion control protocol. It is especially targeted at high-speed, long-distance networks. A sender side modification to the standard TCP congestion control algorithm, it achieves a higher average throughput than the standard TCP, allocates the network resource fairly as the standard TCP, is compatible with the standard TCP,and provides incentives for TCP users to switch. Some more papers are observed such as "one more bit is enough" has implemented simple low complexity protocol called variable structure congestion control protocol (VCP). The congestion removal based algorithm for the heterogeneous users is developed where no explicit feedback is required from network. The algorithm presented is totally window based. Determining near optimal policies when the available bandwidth is unchanging and when bandwidth is changing in restricted manner under the control of an adversary. A novel RED based hop-by-hop congestion control based on packet switched network is developed that is totally based on the coordination of the routers and hosts. The fairness and efficiency balancing is achieved by Protocol design with binomial congestion control protocols is observed in some papers. The TCP friendly congestion control mechanism for many-to-many communication environment targeted unicast WAN and Multicast protocol (TFRC) has solved the sort of problem for competing resources.

2. BACKGROUND

In many networks for traffic and telecommunications, minimizing delays from entry to exit is a major concern of users. In user-optimal routing, each user chooses a path minimize delay form entry to exit, given the existing paths chosen by all other users. Under user-optimal routing, at equilibrium all users experience the same delay. Many Networks, especially data networks, are commonly modeled as networks of single-server queues. Single-server queuing networks with user-optimal routing in which adding servers or increasing the capacity of existing servers worsens the delay experienced by all users. In continuation to this, the connection oriented protocols requires the virtual circuit Connection for the duration of the entire communication of the both hosts. The statistical data of rising numbers will indicate the Congestion occurred. The factor under concentration under the measurement for such congestion control is as Average packet delay, the number of packets that time out and retransmitted standard deviation of packet delay, Percentage of all packets discarded for lack of buffer space, average queue length. If we are able to reduce these quantities then it are definitely controlling congestion in the network. When users are connected they form a virtual circuit in connection oriented protocol. Some times the clients are idle and not communicating with the server i.e. wastage of the bandwidth resource. The time required to complete the request, duration of the entire communication, will gives the important information regarding communication scenario. While working with the congestion controlling on the homogeneous and heterogeneous networks we have tested the different queuing disciplines and their impact on the congestion control. The work we already presented in the role of Markova queuing discipline in congestion control. Meanwhile discussion with many researchers and after survey of the literature we came to the conclusion that how we can verify the results about their consistency and better output with respect to other algorithms? To resolve this query we have tested our simulations across two different simulators. The simulations technique we applied by simulators OMNeT ++ and OPNET. This technique we applied by discrete event simulation of additive increase multiplicative decrease. Still the results on the actual network are always different than the simulated results .To overcome the flaws in the simulation the work presented here is carried on the actual network. The dynamic (changing) behavior of the network elements may Produces the different results.

3. METHODOLOGY

For experiment we have selected the five clients and one server. The network is heterogeneous network. Clients and servers are of connection oriented type. The clients and servers are created by using socket programming. The time of client's requests and servers responses in the given time intervals is measured. The time differences are calculated so that the series shows the behavioral for the future predictions. The log files for recording the times of different events in the network are maintained at client's side and server side. While experimentation we have chosen the computer systems from the well established network with the systems are connected to the server by the switches. So as the packets thrown are passed through the switches. While performing experiments we have created multithreaded server and many clients can connect to it. We maintained the time of events in the network activities. The aim is to avoid irregularities in the connection and unwanted connections for the long time of the span. We are maintaining the database of the different events. The database is used as the data warehouse. By applying the different operations on the data we can predict the future values of the traffic intensity and probability of the congestion in the network. Depending on the predictions the countermeasures can be applied for the future enhancements in the network.The process of the data collection, selection of the data, preprocessing and transformations in the data, and inferring the knowledge base from the database. Selection: The data needed for data mining process obtained from many the routing tables and times series stored at various hops in the network/subnet. We are obtaining data from different clients and servers in the network. The data collected by our programs that are in Proper format, hence no necessary to preprocess. Similarly transformations for data reduction and reformatting are not necessary as the analyzed data we are storing in the data marts.

Data mining: As a part of KDD, we may observe the data mining as the main activity for the future predations about the traffic intensity and in particular period of time. The interpretation and evaluation is important because usefulness of results for the congestion control is depends on the same. Shows data mining approach where during analysis the time series is observed creating a set of attributes values over period of time. Time series consist of only numeric values at specific, evenly spaced intervals. The values usually are obtained as evenly spaced time plots. There are three basic functions performed in time series analysis. In one case distance measures are used to determine the similarity between different time series. In second case the Structure of the line is examined to determine and perhaps classify its behavior. Estimation and prediction may be viewed as types of classification. Prediction can thought of as classifying an attribute value into one of a set of possible classes. It is often viewed as forecasting a continuous value, while classification forecasts a discrete value. All approaches to perform classification assume some knowledge of the data. Often a training set is used to develop the specific parameters required by the technique. Training data consist of sample input data as well as the classification assignment for the data. Domain experts may also be used to assist in the process. The classification can be defined as given database $D = \{t1, t2, ...tn\}$ of tuples(items, records) and a set of classes $C=\{C1, C2...Cm\}$, the classification problem is to define a mapping f: $D \bullet C$ where each ti is assigned to one class. A class Cj, contains precisely those tuples mapped to it; that is $Cj = \{ti \mid f(ti)=Cj, 1 = i = n$, and ti å $D\}$. The mapping from the database to the set of classes where each tuple in the database is assigned to exactly one class. The classification algorithms are available with statistical based, distance based, decision tree based, neural network based, rule based and combined techniques. While looking in deep for the clustering technique the hierarchical algorithms, partition algorithms, clustering large databases are available for the predictions.

A third application would be to use the historical time series plots to predict future values. The time series data May be continuous or discrete. Time series prediction is the Use of model to predict future events based on known past Events. For investigation purpose a time series is considered as consisting only numeric values. After finding out similarity of the time series they classified or Clustering. Given several time series we may want to determine which time series are like each other (clustering). Alternatively, we may give a time series to find which time series from a set are like this one (classification). A special type of similarity analysis is identifying patterns within time series. Here we have created two variants of the same algorithm. In first algorithm we have used the one separate Process/thread for collecting data in the data mart and another process/thread to refine data to create knowledge base. These both of the threads are running one after another. In second algorithm we have proposed the thread model for both activities running simultaneously and to view the results to enhance network performance and remove congestion. The comparative results are showing Compromise between resource allocations at operating system level and speed/performance in decision making.

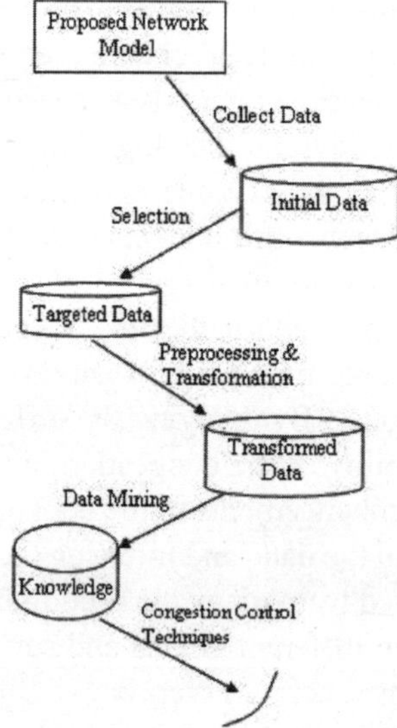

Fig. 1 Data Mining (KDD) in Congestion Control

4. ALGORITHM

1. Generate traffic patterns for 'n' number of clients at different time. Store the time of connection for whole Communication. As well as store starting time and end time for connection (i.e. used for time series analysis.)

2. Create routing table with different hops in the path of destination.

3. Analyze the data stored in the data mart (here we have considered the information stored at the 'deflector' and Time series as part of data mart). Create knowledge base for further congestion controlling algorithm. The clustering and/or classification can be done by using this approach.

4. The information is used for the decision making and predictions for the future traffic intensity. Apply counter measures for the congestion control in high traffic time spans. Here the 'deflector' is 'cute young deflector' in the initial stages. As time passes the information from the data m arts can be refined and used to become 'smarten the deflector'.The cuteness and smartness depends on the knowledge present in the knowledge base. "More knowledge more the Smartness". More refinements on the database tuples will Gives more useful knowledge for he future enhancements of the predictions by the classification and clustering of the Time series. The control

measures are applied to prevent Congestion and proper balance of resource allocation by fairness criteria can be done for the further refinements in the criteria. The 'n' iterations of the above algorithm can gives more and more knowledge in the form of tuples.

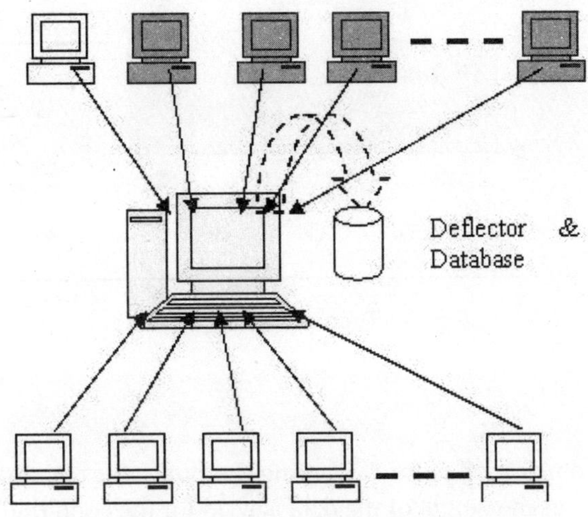

Fig. 2 The Model with topology

5. IMPLEMENTATION, ANALYSIS AND RESULTS

Table 1 Time shown as data from log files

	Server Starting Time: 10: 47: 40 IP-Address: 172. 16. 1. 16				
IP Clients	New Request Received @ server	Client Started	Sub Request Received @ Server	Request from client	End time
(1)	(2)	(3)	(4)	(5)	(6)
172.16.1.17	10:49:52	10:49:52	10:49:57	10:49:59	10:50:03
172.16.1.18	11:04:42	11:04:42	11:04:45	11:07:31	11:07:39
172.16.1.21	11:20:48	11:20:48	11:20:54	11:23:40	11:23:48
172.16.1.19	11:24:52	11:24:52	11:24:58	11:26:26	11:26:34
172.16.1.14	11:35:13	11:35:13	11:35:16	11:35:59	11:36:06

Table 2 Transformed data of time series from Table1

	Server Starting time: 10:47:40 IP-Address: 172.16.1.16						
IP Client (1)	(4 – 3) sec	(5 – 3) sec	(5 – 4) sec	(6 – 3) sec	(6 – 4) sec	(6 – 5) sec	(6 – 2) sec
172.16.1.17	05	07	02	11	06	04	11
172.16.1.18	03	169	166	167	174	09	177
172.16.1.21	06	172	166	180	174	08	180
172.16.1.19	06	94	88	102	96	08	102
172.16.1.14	03	46	43	53	50	07	53

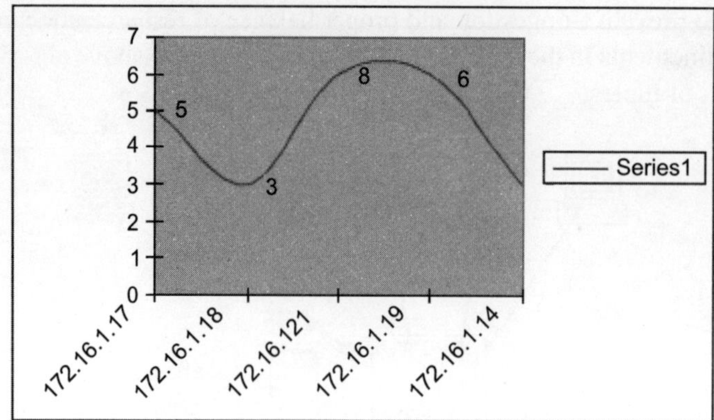

Fig. 3 Time series of (4-3) sec

6. CONCLUSION

Data mining approach used in the congestion is for Clustering the time series is useful for the future predictions. After adding more clients with time series as the output of the data is used for the condition after some time span. Association/ pattern matching rules to optimize the network performance. After applying one of the algorithms on the data of log files of client and server. (User log files as data Warehouse). Use the KDD (Knowledge Discovery over the Database) technique and improve the performance of the Network.

7. FUTURE WORK

The work carried is measuring the time in seconds. If the Time is measured in milliseconds then it may produces the Better and useful information for the connections and relatively for congestion control. For comparative study of the algorithms simulations may be done in future.

8. APPENDIX

(Contents of auto generated log files)
Sat Mar 31 10:47:40 GMT + 05:30 2010
Server Socket[addr = 0.0.0.0/0.0.0.0, port = 0, localport = 8189]
Client1
Socket socket[addr = /172.16.1.17, port = 1182, localport = 8189]
New Request Received: Sat Mar 31 10:49:52 GMT + 05:30 2010
Sat Mar 31 10:49:52 GMT + 05:30 2010
Sub Request Received: Sat Mar 31 10:49:52 GMT + 05:30 2010
File size in bytes: 2411
Sub Request Received: Sat Mar 31 10:49:53 GMT + 05:30 2010
Client2
Socket Socket[addr = /172.16.1.18,port = 1197,localport = 8189]
New Request Received: Sat Mar 31 11:04:42 GMT + 05:30 2010
Sat Mar 31 11:04:42 GMT + 05:30 2007
Sub Request Received: Sat Mar 31 11:04:42 GMT + 05:30 2010
File size in bytes: 2411

Sub Request Received: Sat Mar 31 11:07:28 GMT + 05:30 2010
Client3
Socket Socket[addr = /172.16.1.21,port = 1133,localport = 8189]
New Request Received: Sat Mar 31 11:20:48 GMT + 05:30 2010
Sat Mar 31 11:20:48 GMT + 05:30 2010
Sub Request Received: Sat Mar 31 11:20:48 GMT + 05:30 2010
file size in bytes:2411
Sub Request Received: Sat Mar 31 11:23:35 GMT + 05:30 2010

8.1   Client1 Logs

C:\j2sdk1.4.1 \bin > java echoclient itlab1pc16
Local Host IP-Address = itlab1pc17/172.16.1.17
Connection to
ServerSocket[addr = itlab1pc16/172.16.1.16,port = 8189,localport = 1182]
Sat Mar 31 10:47:57 GMT + 05:30 2010
requiredfile.java
File Request from client sent onSat Mar 31 10:49:32 GMT + 05:30 2007
End time: Sat Mar 31 10:50:03 GMT + 05:30 2010

8.2   Client2 Logs

C:\j2sdk1.4.1 \bin > java echoclient itlab1pc16
Local Host IP-Address = itlab1pc18/172.16.1.18
Connection to
ServerSocket[addr = itlab1pc16/172.16.1.16, port = 8189, localport = 1197]
Sat Mar 31 11:04:45 GMT + 05:30 2010
File request from client sent onSat Mar 31 11:07:31 GMT + 05:30 2007
End time: Sat Mar 31 11:07:39 GMT + 05:30 2010

8.3   Client3 Logs

C:\j2sdk1.4.1 \bin > java echoclient 172.16.1.16
Local Host IP-Address = itlab1pc18/172.16.1.21
Connection to
Server Socket[addr = /172.16.1.16,port = 8189,localport = 1133]
Sat Mar 31 11:20:54 GMT + 05:30 2010
File request from client sent onSat Mar 31 11:23:40 GMT + 05:30 2007
End time: Sat Mar 31 11:23:48 GMT + 05:30 2010

References

1. Lefteris Magmata's, Tobias Harks et.al, "Approaches to Congestion Control in packet Network", Journal of Internet Engineering, Vol. 1 No.1, January 2007.pp.22-33.
2. Margaret H. Dunham,"Data Mining-Introductory and Advanced Topics" person Education, LPE, ISBN 81-7808-996-3.Year 2003.

3. Joel E. Cohen and Clerk Jeffries, "Congestion Resulting from Increased Capacity in Single-Server Queuing Network", IEEE/ACM Transactions on Networking, vol.3 No.2, April 1997.pp.305-310.

4. www.wikipedia.org

5. R. Jain, "Myths in Congestion Control in High Speed Networks", Digital Equipment Corporation, pp1-24.

6. Manoj Devare, Ajay Kumar, "Role of Markovian Queuing Discipline in Congestion Control in Homogenous and Heterogeneous Networks", Proceedings of International Conference On Systemic, Cybernetics' and informatics", ICSCI-2007. PP.436 - 439.

7. Manoj Devare, Ajay Kumar, "Congestion and flow Control in Homogeneous Heterogeneous Networks: Discrete Event Simulation

CHAPTER 44

Extraction of Genetic Features Using Speech Recognition

A.R. Punjabi[1], Santosh Gaikwad[2] and B.W. Gawali[2]
[1]Z.B. Patil College, Dhule, (M.S.), [2]Department of Computer Science & Information Technology,
Dr. Babasaheb Ambedkar Marathwada University Aurangabad (MS), India
E-mail: santosh.gaikwadcsit@gmail.com, bharati_rokade@yahoo.co.in

ABSTRACT

Human Genetics describes the study of inheritance as it occurs in human beings. Genes can be the common factor of the qualities of most human-inherited traits. Study of human genetics can be useful as it can answer questions about human nature, understand the diseases and development of effective disease treatment. No two humans are genetically identical, causes of differences between Individuals include the exchange of genes. The study of human genetic variation has both evolutionary significance and medical applications. The study can help scientists understand ancient human population migrations as well as how different human groups are biologically related to one another. From a medical perspective the study of human genetic variation may be important because some disease causing alleles occur at a greater frequency in people from specific geographic regions. This paper describes performance of genetic feature in speech, how mother's speech is related to daughter and father's speech is like children.

Keyword: molecular genetics, biochemical genetics, genomics, population genetics, developmental genetics, speech recognition.

1. INTRODUCTION

Human genetics encompasses a variety of overlapping fields including: classical genetics, cytogenetic, molecular genetics, biochemical genetics, genomics, population genetics, developmental genetics, clinical genetics, and genetic counseling. Genes can be the common factor of the qualities of most human-inherited traits. Study of human genetics can be useful as it can answer questions about human nature, understand the diseases and development of effective disease treatment, and understand genetics of human life [1, 2]. Human Genetics presents original and timely articles on all aspects of human genetics. Coverage includes gene structure and organization; gene expression; mutation detection and analysis; linkage analysis and genetic mapping; physical mapping; cytogenetic and genomic imaging; genome structure and organization; disease association studies; molecular diagnostics; genetic epidemiology; evolutionary genetics; developmental genetics; genotype-phenotype relationships; molecular genetics of tumor genesis; genetics of complex diseases and epistemic interactions; ethical, legal and social issues and bioinformatics. [3]

1.1. Genes

Genes are a fundamental unit of inheritance. Genes can be defined as a sequence of DNA in the genome that is required for production of a functional product. Genes have both minor and major effects on human characteristics. Human genes have become prominent in the nature versus nurture debate.

1.2. Human genetic variation

Human genetic variation is the genetic diversity of humans and represents the total amount of genetic characteristics observed within the human species. Genetic differences are observed between humans at both the individual and the population level [5, 6]. There may be multiple variants of any given gene in the human population (alleles), leading to polymorphism. Many genes are not polymorphic, meaning that only a single allele is present in the population: that allele is then said to be fixed. No two humans are genetically identical. Causes of differences between Individuals include the exchange of genes [8, 9, 2].

1.3. Speech Recognition

Speech is a natural mode of communication for people. We learn all the relevant skills during early childhood, without instruction, and we continue to rely on speech communication throughout our lives

1.4. Speech Production

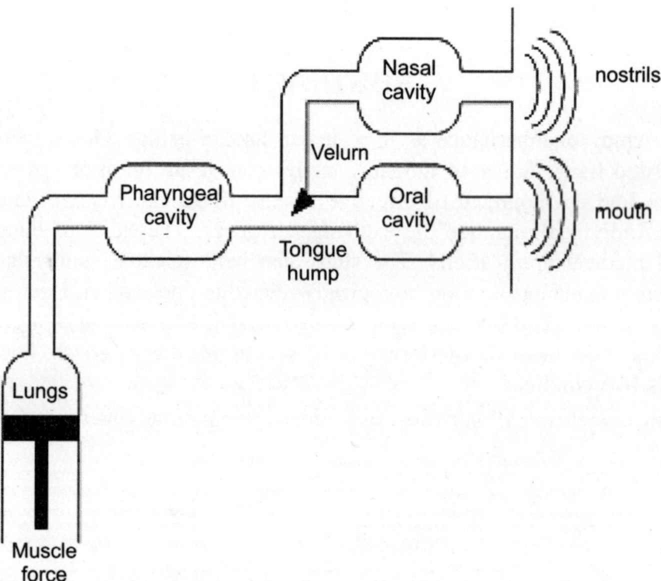

Fig. 1 A block diagram of Human Speech Production

2. FAST FOURIER TRANSFORMATION

Fast Fourier transformation (FFT) is an efficient algorithm to compute the discrete Fourier transform (DFT) and its inverse. There are many distinct FFT algorithms involving a wide range of mathematics, from simple complex-number arithmetic to group theory and number theory; this article gives an overview of the available techniques and some of their general properties, while the specific algorithms are described in subsidiary articles linked below. A DFT decomposes a sequence of values into components of different frequencies. This operation is useful in many fields (see discrete Fourier transform for properties and applications of the transform) but computing it directly from the definition is often too slow to be practical. An FFT is a way to compute the same result more quickly: computing a DFT of N points in the naive way, using the definition, takes $O(N2)$ arithmetical operations, while an FFT can compute the same result in only $O(N \log N)$ operations. The difference in speed can be substantial, especially for long data sets where N may be in the thousands or millions—in practice, the computation time can be reduced by several orders of magnitude in such cases, and the improvement is roughly proportional to $N / \log(N)$. This huge improvement made many DFT-based algorithms practical; FFTs are of great importance to a wide variety of applications, from digital signal processing and solving partial differential equations to algorithms for quick multiplication of large integers. The most well known FFT algorithms depend upon the factorization of N, but (contrary to popular misconception) there are FFTs with $O(N \log N)$ complexity for all N, even for prime N. Many FFT algorithms only depend on the fact that is an N th primitive root of unity, and thus can be applied to analogous transforms over any finite field, such as number-theoretic transforms. Since the inverse DFT is the same as the DFT, but with the opposite sign in the exponent and a $1/N$ factor, any FFT algorithm can easily be adapted for it. It is very common in science and engineering to view a signal's amplitude vs. time. For example, imagine that a doctor is watching a patient's heartbeat on an electrical device. He might see peaks in the heartbeat signal every 1 second if the patient's heart beats 60 times a minute.If the doctor wishes to calculate the patient's heart rate (assuming it is perfectly steady), he can try to measure the time between successive peaks on the screen (1 second in this case) and calculate the heart rate from that information. However, there is an easier way.Any signal (electrical or otherwise) can be viewed as a number of sine waves at different frequencies with various amplitudes and phase shifts. Simply put, a graph can be made that shows amplitude vs. frequency instead of amplitude vs. time. In the doctor's case above, it would be very convenient for him to have a graph of amplitude vs. heart rate frequency. If the patient's heart rate is approximately 1 Hz as noted above, then the amplitude vs frequency plot should show a peak somewhere near 1 Hz as well. Now, the doctor can simply glance at the graph to see the heart beat frequency [11, 12]

3. DATABASE CREATION

In this study we visited a family, and asked father & son to say word **"OM"**. Their voices were recorded with the help of laptop & microphone. For recording voice sound recorder software was used. Their voice was saved in male group (folder). Later we asked mother & daughter to say word "OM" & their voices were stored in female group. Similarly voice samples of daughter-daughter, son-son combinations were also recorded & stored in respective male & female groups. While recording or collecting samples age difference between samples was one of the major factors & was considered. Since voices of small children or adult persons varies from voice of young person. So family members having less age difference were visited & their voice was recorded.in database we collected sample 10 families and test their result.

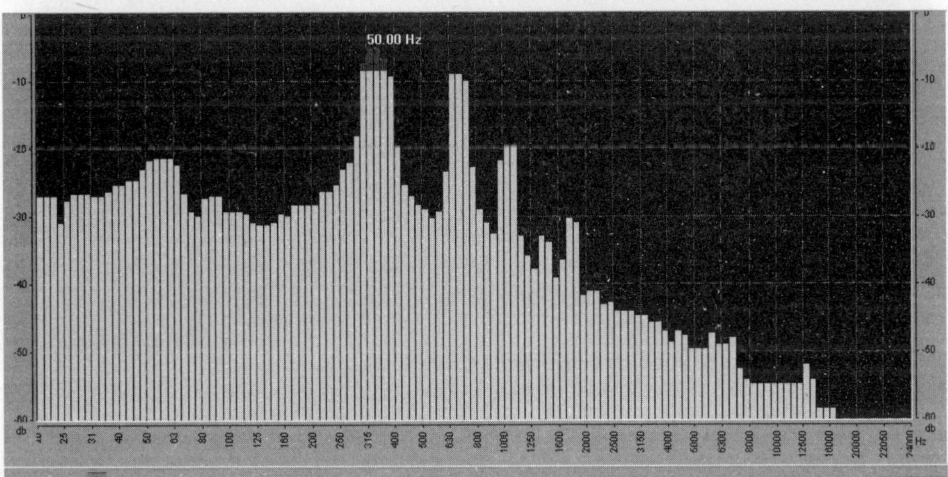

Fig. 2 Speech signal of Mother

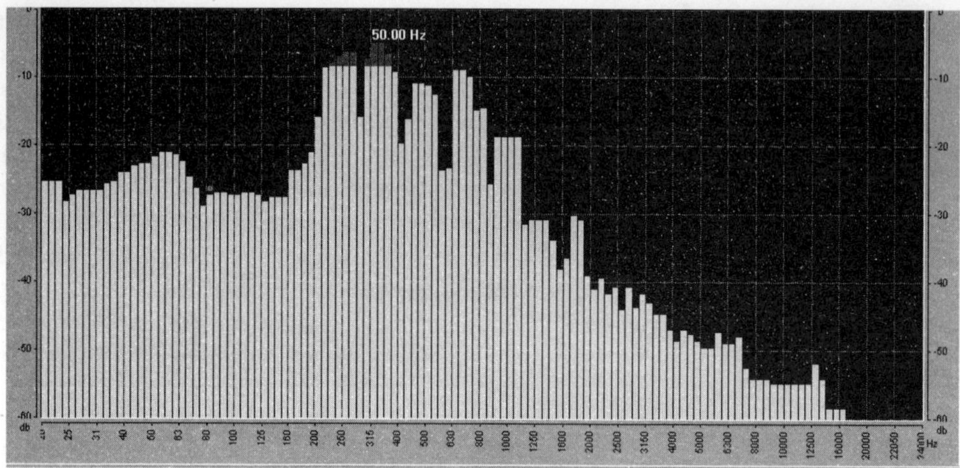

Fig. 3   Speech signal of Daughter

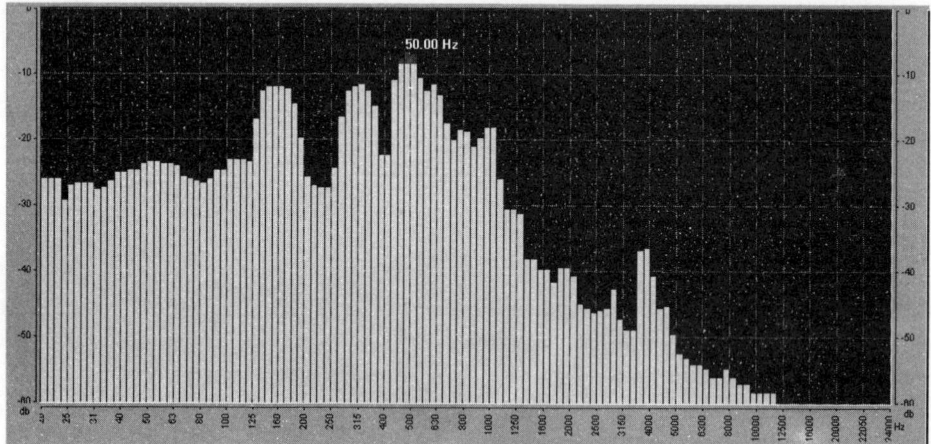

Fig. 4   Speech signal of Father

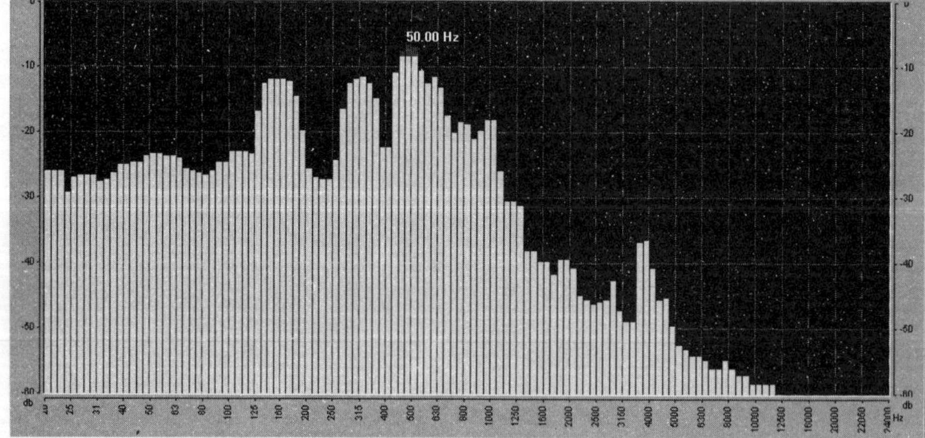

Fig. 5   Speech signal of Son

Time is universal constant that leaves different impacts on every momentum in our everyday life[13,14]. We see things moves as a function of time. So it becomes an important factor for every living & non living transactions of life. We describe a vocabulary of creation of "OM" word database. So voice samples of large number of parent-offspring combinations such as Father-Son, Mother-Daughter, Son-Son, Daughter-Daughter samples. The feature extraction is done by using Fast Fourier Transform on enrolled 40 samples (20 males & 20 females). To cope up with situation, the following comparisons were done. In result we extract feature of speech signal using a Fast Fourier Transformation and apply statics as Mean and standard deviation .using that Mean and Standard deviation we describe a distance matrix.

Table 1   distance matrix of mother and daughter

		Mother	*Daughter*
Mother	Mean	**0**	0.07
	STD	**0**	15.86
Daughter	Mean	0.07	**0**
	STD	15.86	**0**

Table 2   distance matrix of mother and daughter

		Mother	*Daughter*
Mother	Mean	**0**	0.06
	STD	**0**	3.61
Daughter	Mean	0.06	**0**
	STD	3.61	**0**

Table 3   distance matrix of mother and daughter

		Mother	*Daughter*
Mother	Mean	**0**	0.109
	STD	**0**	91.49
Daughter	Mean	0.109	**0**
	STD	91.49	**0**

Table 4   distance matrix of mother and daughter

		Mother	*Daughter*
Mother	Mean	**0**	0.03
	STD	**0**	9.05
Daughter	Mean	0.03	**0**
	STD	9.05	**0**

Table 5   distance matrix of mother and daughter

		Mother	*Daughter*
Mother	Mean	**0**	0.03
	STD	**0**	9.05
Daughter	Mean	0.03	**0**
	STD	9.05	**0**

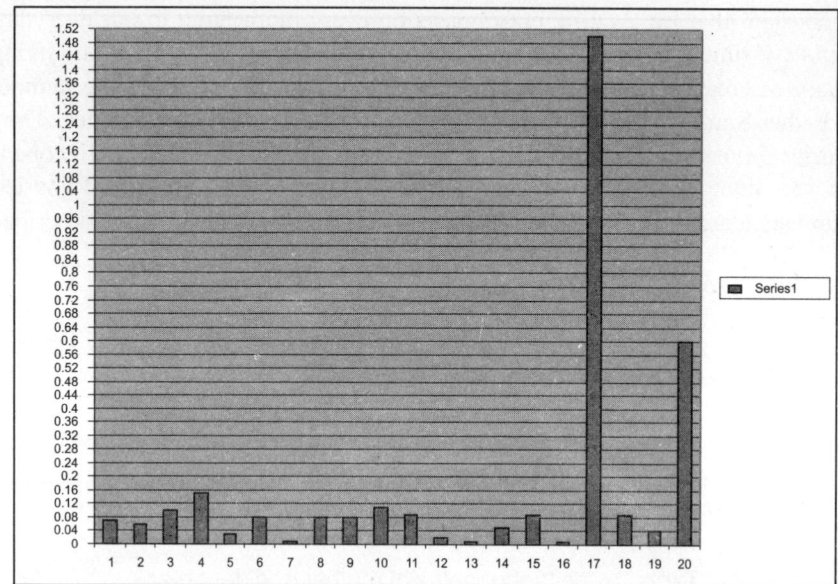

Fig. 6 Differences Mean of Collected Female Sample

- Out of 20 enrolled male samples comparison of Father-Son belonging to same family, 11 samples of male were having much more recognition rate. As it is observed that similarity between these samples are more than 50% we can conclude genetics signatures comes in voice of son from their father.

- Out of 20 female samples comparison of Mother-Daughter belonging to same family, 12 samples of female were having more recognition rate. As it is observed that similarity between these samples is more than 50% we can conclude genetics signatures comes in voice of daughter from their mother.

- As per data collected from father & son of one family and father of one family & son of another family we found the result that the son belonging to same family is much more similar than that of son belonging to another family. Thus it shows that genetics surely comes in blood relation.

The performance of system can be improved further by increasing number of voice samples having less age difference.

References

1. "Human Genetics "[online] source: http://en.wikipedia.org/wiki/Human_genetics viewed on 12 sept 2010.
2. "Human genetics Variation" [online] Source http://en.wikipedia.org/wiki/Human_genetic_variation
3. Young Neustein, International Journal of Speech Technology Source: http://www.springer.com/engineering/signals/journal/
4. Physics Cochran, W. Cooley June 1967 Available from http://wwwclasses.usc.edu/engr/ce/402/fft..pdf
5. Research and Development, 2006. SCOReD 2006. 4th Student Conference on Issue Date: 27-28 June 2006 "Analysis of the Sound Computer Music Synthesis"
6. Acoustics, Speech, and Signal Processing, 1988. ICASSP-88., 1988 International Conference Issue Date: 11-14 Apr 1988 Min, K. Chien, D. Li, S. Jones, C. (14 April 1988)"Automated two speaker separation system".
7. Yunik, M. Boyanov, B. MacDonald, R. Rahardjo, B. (2 Jun 1989)" Spectral analysis of vowels and musical sounds by means of the fast Walsh transform"
8. Seireg, R.H. Barbour, A.E., Electron. Dept., Mil. Tech. Coll., Cairo "A new algorithm for pattern recognition of voices"(12 A1992)

9. Moriyama, T. Kimura, K., Tokushima Bunri Univ. "Recognition on voice-prints of elder persons" (31 Jul 1997)

10. Medan, Y. Yair, E. (Sep 1989)" Pitch synchronous spectral analysis scheme for voiced speech"

11. Eun Ho Kim Kyung Hak Hyun Soo Hyun Kim Yoon Keun Kwak (Aug. 2007) "Speech Emotion Recognition Using Eigen-FFT in Clean and Noisy Environments"

12. Samra, A.S. El Taweel Gad Allah(Dec. 2003)" Face recognition using wavelet transform, fast Fourier transform and discrete cosine transform"

13. Wenjun Zhou Yanling Hao, Coll. of Autom., Harbin Eng. Univ. "Disquisition of Speech Recognition In VDR" (23 October 2006)

14. http://hyperphysics.phyastr.gsu.edu/HBASE/Math/fft.html

CHAPTER 45

Knowledge Discovery in Agriculture Crop Production

Kavita Bhosle[1], S.R. Chaudhary[1] and Madhu Jaiswal[1]
[1]CSE Department, MIT, Aurangabad (MS), India
E-mail: kvbcse@gmail.com, schary03@gmail.com, jaiswalmadhu4@gmail.com

ABSTRACT

A time series is a chronological sequence of observations on a particular variable. Usually the observations are taken at regular intervals (days, months, years), but the sampling could be irregular. A time series analysis consists of two steps- building a model that represents a time series, and using the model to predict (forecast) future values. In agriculture sector, productivity analysis is important in order to give suggestion and motivation to farmers. Agriculture department has lot of data still there expected production not matching with actual production. They need several types of comparison. I propose C4.5 decision tree based algorithm to analyze periodical data and give expected result.

1. INTRODUCTION

A temporal database typically stores relational data that include time-related attributes. These attributes may involve several timestamps, each having different semantics. A sequence database stores sequences of ordered events, with or without a concrete notion of time. A time-series database stores sequences of values or events obtained over repeated measurements of time like hourly, daily, weekly data. This WEKA-based analysis and application construction process is illustrated through a case study in the agricultural domain—crop productivity [1].

The data mining expert collaborate to transform the cleansed data into a form that will produce a readable, accurate data model when processed by a data mining algorithm. These two analysts may, for example, hypothesize that one or more attributes are irrelevant, and set aside these extraneous columns. Attributes may be manipulated mathematically, for example to convert all columns containing temperature measurements to a common scale, to normalize values in a given column, or to combine two or more columns into a single derived attribute [2].

2. TIME SERIES DATA ANALYSIS

If a time series has a regular pattern, then a value of the series should be a function of previous values. If Y is the target value that we are trying to model and predict, and Y_t is the value of Y at time t, then the goal is to create a model of the form [3].

$$Y_t = f(Y_{t-1}, Y_{t-2}, Y_{t-3}, ..., Y_{t-n}) + e_t$$

where Y_{t-1} is the value of Y for the previous observation, Y_{t-2} is the value two observations ago, etc., and e_t represents noise that does not follow a predictable pattern (this is called a random shock). Values of variables occurring prior to the current observation are called lag values. If a time series follows a repeating pattern, then the value of Y_t is usually highly correlated with $Y_{t\text{-cycle}}$ where cycle is the number of observations in the regular cycle. For example, monthly observations with an annual cycle often can be modeled by

$$Y_t = f(Y_{t-12})$$

The goal of building a time series model is the same as the goal for other types of predictive models which is to create a model such that the error between the predicted value of the target variable and the actual value is as small as possible. The primary difference between time series models and other types of models is that lag values of the target variable are used as predictor variables, whereas traditional models use other variables as predictors, and the concept of a lag value doesn't apply because the observations don't represent a chronological sequence [4].

To select the model for time series analysis is also difficult task. We propose decision tree model. There are so many model suitable for temporal data like Tree Boost (boosted series of decision trees), Multilayer perception neural network General regression neural network (GRNN), RBF neural network, Cascade correlation network, Support vector machine (SVM), Gene expression programming (GEP). Decision tree induction: Decision tree algorithms, such as ID3, C4.5, and CART, were originally intended for classification. C4.5 is a successor of ID3. ID3 technique of building a decision tree is based on information theory and attempts to minimize excepted number of comparisons. Entropy is used to measure the amount of uncertainty or surprise in a set of data when all data in a set belongs to the same class there is no uncertainty – entropy is zero [5].

The objective of decision tree classification is to iteratively partition the given data set into subsets where all elements in each final subset belong to the same class-pure partition

Definition: Given a data set D and probabilities $p1, p2,..., pn$ where $\Sigma pi = 1$, pi is the probability that an arbitrary tuple in D belongs to Class Ci, entropy is defined as [6].

$$H(D) = \Sigma pi \, (\log(1/pi)) = - \Sigma pi \, \log \, (pi)$$

If selection of an attribute A does not result into pure partitions then additional information required in order to arrive at exact classification is measured as

$$\text{info } A(D) = \Sigma \, |Dj|/|D| \times \text{Info } (Dj)$$

The term $|Dj|/|D|$ acts as the weight of the jth partition

Information gained by branching on attribute A

$$\text{Gain } (A) = \text{Info } (D) - \text{Info } A(D)$$

C4.5 improves ID3 in the following ways [7].

1. Missing data- instead of ignoring missing data, the value is predicted based on what is known about the attributes of other records.
2. Continuous data- discredited by dividing data into ranges.
3. Pruning-
   (a) with sub tree replacement, a sub tree is replaced by a leaf node, if this replacement results in an error rate close to that of the original tree bottom up.
   (b) With Sub tree rising, a sub tree is replaced by its most used sub tree. Sub tree is raised to a higher location depending on increase in error rate.
4. Rules - generates both decision tree and the rules set. . Some methods are used to simplify rules such as replacing rule by a simpler version.
5. Splitting – The ID3 approach favors attributes with many divisions and thus may lead to over fitting . An improvement can be made by taking into account the cardinality of each division. The GainRatio is used opposed to Gain [8].

$$\text{GainRatio } (D, S) = \text{Gain } (D, S)/H(|Di|/|D|)$$

C 4.5 uses the largest Gainratio that ensures larger than average Information gain. which attempts to overcome this bias. It applies a kind of normalization to information gain using a "split information" value defined analogously with $Info(D)$. This value represents the potential information generated by splitting the training data set, D, into v partitions, corresponding to the v outcomes of a test on attribute A. Note that, for each outcome, it considers the number of tuples having that outcome with respect to the total number of tuples in D. It differs from information gain, which measures the information with respect to classification that is acquired based on the same partitioning. The gain ratio is defined as

$$GainRatio\,(A) = Gain(A)/SplitInfo(A)$$

The attribute with the maximum gain ratio is selected as the splitting attribute. However, that as the split information approaches 0, the ratio becomes unstable. A constraint is added to avoid this, whereby the information gain of the test selected must be large at least as great as the average gain over all tests examined [9].

3. CASE STUDY

In agriculture sector, farmer is our main focus. Productivity analysis is important in order to give suggestion and motivation to farmers. Agriculture department has all current data still there expected production not matching with actual production.

Department has last 10 yrs area wise production data. They need

1. Comparison of last year production with best production year.
2. Comparison of last year production with state average.
3. Comparison of last year production with last 5 years average.
4. Comparison of last year production with production of previous year.
5. Comparison of last year production with best production year.
6. Circle wise or block wise or taluka wise production comparison.
7. Market crises
8. Production Estimation.

Here we propose C4.5 decision tree based algorithm. J48 is clone of C4.5. WEKA support J48 classifier [10]. A time series is a chronological sequence of observations on a particular variable. Usually the observations are taken at regular intervals (days, months, years), but the sampling could be irregular. A time series analysis consists of two steps- building a model that represents a time series, and using the model to predict (forecast) future values [11].

Algorithmically:

Let n be the number of instances in the training data in each year

Cleansed data are then processed by the data mining schemes.

For each of t iterations do

Randomly sample n instances

Apply a C4.5 to build a model from the sample

Store the model

End

4. CONCLUSION

C4.5 decision based model is more efficient. As the technology of machine learning continues to develop and mature, learning algorithms need to be brought to the desktops of people who work with data and understand the application domain from which it arises. It is necessary to get the algorithms out of the laboratory and into the work environment of those who can use them. WEKA is a significant step in the transfer of machine learning technology into the workplace.

References

1. Mark Hall Eibe Frank, Geoffrey Holmes, Bernhard Pfahringer, Peter Reutemann, Ian H. WittenThe WEKA Data Mining Software: An Update.

2. Sally Jo Cunningham and Geoffrey Holmes, Department of Computer Science, University of Waikato, Developing innovative applications in agriculture using data mining

3. Fayyad U.M., Piatetsky-Shapiro G., Smyth P., "From Data Mining to Knowledge Discovery: An Overview", In Advances in knowledge Discovery and Data Mining, pp. 1-30, AAAI / MIT Press 1996.

4. Antunes C.M., Oliveira A.L., "Temporal Data Mining: An Overview", Workshop on Temporal Data Mining ACM SIGKDD 2001, San Francisco, California (USA), August 2001.

5. Jiawei Han, Micheline Kamber, "Data Mining: Concepts and Techniques", 2nd Edition, 2006.

6. Rousseeuw, P.J. and Leroy, "Robust regression and outlier detection", John Wiley & Sons, Inc., New York, NY, USA, 1987.

7. Aparna S. Varde, Challenging Research Issues in Data Mining, Databases and Information Retrieval

8. Eamonn Keogh Shruti Kasetty, On the Need for Time Series Data Mining Benchmarks: A Survey and Empirical Demonstration.

9. Leonidas Karamitopoulos, Georgios Evangelidis, Recent Developments in Time Series Data Mining: Similarity Measures & Representations.

10. Dan Li, Sherri Harms, Steve Goddard, William Waltman, Jitender Deogun, Time-Series Data Mining in a Geospatial Decision Support System.

11. Eamonn Keogh, Data Mining and Information Retrieval in Time Series/Multimedia Databases.

CHAPTER 46

A Review Paper on Data Mining: A Tool for Earthquake Prediction

Jagruti Mahure[1], Snehal Suryavanshi[2] and Swati Ganar[3]

K.C. College of Engineering, Thane (MS)-400-603, India

E-mail: jagruti.mahure@gmail.com[1], snehalss_11@yahoo.com[2], swati_gnr@rediffmail.com[3]

ABSTRACT

Data mining consists of evolving set of techniques that can be used to extract valuable information and knowledge from massive volumes of data. This paper aims at further data mining study on scientific data. This paper highlights the data mining techniques applied to mine for surface changes overtime (e.g. Earthquake rupture). The data mining techniques help researchers to predict the changes in the intensity of volcanoes. This paper uses predictive statistical models that can be applied to areas such as seismic activity , the spreading of fire. The basic problem in this class of systems is unobservable dynamics with respect to earthquakes. The space-time patterns associated with time, location and magnitude of the sudden events from the force threshold are observable. This paper highlights the observable space time earthquake patterns from unobservable dynamics using data mining techniques, pattern recognition and ensemble forecasting. Thus this paper gives insight on how data mining can be applied in finding the consequences of earthquakes and hence alerting the public.

1. INTRODUCTION

The field of data mining has evolved from its roots in databases, statistics, artificial intelligence, information theory and algorithms into a core set of techniques that have been applied to a range of problems. Computational simulation and data acquisition in scientific and engineering domains have made tremendous progress over the past two decades. A mix of advanced algorithms, exponentially increasing computing power and accurate sensing and measurement devices have resulted in more data repositories

Advanced technologies in networks have enabled the communication of large volumes of data across the world. This results in a need of tools &Technologies for effectively analyzing the scientific data sets with the objective of interpreting the underlying physical phenomena. Data mining applications in geology and geophysics have achieved significant success in the areas as weather prediction, mineral prospecting, ecology, modeling etc and finally predicting the earthquakes from satellite maps.

An interesting aspect of many of these applications is that they combine both spatial and temporal aspects in the data and in the phenomena that is being mined. Data sets in these applications come from both observations and simulation. Investigations on earthquake predictions are based on the assumption that all of the regional factors can be filtered out and general information about the earthquake precursory patterns can be extracted. [6]

Feature extraction involves a pre selection process of various statistical properties of data and generation of a set of seismic parameters, which correspond to linearly independent coordinator in the feature space. The seismic parameters in the form of time series can be analyzed by using various pattern recognition techniques.

Statistical or pattern recognition methodology usually performs this extraction process. Thus this paper gives insight of mining the scientific data.

2. DATA MINING-DEFINITIONS

Data mining is defined as process of extraction of relevant data and hidden facts contained in databases and data warehouses.

It refers to find out the new knowledge about an application domain using data on the domain usually stored in the databases. The application domain may be astrophysics, earth science or about solar system.

Data mining techniques support to identify nuggets of information and extracting this information in such a way that, this will support in decision making, prediction, forecasting and estimation. [4]

3. DATA MINING GOALS

Bring together representatives of the data mining community and the domain science community so that they can understand the current capabilities and research objectives of each other communities related to data mining.

Identify a set of research objectives from the domain science community that would be facilitated by current or anticipated data mining techniques.

Identify a set of research objectives for the data mining community that could support the research objectives of the domain science community.[4]

4. DATA MINING MODELS

Data mining is used to find patterns and relationships in data patterns. The relationships in data patterns can be analyzed via 2 types of models.

Descriptive models: Used to describe patterns and to create meaningful subgroups or clusters.

Predictive models: Used to forecast explicit values, based upon patterns in known results.

In large databases data mining and knowledge discovery comes in two flavors:

4.1 Event Based Mining

- Known events/known algorithms: Use existing physical models (descriptive models and algorithms) to locate known phenomena of interest either spatially or temporally within a large database.
- Unknown events/known algorithms: Use expected physical relationships (predictive models, Algorithms) among observational parameters of physical phenomena to predict the presence of previously unseen events within a large complex database.
- Unknown events/unknown algorithms: Use thresholds or trends to identify transient or otherwise unique events and therefore to discover new physical phenomena.

4.2 Relationship Based Mining

- Spatial Associations: Identify events (e.g. astronomical objects) at the same location. (e.g. same region of the sky)

- Temporal Associations: Identify events occurring during the same or related periods of time.
- Coincidence Associations: Use clustering techniques to identify events that are co-located within a multidimensional parameter space.[4]

User requirements for data mining in large scientific databases

- Cross identifications: Refers to the classical problem of associating the source list in one database to the source list in another.
- Cross correlation: Refers to the search for correlations, tendencies, and trends between physical parameters in multidimensional data usually across databases.
- Nearest neighbor identification: Refers to the general application of clustering algorithms in multidimensional parameter space usually within a database.
- Systematic data exploration: Refers to the application of broad range of event based queries and relationship based queries to a database in making a serendipitous discovery of new objects or a new class.

5. DATA MINING TECHNIQUES

The various data mining techniques are

1. Statistics
2. Clustering
3. Visualization
4. Association
5. Classification & Prediction
6. Outlier analysis
7. Trend and evolution analysis

Statistics

- Data cleansing i.e. the removal of erroneous or irrelevant data known as outliers.
- EDA Exploratory data analysis e.g. frequency counts histograms.
- Attribute redefinition e.g. bodies mass index.
- Data analysis is a measure of association and their relationships between attributes interestingness of rules, classification, prediction etc.

Visualization

- Enhances EDA, make patterns visible in different views .

Clustering (Cluster Analysis)

- Clustering is a process of grouping similar data. The data which is are not part of clustering are called as outliers. How to cluster in different conditions,
- Class label is unknown: Group related data to form new classes, e.g., cluster houses to find distribution patterns
- Clustering based on the principle: maximizing the intra-class similarity and minimizing the interclass similarity
- It provides subgroups of population for further analysis or action –very important when dealing with large databases.

Association (Correlation and Causality)

- Mining association rules finds the interesting correlation relationship among large databases.

Classification and Prediction

- Finding models (functions) that describe and distinguish classes or concepts for future prediction e.g., classify countries based on climate, or classify cars based on gas mileage
- Presentation: decision-tree, classification rule, neural network
- Prediction: Predict some unknown or missing numerical values
- Outlier analysis
- Outlier: A data object that is irrelevant to general behavior of the data ,it can be considered as an exception but is quite useful in fraud detection in rare events analysis

Trend and Evolution Analysis

- Trend and deviation: regression analysis
- Sequential pattern mining, periodicity analysis
- Similarity-based analysis[4]

6. EARTHQUAKE PREDICTIONS

1. Ground water levels
2. Chemical changes in Ground water
3. Radon Gas in Ground water wells.[2]

Ground Water Levels

Changing water levels in deep wells are recognized as precursor to earthquakes. The pre-seismic variations at observation wells are as follows.

1. A gradual lowering of water levels at a period of months or years.
2. An accelerated lowering of water levels in the last few months or weeks preceding the earthquake.
3. A rebound, where water levels begin to increase rapidly in the last few days or hours before the main shock.

Chemical Changes in Ground Water

1. The Chemical composition of ground water is affected by seismic events.
2. Researchers at the University of Tokyo tested the water after the earthquake occurred, the result of the study showed that the composition of water changed significantly in the period around earthquake area.
3. They observed that the chloride concentration is almost constant.
4. Levels of sulphate also showed a similar rise.

Radon Gas in Ground Water Wells

1. An increase level of radon gas in wells is a precursor of earthquakes recognized by research group. Although radon has relatively a short half life and is unlikely to seep the surface through rocks from the depths at which seismic is very soluble in water and can routinely be monitored in wells and springs often radon levels at such springs show reaction to seismic events and they are monitored for earthquake predictions. [1]

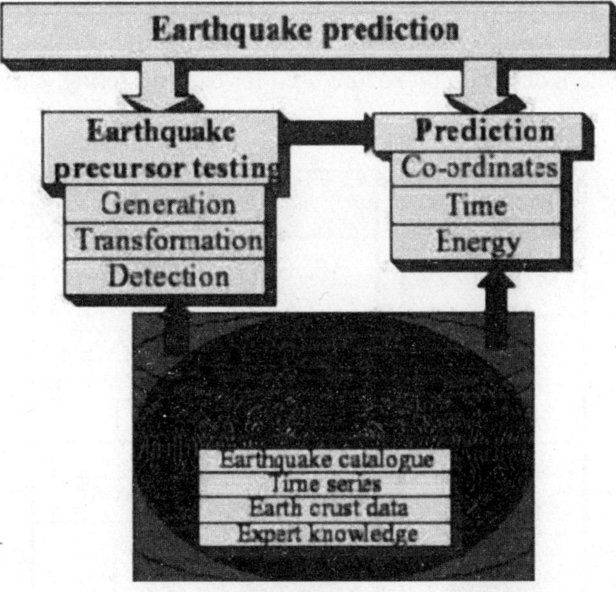

Fig.1

2. There is no effective solution to the problem.
3. To solve this problem earthquake catalogs, geo-monitoring time series data about stationary seismo-tectonic properties of geological environment and expert knowledge and hypotheses about earthquake precursors

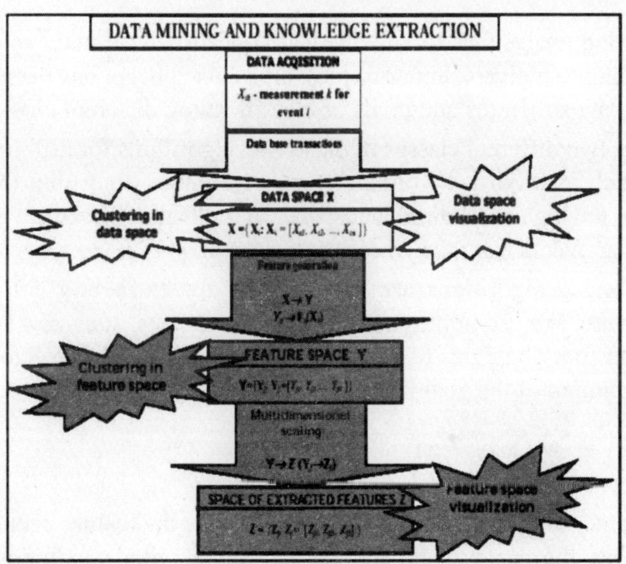

Fig.2

This proposes a multi-resolutional approach, which combines local clustering techniques in the data space with a non-hierarchical clustering in the feature space. The raw data are represented by n-dimensional vector Xi of measurements Xk. The data space can be searched for patterns and can be visualized by using local or remote pattern recognition and by advanced visualization capabilities. The data space X is transformed to a new abstract space Y of vectors Yj. The coordinates Yl of these vectors represent nonlinear functions of measurements Xk, which are averaged in space and time in given space-time windows. This transformation allows for coarse graining of data (data quantization), amplification of their characteristic features and suppression of the noise and other random components. The new features Yl form a N-dimensional feature space. We use multi-dimensional scaling procedures for visualizing the multi-dimensional events in 3D space. This transformation allows a visual inspection of the N-dimensional feature space. The visual analysis helps greatly in detecting subtle cluster structures which are not recognized by classical clustering techniques, selecting the best pattern detection procedure used for data clustering, classifying the anonymous data and formulating new hypothesis.[1]

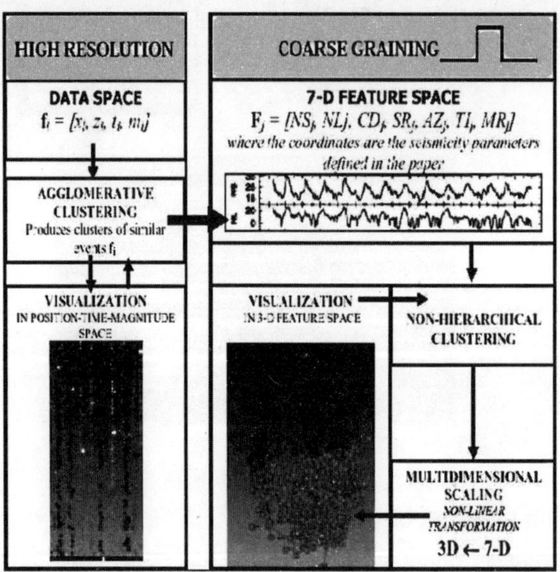

Fig.3

Clustering schemes Clustering analysis is a mathematical concept whose main role is to extract the most similar separated sets of objects according to a given similarity measure. This concept has been used for many years in pattern recognition. Depending on the data structures and goals of classification, different clustering schemes must be applied.

In our new approach we use two different classes of clustering algorithms for different resolutions. In data space we use agglomerative schemes, such as modified Mutual Nearest Neighbor algorithm (MNN). This type of clustering extracts the localized clusters in the high resolution data space. In the feature space we are searching for global clusters of time events comprising similar events from the whole time interval. [1]

The non-hierarchical clustering algorithms are used mainly for extracting compact clusters by using global knowledge about the data structure. We use improved mean based schemes, such as a suite of moving schemes, which uses the k-means procedure and four strategies of its tuning by moving the data vectors between clusters to obtain a more precise location of the minimum of the goal function:

$$j(w, n) = \sum_j \sum_{i \varepsilon Cj} |x_i - z_i|^2$$

where zj is the position of the center of mass of the cluster j, while xi are the feature vectors closest to zj. To find a global minimum of function $J()$, we repeat the clustering procedures at different initial conditions. Each new initial configuration is constructed in a special way from the previous results by using the methods. The cluster structure with the lowest $J(w, n)$ minimum is selected [1] [4]

Hierarchical Clustering Methods

A hierarchical clustering method produces a classification in which small clusters of very similar molecules are nested within larger clusters of less closely-related molecules. Hierarchical *agglomerative* methods generate a classification in a bottom-up manner, by a series of agglomerations in which small clusters, initially containing individual molecules, are fused together to form progressively larger clusters. Hierarchical agglomerative methods are often characterized by the shape of the clusters they tend to find, as exemplified by the following range: single-link - tends to find long, straggly, chained clusters; Ward and group-average - tend to find globular clusters; complete-link - tends to find extremely compact clusters. Hierarchical *divisive* methods generate a classification in a top-down manner, by progressively subdividing the single cluster which represents an entire dataset .Monothetic (divisions based on just a single descriptor) hierarchical divisive methods are generally much faster in operation than the corresponding polythetic (divisions based on all descriptors) hierarchical divisive and hierarchical agglomerative methods, but tend to give poor results. One problem with these methods is how to choose which clusters or partitions to extract from the hierarchy because display of the complete hierarchy is not really appropriate for data sets of more than a few hundred compounds.[5].

Non--Hierarchical Clustering Methods

A non-hierarchical method generates a classification by partitioning a dataset, giving a set of (generally) non-overlapping groups having no hierarchical relationships between them. A systematic evaluation of all possible partitions is quite infeasible, and many different heuristics have described to allow the identification of good, but possibly sub-optimal, partitions. Three of the main categories of non-hierarchical method are single-pass, relocation and nearest neighbor. Single-pass method (e.g. Leader) produce clusters that are dependent upon the order in which the compounds are processed, and so will not be considered further. Relocation methods, such as k-means, assign compounds to a user-defined number of seed clusters and then iteratively reassign compounds to produce the better clusters result. Such methods are prone to reaching local optimum rather than a global optimum, and it is generally not possible to determine when or where the global optimum solution has been reached. Nearest neighbor methods, such as the Jarvis-Patrick method, assign compounds to the same cluster as some number of their nearest neighbors. User-defined parameters determine how many nearest neighbors need to be considered, and the necessary level of similarity between nearest neighbor lists. Other non-hierarchical methods are generally inappropriate for use on large, high-dimensional datasets such as those used in chemical applications. [5]

6.   DATA MINING APPLICATIONS

1. In Scientific discovery – super conductivity research, For Knowledge Acquisition.
2. In Medicine – drug side effects, hospital cost analysis, genetic sequence analysis, prediction etc.
3. In Engineering – automotive diagnostics expert systems, fault detection etc.,
4. In Finance – stock market perdition, credit assessment, fraud detection etc.[4]

7.   FUTURE ENHANCEMENTS

The future of data mining lies in predictive analytics. The technology innovations in data mining since 2000 have been truly Darwinian and show promise of consolidating and stabilizing around predictive analytics. Nevertheless, the emerging market for predictive analytics has been sustained by professional services, service bureaus and profitable applications in verticals such as retail, consumer finance, telecommunications, travel and leisure, and related analytic applications. Predictive analytics have successfully proliferated into applications to support customer recommendations, customer value and churn management, campaign optimization, and fraud detection. On the product side, success stories in demand planning, just in time inventory and market basket optimization are a staple of predictive analytics. Predictive analytics should be used to get to know the customer, segment and predict customer behavior and forecast product demand and related market dynamics. Finally, they are at different stages of growth in the life cycle of technology innovation.

8.   CONCLUSIONS

The problem of earthquake prediction is based on data extraction of pre-cursory phenomena and it is highly challenging task various computational methods and tools are used for detection of pre-cursor by extracting general information from noisy data.

By using common frame work of clustering we are able to perform multi-resolutional analysis of seismic data starting from the raw data events described by their magnitude spatio-temporal data space. This new methodology can be also used for the analysis of the data from the geological phenomena e.g. We can apply this clustering method to volcanic eruptions.

References

1. W. Dzwinel et al "Non multidimensional scaling and visualization of earth quake cluster over space and feature space, nonlinear processes in geophysics" 12[2005] pp1-12.
2. C. Lomnitz. "Fundamentals of Earthquake prediction" [1994]
3. B.Gutenberg & C.H. Richtro, "Earthquake magnitude, intensity, energy & acceleration" bulseism soc. Am 36, 105-145 [1996]
4. C. Brunk, J. Kelly & Rkohai "Mineset An integrate system for data access, Visual Data Mining & Analytical Data Mining", proceeding of the 3rd conference on KDD 1997.
5. Andenberg M.R. Cluster "Analysis for application", New York, Acedamic, Press 1973.
6. "Data Mining: A Knowledge Discovery Approach" Krzysztof J. Cios, Witold Pedrycz, Roman W. Swiniarski, and Lukasz A. Kurgan

Websites

www.dmreview.com
www.aaai.org/Press/Books/kargupta2.php
www.forrester.com
www.ftiweb.com

CHAPTER 47

Comparative Study of Credit Card Fraud Detection Using HMM and Neural Network

Pukhraj P. Shrishrimal, Sunil A. Khillare, Vishal B. Waghmare, C. Namrata Mahender and R.R. Deshmukh
Department of Computer Science & Information Technology, Dr. Babasaheb Ambedkar Marathwada University,
Aurangabad (MS), India
E-mail: pukhraj.shrishrimal@gmail.com, sunil1.khillare@gmail.com, vishal.pri12@gmail.com, nam.mah@gmail.com,
ratnadeep_deshmukh@yahoo.co.in}

ABSTRACT

As the new era is of Electronic Commerce (e-commerce) the whole world is moving towards the more usage of Credit card. The popularity of credit card has increased dramatically as it can be used for both online as well as for regular shopping, so the number of fraud cases taking place is also more. This paper compares the two techniques used for detecting Credit card Frauds HMM (Hidden Markov Model) and NN (Neural Network). It is observed that the accuracy of detecting fraud using Neural Network is more than the Hidden Markov Model.

Keywords: Internet, Credit cards, E-commerce Security, Fraud Detection, Hidden Markov Model, Neural Network.

1. INTRODUCTION

The Craze of online shopping is rapidly growing day by day. As the economy is growing the expenditure of the people is increasing. The credit cards are not only used for online shopping but also for the regular shopping. One can imagine the popularity of credit card usage by the number of transactions reported by Barclays by the end of the last century which tells that 350 million card transactions were recorded per year. It is nothing but the world's biggest retail chain Wal-Mart records more than 7 Billion transaction per year [1]. The transactions happening online as well as regular transaction are increasing rapidly. As the number of credit card users is increasing the chance for the attacker to get the card details and do fraudulent transactions is also increasing.

The card transactions can be classified in two different categories: (i) Virtual or Online and (ii) Physical. In the First type the attacker get the necessary card details (such as Credit Card Number, Date of Expiry, CVV2 Security number, and in few cases the online account details of the card holder). Mostly this type of the Card fraud is done over Internet and Phone. In the Second category to perform a card transaction or purchase the cardholder needs to present the card for shopping to retailer. For such type of transaction one need to steal the credit card. If the card holder does not come to know that the card is lost than the Credit card Company has to suffer a substantial financial loss. In the first type the card holder comes to know that his or her card is being used by other person when the Credit card statement is received.

The credit card fraud is becomes the nightmare for the all parties involved. Also, the credit card fraud losses are increasing daily [2]. Experts from Visa International predict annual growth of some fraud types up to 65% [4]. For the credit card industry, fraud accounts for over $850 million dollars in losses each year in the United States and $10 billion worldwide [5].

The occurrence of fraudulent transactions can be discovered by inconsistent spending patterns. The detection of the fraud gets more difficult if the frauds occurred is having similar spending pattern as that of the card holder. To find the inconsistent spending patterns there are many different techniques which can be applied. The most popular techniques used are Neural network and HMM (Hidden Markov Model).

This paper is organized as follows: Section 2 helps us to know what is meant by Credit card Fraud Detection and the most common Problems Faced. Section 3 displays the HMM (Hidden Markov Model) model. Section 4 displays the Neural Network Techniques in credit card fraud detection. Section 5 includes the comparison between the HMM and Neural Data Mining techniques. Finally, Section 6 contains the conclusion of the paper.

2 CREDIT CARD FRAUD DETECTION

In this section of paper deals with the study of the Credit Card Fraud and the problems that are been faced in the Fraud Detection System (FDS). Here we are clearing the idea about Credit card only but it also applies for the Debit Cards which is similar to that of Credit Card Fraud.

2.1 Meaning of Credit Card Fraud

Whenever the Credit card holder does not perform a transaction using his or her Credit card is known as a fraudulent transaction. The more use of Credit card in the daily life has provided many luxuries to the human being as they are having credit card with them they can purchase when they are short of cash and can pay later to the Credit card company within the given time without incurring any interest. The Credit card has given the bad people or fraudsters a good opportunity to get handsome reward without paying a single penny from their pocket.

The Credit card fraud is attracting more attackers as no one can find them easily as the fraud detected after 2 to 3 weeks of the Fraud. Generally, the online Card fraud is increasing as no one can see who as actually done the purchase of good or who have done registration. Fraud is almost always directed toward cash or items that can be converted into cash and compressed in time [5]. The most common Fraud techniques are

(a) Getting the copy of the card and get hold PIN number of the card [3]

(b) To get hold of card details (like Card number, Expiry Date and CVV2 Security Code).

(c) Vendors charging more money than agreed to the customer, without notice to the customer.

The Credit card fraud leads to the financial loss of the financial organization and the customers. The customer or Cardholder face a partial (possibly complete) pay for the loss by paying the higher interest rates, reduced benefits and high membership fees [3]. To reduce the Card fraud is in the interest of Bank or Financial organization and card holder which resulted in the Fraud Detection System.

2.2 Problems in Credit card Fraud detection

The biggest problem of the Fraud detection system is lack of the real world data for academic researcher for performing the experiment. It is because fraud detection is associated with the sensitive financial data of the customers of the financial organization which is confidential as per the policy of the customer privacy [3].

The another problem is to find the inconsistent pattern of spending in which sometimes the transaction of the cardholder which can be genuine can also get declined. Another problem in Credit card Fraud detection is what if the fraudulent amount is similar to that of the spending pattern of the cardholder then it can bypass the Fraud Detection System.

The qualities that should be possessed by the Fraud detection system are

(a) It should be able to identify the inconsistent pattern of spending as the number of actual fraudulent transaction is few percent of total transactions.

(b) The system should be able to adapt to new kind of frauds [3].

(c) It should be able to separate the overlapping data i.e. those transactions which are genuine but similar to the fraudulent one and fraudulent one similar to the genuine transaction [3].

3. HIDDEN MARKOV MODEL

A Hidden Markov Model is a double embedded stochastic process with two hierarchy levels. It can be used to model much more complicated stochastic processes as compared to a traditional Markov model. HMM has a finite set of states governed by a set of transition probabilities. In a particular state, an outcome or observation can be generated according to an associated probability distribution. It is only the outcome and not the state which is visible to an external observer [6]. Hidden Markov model based applications are common in various areas.

An HMM can be characterized by the following [6]

(i) N, the number of states in the model. We denote the set of states $S = \{S1, S2 \dots SN\}$, where Si, $i = 1, 2 \dots N$ is an individual state. The state at time instant t is denoted by qt.

(ii) M, the number of distinct observation symbols per state. The observation symbols correspond to the physical output of the system being modeled. We denote the set of symbols $V = \{V1, V2 \dots VM\}$, where Vi, $i = 1, 2 \dots M$ is an individual symbol.

(iii) The state transition probability matrix $A = [a_{ij}]$, where

$$aij = P\,(qt + 1 = Sj \mid qt = Si),\ 1 \le i \le N,\ 1 \le j \le N;\ t = 1, 2 \tag{1}$$

For the general case where any state j can be reached from any other state i in a single step, we have $aij > 0$ for all i, j. Also,

$$\sum_{J=1}^{N} a_{ij} = 1,\ 1 \le i \le N$$

(iv) The observation symbol probability matrix $B = [b_j\,(k)]$, where

$$b_j\,(k) = P\,(V_k \mid S_j),\ 1 \le j \le N,\ 1 \le k \le M \text{ and } \sum_{k=1}^{M} b_j\,(k) = 1,\ 1 \le j \le N \tag{2}$$

(v) The initial state probability vector $p = [p_i]$ where

$$p_i = P\,(q_1 = S_i),\ 1 \le 1 \le N,\ \text{such that } \sum_{i=1}^{N} \Pi_i = 1 \tag{3}$$

(vi) The observation sequence $O = O1, O2, O3, \dots OR$, where each observation Ot is one of the symbols from V and R is the number of observations in the sequence.

It is evident that a complete specification of an HMM requires the estimation of two model parameters, N and M, and three probability distributions A, B and p. We use the notation $= (A, B, p)$ to indicate the complete set of parameters of the model, where A, B implicitly include N and M.

An observation sequence O as mentioned above, can be generated by many possible state sequences. Consider one such particular sequence.

$$Q = q_1, q_2 \dots q_R \tag{4}$$

where q_1 is the initial state.

The probability that O is generated from this state sequence is given by:

$$P(O \mid Q, \lambda) = \prod_{t=1}^{R} P(O_t \mid q_t, ?) \tag{5}$$

where statistical independence of observations is assumed. Eq. 5 can be expanded as.

$$P(O \mid Q, \lambda) = bq1\ (O1).\ b\ q2\ (O2)...\ b\ qR\ (OR) \tag{6}$$

The probability of the state sequence Q is given as.

$$P(Q \mid \lambda) = \pi\ q1\ a\ q1\ q2\ a\ q2\ q3\ ...\ a\ qR\text{-}1\ qR \tag{7}$$

Thus, the probability of generation of the observation sequence O by the Hidden Markov Model specified by ? can be written as follows.

$$P(O \mid \lambda) = \sum_{allQ} P(Q, \lambda)\, P(Q \mid \lambda) \tag{8}$$

Deriving the value of $P(O \mid ?)$ using the direct definition of Eq. 8 is computationally intensive. Hence, a procedure named as Forward-Backward procedure [6] is used to compute $P(O \mid ?)$.

4. NEURAL NETWORK

Neural networks are an extension of risk scoring techniques. They are based on the statistical knowledge contained in extensive databases of historical transactions, and fraudulent ones in particular.

These neural network models are basically 'trained' by using examples of both legitimate and fraudulent transactions and are able to correlate and weigh various fraud indicators (e.g., unusual transaction amount, card history, etc) to the occurrence of fraud.

A neural network is a computerized system that sorts data logically by performing the following tasks.

(a) Identifies cardholder's buying and fraudulent activity patterns.

(b) Processes data by trial and elimination (excluding data that is not relevant to the pattern).

(c) Finds relationships in the patterns and current transaction data.

The principles of neural networking are motivated by the functions of the brain especially pattern recognition and associative memory. The neural network recognizes similar patterns, predicting future values or events based upon the associative memory of the patterns it has learned.

The advantages neural networks offer over other techniques are that these models are able to learn from the past and thus, improve results as time passes. They can also extract rules and predict future activity based on the current situation. By employing neural networks effectively, banks can detect fraudulent use of a card, faster and more efficiently [7].

5. COMPARISON OF HIDDEN MARKOV MODEL AND NEURAL NETWORK FOR CREDIT CARD FRAUD DETECTION

While doing the study of credit card fraud detection using Hidden Markov Model it was been observed that an accuracy of approximately 80% was achieved using Hidden Markov Model [8]. The accuracy achieved by the Neural Network was 92.50% for the training database used for the study [9].

The Learning time for the Artificial Neural Network can be more. While learning time for Hidden Markov Model depends upon the type of clustering algorithm used.

6. CONCLUSION

From the above comparison came to know that the Credit card Fraud Detection using Neural Network is having more accuracy than Credit card Fraud Detection Hidden Markov Model. The Research carried out on Credit card Fraud detection is carried on imaginary dataset not on the real data so the chance to test the result on real data is difficult due unavailability of Data.

References

1. D.J. Hand, G. Blunt, M.G. Kelly, and N.M. Adams, "Data Mining for Fun and Profit," Statistical Science, vol. 15, no. 2, pp. 111–131, 2000.
2. Dr. Saleh Al-Furiah Lamia AL-Braheem , "Comprehensive study on methods of fraud prevention in credit card e-payment system"
3. Sam Maes, Karl Tuyls, Bram Vanschoenwinkel, Bernard Manderick, "Credit card Fraud detection using Bayesian and Neural Networks".
4. Vladimir Zaslavsky and Anna Strizhak ,"Credit card Fraud Detection using self organizing maps".
5. Robert J. Richardson, "Monitoring Sale Transactions for Illegal Activity".
6. L.R. Rabiner, "A Tutorial on Hidden Markov Models and Selected Applications in Speech Recognition,"
7. Tej paul Bhatla, Vikram Prabhu, Amit Dua, "Understanding Credit Card Frauds"
8. Abhinav Srivastava, Amlan Kundu, Shamik Sural, Arun K. Majumdar, "Credit card Fraud Detection using Hidden Markov Model"
9. S. Gosh, D.L. Reilly, "Credit card Fraud Detection with a Neural Network"

Author Index